Library of
Davidson College

Ethnic Adaptation and Identity:
The Karen on the Thai Frontier with Burma

Charles F. Keyes, editor

Ethnic Adaptation

THE KAREN ON THE THAI FRONTIER WITH BURMA

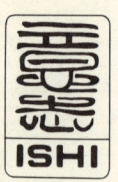

A Publication of the
Institute for the Study of Human Issues
Philadelphia

and Identity

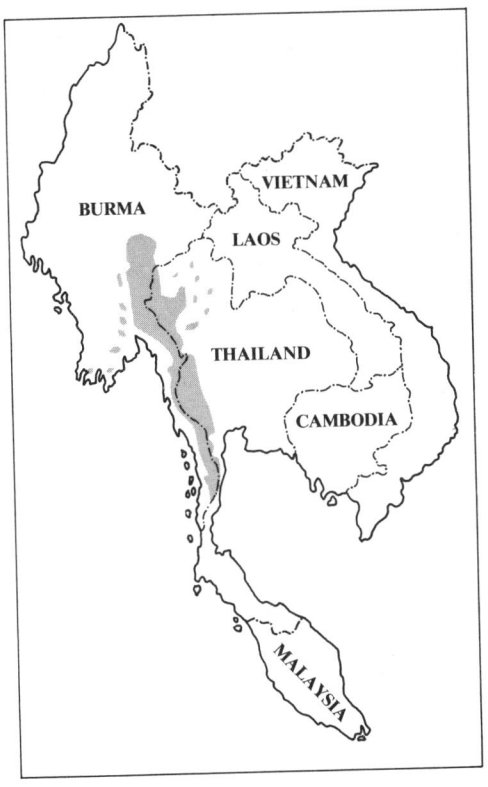

Copyright © 1979 by ISHI,
Institute for the Study of Human Issues, Inc.
All Rights Reserved
No part of this book may be reproduced in any form or by any electronic or mechanical means including information storage and retrieval systems without permission in writing from the publisher, except by a reviewer who may quote brief passages in a review.

Manufactured in the United States of America

Library of Congress Cataloging in Publication Data:

Main entry under title:

Ethnic adaptation and identity.

    Includes bibliographical references and index.
    1. Karens—Ethnic identity. 2. Thailand—Social life and customs.
I. Keyes, Charles F.
DS570.K37E86   301.45'1'04209593   79-12448
ISBN 0-915980-67-3

For information, write:

Director of Publications
ISHI
3401 Science Center
Philadelphia, Pennsylvania 19104
U.S.A.

Contents

Preface   vii
A Note on Transcription   ix

Introduction   1
CHARLES F. KEYES

Ethnic groups: some theoretical considerations, *1* / Ethnic identity and adaptation of Karen in Thailand, *8*

The Karen in Thai History and the History of the Karen in Thailand   25
CHARLES F. KEYES

Were the Karen an autochthonous people in northern Thailand? *26* / Origins of Karen relationships with Siamese and Yuan, *31* / Emergence of the Karen in the worlds of the Yuan and Siamese, *36* / The structure of Karen relationships with the Yuan and Siamese, *46*

A People Between: The Pwo Karen of Western Thailand   63
THEODORE STERN

The northern Pwo, *67* / The central Pwo, *69*

The Karen, Millennialism, and the Politics of Accommodation to Lowland States   81
PETER HINTON

Lowland relations with the Pwo Karen, *82* / Lowland relations with the Kayah Karen, *87* / The Pwo and Kayah compared, *89* / The role of millennial movements, *90*

v

Ethnic Identity and Sociocultural Change Among Sgaw Karen in Northern Thailand   99

SHIGERU IIJIMA

Sociocultural change in hill and plains Karen villages, *99* / The religious basis of ethnic identity, *107* / Sociocultural change and ethnic identity, *115*

Ethnic Group, Category, and Identity: Karen in Northern Thailand   119

PETER KUNSTADTER

Methods and evidence, *123* / The Karen at home, or who are the Karen? *125* / Karen in Mae Sariang district, *126* / Ethnic stability and cultural change, *130* / Karen economic status and ethnic identity, *134* / Extra-village relationships, *137* / Conclusions, *157*

In the Mosaic: The Cognitive and Structural Aspects of Karen-Other Relationships   165

DAVID H. MARLOWE

The behavioral basis of ethnic categorical usage, *168* / Karen social structure in comparison to Northern Thai, *176* / Karen-other group relationships, *180* / Hierarchy of social relationships involving Karen, *189* / Transformation of hierarchical to pluralistic society, *202*

Who Are the Karen, and If So, Why? Karen Ethnohistory and a Formal Theory of Ethnicity   215

F. K. LEHMAN

Karen origins: ethnolinguistic and historical evidence, *217* / Ethnic category words and their shifting application: did "Karen" always mean the people it means now? *229* / A general theory of ethnicity, *232* / Applications of the theory to Karen identity, *238* / The contemporary dynamics of Karen ethnicity: the Kayah example, *241* / Culture change and ethnic identity: some conclusions, *247*

References   255
Notes on the Contributors   268
Index   269

Photographs (by Charles F. Keyes) appear on pages 95–98.

Preface

This book had its beginnings in 1967–68 when several of the contributors (Kunstadter, Marlowe, Hinton, Lehman, and myself) were all engaged in field work among the Karen in northern Thailand. Our periodic meetings gave us the opportunity to compare notes, to argue, and to find common themes in our research. In 1971 I organized a symposium on the topic of "A Pivotal or Marginal People: The Place of the Karens in Southeast Asia," which was held at the annual meeting of the Association for Asian Studies in Washington, D.C. At the session, Peter Kunstadter, David Marlowe, Theodore Stern, and I delivered preliminary versions of the essays that appear here. F. K. Lehman, who served as discussant at the symposium, subsequently elaborated upon his remarks in the chapter presented here. Following the symposium, I sent copies of the essays to a number of people, soliciting their comments. After having read the works, Peter Hinton and Shigeru Iijima accepted my invitation to prepare contributions of their own. I was able to discuss their essays with them on visits to Australia and Japan in 1972 and 1973 respectively.

Although work on this volume was mainly completed in 1974 and it was originally scheduled for publication in 1977, a combination of circumstances has prevented its being published until now. Given the delay, the contributors to this volume have not been able to take into account all of the relevant literature on the Karen. For example, James W. Hamilton's study, *Pwo Karen: At the Edge of Mountain and Plain* (Hamilton 1976), appeared after all the contributors had completed their chapters. In the past few years, also, a new generation of scholars interested in the Karen, and particularly in the Karen in Thailand, has begun to emerge. I should like to call attention especially to the research carried out by Mr. Ronald Renard from the University of Hawaii on the history of Karen in Thailand, by Anders Baltzer Jørgensen and Kirsten Ewers Andersen of the Institut for Ethnologi og Antropologi, Copenhagen University, on economic and ideological aspects of Pwo Karen life, and by Michael Mahda of Cambridge University on economic aspects of Sgaw Karen life.

This work was conceived, as my introductory essay and several chapters by other contributors indicate, as a contribution not only to knowledge about the Karen but also to the efforts to construct theoretical interpretations of ethnic group relations. In my Introduction, I have attempted to formulate an approach to the study of ethnic group relations that takes into account both the structure of intergroup relations and the cultural meanings people attach to their ethnic identities. In an essay written subsequent to this one (Keyes 1976), I have attempted to explore other logical implications of my position and I have pursued the argument in yet another essay that has recently been completed (Keyes, forthcoming).

Many debts have been incurred in the effort to see this work finally into print and I can but acknowledge only the more obvious ones. All of the authors, myself included, are very grateful to the government of Thailand for permitting us to carry out our respective researches. I should like also to express my personal gratitude to the National Science Foundation whose support enabled me to carry out the research on which my own contributions are based and to begin the task of preparing the book. I am also indebted to the Faculty of the Social Sciences at Chiang Mai University (where I served as a visiting lecturer in 1972–74), to the Department of Anthropology, University of Washington, and to the Program for the Comparative Study of Ethnicity and Nationality, University of Washington, for arranging for the typing of the manuscript. I benefited greatly from the comments made by members of the Program in the Comparative Study of Ethnicity and Nationality at the University of Washington on my introductory essay and from the discussions I have had with them about various aspects of ethnic group relations. This program also made it possible for Mr. Richard Trottier to work with me in constructing an index to the work. Finally, I should like to thank each of the contributors for their patience, understanding, and tolerance throughout the long period during which this book has been in gestation.

CHARLES F. KEYES

A Note on Transcription

Since there is no generally accepted transcription of Karen words, I have allowed each author to use his own method. This means that the same term may appear quite differently in the various chapters. For example, the Sgaw expression, "to feed the ancestral spirits," is rendered *au xhre* by Marlowe, *awkre* by Kunstadter, and *oxe* by Iijima. Fortunately, the Karen words are few and the contexts are, so far as I can tell, sufficiently clear to permit identification of corresponding words as used by the different authors.

For words in Thai (standard Thai) and Northern Thai, I have followed a modified version of the system developed by the Thai Royal Institute, which is used for transcribing from standard Thai orthography. I have attempted to apply this system consistently throughout the book and have used it even for Northern Thai words, except when a form that more closely represents the speech form is specified. Thus, for example, the Northern Thai term for "Karen" is usually transcribed as *yang,* from the orthographic form, rather than *njang,* from the spoken form.

CHARLES F. KEYES

Introduction

Charles F. Keyes

> It is worthy of observation that, although residing in the midst of the Burmese and Peguans, they not only retain their own language, but even in their dress, houses, and everything else are distinguished from them; and what is more remarkable, they have a different religion. —Father Sangermano, writing of the Karen of Burma at the end of the eighteenth century.

Ethnic Groups: Some Theoretical Considerations

The observation made by Father Sangermano at the end of the eighteenth century provides us with the question that underlies all of the essays in this volume: How can 3 to 3.5 million people, living in Thailand and Burma,[1] retain a distinctive ethnic identity even though they are culturally diverse, have never had an independent nation-state, and have always been subjected to pressures exerted upon them by the politically and economically more powerful peoples with whom they live? Although the people known as the Karen are intrinsically interesting in their own right, the question posed here about them has implications that are not limited to the ethnography of Southeast Asia. Ethnic pluralism, once thought to reflect "primordial attachments" that give way as modernization occurs (cf., for ex-

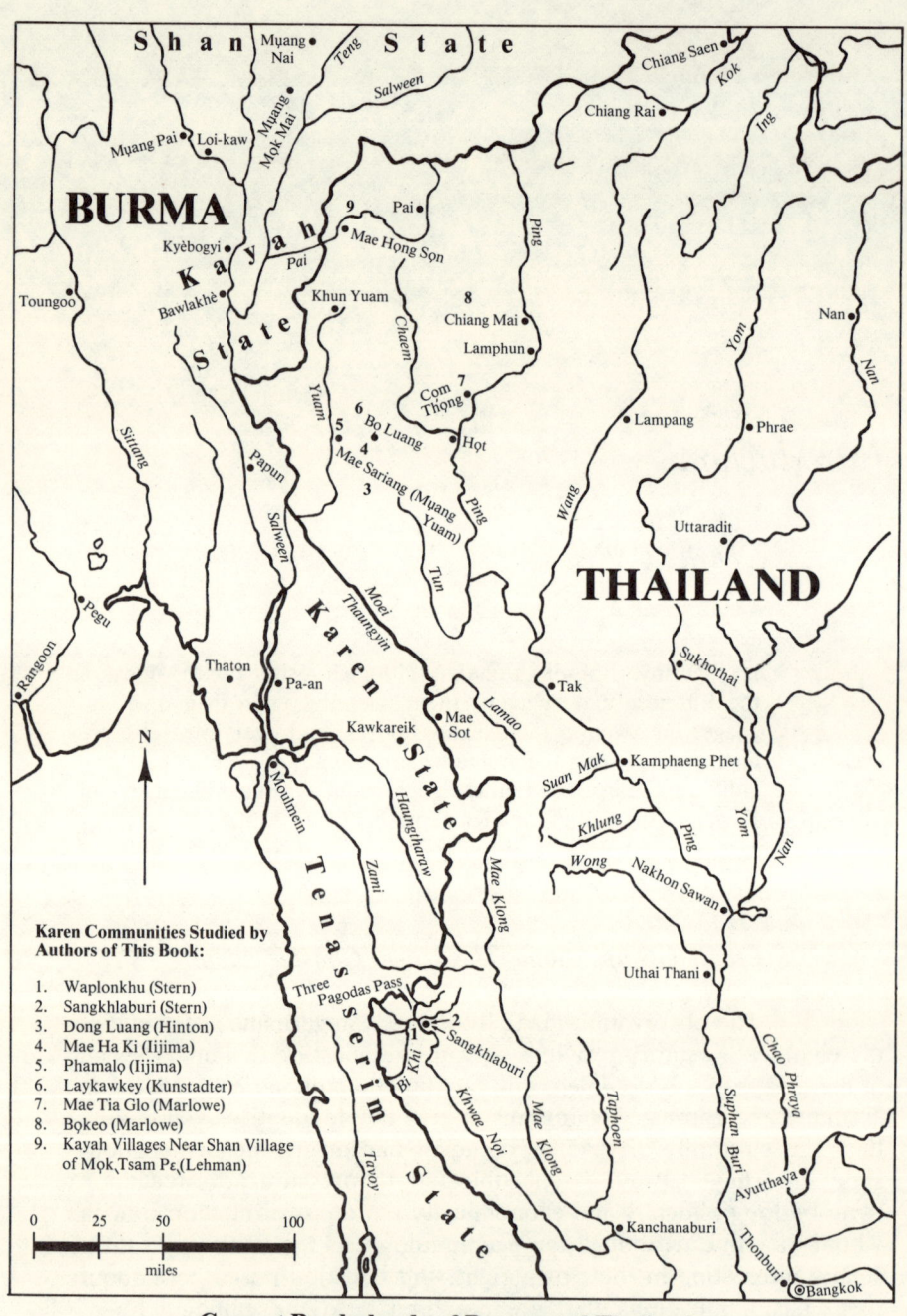

Current Borderlands of Burma and Thailand,
Including Areas of Karen Settlement

ample, Geertz 1963), has reemerged as a significant, and sometimes explosive, factor in advanced industrialized society. In this introduction, I should like to attempt to pull together some of these implications, first in general theoretical terms and then with specific reference to the Karen as described in the following chapters.

The conventional, and still popular, conception of an ethnic group is that of people who share a common culture, speak a common language, and belong to a common society. This conception has been sharply challenged by a number of anthropologists who have been confronted with particular ethnographic situations where the application of this conception would produce a highly distorted analysis. Perhaps the most well-known of such ethnographic situations is that of highland Burma. E. R. Leach, who carried out research in this area, found that the Kachin, recognized by those of the area as well as by the anthropologist as one of the two major ethnic groups of the region, included people who spoke a variety of mutually unintelligible languages and who displayed marked variations in culture. Rather than forcing his data into conventional categories, Leach concluded that "the ordinary conventions as to what constitutes *a* culture and *a* society are hopelessly inappropriate" (Leach 1954: 281). Leach argued, instead, that ethnic groups, such as the Kachin, should be conceived of as social, not cultural, entities, whose definition is a function of structural opposition to other such social entities. In the Kachin Hills of northern Burma, Leach found there was a fundamental opposition between two groups, Kachin and Shan, in their relative access to political power.

Following Leach, a number of other students of Southeast Asian ethnography have also analyzed ethnic group relations in terms of structural oppositions (see Lehman 1967A, 1967B; and Moerman 1965, 1968). Moreover, this view has gained wide acceptance in anthropology at the expense of the view that the world can be divided into discrete ethnic groups or "cultunits" (Naroll 1964) that possess common distinct cultures and common distinct languages. Recently, Fredrik Barth has attempted a general theoretical formulation for use in the study of ethnic groups and boundaries. For Barth, ethnic groups are also societal entities that result from a structural differentiation between interacting groups (Barth 1969B: 10). Determination of group membership is not a function of a shared common culture but of "ascription and identification by the actors themselves" (p. 10). Such ethnic identity, Barth further argues, "classifies a person in terms of his basic, most general identity, presumptively determined by his origin and background" (Barth 1969B: 13).

Barth also observes that the members of an ethnic group will share some features of culture; however, he suggests that this shared common culture is best regarded "as an implication or result, rather than a primary and definitional characteristic of ethnic group organization" (Barth 1969B: 11). Here I must disagree with Barth. It is not necessary to insist, as Barth seems to think those who see ethnic groups as culture-bearing units do, that members of ethnic groups share a total "assemblage of cultural traits" (Barth 1969B: 12) for culture to be a defining characteristic of ethnic groups.[2] Rather, ethnic identity itself provides the defining cultural characteristic of ethnic groups. The "origin and background" of individuals, from which, Barth says, ethnic identity is derived, are not communicated genetically or in some mysterious way. Rather, they are communicated, and constantly revalidated, in cultural expressions such as myth, religious belief, ritual, folk history, folklore, and art. These cultural expressions, these symbolic formulations of ethnic identity, provide individuals with the meanings that make relationships between ethnic groups meaningful. These cultural expressions of ethnic identity, and not some arbitrary list of cultural traits, provide the culturally distinctive character of ethnic groups.

Although it may offend certain modes of Western thought that would have ethnic identities be mutually exclusive, it is both theoretically possible and empirically verifiable that individuals may hold more than one ethnic identity concurrently. Take the case of villagers in northeastern Thailand with whom I have carried out research (Keyes 1966A, 1966B, 1967). Such villagers sometimes identify themselves as "Lao" when interacting with Thai government officials or with others from central Thailand. This identity finds expression in a folk history wherein they trace their origins to a common source with the Lao of Laos, in their beliefs that certain of their cultural traits—for example, the ceremony of calling the "soul-stuff" (*su khuan*)—are shared by the Lao of Laos and not by the Central Thai (whether all of these traits are distinctive is irrelevant; see Moerman 1968), and in one version of their folk ethnic taxonomy. On the other hand, when such villagers make visits to present-day Laos, which not a few of them do, they often identify as "Thai." This identity finds expression in the history villagers learn in school (education is compulsory for four and in some areas seven years), in rituals that link them as subjects to the king of Siam, and so on. Finally, on some occasions, in both Thailand and Laos, northeastern villagers will identify as "Isan," a term that means "northeasterner." This identity is more than merely regional, for to villagers it implies a distinctive cultural heritage drawn in part from the Lao, in part from the Thai, and in part (as manifest in folklore, various legends, etc.) from a local tradition found only in northeastern Thailand. Most villagers in northeastern Thailand have a choice of which of these three identities to use and many will use all three in different contexts. Groups that can draw upon more than one ethnic identity have a flexibility in adapting to multiethnic contexts which is not available to groups that are restricted (or that feel restricted) to a single identity. This point is particularly relevant to the Karen case, as we shall see below.

Although the cultural distinctiveness an ethnic identity provides is a necessary condition for the existence of an ethnic group, it is not a sufficient condition. As we have already seen, there must also be structural oppositions between groups for ethnic boundaries to exist. Following J. S. Furnivall (1939, 1956), many students of ethnic group relations have argued that the significant (and for some, the only) structural opposition is that which divides people in their access to productive resources and/or to wealth. To my mind, viewing ethnic groups as being the product of a "cultural division of labor" (to use a phrase suggested by Michael Hechter[3]) is too constricting. For example, in the case of the Kachin and Shan discussed by Leach (1954), the structural opposition was fundamentally a function of differential access to power in the Kachin Hills of northern Burma. In contemporary American society, structural oppositions have emerged between ethnic groups competing for access to knowledge as communicated within the educational system. In other cases, the opposition has been between those who have differential access to legal rights as citizens and/or before the bar of justice. In numerous cases known to anthropologists (see Lévi-Strauss 1949), the critical distinction is made on the basis of who should have access to the reproductive capacities of particular women. All of these examples have in common a structural differentiation between groups in their competition for scarce resources. That is, the members of an ethnic group share a common interest situation as well as a common cultural identity. It is in these terms that I view the structural opposition between ethnic groups.

Ethnic groups may stand in structural opposition to several different groups in relation to different resources. In Thailand, for example, an individual may be Chinese in contrast to Thai when seeking a job, but may also be Thai in contrast to other Southeast Asians in competing for a fellowship to study in a foreign country. The situation where all ethnic group boundaries fall along the same cleavage is the limiting, not the type, case.

Given the structured opposition between groups, ethnic identities serve to make meaningful the interaction among groups or their members. The Ban Ping villagers of Chiengkham district in northern Thailand, whom Michael Moerman has studied, explain (to themselves and to others) that the differences in various practices between themselves and townspeople is a function of their "Lueness." Such an explanation is functional, as Moerman shows, since villagers thereby "avoid opprobrious class identification through asserting the higher priority of a non-stratifiable ethnic identification" (Moerman 1968: 162). The villagers' practices are not indicators of class inferiority but, on the contrary, "the foci of ethnic pride" (p. 162). Ethnic identities serve not only to invest long established social relations with meaning but also to guide those who hold them in coping with new types of social relations. Following the end of British rule in Burma, the relationships between a variety of ethnic groups and the demographically and politically dominant Burmans underwent radical change. Many of those who carried the identity "Indian" were forced to "return home to India" even though some were second and third generation Burmese. Many Karen, like segments of many other ethnic groups, took up arms and began to demand political autonomy *as Karen*. Indeed, Burma today still probably has more "ethnic rebellions" than any other country in the world. In sum, ethnic identities serve as adaptive strategies for people faced with certain types of social experiences. As Clifford Geertz has noted of the relationship between culture and society in general, ethnic identities—or, more precisely, the symbolic expressions of such identities—can serve as both "models of" and "models for" such social experiences (Geertz 1966B).

As social circumstances change, preexisting ethnic identities may become less adaptive. If the significant structural oppositions between groups are eliminated, even marked cultural differences may be overcome and assimilation of individuals or groups to another ethnic group may occur. Such is the case with the Lua' or Lawa who live, and have lived for centuries, in the upland areas of northern Thailand. For the Lua', the significant structural contrast between themselves and the Northern Thai appears to be ecological, that is, the Lua' are swidden upland cultivators and the Northern Thai lowland wet-rice cultivators. Even though Lua' and Northern Thai cultures are markedly different (the Lua' language belongs to the Mon-Khmer language family and the Northern Thai language belongs to the Tai family; the Lua' are animistic, the Northern Thai Buddhist; and so on), Lua' who move from the hills to the lowlands can literally shed their identity as Lua' overnight. That such radical change in identity is possible indicates that nearly all Lua' have internalized much of Northern Thai culture and the codes of communication used by Northern Thai so little learning has to take place when identities are changed. However, the elimination of the structural opposition between Lua' and

Northern Thai that a move from the upland to the lowland accomplishes is the *causa efficiens* for ethnic change. In marked contrast, two groups can become increasingly alike in culture and still remain ethnically distinct if the structural opposition that separates them remains. Thus, the Ban Ping villagers studied by Moerman have remained Lue even though their culture has come to differ little from that of their Northern Thai neighbors. The Ban Ping villagers remain Lue in contrast to Northern Thai presumably (Moerman is not entirely clear on this point) because it is more practical to be ethnically different than (as is the case with the Northern Thai) to be rural Thai peasants (Moerman 1968: 162).

In contrast to the Lue case, Northeastern Thai villagers have taken on the identity of Thai (at least in some situations) even though the same structural difference between themselves and officials and townspeople also exists. In some situations, rural Northeastern Thai villagers are willing to think of themselves in class rather than ethnic terms.[4] To summarize the above argument, assimilation, which implies a change of ethnic identity, is not a function of the relative degree of difference between two groups in their cultures and languages. To think of assimilation in such a way would not only obfuscate our understanding of such cases of ethnic change or nonchange discussed above, but would also force us to ignore the marked cultural and linguistic variation that can and does exist among those who are members of the same ethnic group (cf. Barth 1969B; Hymes 1968). Rather, assimilation requires that the structural difference that separates two groups either be eliminated or redefined in nonethnic terms. Whether such redefinition takes place depends on the relative advantage of membership in an ethnic group as distinct from membership in some other type of social entity.

Just as structural contrasts may be eliminated or redefined, thereby making assimilation possible, new structural contrasts may emerge or old ones be redefined, thereby leading to the formation of new ethnic identities or the application of old identities in new ways. In Thailand, before the end of the eighteenth century, the label Chinese designated people from a foreign country and also was applied to a small, specifically "alien" or "stranger" population living in the country. With the great influx of migrants from China in the nineteenth century and the first part of the twentieth century, the term Chinese also came to be applied to an ethnic group within Thailand that held certain types of jobs (mainly proletarian and middlemen) (Skinner 1957). The influx of large numbers of migrants who have settled in the hills of northern Thailand together with the institution of new laws in Thailand regarding land use in the upland regions has led to the emergence of a new ethnic category, *chao khao* ("hill tribe"), used by Thai officials. Some of the people so classed, mainly Lua' and Karen, have been subjected to more disadvantages than they experienced with their previous ethnic status.

From the foregoing, it should be apparent that in studying ethnic group relations either as ongoing systems or in the process of change, both the cultural definition of groups (i.e., the ethnic identity or identities available to members) and the structural oppositions that separate groups must be treated as problematical. I now wish to turn to a specific body of ethnographic material, namely, that presented in this book, to examine how a particular ethnic identity, Karen, has been used in the adaptation of ethnic groups to a variety of social contexts found in Thailand, both past and present.

Ethnic Identity and Adaptation of Karen in Thailand

The vast majority for whom the term Karen is appropriate live in Burma, and it is from Burma that the first studies of the Karen come. Unfortunately, it has been next to impossible for anthropologists, linguists, historians, and others to carry out any research among the Karen of Burma since before World War II. The war itself, followed by the Karen rebellion against the newly established Union of Burma, the persistence of rebellion in a number of Karen areas, and the closing of Burma to outside scholars after the establishment of military rule in 1962 have prevented almost any research being undertaken among Karen populations. Among the very few research studies of the several types of Karen since the war are an anthropological study of the Pa-O or Taungthu Karen by William Hackett (1953), a man who served as a missionary to the Pa-O, a study of Karen language by R. B. Jones (1961A), who worked with informants in Moulmein and in the United States, and an ethnohistorical and ethnographic study of the Kayah by F. K. Lehman (1967A, 1967B), who was fortunate in being able to undertake seven months of research in Kayah State.

Although Burma has been closed, a number of linguists and anthropologists have in the last two decades made studies among Karen living in Thailand. Among the first postwar studies of Karen in Thailand were anthropological studies made by Addison Truxton (1958) and James Hamilton (1963, 1965) and a linguistic study by Joseph Cooke, J. Edwin Hudspith, and James Morris (1976). The essays contained in this volume all report upon recent research made among various Karen populations in Thailand mainly during the 1960s. This research has been made in the major areas of Karen settlement: Kan-

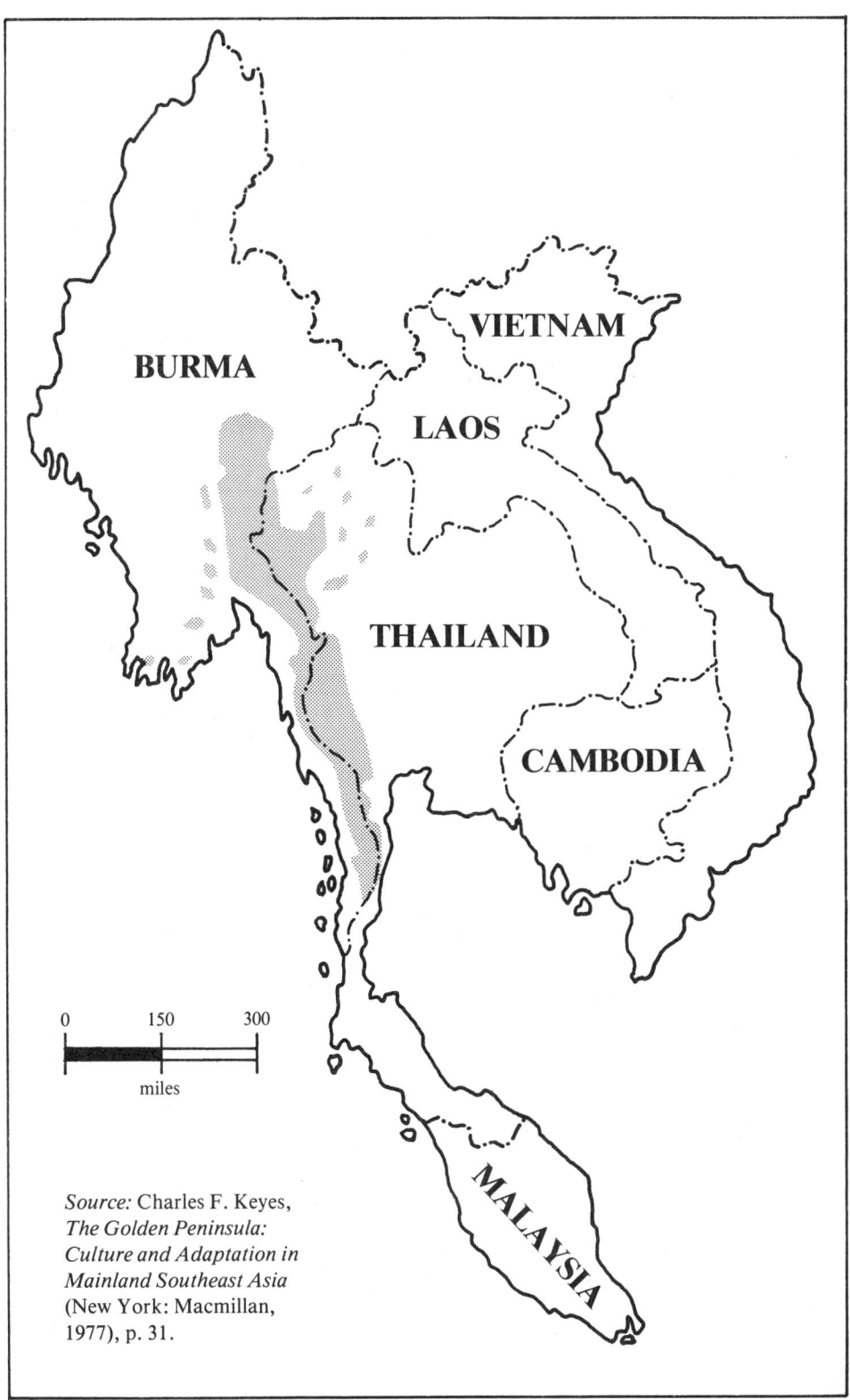

Source: Charles F. Keyes, *The Golden Peninsula: Culture and Adaptation in Mainland Southeast Asia* (New York: Macmillan, 1977), p. 31.

Location of Karen Populations

chanaburi province in central Thailand (Stern) and Chiang Mai (Marlowe) and Mae Hong Son provinces (Kunstadter, Iijima, Keyes, Hinton, and Lehman) in the north. In addition to anthropological and ethnolinguistic field research, a number of the authors have also undertaken research on historical sources. With all of the research taken together, it can be said that much of the relevant data on the Karen in Thailand to be found in the India Office, in the Thai archives, and in Thai chronicles and annals has been considered here. This totality of research—anthropological, linguistic, and historical—makes possible a balanced assessment of the adaptation of Karen in Thailand.

THE NATURE OF KAREN ETHNIC IDENTITY

Whether any particular local group can be considered ethnically Karen depends both upon whether members of the group so identify themselves and whether those with whom this group interact also identify them as such. There is no logical reason why self-identification and assigned identity should always coincide since the two identifications belong to different cultural sets. In fact, as we shall see, they do not always coincide.

Karen self-identity finds cultural expression in the beliefs that certain traits are culturally diagnostic and in myths and folk histories wherein Karen are distinguished from other ethnic groups. These cultural expressions of Karen identity are described by a term that, although having different forms in different Karen languages, means "person," "people," or "human being" in each language.[5]

Foremost among the cultural traits that local groups of "the people" see as diagnostic is that of language. What Theodore Stern says in his essay about the Pwo of Kanchanaburi could probably be said of all Karen groups in Thailand. The language of these Pwo, Stern says, is "significant in their own definition of their ethnic group" and "serves to locate them within the larger family of Karen speakers." It so happens that Karennic languages are highly distinctive and their relationship to other languages in Southeast Asia is still uncertain. Gordon Luce, the pioneer student of Karen languages, has suggested that despite the conventional identification of these languages as being Tibeto-Burman, they may be more closely related to Thai languages (Luce 1959A). R. B. Jones, who has made the most intensive studies of any linguist of Karen languages and dialects, tends to agree with Luce:

> Mon influence has apparently been very small; clear Sino-Tibetan words are also relatively few; many words are Burmese; they do not correspond for tone and are no doubt borrowings (in my

opinion). . . . I myself lean rather toward a Karen-Thai relationship, but still without any solid evidence. . . .[personal communication, March 1971].

Lehman's essay is rather critical of this postulated relationship between Karennic and Thai languages. Yet, whatever the ultimate connections of Karennic to other languages in Southeast Asia, the fact is that Karennic languages do remain highly distinctive in comparison to other languages in the region.

I have belabored the point about the distinctive nature of Karennic language since this characteristic is often pointed to as the fundamental element of Karen identity. Yet even for the Karen this would be a false conclusion. It is the *cultural belief* held by Karen people that their language is distinctive, and not the linguistic fact of the objective distinctiveness of Karen languages, that is relevant to the definition of Karen identity. Although the linguistic and cultural facts are unquestionably related, there are Karen speakers whose identity as Karen is rather dubious (some Taungthu interviewed in Mae Sariang thought of themselves as a type of Shan), and there are domestic speakers of languages other than Karen (e.g., some of the leaders of the Karen who use English they learned in missionary schools) who are unquestionably ethnically Karen.[6]

The identity of the Karen derives not only from their cultural belief in being speakers of the same language, but also from myths and folk history that define them as different from other neighboring groups. Common to these myths and histories is the cultural belief, constantly reiterated, that "the people" are in some way (in power, in wealth, in knowledge) inferior to the dominant lowland people. This is clear, for example, in the myth (versions of which Marlowe and Kunstadter provide) wherein the Karen lose the gift of a book (i.e., a literary tradition) given by God (*ywa*), but the Burmese, the Thai, Westerners, and the Chinese retain it. Both Peter Hinton and David Marlowe also show that the Pwo of Mae Sariang and the Sgaw of Chiang Mai today still retain memories, encompassed in their folk histories, of their subordinate position within Burmese society. With the apparent exception of the Pwo studied by Hinton, all of the Karen with whom the various authors in this book worked retain fairly concrete memories of their subordinate positions in premodern Thailand. In this latter guise, the Karen are not unique. Thus, it is not surprising to find the Karen of northern Thailand, for example, feeling a strong sense of kinship to the Lua' whose position in traditional Northern Thai society was very much the same as that of the Karen (see Marlowe's, Kunstadter's, and my own essay in this connection).

Although accepting a structurally subordinate position to the dominant lowlanders, at least some Karen hold the belief that they are morally superior, pointing specifically to lax sexual behavior on the part of the Thai as compared with the Karen (Kunstadter). In this the Karen echo the Lue, who Moerman also found use their ethnic identity as a mechanism for avoiding class considerations and for asserting a pride in their moral behavior (Moerman 1968: 162).[7]

It is important to observe at this point that, unlike Father Sangermano in the eighteenth century, those who have studied the Karen in Thailand have not found that the Karen associate their identity with a distinctive religion. Rather, Karen follow a number of different religions while still remaining Karen: traditional forms of spirit and ancestor worship, a tattooing cult (*cekosi*), several varieties of millennialism (cf. Stern 1968A), Christianity, and different types of Buddhism. That there is no single Karen religion does not make religion irrelevant to our considerations; quite the contrary, as we shall see below. However, for the moment, it is worth noting that few, if any, local groups of Karen in Thailand hold that particular religious forms distinguish Karen from non-Karen.

Each local group of Karen also appears to have a list of other cultural traits it believes distinguishes it (see, for example, Kunstadter's and Iijima's chapters). Again, it is not important whether these traits are shared exclusively by all Karen—they are not—but that they are believed to be distinctive (again, cf. Moerman [1968] who makes the same point regarding the Lue of Chiengkham).

Whether local groups in Thailand are identified as Karen by non-Karen depends upon what characteristics are considered distinctive in the ethnic taxonomies used by non-Karen groups. As I show in my chapter, it does not appear that the category Karen emerged as a significant one for either the Siamese of central Thailand or the Northern Thai until the eighteenth century. It is probable that before the eighteenth century people who carried the self-identity Karen were identified as Mon, Lua' or Lawa, or Shan by the Siamese and Northern Thai since the cultural characteristics of these categories could be applied to the Karen with whom they had contact. It is also possible that in certain local situations in premodern Thailand, Karen may also have been recognized by Thai as Karen.

By the nineteenth century, the groups Northern Thai and Siamese identified as Karen mainly coincided, insofar as we can tell from the historical record, with the groups who identified themselves as Karen. One exception appears to be the Taungthu (called Tǫngsu by the Siamese and Northern Thai) who appeared in Thailand as traders. The Taungthu were either specifically distinguished or were lumped together with the Shan. The unique status of the Taungthu for the Siamese and Northern Thai echoes the marginal place they occupy as Karen in the eyes of other Karen (cf. the Sgaw Karen legend given by Jones 1961A: 232–33) and even in their own eyes.

Since World War II, the Karen of Thailand have become increasingly subsumed, at least from the vantage point of the Thai government, in a general category of "hill tribes" (*chao khao*) (see Kunstadter's and Marlowe's essays). For the Thai government, and its representatives, those who are hill tribes are distinguished by their practice of upland swidden cultivation, by their production of opium, by their low level of economic development relative to the rest of the Thai population, and by their "alien" status as recent, and illegal, migrants into Thailand (see Suwan Ruenyote 1969: 12–13). As Peter Kunstadter notes, this definition of the distinctive characteristics of hill tribes tends to be drawn from the Thai image of Meo. It is a definition that grossly misrepresents the Karen: only part of the population are swidden cultivators; they are rarely cultivators of opium; their economic position is no worse than that of a large sector of the country's rural population who are ethnically Thai; and, for the most part, they are native-born residents of Thailand.

Insofar as the self-identity of Karen and the identification assigned to them by non-Karen coincide, the structure of intergroup relations is formed by common cultural understandings on both sides. However, when these do not coincide, as is the case at present when Karen are sometimes assimilated into the larger category of hill tribes, cultural misunderstanding may ensue. We will return to this point when we take up the question of the change in ethnic group relations between Karen and others in Thailand.

KAREN IDENTITY WITH RESPECT TO OTHER GROUPS

The main focus on ethnic group relations in this book is on the relationship between the Karen and the dominant peoples of Thailand. In premodern Thailand, these dominant peoples were the Siamese in central Thailand and the Yuan or Khon Muang (also called the Northern Thai) in northern Thailand. Today, most authors distinguish between locally resident Thai populations and the officials of the Thai state. In addition, almost all of the authors have made some observations on the relationships between the Karen and ethnic groups other than one of the Thai groups who live in the same area. I shall discuss the relationships between Karen and non-Karen with reference to structural differentiation in access to a number of different scarce resources.

Although a number of the authors found that Karen could marry with non-Karen, there is a marked preference among Karen for ethnic endogamy (see, especially, Kunstadter's comments on this point). Karen prefer to restrict access to the reproductive capacities of Karen women to Karen men. The example given by David Marlowe of a young Karen man who had been "married" to several Thai wives, but who said that when he "really" married it would be to a Karen, is instructive here. Ethnic endogamy is one of the main structural mechanisms for maintaining boundaries with other ethnic groups.

The Karen do not occupy a wholly distinctive ecological niche within Thai society but are limited in the type of economic roles they can fill while retaining an exclusive identity as Karen. The majority of Karen are agriculturalists, and the biggest percentage of these are swidden cultivators living in the hills of northwestern and west central Thailand. These swiddening Karen share the hills with a variety of other ethnic groups: Meo, Lua', Lahu, Lisu, to mention but a few. As Kunstadter shows, the boundaries between the Karen and other groups are distinct, even vis-à-vis the Lua' with whom some Karen have had very intensive relationships over several generations. These boundaries between various upland-dwelling peoples are not, however, well-known to many Thai. Particularly among Thai officials, there is a tendency to lump together all those who live by swidden agriculture in the hills under the rubric of hill tribes. The use of land for swidden cultivation is specifically proscribed by Thai law and it has been the policy of the Thai government since at least the early 1960s "to prevent the destruction of forest and courses of natural streams by encouraging stabilised agriculture to replace the destructive shifting cultivation practised by the hill tribes" (Suwan Ruenyote 1969: 13). Although the Thai government has tended to move rather slowly in enforcing this policy, its existence implies that all hill tribes, including Karen, are engaged in illegal acts and, therefore, subject to having their rights of access to their traditional means of livelihood summarily eliminated.

Those who are hill tribes are also considered, by definition of the Thai government, to be cultivators of opium. As such, they are again thought to be engaged in illegal acts that Thai policy seeks to end, albeit through a process of crop substitution rather than through force. Although Karen are included among the people for whom policies designed to eliminate opium production have been developed, a very small number of Karen actually engage in production of opium. Those who produce opium appear to have begun only in the past few years (Marlowe 1973), although other Karen, particularly those addicted to opium, have for some time worked as laborers in the fields of other groups such as the Meo, which do produce opium on a significant scale.

Although we have no precise information, there is no question but that a far bigger percentage of Karen than of any other so-called hill tribe of Thailand live in lowland villages and practice wet-rice agriculture. Moreover, Karen have lived in such lowland communities for at least several generations, a length of time sufficient for both upland- and lowland-dwelling Karen to think of such communities as part of the established world in which Karen live. Karen who move from the uplands to the lowlands do not associate such an ecological change with an ethnic change as do, for example, the Lua' (see Kunstadter's and Iijima's chapters). To be peasant farmers just like Thai who are peasant farmers poses no strain, it is apparent, on Karen ethnicity (see Marlowe's essay). Indeed, peasant farmers in Thailand can, and do, hold a variety of ethnic identities other than "Thai"—Lao, Shan, Lue, Mon, Chinese, Vietnamese, Khmer, Malay, for example.

Although ethnic considerations are not associated with agricultural occupations, they are relevant for occupations outside of agriculture. The Karen have something of a monopoly on the jobs associated with extracting teak from the forests of northwestern Thailand. In the recent past, when the teak industry was carried out on a wider scale in north Thailand than it is today, groups other than the Karen—the Khamu for example—also engaged in such jobs, but today the Karen have few, if any, competitors for these jobs. In Mae Sariang district, the elephants used for this work are owned by Karen, the labor is recruited exclusively from among the Karen, and the organizers and managers of the work parties are also Karen (cf. Kunstadter's chapter).

A few Karen involved in the teak trade have been able to accumulate capital that they have then invested in Mae Sariang, at least, in small-scale lumber mills and in commercial enterprises. It is significant that the handful of Karen capitalists in Mae Sariang, numbering not much more than a half dozen, also identify as Thai and are able to maintain this identity, when necessary, because they have acquired through education in Thai schools and through constant interaction with Thai the ability to make their actions as Thai appropriate, and because since they are Thai citizens and have a loyalty to the Thai king, they also have a cultural basis for a self-identity as Thai.

Some Karen in Mae Họng Sọn and Tak provinces have become wage laborers in local mines. Most such labor seems to be drawn from the poorest sector of Karen society and, often, from Karen whose homes are actually in Burma. Such labor, carried on as it is in areas surrounded by Karen villages, requires no new adjustments in ethnic identity.

A few Karen have taken on white-collar jobs and have still remained Karen. However, such jobs are limited almost exclusively to those of schoolteacher and Christian pastor, the latter being within the Karen Baptist Church. Those few Karen who have become schoolteachers have been educated within the Thai system but have returned to serve in Karen village schools. One major exception of a Karen who has taken on a job outside local Karen society and has still retained his identity as Karen is the manager of a major bank in Chiang Mai city in northern Thailand. This man, it should be quickly added, carries the identity of Thai as well as Karen. With the exception of those who have jobs within the teak industry, only those who have occupations that keep them within village society can maintain identity as Karen to the exclusion of all other identities.

The political position of the Karen within Thailand is very similar to their economic position. At the village level, leadership is ethnically Karen, although even here the role of village headman is conditioned by the fact that it must articulate with the Thai system of local administration. Beyond the village, no place is allowed for any degree of political autonomy for ethnic groups. This was not always the case; under the premodern political system Karen held office as feudal-like chiefs over political units in Kanchanaburi province that were recognized by the Thai government as being Karen units (see Stern's essay, pp. 66–67; and Stern 1971). However, such units were abolished in the wake of the administrative reforms instituted at the end of the nineteenth century (Tej Bunnag 1968). A number of the leaders of the Karen rebellion against the Burmese government have taken refuge in Thailand, some legally, others illegally. Moreover, elements of the Karen rebel forces operate from bases in Thailand. However, the rebels and their leaders seek to achieve political autonomy vis-à-vis the Burmese, not the Thai, authorities. Although some Thai Karen support the objectives of the Karen rebellion in Burma, there is no evidence to suggest there is any support for greater political autonomy for the Karen in Thailand. Insofar as they are allowed, Karen appear willing to participate as voters and as candidates for elected office in Thailand with reference to locality (as provided for in Thai law) rather than with reference to ethnic identity. In 1968 and 1969, as Kunstadter observes, some Karen in Mae Sariang voted, along with the other residents of the district, for a member of Parliament and for members of the Provincial Assembly. Two Karen stood for election to the Provincial Assembly, and one was elected. Both men, who, like the banker mentioned above, identified as Thai as well as Karen, fully accepted that they would represent the interests of the total constituency and not those of the Karen alone.

The application by Thai officials to the Karen of the identification as hill tribes has resulted, in some cases, in the total exclusion of Karen from the Thai political system beyond the village level. In official eyes, all hill-tribe peoples are, unless strong, documented evidence to the contrary exists, considered as "aliens" who have illegally settled within the borders of Thailand. Therefore, they do not have the right to obtain Thai citizenship. Even though very few Karen villages in Thailand include recent migrants from Burma, many upland Karen are not allowed to claim Thai citizenship. The potential explosiveness of this situation has been offset, in part, by the fact that most Karen so denied citizenship live in the most traditional of Karen hill villages. So far as we know, no lowland-dwelling Karen (other than self-proclaimed refugees from Burma) have been denied citizenship. In addition, the king of Thailand himself has taken a particular interest in the people living in the hills and has helped some Karen, as well as other upland-dwelling people, to gain rights as citizens.

Although the Karen, according to their own myths, did not obtain the gifts of writing and literacy at the same time as did their neighbors, a Karen literature did develop in Burma in the mid-nineteenth century following the success missionaries had in converting Karen to Christianity. American Baptists who worked primarily among Sgaw-speaking Karen helped devise an adaptation of Burmese script for use in writing Karen. This script subsequently gained greater popularity than its competitor, a Roman script devised by Catholic missionaries. Today, it is thought of by many Karen, even if they are not Christian and even if they speak dialects other than Sgaw, as the Karen script. The literature written in this script was, at the beginning, limited mainly to religious works; however, since early in the twentieth century, a secular literature has developed. Today, Karen presses in Burma continue to publish a large corpus of books, magazines, newspapers, and pamphlets on both religious and secular subjects.

There was apparently some debate after World War II within the missionary community in Thailand as to the advisability of using the Karen script rather than a Thai script for work among Karen. In the end, the Baptist missionaries decided to use this script because of the literature already available in Karen once literacy was attained. On the other hand, the Catholic missionaries have continued to use a Roman script and missionaries working among the Pwo Karen have developed a Thai script for transcribing Pwo. Despite the existence of several alternative scripts for Karen languages, literacy in Karen can be assumed, except in very rare cases, to mean literacy in the Karen using the Burmese-adapted script for Sgaw.

Most of the Karen who have achieved literacy in Karen have done so through association with the Karen Baptist Church, although a few non-Christian Karen apparently have picked up some knowledge of the language for writing love poems and love letters. Such cases notwithstanding, literacy in Karen can be said to orient those who possess it to a Karen Christian world. Such literacy has no functional value in Thai society outside of Karen communities. On the other hand, literacy in Thai, which is available to some Karen through government schools located in Karen villages or in towns to which Karen children are sent to live, makes possible much more varied involvement in Thai society. Such literacy is essential for any Karen who wish to obtain training in almost any skill other than the limited repertoire available in the village or through the church. Such literacy is also essential if any Karen aspires to a political role higher than that of village headman. In other words, the lack of literacy in Thai restricts a Karen to participating fundamentally only in a village-based society. Literacy in Karen does open an avenue for participation in a somewhat larger society, that of the Karen church. It may also orient the Karen towards Karen society in Burma, although it is not clear whether this actually occurs. Only literacy in Thai will afford the Karen an opportunity to participate in a national society, that of Thailand.

To identify exclusively as a Karen defines for one the population from whom one should choose a spouse, limits the economic roles one may play to those found in agricultural villages or in the teak trade, prevents one from acquiring power and authority over anything larger than a village, and affords one access to a literate education that, at best, prepares one for activity within the Karen church and that may orient one towards a country other than that in which one presently lives. Moreover, as a Karen, one may also be categorized by Thai officials as a member of the hill tribes. As such, one may not have the same legal rights as other residents of Thailand who are recognized as "citizens" and one may also be vulnerable to forcible disruption of one's livelihood. These considerations are relevant for our understanding of how Karen identity has been adapted to various situations in Thailand.

ETHNIC ADAPTATION AND CHANGE

Karen identity, when held exclusively, is today, as it has been for some time in the past, adaptable for those whose lives are confined to village-level society. But identity as Karen, while permitting some flexibility in adaptation, is obviously restricted when compared to identity as Thai. Those who experience structural constraints may cope with them in several ways. One possible resolution is assimilation, that is, the exchanging of one's present identity for an alternative identity that does not constrain one, at least in the same ways. There is evidence in the case of the hill-tribe people that the Thai government has made their structural position increasingly difficult while at the same time offering the carrot of assimilation (cf. Hinton 1969; Keyes 1971; Suwan Ruenyote 1969). The Thai government has promoted programs such as the establishment of Thai schools in tribal villages and has supported programs such as the Buddhist mission to the tribal peoples that serve as mechanisms of assimilation. Lehman's chapter provides an example of the Kayah of Mae Hong Son province whose position has become so untenable in their own eyes that they are willing to assimilate to almost any other group provided they can be assured of advantages if they do so. However, despite the pressures on the Karen to assimilate, the existence of mechanisms that could facilitate assimilation, and even (if the Kayah case could be generalized) the apparent desire to assimilate, actual cases of "total assimilation," that is, of Karen becoming Thai, are exceedingly rare. The reason for this is really quite simple: official policy notwithstanding, it is not necessary in Thai society for one to hold an exclusive ethnic identity. One can be *both* Thai and Chinese, Thai and Khmer, Thai and Lao, and so on. Similarly, one can be both Thai and Karen. Given the social pressures to remain Karen within domestic groups, within village society, within the church if one is Christian, and/or within the lumber industry, it is quite rational for one to restrict identity as Thai to those contexts, such as in interaction with government officials, in politics, in banking, and in other economic spheres, where it is more advantageous and more efficient for social relations to hold such an identity.

This possibility of being both Thai and something else is not fully accepted by all who identify exclusively as Thai. A local deputy district officer in Mae Sariang, for example, in the course of an argument with an American Baptist missionary, asserted that, "To be Thai is to speak only Thai, to be Buddhist." There are even some people who would make such an idea legally binding on the people of the nation. It has been such people who have periodically fanned the flames of anti-Chinese feeling and, more recently, of anti-Malay and antitribal feelings. Fortunately, to date, such people have always been in a distinct minority and Thai society has been able to accommodate happily those who hold two and even three or more ethnic identities concurrently.

There are also those within Karen society who would insist on being Karen in all contexts. Some Karen who feel the structural limitations of their position are nevertheless unable and/or unwilling to adopt a superordinate identity as Thai. These people may not have the mechanisms for acquiring such an identity. They may have been influenced by the objectives of the Karen independence movements in Burma. Or they may simply not understand that it is possible within Thai society to hold more than one ethnic identity. For those who do perceive the limitations of their structural position as Karen and who also insist on or have no choice but to accept an exclusive identity as Karen, the only resolution is to effect a restructuring of their position. This could mean, and in Burma certainly has meant, a resort to armed rebellion. However, since the eighteenth century, at least, the more typical response of Karen caught in such constraints has been religious, especially, but not exclusively, manifest in the form of millennial religious movements. As Theodore Stern has shown in his superb study of Karen millennialism (Stern 1968A) and as is evident from the data presented here (see especially Hinton's and Stern's essays), millennialism has long been endemic among Karen of both Burma and Thailand. For the Karen in Thailand, the movements have included the Telakhon sect in Kanchanaburi province and the movement focused on the "white robed teacher" (*khruba khao*), which several authors in this book observed in areas of northern Thailand. In addition, I have found evidence of other local Karen millennial movements including one that had its florescence in 1967–70 in northern Tak province and that centered on a young Karen boy who had taken to wearing white robes. Yet another movement was still going strong in 1974 in Lamphun province where a large number of Karen from Chiang Mai had gathered around a charismatic Northern Thai monk. Millennialism represents an effort, culturally expressed, to escape structural binds or to come to grips with radical structural change (cf. Keyes 1973, 1977). However, millennialism ultimately always fails as millennialism since the millennium never comes.

On the other hand, religious change that provides for a new definition of reality and that is not millennial can serve to resolve the structural problems people face. The widespread embrace of Christianity by Karen certainly has its roots in the social constraints many Karen experienced. Moreover, the particular place that association with Western missionaries in Burma gave the Karen provided not only a cultural solution to their difficulties but also a social solution as well. Unfortunately, the solution was only temporary since the special place of the missionaries was eliminated following the end of colonial rule in Burma. In this sense, the success of Christian missionaries among the Karen must be seen as one of the most significant causes for the emergence of the Karen rebellion following the British recognition of an independent Burma.

In Thailand, Christian missionaries have also had some significant success in their work among the Karen, particularly Sgaw-speaking Karen. Conversion to Christianity has also had the effect in Thailand, as in Burma, of strengthening the ethnic boundaries between Karen and others. However, unlike the case in Burma, in Thailand the missionaries and the leadership of the Karen church seem to be aware of this fact and are concerned not to have the Karen Christian community stand apart from Thai society. Thus, in recent years, the Karen Baptist Church has affiliated with the Church of Christ in Thailand whose leadership is ethnically Thai. Moreover, the Karen Baptist Church no longer sponsors schools of its own, but provides hostels so Karen can attend Thai schools. In other words, there have been some efforts on the part of missionaries and Christian leaders among the Karen in Thailand to make the Karen Baptist Church another mechanism whereby Karen can acquire a superordinate identity as Thai. Whether these efforts will succeed in the face of strong countervailing pressures to keep the Karen Baptist Church distinctively Karen, as is exemplified in its continued use of Christian literature in Karen rather than in Thai, is not yet certain.

Embrace of millennialism and conversion to Christianity are not the only forms of religious change to be found among the Karen in Thailand. A number of writers mention a recent cult movement, known as *cekosi,* whose members are released from obligations to serve the spirits after having been ritually tattooed. The information on this cult is too sketchy as yet to permit us to understand what cultural explanations are offered as replacement for the belief in spirits. Nonetheless, it should be noted that the movement has attracted a fairly sizeable following in Mae Hong Son and Chiang Mai provinces.

A number of Karen today identify themselves as Buddhists, although many who do have rather different ideas about what Buddhism is than do the Thai or the Burmese. From the studies reported here, it would appear that Karen adherence to Buddhism is strongest among the Karen in Kanchanaburi province (see Stern's chapter). In Mae Sariang district, it appears that until recently those Karen who were Buddhists tended to follow Burmese rather than Thai forms of the religion. This was true in part because of the connection of Karen with Burma and in part because the owners of the teak company in Mae Sariang, for whom many Karen work, were followers of Burmese Buddhism rather than Thai Buddhism. However, in the past decade or so, a small but steady number of Karen have been ordained as novices and occasionally as monks in the Thai order. As these Karen leave the order to take their places in lay society (the Thai order encourages men to spend temporary periods as novices or monks), they become the nuclei of lay Buddhist groups that are now oriented towards Thai Buddhism. It seems probable that the percentage of Buddhists following the Thai Buddhist forms will continue to increase among the Karen in all parts of the country. It should be noted, however, that becoming Thai Buddhists does not require that Karen cease to be Karen. Rather, what is occurring, as my own work in Mae Sariang district revealed, is the emergence of a Karen Buddhist community that is structurally linked to the Thai ecclesiastical hierarchy but that culturally is adapted to the experiences of Karen villagers.

The adaptation of Karen to Thai society has undergone marked changes in the two centuries or so since they have lived in association with the other peoples of Thailand. In the nineteenth century, Karen were able to develop locally autonomous entities that were distinctively Karen. The administrative reforms at the end of the century eliminated the right to local political autonomy beyond the village level. The emergence of the Thai official attitudes towards hill tribes, a category often applied to the Karen, has led to the Karen being placed at a disadvantage relative to other groups in Thai society in regard to access to land and to the rights accorded Thai citizens. For many Karen, the response to the growing untenableness of their position has been to turn to new religious explanations, a response we now recognize (thanks to Stern's work) as being characteristic of Karen when placed in such a position. The embrace of millennialism has, as Peter Worsely (1968) has observed in his study of Cargo cults, a strong element of incipient nationalism. Karen nationalism has been fed further, although apparently only to a small degree, by the persistence of Karen rebellion against the Burmese government. In short, both the reasons for increased ethnic conflict and the mechanisms for nationalistic expression of such conflict exist among the Karen of Thailand.

Such conflict need not become the prevailing characteristic of Karen relations with the Thai. To date, it has not become an imperative for those living in Thai society to be ethnically Thai in all spheres of social action. Karen, and other non-Thai ethnic groups, do not choose between total assimilation and separatism. Rather, Karen can remain Karen in much of their social life, while becoming Thai for those sectors of social action wherein such an identity is required. Whether Karen choose this route in accommodating to Thai society depends in part on how successful the Thai government and other institutions such as the Karen Baptist Church are in establishing mechanisms, such as schools, whereby Karen can acquire those attributes that make identification as Thai possible and acceptable. It also depends in part on these institutions not erecting barriers—such as denying Thai-born Karen the right of citizenship or insisting on the distinctiveness of the Karen church—that preclude the acquisition of the additional identity as Thai. It is impossible to predict whether an accommodation that permits the Karen to be both Karen and Thai or whether conflict between Karen and Thai will characterize the future of the Karen in Thailand. However, the strong effort undertaken by King Phumiphon in the past few years to make a place for the hill tribes within Thai society that does not necessitate their total assimilation bodes well for the future.

Notes

1. Perhaps the 1973 census figures, when known, will permit a satisfactory estimate of the number of Karen in Burma, but for the moment only estimates can be made. In 1931 the Karen in Burma were estimated to number 1,340,000 (LeBar, Hickey, and Musgrave 1964). Extrapolating in analogy with population increases elsewhere in Southeast Asia, it is probable that Karen in Burma today number over 3 million. In Thailand various estimates made by government officials I interviewed in Chiang Mai placed the Karen population in Thailand in 1970 between 100,000 and 150,000.

2. I am indebted to Professor James B. Watson, my colleague in the Department of Anthropology at the University of Washington, for first pointing out to me the implications of Barth's position regarding the relationship between ethnic groups and culture.

3. Michael Hechter's approach focuses upon "the salience of cultural distinctions in the system of stratification. . . . When individuals are assigned to specific types of occupations and other social roles on the basis of observable cultural traits, or markers, this may be appropriately termed a 'cultural division of labor' " [Hechter 1974B: 1154; also see Hechter 1971, 1974A].

4. I suspect this is also the case for Michael Moerman's Ban Ping villagers as well. Certainly in situations wherein tribal people are involved, Ban Ping villagers would rather be thought of as members of a class of Thai society than as one of the tribal groups whose status in Thai society is marginal.

5. In Sgaw Karen, the relevant term is /pyakəʔ ñɔ́/ and in Pwo, /phó/, which is cognate with Sgaw /pyò/ (Jones 1961). In Kayah, the relevant term is /kəʔyà/ (see Lehman's chapter).

6. James B. Watson (personal communication) informs me that in the central highlands of New Guinea there is a group that denies that some speakers of mutually intelligible dialects actually speak the same language.

7. F. K. Lehman (personal communication) has pointed to a similar pattern among the Chin of Burma: The "Southern Chin work hard to maintain their separate identity on the grounds that psychologically it is more acceptable to define goals and standards that one can live up to than to accept goals and standards that one is too poor to live up to; that is, it is better to have the chance to be a successful Chin than a half-arse Burman" (also see Lehman 1963).

The Karen in Thai History
and the History of the Karen in Thailand

Charles F. Keyes

In the records of Thai history, that is, in the records of the Siamese kingdom of central Thailand and of the Yuan or Lannathai principalities of northern Thailand,[1] one finds occasional reference to people who are labelled *kariang* in Siamese and *yang*[2] in Yuan. On the basis of present-day usage, these labels would appear to indicate the presence in certain historical contexts of Karen-speaking people. Although not all Karen-speaking people referred to in the records of traditional Thailand are labelled *kariang* or *yang*[3] and although, in one case at least, the label *yang* does not indicate Karen-speaking people,[4] the usage of these labels can generally be taken as referring to Karen-speaking people. Thus, the appearance of these labels in the records provides clues for one interested in the history of the Karen in Thailand.

While serving to answer one question, the use of the labels *kariang* and *yang*, as with the use of any ethnic group designations found in primary historical documents, raises another question. Why did those who compiled the records find it necessary or useful to employ these labels? Why, in other words, do Karen-speaking people appear under distinctive ethnic labels in Thai history?

In this essay, I concern myself with these questions. On the one hand, I attempt to use Thai historical records to throw light on the history of the movement and settlement of Karen-speaking people within the present-day borders of Thailand. On the other hand, I attempt to identify the structures of intergroup relationships that prompted the compilers of Thai histories to use labels designating Karen-speaking people. The focus is particularly on the relationship of the Karen to the Yuan and Siamese, both Tai-speaking peoples.

Were the Karen an Autochthonous People in Northern Thailand?

In some Yuan accounts, there are references to a relationship between Karen-speaking people and Tai-speaking Yuan that was forged at a time when the Yuan were first establishing themselves in northern Thailand. Bunchuai Sisawat, in his study of the hill people of Thailand, has summarized these accounts as follows:

> The Karen lived in the area of [present-day] Thailand before the Thai moved down into the Suwannaphummi Peninsula. But their numbers were few and they arrived after the Lawa or Lua?. In several histories of reliquaries (*phrathat*) and in the northern chronicles, it is mentioned that after the Lua? or Lawa there was a Yang or Karen group living in the forests around the *muang*. The Karen themselves say that they are the elder siblings of the Thai [Bunchuai Sisawat 1963: 66; my translation].

In searching through Yuan texts, I have been able to trace three sources that appear to support Bunchuai's conclusions.

The first is the *Camdevivaṁsa,* a chronicle of Haripuñjaya, the first kingdom of record in northern Thailand. This chronicle was written, in Pali, by a Yuan monk living in Chiang Mai, in what is today northern Thailand, in the late fourteenth or early fifteenth century (Coedès 1925: 12–13). In the published Thai version of this chronicle, it is stated that *kariang,* along with Lua', lived in the forests around the site upon which the old city of Chiang Mai is said to have first been built in the eighth century A.D. (Pọriyat Thammathada and Phra Yanwicit 1967: 54–55). A similar piece of evidence comes from the Yuan history, the Chronicle of Mahathera Fạ Bŏt, which has been published in French translation by Camille Notton.[5] In a footnote to a passage concerning the founding of Chiang Mai by one Phraya Lua' (Lord Lawa), Notton quotes a variant version to the effect that the Lord made offering to the spirits of both the Lua' and the Yang (Notton 1926: 35–36).

The most extended account of early Yuan-Karen relations occurs in a Yuan legend summarized by Charles Archaimbault in his 1961 study, "L'histoire de Campasak":[6]

> Formerly, in Lanna, there were two petty kingdoms which were allies. One was Mu'ang Yu, which was ruled by K'ulah and his wife Mahko'n, and the other was Mu'ang Yong[7], ruled by Ko'ng Cau and his wife Ngau H'on. The two kings were deceived by a tribal chief belonging to the aboriginal Karen and were forced to abandon their kingdoms. They took refuge in the region of Chiang Rai where they became agriculturalists. Mahko'n had a son, K'ulu, while Ngau H'on had given birth to a daughter, Nang Ua. When they grew up, K'ulu fell in love with his friend, but she did not feel for him even as she would for an elder brother.
> She met the son of the Karen chief and fell in love with him. However, when her mother revealed to her the treason which the father of the young man had committed, Nang Ua then turned her attention to K'ulu. They vowed that they would commit suicide if they ever broke their promise of fidelity. On the day of the wedding, the son of the Karen chief used a narcotic to put all the guests to sleep. On the following morning when K'ulu arose, he discovered that his fiancée had disappeared. He found her in a woods and he killed himself [Archaimbault 1961: 527–28; my translation].

Archaimbault observes (pp. 527f.) that this myth is one of a type that defines the relationship between those who founded lowland states *(muang)* and an aboriginal tribal people who live in the same area.[8]

The accounts found in the legends and records of the Yuan would appear to be the source for the theory, found in a number of versions in both Western and Thai writings, that the Karen were among the autochthonous inhabitants of Thailand. James Scott and J. P. Hardiman, in the *Gazeteer of Upper Burma and the Shan States,* for example, quote an unspecified source as asserting that:

> The best authorities believe the Siamese to have migrated, only shortly before the founding of Ayuthia, from the hill country towards the north and to have displaced the aboriginal Karens, by whom the country now called Siam was inhabited [Scott and Hardiman 1900: I, 259].[9]

This theory finds some support in Karen legend as well. Stern has reported a Pwo Karen myth, current today, that deals with the legendary migrations of the Karen.

> [These migrations were] led initially by Htaw Meh Pa, with his magical comb—or gold and silver combs—of immortality, until he

> went on ahead and vanished from sight. Thereafter, the Karen split from one another . . . the Pwo from the Taungthu at the Valley of Five Piles of Paddy Husks, in western Thailand [Stern 1968A: 303].

There is also a Kayah Karen legend, given by Francis Mason, that makes the relationship between Yuan and Karen more specific. Mason is discussing the migration of the ancestors of the Kayah to what is now the Kayah state of Burma:

> [This migration] occurred about the time the Shans [i.e., Tai-speaking peoples] first settled in Labong [Lamphun] and Zimmay [Chiang Mai]; because tradition represents the [Kayah] chieftain to have come over [to northern Thailand] first with an exploring party, and they selected the region around Labong and Zimmay for their future home; but when he returned with his nation, he found it occupied by the Shans [Mason 1860: 72].

Professor Gordon Luce has also speculated, on the basis of his study of Karen languages, that "it is Thailand . . . more than Burma, which holds the key to the secret of Karen origins" (Luce 1959A: 3). Professor Luce based his argument on the linguistic theory that the area of greatest linguistic diversity in a language family is likely to be the area in which that family has existed for the longest time. For Karen languages, this area of greatest diversity appeared, to Luce, to lie in a hill area on the border between Burma and northern Thailand:

> Though unimportant numerically, it is the Karens of these eastern hills of southern Burma and Siam, who provide the greatest linguistic interest and variety. These hills are the nursery from which the Karens as a whole have spread and multiplied all over the plains of Lower Burma [p. 3].

R. B. Jones, another student of Karen languages, accepts the same theoretical position as that taken by Professor Luce, but he points out that it is not Thailand where Karen languages are found in greatest diversity. Rather, Jones has written:

> Dialectological evidence would place [the Karen] "Urheimat" in roughly the Southern Shan States area, for there we find the greatest number of distinct dialect groups which differ widely from each other.[10]

Jones then offers a speculative reconstruction of early Karen history—a reconstruction he says depends heavily on Professor Luce's studies of the geopolitical history of Burma:

> My own guess, and it is no more than that, is that in these early years of our era the Mon were dominant in the South [of Burma], the Pyu in the West-Central, and Karens in the Eastern hill area, and that the coming of the Shans precipitated the movement of some of them (especially Sgaw and Pho) to the plains and southwards, possibly accounting for their presence in the Pyu area.[11]

Professor Jones also observes, on the basis of linguistic data, that the Karen who live in Thailand appear to have settled in this country comparatively quite late. This observation is strongly supported by historical data, to be presented below, that indicate Karen-speaking people did not begin to settle in what is today Thailand until the end of the eighteenth century. Indeed, after the reference to *yang* in the early accounts of the Yuan, no other references to Karen occur in Thai sources, so far as I have been able to check, before the seventeenth century.

We are left, then, with a puzzle. Both Yuan and Karen sources point to some relationship between the Tai and the Karen at a period (thirteenth century and earlier) when the Tai were becoming the dominant people in northern Thailand. Subsequently, the Karen disappear from the Tai records, a fact that on the surface also appears strange since Karen were known to live in the border region between the Mon, Burman, and Shan states, which are mentioned in the chronicles.

In attempting to solve this puzzle, we must first think of the categories of Karen, Yuan, Siamese, and so on as belonging to a matrix (or matrices) of ethnic group relations rather than as designating distinctive "culture-bearing units" (Barth 1969B; Lehman 1967A). This is not to say that the Karen are not culturally distinctive from the Yuan or Siamese. Indeed, some cultural and linguistic differences are presupposed whenever ethnic distinctions are made. The point is that cultural and linguistic differences do not themselves determine that a group will be ethnically distinct. For ethnic distinctions to emerge and be perpetuated, there must be structural divisions among people who live in close proximity and maintain regular interaction in regard to religious truth, power, and/or wealth. The access to one or all of these is recognized by the people concerned as being the right of those who share some common set of cultural traits not shared by others. The traits that are manipulated in determining ethnic affiliation vary from one case to another and may, in fact, not be particularly distinctive even though they are believed to be (Moerman 1965). What remains constant is the structural division of access to religious truth, power, and/or wealth.

In traditional Southeast Asia, that is, before the eighteenth and nineteenth centuries when structural bases for economic, political, and religious action began to be seriously challenged and then culturally altered, there was a type of structural division of access to wealth, power, and religious truth that was very widespread.[12] Two "ethnic groups" lived in symbiotic relationship, the one having wet-rice cultivation as its economic base and being organized into states or quasi-feudal polities, the other having upland swidden cultivation as its main system of production and having no stable political organization that brought together more than a few villages. Each of these groups also followed distinctive religious traditions, the first adhering to a tradition in which ultimate causation was disassociated from the immediate sociospatial world in which people lived and the second still following a tradition in which the most important sources of supernatural power were linked with locality and family. Such religious distinctions served both to reinforce cultural conceptions of access to power and wealth and to orient the adherents to some types of social action that could be termed religious (Geertz 1966B). As E. R. Leach (1954) has shown, there may be considerable objective cultural and linguistic variation among the people who are thought of and think of themselves as belonging to one or the other of ethnic groups in such a pair.

The best-known examples of dichotomized ethnic groups that are both linked and separated by the structural divisions outlined in the model include Kachin-Shan (Leach 1954), Chin-Burman (Lehman 1963), Lua'-Yuan or Khon Muang (Kraisri 1965A; Kunstadter 1965), and Kha-Lao (Archaimbault 1964, 1973: 77–96). Before the eighteenth century, Karen-speaking people also maintained similar symbiotic relationships although given their numbers and distribution, there was not just one other member of the other category. In lower Burma, the relationship was with the Mon; in Central Burma, it was with the Burmans; and in upper Burma, it was with the Tai-speaking Shan. It is my thesis that the early use in Northern Thai sources of the term *yang*, a term that is paired with *tai* in the southern Shan states, indicates not that Karen-speaking people were present in northern Thailand at the time when the Tai-speaking people assumed dominance but that Shan from the southern Shan states were.

When Tai-speaking people became the dominant people in northern Thailand, most would appear to have adopted the conception of dichotomous ethnic group relations that had been held by their Mon predecessors. In Tai terms, this structure came to be formulated as Lua' or Lawa-Yuan or Khon Muang. However, some of the early Tai who helped found the principalities of Lannathai may have brought with them another conception, that of Yang-Tai, which had evolved in the southern Shan states, an area that appears, on linguistic evidence, as we have seen, to have been the area of greatest Karen concentration.

Since no Karen-speaking people, or at least no significant numbers of Karen, moved into the domains of the Yuan of northern Thailand before the eighteenth century, and since the category Yang did not supplant the older category Lua', reference to Yang soon disappeared. When the category reappeared, it was in the context of a new matrix of ethnic group relations in northern Thailand.

Origins of Karen Relationships with Siamese and Yuan

Even though Karen-speaking people were probably not among the earliest inhabitants of Thailand, they did live in hill areas along the borders of the old Yuan and Siamese states from the beginnings of these states in the thirteenth century. Despite the proximity, Yuan and Siamese chroniclers made no references to the Karen in their accounts until the seventeenth century, and even these references are rather problematic. It was only with the major political upheavals of the eighteenth century that the Karen began to come to the attention of the Siamese and Yuan; that is, it was only when events forced the Siamese and Yuan to restructure their conceptions of ethnic group relations that Karen became a significant category for them.

Prince Damrong in his study, *Thai Wars with Burma,* mentions, in a footnote, that one Saen Phumilokaphet, who was a commander of troops under King Naresuan during the Siamese attack on Toungoo in 1600, was probably a *kariang* (Prince Damrong 1962: 172; cf. Prince Damrong 1957: 190). Unfortunately, this fact is not corroborated by either the Siamese or Burmese chronicles I examined.[13] Since Mon had at this time been included in special units of the Siamese forces, it would seem possible that Saen Phumilokaphet had risen to his position because of the association of Karen with the Mon. However, there is no evidence for this conjecture.

In 1661, again according to Prince Damrong, a Siamese force invaded northern Thailand and captured a number of northern principalities *(muang).* Included among these were "many principalities of Karen and Lawa which were under the rule of Chiang Mai, for example, Muang Inthara Khiri [Skt. Indra Giri], Muang Ramtri, and Muang Umluk, a border post" (Prince Damrong 1962: 233–34; Prince Damrong 1957: 234–35). Neither the Yuan chronicles (which date the events in 1662) nor the Ayutthayan chronicles mention the names of the places nor the fact that Karen principalities were then under the suzerainty of the Yuan state of Chiang Mai (*Phra ratchaphongsawadan krung Ayutthaya* 1962: 447; Prachakitcakoracak 1964: 411–12; Sanguan 1972B: 104). This reference is most intriguing since it suggests that in the seventeenth century, Karen were included in the political domain of Chiang Mai and that they (along with the Lua') were organized at least symbolically into political units *(muang)* comparable to those of the Yuan themselves.[14]

There is some evidence, from sources other than those of the Siamese or Yuan, which might throw light on this reference to the Karen in the seventeenth century. In the history of the southern Shan principality of Muang Pai (Mobyè in Burmese), Karen are mentioned as having been a component in the population in the middle of the sixteenth century when the principality was founded. Since Muang Pai is located near the border of the Yuan state of Chiang Mai, its emergence could not have been without interest to the Yuan rulers even though the principality is not mentioned in Yuan chronicles until a much later date. It is possible that when Muang Pai was founded, the Yuan moved to extend their influence over border populations to safeguard their interests. The importance of the Karen of this area at the end of the seventeenth century is indicated by the fact that Karen destroyed the ruling house of Muang Pai in 1692 and were able to withstand a Burmese attack mounted in 1696.[15] This Karen revolt of the late seventeenth century might represent the beginnings of political change that were to lead to the formation of the Kayah principalities.

Whatever we are to make of the reference to the Karen in Prince Damrong's works referring to the late seventeenth century, the fact remains that the Siamese and Yuan chronicles are totally lacking in any reference to Karen, save for the early legendary references already discussed, before the eighteenth century. It is the upheaval in both Burma and the Tai states in the eighteenth century that finally catapults Karen onto a stage where both Siamese and Yuan take significant notice of them.

At the beginning of the eighteenth century, we know that Karen-speaking people were living primarily in the hills of the southern Shan states and along the eastern frontier of Burma down into the Tenasserim Peninsula. In the southern part of this region, the major valley people with whom Karen had contact were Mon and to a lesser extent Burmans; in the central region, contacts with Burmans were greater than those with any other "civilized" people; and, in the north, contacts were primarily with Shan. Such contacts between Karen and lowland peoples ranged from intensive to almost none in the case of the Karen living in hills in the interior.[16]

Ultimate power over all the lowland people of Burma plus over all upland people who maintained symbiotic relations with the lowlanders lay nominally with the Burman kings at Ava. In fact, at the outset of the eighteenth century, these kings were so weak that effective power was very localized. Karen, at this time then, probably knew of no higher authority than Mon and Burman *myothugyis* (officials in charge of administrative districts) and Shan *sawbwas* (local "lords"). To the east of Burma, the Siamese state of Ayutthaya had also fallen into a decline following the "Golden Age" of King Narai who died in 1688. The local prince of Chiang Mai in northern Thailand had taken advantage of weak Burmese rule to attain effective independence in the early part of the eighteenth century. In short, in the world surrounding the Karen in the early part of the eighteenth century, the power of the lowland civilizations was markedly fragmented.

Out of this context emerged several new claimants to power. The movements they led had strong millennial overtones, a fact that is far from unimportant in what happened to the Karen during the middle and latter part of the eighteenth century.

The first significant attempt to resurrect a strong throne was made by the people of lower Burma who rose in rebellion against Ava in 1740. The prevailing interpretation of this uprising and the subsequent struggle between upper and lower Burma for political supremacy considers these events in terms of ethnic nationalism with the Mon of lower Burma pitted against the Burmese of upper Burma (see Hall 1968: 385f.; Steinberg et al. 1971: 97–98). Although it is true that the old Kingdom of Pegu (Haṁsavati), which had been subjugated by the Burman kingdom of Ava in the sixteenth century, had been ruled and mainly populated by Mon, by the eighteenth century, ethnic Burmans most certainly outnumbered the Mon in lower Burma (Brailey 1970: 44). Moreover, the first king of a resurgent Pegu, Smin Htaw Buddhaketi, was neither Mon nor Burman by origin. Nigel Brailey (1970: 34–35) has attempted to prove that Smin Htaw Buddhaketi was a Karen and, by implication, that the resurrection of Pegu represented the emergence of a Karen power previously unknown. Although it is possible that Smin Htaw Buddhaketi may have been a Karen by origin,[17] the most salient characteristic about him was that he was a monk at the time of the founding of the new Pegu. The revolt of lower Burma against the king of Ava was ideologically, not ethnically, motivated. Smin Htaw Buddhaketi's claim to power was almost certainly grounded in ideas of Buddhist millennialism.[18]

Once in power, Smin Htaw Buddhaketi moved to reinforce his claim to power through the more traditional means of producing genealogical evidence linking him with former kings of Pegu and of making strategic marriages such as that between himself and the daughter of the ruler of Chiang Mai. Such acts and his popularity notwithstanding, Smin Htaw Buddhaketi was not an effective king at a period when dynamic leadership was demanded. In 1747 he either abdicated or was forced to abdicate in favor of his general, Binya Dale.[19]

After Smin Htaw Buddhaketi's abdication, Peguan forces enjoyed a period of success in pressing their cause against the Burman king at Ava. Indeed, a Peguan force sacked Ava and brought an end to the Toungoo dynasty that ruled there. In the wake of this event, another millennial figure, this time a Burman from Shwebo, emerged and led a counteroffensive against the Peguan forces. This new Burman king, who took the name Alaungpaya, "Embryonic Buddha," was able to attract a sufficient following both to repulse the Peguan attackers and then to reunite Burma under his rule.

For a full half-century after Alaungpaya first raised his standard at Shwebo in 1752, Burma and Thailand were in constant turmoil. Of major concern to Alaungpaya and his successors was the elimination of threats from lower Burma. Although Pegu was captured in 1757, the Burmese army had to put down successive revolts in lower Burma in 1758–59, in 1773, and in 1784. Alaungpaya also renewed the Burmese dream of subjugating all the neighboring Tai polities. In 1755 Alaungpaya established a Burmese viceroy at Mµang Nai (Monè) to exercise Burman authority over the southern Shan states. Subsequently, in 1759–63 the principality of Mµang Pai, which bordered on both what was to become Kayah State and on northern Thailand, was reestablished under the Burmese (Brailey 1970: 47). In 1760 Alaungpaya himself led an unsuccessful attack on the Siamese capital of Ayutthaya. Although he died in the attempt, his son Hsinbyunshin was able to fulfill the objective in 1767 by capturing and destroying Ayutthaya. However, a Siamese general, Taksin, whose career is remarkably similar to that of Alaungpaya (including a claim to being a bodhisattva), was able to command a sufficient force to prevent the Burmese from consolidating the gain in Siam. Taksin founded a new capital at Thonburi and then began a series of conquests of his own.

Northern Thailand next became the scene for a major struggle between the Siamese and Burmese. From 1767 to 1802 the Siamese fought with their Yuan allies to end Burmese domination of the region. The Yuan allies of the Siamese were the sons and grandsons of the ruler of Lampang, Thip Chang, himself a man linked with Buddhist millennialism.[20]

Karen-speaking people were caught in the turmoil of events in the period between 1740 and 1802. Most obviously, many Karen communities lay along the routes through which the various armies passed. Such Karen were forced to provide provisions, were recruited as guides and spies, and were taken as captives. Other Karen had been among the supporters of the Peguan resurgence and suffered accordingly when Burmese forces finally brought Peguan resistance to an end. In the new order established by the Burmese rulers, Karen were apparently subjected to particularly heavy taxes.[21] Perhaps most significantly, Karen during this period were also exposed to the rampant millennialism which was found in both Burma and Thailand. Millennial movements were characterized by the emergence of individuals who were believed to have powers to effect an immediate improvement in the conditions of life of their followers. Such a radical transformation of life, comparable to the Christian belief in the establishment of a millennium of peace under Christ, was believed to be possible through the observance of magico-religious practices instituted by the leaders of the movements. Such millennialism found responsive chords in Karen culture since the traditional role of religious prophet lent itself to manipulation in millennial terms. The troubled times gave the messages of new Karen prophets—messages that often borrowed from the Buddhism of neighboring peoples—an appeal they might not otherwise have had. Together, millennial aspirations and the troubled times served as a crucible for the forging of new political statuses for the Karen of the Thai-Burman frontier.[22]

In addition to the changes in the politico-religious context in which the Karen lived, there may also have been internal forces operating within Karen culture that were important in spurring the Karen to adopt new roles. It is possible, for example, that the Karen population had begun to grow too large to be supported by the traditional modes of upland cultivation in the areas in which they then lived. Unfortunately, there is no evidence to determine whether initial expansion by the Karen was caused by demographic and economic factors within Karen society as well as by the crisis in power that pervaded the Tai and Burmese worlds of the period. It is clear, however, that demographic increase did become important in subsequent expansion.

Although physical expansion brought Karen into closer contact with people living in the territories of Lannathai and Siam, it was not this contact alone that made the Karen significant to the Tai. Recognition of a distinctive Karen ethnic element by the Tai followed from the unique adaptation—religious, political, and economical—that Karen-speaking people made to the worlds dominated by the Tai. It is to the historical development of such adaptation that we now turn.

Emergence of the Karen in the Worlds of the Yuan and Siamese

Karen began playing significant roles for the Yuan who dominated northern Thailand during the turbulent years at the end of the eighteenth century. One role was played by those Karen who succeeded in forming the small principalities of Karenni in what is today the Kayah state of Burma. These Kayah or Red Karen principalities, and particularly that of Kantarawady or Eastern Karenni, were important to the Yuan because of their political dominance in a border region and also because of their economic significance in the teak and "slave" trades. Other Karen, mainly Sgaw and Pwo, together with a small number of Kayah, settled in areas within the domains of the Yuan rulers. These Karen came to dominate the upland areas of the western portion of the Lannathai principality of Chiang Mai. In addition, they also developed specialized roles in the teak trade, which was so important economically to the rulers of northern Thailand.

In 1764 Burmese forces under King Hsinbyunshin captured Chiang Mai, the Yuan capital of the principality that lay in the Mae Ping valley. Thus, the Burmese succeeded in bringing most of northern Thailand under Burmese rule once again. Although many Yuan resisted Burmese domination, many others accepted it; Yuan levies were among the Burmese troops that captured and destroyed the Siamese capital of Ayutthaya in 1767. To deny the Burmese their bases of support in northern Thailand, the resurgent Siamese, under King Taksin, sent troops to northern Thailand in 1771. In addition to wanting to rid the region of Burmese control, Taksin also wanted to make the Yuan principalities vassals of Siam.

The ensuing struggle in northern Thailand, like the preceding struggle between upper and lower Burma, has long been interpreted in ethnic terms. That is, it has been seen as a struggle between the Tai on one side—that is, the Siamese and Yuan—against the Burmans on the other. More correctly, it was a struggle between two powerful kingdoms over the question of which should control a particular group of vassal principalities. The struggle was by no means limited to northern Thailand but extended into what is today Laos and into an area of the present-day Shan states. In the case of the Yuan, some of the local rulers, including the ruler of Chiang Saen, whose principality was located in what is today northern Chiang Rai province, and the ruler of Fang, who controlled an area in northern Chiang Mai province, continued to maintain their allegiance to the Burmese throne. The rulers of the principalities of Nan and Phrae in the upper Nan and Yom valleys attempted to follow a policy of neutrality and hoped that they would be ignored. It was in the valleys of the Ping and Wang that the struggle of the 1770s took place.

In 1774 a Yuan force under the leadership of the rulers of Lampang together with a Siamese force sent by King Taksin succeeded in taking Chiang Mai. However, the battle left the capital city virtually in ruins. Following the capture of Chiang Mai, King Taksin of Siam appointed two Yuan vassal rulers, both of whom were to be important in the unfolding story of the Karen in the Yuan world. Ca Ban, a son of Thip Chang of Lampang, was made ruler *(phraya)* of the principality of Chiang Mai in the Mae Ping valley. Kawila, a nephew of Ca Ban and grandson of Thip Chang, was invested as the ruler of the principality of Lampang in the Mae Wang valley. King Taksin also appointed as *upparat,* or deputy ruler, of Muang Chiang Mai one Kon Kaeo who was yet another nephew of Ca Ban and grandson of Thip Chang. It was Kon Kaeo, so it appears, who provided the first link in an evolving Karen-Yuan relationship.[23]

Kon Kaeo had considerable influence among the Lua' (Lawa) hill people of northern Thailand. Moreover, he had acquired mercenaries from a group (or groups) who are described as "red-turbaned" *(hua daeng)* and as being from Papun (Muang Thalang in the Tai chronicles) in what is today the Karen state of Burma. In a passage in the Northern Thai chronicles regarding these followers of Upparat Kon Kaeo at a time (1783) after Kon Kaeo's death, they were identified as "Karen" *(yang)* (Prachakitcakoracak 1964: 452; Sanguan 1972B: 128). We shall leave open for the moment the question of what type of Karen they were.

In 1775 Phraya Ca Ban, the ruler of Chiang Mai, had his nephew Upparat Kon Kaeo killed, ostensibly because he was slow in arranging for provisions for troops engaged in fighting with the Burmese. The "red-turbaned" Karen mercenaries then fled, some going, according to the chronicles, to Muang Pon, Muang Yuam, and Thatafang[24] on the eastern side of the Salween, and some across the Salween to Tha Sitho, Tha Sithae, Ban Mae Paphaku, and Muang Thalang[25] (Prachakitcakoracak 1964: 452; Sanguan 1972B: 129). Here they remained until 1783 when they once again appear in Northern Thai history.

Between 1775 and 1779, Phraya Ca Ban was never able to gain the initiative in the continuing war with the Burmese. In 1779 he was called to Bangkok where King Taksin had him jailed, ostensibly for the murder of Kon Kaeo.[26] Ca Ban died in jail shortly after King Rama I ascended to the throne. In 1782 the new Siamese monarch appointed Kawila, formerly ruler of Lampang and nephew of Ca Ban, to be the ruler of the principality of Chiang Mai. Kawila followed the precedent of Ca Ban and established his capital at a place other than Chiang Mai city, in this case at Pa Sang in present-day Lamphun province. However, Kawila was fully intent upon restoring Chiang Mai city as the capital of a reconstructed state.

Kawila was faced by two major problems. The first, and most pressing, was the security of his borders. The Burmese threat had far from subsided. In addition, he may have been further concerned by abortive revolts against the Burmese staged in 1782 and 1783 by Shan and Karen under the *sawbwa* of Muang Pai.[27] The second major problem facing Kawila was the underpopulation of his kingdom brought about both by the devastation caused by wars with Burma and by the movement of people from the region either into Burma (mainly as a consequence of forced migration) or away from the areas that the Burmese armies were constantly travelling through. In his efforts to overcome both of these problems, Kawila established new relationships with the Karen.

In 1783 Kawila sent representatives to ensure the loyalty of those who held local power in the region along the eastern border, which at this time appears to have been the Salween River. He also sent small forces to the same area and further across the Salween to capture or persuade people there to move into his domains, presumably in the Mae Ping valley and surrounding hills. The following record from the Chiang Mai Chronicle explains the contacts in 1783 between Kawila's emissaries and Karen of the eastern border region:

> In Culasakaraj 1445, *ka-mao* year [1783] the prince who was chief [Kawila] and the three other princes[28] delegated Phraya Samlan to take 30 retainers and go present 40 beautifully decorated bowls (*thuai lai ngam*) to the Karen *kang*[29] [who wears] a turban with silver thread *(yang kang hua tat)* and who is a border chief *(hua dan)*. The Karen *kang* [who wears] a turban with silver thread was persuaded by this gift to be friends [lit., "at heart"] with Phraya Samlan.[30] [This Karen chief then led] a sneak attack on the village of Tongpho or Tongpu whose populace was sent to the capital.[31] This was the first time.[32]
>
> At the same time, [Kawila] ordered the Cao Upparatcha and the Cao Ratana Huamuang Kaeo[33] to take a message to persuade Fa Noi Mot[34] of Muang Thalang [Papun] [to align himself with Kawila]. [These emissaries first[35]] took 30 beautifully decorated bowls and cloth[36] to present to Kang Saen Luang,[37] the Karen *(yang)* border chief on the western side of the Salween River.[38] Kang Saen Luang agreed [lit., "to be of heart"] to send the message [on] to Fa Noi Mot. Fa Noi Mot was pleased to offer his fealty [to Kawila]. The emissaries thus sent Fa Noi Mot to the capital.[39] This was the second time.

[Kawila] and the three princes who were his younger brothers were clever. They had boldly brought their enemies into their grasp and had expanded their territories. Being normally a small [principality], they had resolved to take all the small and large villages and principalities which were dependencies of Ava and to attach their populations firmly to their own villages and principalities.[40]

At that time [Kawila] appointed Nai Cantharecha as commander of a force which attacked and seized Ban Thafang[41] on the eastern shore of the Salween and captured the Phǫ Mųang[42] of Mųang Thu, the Phǫ Mųang of Mųang Kiti,[43] the Phǫ Mųang of Mųang Yan,[44] Acan Nan Tho[45] and drove the population [of these districts] back to the country [of Chiang Mai] [Sanguan 1972B: 129–30; my translation].[46]

With this text, we can now say something about the Karen who first appear as mercenaries in the mid-1770s under the Upparat of Chiang Mai and the Karen who later in 1783 are brought under the control of Kawila, then the ruler of Chiang Mai.[47] Apparently on the basis of the designation "red-turbaned," Brailey (1970: 41) has identified these mercenaries as "Red Karen," that is, Kayah. This identification finds support in the characterization of the Kayah by A. W. Moore, who wrote of them in 1879 as being a people "who wear red turbans and red drawers" (1879: 1). However, the area from which the people are said to have come is clearly in present-day Karen State, inhabited primarily by Sgaw and Pwo, and not in present-day Kayah State. Moreover, the term *yang daeng* does not appear in the passages considered thus far, although in subsequent references in the Yuan chronicles, it is used when the Kayah are being referred to.[48]

All we can say, then, is that some Karen-speaking people were employed as mercenaries by the Yuan in the 1770s. In 1783 leaders of rather small communities of Karen (who in this case, I suspect, were Sgaw) living west of the Salween recognized the overlordship of Kawila of Chiang Mai. So, too, did the ruler of Papun who is, significantly, not identified as a Karen. Some Karen (probably Sgaw) were forcibly resettled, along with other frontier peoples, in the heartland of Chiang Mai. These resettled Karen may be, I suggest, the ancestors of Sgaw populations living today in the hills flanking the Ping valley.

Although Kawila and his brothers may have thought of themselves as clever in sending emissaries and forays across the Salween to win over those who had once been (nominal at least) subjects of Burma, Burma had not yet relinquished its claims to authority over either these peoples or over northern Thailand itself. In 1784 another major Burmese campaign was undertaken in northern Thailand, and for the two decades following, there was almost constant warfare in the region between the Burmese and their Yuan ally, Chiang Saen, on one side and the Siamese and their Yuan allies, led by Chiang Mai, on the other. Although the Burmese never again succeeded in reestablishing their control over the whole region, they did continue to maintain a stronghold at Chiang Saen until 1804, when a Chiang Mai force finally succeeded in capturing and destroying this city. With Burmese influence in northern Thailand finally ended, the rulers of Chiang Mai again turned their attention to their western frontier. In doing so, they came into contact with the Kayah or Red Karen who had formed their own principalities in the area.

The history of the foundation of the Karenni or Kayah statelets, and particularly the foundation of Kantarawady or Eastern Karenni with which Chiang Mai was to develop relations, is rather obscure. F. K. Lehman, who has provided an excellent analysis of the origins of the Kayah statelets, speculates that the "Kayah system is the political culmination of Karen millennialism" that took place in the 1820s (Lehman 1967B: 20). Although concurring fully with his conclusion regarding millennialism, I would suggest on the basis of evidence I have gathered that the date at which Kantarawady was founded was perhaps two or three decades earlier. My main basis for making this assertion is a treaty made between Chiang Mai and Kantarawady in 1809 or earlier.

This treaty appears in both Yuan accounts[49] and in the accounts given by some Kayah who were interviewed by British members of the Anglo-Siamese Border Commission of 1890.[50] Although one of the reports gathered by the commission places the date of it around 1790, the Yuan sources date it as occurring in the year when King Rama II ascended to the throne of Siam, 1809.

In 1809, according to the Yonok Chronicle,

> The ruler of Chiang Mai [Kawila] ordered the Upparat to make an inspection of the border from Muang Yuam[51] to the west to the Salween.[52] The Upparat observed that Muang Yang Daeng lay on the western side of the Salween and that it was not a dependency of Ava. The Upparat persuaded Fa Fo or Phra Pho,[53] the Cao Muang[54] of Muang Yang Daeng, to agree to a treaty of friendship [Prachakitcakoracak 1964: 479; my translation].

In a Yuan-Siamese document whose title translates as "Records of Treaty Making between Chiang Mai and the Red Karen Country," it is said that the purpose of the treaty was to enlist the aid of the Kayah in providing the Yuan with early warning of advancing Burmese armies (Sanguan 1972B: 546). The Yonok Chronicle then continues:

> An oath-taking ceremony, following Red Karen custom, was then held at Tambon Saya,[55] which is a crossing on the Salween. The ritual consisted of the killing of a carabao, taking its blood, and mixing it with liquor to create the "liquid of truth." The horns of the carabao were divided, one being given to Muang Yang Daeng and the other to Chiang Mai to keep. The following vow was made by both parties: "So long as the waters of the Salween do not disappear, the horns of the buffalo do not straighten, and the White Elephant cave does not shrink, Muang Chiang Mai and Muang Yang Daeng will be allies." From then on, Muang Yang Daeng and Muang Chiang Mai were allies [Prachakitcakoracak 1964: 479; my translation].

Two versions of the treaty are given in the reports of the Anglo-Siamese Commission. J. C. Scott, then superintendent of the Shan states, gives the following account, based on information supplied by some unidentified Karenni leaders:

> It is . . . asserted that very many years ago representatives of Chiengmai and Eastern Karenni met to determine their frontier line east of the Salween.[56] Great numbers of buffaloes were killed, their blood drunk, and their flesh eaten by the two parties, and both Laos and Karenni carried off a horn as an outward sign and symbol of the boundary agreed upon. This is said to have been determined by letting loose a buffalo on the summit of a range and erecting marks on the line which he followed. The place of meeting was called Kwègyo Taung[57] in memory of the settlement and the horn taken by the Karenni is still preserved at Sowlon.[58] The skeletons of the slaughtered buffaloes are said to be still in a cave on the Kwègyo Taung. Where this hill is I have been unable to determine, but it seems to lie southeast of Muang Sè (Muang Ché of the Siamese). The corresponding horn ought, it is said, to be found in Chiengmai [Government of India, Foreign Department, 1890: 1059].

W. A. Archer, also one of the commissioners and British vice-consul at Chiang Mai, obtained another account from Kayah living in the Mae Pai valley east of the Salween and west of Mae Hong Son:

> [T]he Karennis and Chiengmai made an agreement to the effect that a buffalo should be shot and that if it fell on its right or east side, the Karennis should have the country up to Kun Yuam and Mèhongson,[59] but if it fell on its left or west side, they should only get the country adjoining the Salween. The buffalo fell on its west side and the Karennis got only the territory they now occupy. One of the horns of the buffalo was kept respectively by Chiengmai and Karenni, on the understanding that peace should

be preserved on both sides until the horns became straight (i.e. for ever) [Government of India, Foreign Department, 1890: 1096].

According to the Yuan-Siamese account in the "Records of Treaty Making," during the period when Phraya Chang Phuak ruled over Chiang Mai (1813–21), he sent his son "to make an inspection of the border area and to have Phapho [Papaw] take the water [of allegiance]. The ruler of the Red Karen Country was at Tha Saya as before" (Sanguan 1972A: 546). This suggests that Kantarawady was considered a vassal rather than an ally, a position the Kayah would most probably not have accepted. The basis of the relationship, at the initial stage, was likely to have been a mutual concern about future Burmese attacks. Papaw would have wanted to safeguard his nascent statelet, and the Chiang Mai ruler wanted to protect his own borders.

In 1836 a Kayah, whom the British accounts call Sawlasa and the Tai accounts Rasa, brought some followers and settled at Mae Samat near present-day Mae Hong Son. Sawlasa (i.e., *cao rasa*) is said to have been the son of Papawgyi, the man who founded Kantarawady, and also his successor. According to an account given to the British by the chief Buddhist monk of Kantarawady, Sawlasa asked prior permission from the ruler of Ava (who, most improbably, was said to be Alaungpaya) and those of Chiang Mai and the Shan state of Muang Nai (Moné) before establishing his settlement.[60] The Yuan-Siamese account says that Sawlasa broke with his father and then led his followers to create the new community. Having done so, he was taken in 1837 on the order of the ruler of Chiang Mai to Bangkok where he was given permission by the Siamese monarch to live within his domains. Both of these accounts appear to exaggerate the importance of Sawlasa's settlement, which the Yuan-Siamese account says comprised only twenty households.

Sawlasa later returned to succeed his father and, according to the Siamese-Yuan account, died in 1843. The settlement he founded dwindled first to ten households and finally to nothing. The last ten households "returned to their home" after a Yuan official attempted to gather a tax on trees being cut in the area.[61] Later, Shan from Muang Mok Mai (Mawkmè) established themselves in Mae Hong Son and founded a permanent settlement under Chiang Mai.[62]

Although the first Kayah settlement in Mae Hong Son lasted for not much more than a decade, a few Kayah did subsequently come to settle permanently in what is today Mae Hong Son province. The story of the first settlement may be the basis for the belief of the Kayah who live in Mae Hong Son today that they were once subjects of the prince of Chiang Mai.[63]

Kayah were not the only Karen with whom the Yuan of Chiang Mai developed relations in the early part of the nineteenth century. As noted above, small numbers of Karen, who were probably Sgaw, had been settled, mostly by force, in the domains of Chiang Mai as early as 1783. During the rule of Phraya Chang Phuak (1813-21), two Yuan officials were ordered "to take a force of over a hundred men and to take captives among the Karen [known as the] Yang Suai Krabang who live to the southwest of Chiang Mai. Many prisoners were taken" (Prachakitcakoracak 1964: 482). Although I have not been able to discover what is meant by *suai krabang*,[64] it is likely that these Karen were also Sgaw.

As a result of the Anglo-Burmese war of 1824-26, the British gained control of part of lower Burma, a territory that contained a sizeable population of Sgaw and Pwo Karen. From some of their new subjects, the British discovered that the Yuan had been making raids in the area to capture people (including Mon and some Burmans as well as Karen) who were forced to resettle in the Ping river valley. Some Karen had moved to Chiang Mai after having been persuaded to do so by a man who was styled as the chief of the Karen in the district of Chiang Mai. The British moved to bring an end to the forcible resettlement of people and succeeded in obtaining the repatriation of some who had been captured.[65]

In 1829 Dr. D. Richardson, an emissary of the British commissioner at Moulmein, made the first of several trips to Chiang Mai and the Karenni country. He found Karen living in the Muang Yuam (Mae Sariang) territory in the area between the Yuam and Moei rivers, at the point where they converged. He noted that the Karen were subject to Yuan officials sent from Lamphun (Blundell 1836: 607-10). These Karen were probably Sgaw, although both Pwo and Sgaw were among the Karen forced to settle in northern Thailand (Smeaton 1887: 71). In the territory now included in Mae Sariang district, the Sgaw appear to have preceded the Pwo.

The migration of Karen into the domains of the rulers of Chiang Mai was not all the result of forced migration. During the devastating wars between the Burmese and the Tai, many Yuan who had settled in the border areas fled to safer places or were themselves forced to resettle in Burmese territory. Something of a vacuum was left in the areas vacated by the Yuan and it is quite probable that some Karen moved into these areas of their own volition (Keyes 1970).

Although Karen receive far more mention in the annals of the Yuan than they do in the records of the Siamese, they do begin to emerge as a distinctive ethnic element in Siamese history at about the same time as they do further north. During the wars with Burma, some Karen appear to have assisted the Siamese. In 1775 Karen are said in the Burmese chronicles to have provided Siamese troops stationed near Saiyok in Kanchanaburi province with intelligence regarding the movements of the Burmese army.[66] They played a similar role again in 1786 near the headwaters of the Khwae Nọi River in Kanchanaburi province (Aung Thein 1959: 130, 138; Stern 1971A: 13–14). Also, during this same troubled period, some Karen (mainly Pwo and some Sgaw) migrated into Siam and placed themselves under Siamese rule (Bunchuai Sisawat 1963: 104; Stern 1971: 13–14). In addition, the Siamese appear to have followed the same practice as the Yuan in forcing Karen to settle in their territory (Smeaton 1887: 157–59; Stern 1971A: 10–11).

Karen did not settle (willingly or unwillingly) only in the border areas of Siam. In an old Siamese map, which would seem to date from 1827, five Karen villages appear in the mountains between Saraburi and Khorat far to the east of Bangkok (Kennedy 1970: 325). In 1868 Henri Mouhot stumbled upon one of these villages on a mountain in the Dong Phya Fai range between Saraburi and Khorat:

> In a gorge of this mountain and on a height nearly inaccessible and excessively fever-infested, I found a small tribe of Karens which not long ago inhabited the region of Patawi.[67] In order to conserve their independence, they live nearly secluded because the fear of fever prevents the Siamese from penetrating to them. They have neither temples nor priests. They raise magnificent rice and many varieties of bananas which are found only among tribes of the same origin. Many individuals, although they have come near to them, are ignorant of their existence. It is true that they are somewhat nomadic. Some maintain that they pay an annual tribute consisting of a *rake,* which is either gum lac or Japanese lac. However, contrarily, the governor of Korat and many of the chiefs of Saraburi appear to be in complete ignorance of the subject [Mouhot 1868: 293–94; my translation].

In 1872 C. H. Carpenter, who was a missionary among the Karen of Burma, again "discovered" the Karen who were living in the mountains between Saraburi and Khorat:

> The few Karens in this vicinity are neither indigenous nor are they from the East. Their ancestors were captured by the Siamese in one of their incursions in the Tavoy district, and were brought to this distant place to prevent their escaping. Even here, isolated from the great body of their people, they are entirely free from taxation. They had settled among the Laos, and intermar-

ried with them until the children's children had lost the use of their own language altogether. A dozen or two of the older people could still speak Karen and understand us very well, but that was all [Carpenter 1873: 73].

The mention of Siamese incursions into Tavoy suggests that these furthermost eastern Karen may have been settled as early as the last years of the eighteenth century. If Kennedy's dating of the map is correct, they certainly had settled there before 1827. It would appear that after some fifty to seventy-five years, this small group of resettled Karen had reached the point of total assimilation into the surrounding Tai-speaking groups.

The map published by Kennedy contains the earliest use of the term *kariang* I have been able to find. The Siamese word derives, I believe, from the Mon word *kareang,* which is used by the Mon as a label for Karen-speaking people.[68] This derivation is the more plausible given that Karen (especially Pwo Karen) had long had a symbiotic relationship with the Mon. With the final destruction of the Peguan kingdom of lower Burma, many Mon fled into Siam and some joined with the Siamese armies in their fight with the Burmese. In the frontier areas where the Mon settled and where the battles took place, the Siamese made their initial contacts with the Karen. It is quite likely that these contacts were first mediated by the Mon.

Karen may also have moved into Siam together with the Mon who sought to escape from the oppression of the Burmese (Stern 1968A: 299). In addition, Karen may have been stimulated to move out of their homes as a consequence of millennial ideas that reached a peak in the 1820s (Stern 1968A: 305–6). In other words, the initial settlement of Karen in Siam as in the Yuan territory to the north was a function both of forced migration undertaken by the Siamese and voluntary migration by the Karen in response to events in Burma and to ferment within their own society. Most of the Karen who settled in Siam, with rare exceptions such as those who went to the hills between Saraburi and Khorat, found homes in the hill districts of Kanchanaburi and Tak provinces.

To summarize, the emergence of the Karen as a significant ethnic element in the Tai worlds of the Yuan and the Siamese occurred between the 1770s and the 1820s. The Kayah state of Kantarawady, which had been established on the western borders of Chiang Mai, attracted the attention of the Yuan rulers because of its strategic location. Although the pioneer and temporary settlements of Kayah within the borders of Yuan State did not presage any significant movement of Kayah into northern Thailand, a sizeable number of

Sgaw and Pwo Karen did come, some unwillingly and some willingly, to establish permanent homes in Yuan territory. Sgaw and Pwo also settled, again as a result of both push and pull, in the domains of the Siamese king. As the Karen began to develop regular relationships with the Yuan and the Siamese, new structures whereby these relationships could be ordered began to evolve.

The Structure of Karen Relationships with the Yuan and Siamese

The new relationships that developed between the Karen on the one hand and the Yuan and Siamese on the other during the late eighteenth and early nineteenth centuries had been brought about in part because of the desire of the Yuan and Siamese rulers for more subjects and in part because of the quest undertaken by many Karen for a new politico-religious identity. In the process of adaptation that followed, political and religious considerations were of obvious importance. Of equal importance were economic considerations that developed because of Karen movement into the valleys and because of the response by both Karen and Tai to the growing demand for teak.

Before their expansion out of their homeland, the Karen were predominantly an upland swidden cultivating people. Traditionally, the only salient alternative to swidden cultivation was lowland wet-rice cultivation. As the result of the establishment of a British colony in lower Burma after the Anglo-Burmese war of 1824–26, a new mode of productive activity became a real possibility for a sizeable number of Karen. The demand for teak, which was plentiful in the area where the Karen traditionally lived and in the border regions of western Siam and western Chiang Mai where they had begun to move, grew exponentially after the British developed the port of Moulmein. The court at Bangkok was not slow in recognizing the significance of revenue from teak and it also began to encourage the trade through the port of Bangkok. Although the Yuan rulers began to impose taxes on the teak cut in the forests in their domains, the rapidly increasing demand for teak during the nineteenth century made it possible for many Karen to take on new roles as lumberjacks and as mahouts with elephants who dragged the teak from the forest. The elephants used were also owned, raised, and trained by the Karen. A few Karen became middlemen in the teak trade and the Kayah rulers of Kantarawady openly competed with their neighbors, both Shan and Yuan, for control of teak forests.

The Kayah also took on another role, which the British referred to as "slave trading." In fact, it appears that the Kayah became middlemen for Yuan, Shan, and Burmans in their quest for more subjects. Although the principals themselves ceased to make raids on their neighbors to force people to settle in their domains, the Kayah were willing to perform this service for them. In addition to capturing people, the Kayah also used the occasion of their raids to plunder.

Following the treaty between Kantarawady and Chiang Mai, which took place no later than 1809, there was a period of peace between the two states. Within two decades, however, the Kayah had begun to develop a reputation for being very troublesome neighbors. In 1829 the Yuan border town of Muang Yuam (Mae Sariang) had practically been depopulated by the constant raids made by Kayah dacoits (Hallett 1890: 30). These raids on Muang Yuam continued until the late 1870s (Hallett 1890: 30–31). In 1845 a mission sent to Kantarawady by the ruler of Chiang Mai found the Kayah at war with the Burmese and Shan (Prachakitcakoracak 1964: 489–90). In the 1850s, Kayah migrants began to settle in large numbers in areas east of the Salween. Scott provides the reason for the migration:

> It was noticeable that all along the Salween about this time the forest country was being rapidly taken up by the Western Chiefs [of the Kayah]. The cause was no doubt the occupation of Lower Burma by British arms. There arose a great demand for teak. Previously it had only been rarely wanted for the erection of a monastery or a Chief's palace. Now there was a constant and increasing demand [Government of India, Foreign Department, 1890: 1059].[69]

Such settlement of Kayah east of the Salween continued into the 1870s and early 1880s.[70]

The constant raiding by the Kayah together with their claims to lands east of the Salween brought them into open conflict with the Yuan of Chiang Mai in the 1870s (Moore 1879: 23–24). In 1882 representatives of Kantarawady and of Chiang Mai met in Mae Hong Son and negotiated a new treaty.[71] The British later became sceptical of whether this treaty had ever been signed since it clearly specified that the Salween River was the border between Kantarawady and Chiang Mai, but the scepticism appears to have been born of special pleading on the part of the Kayah.[72] In addition to establishing the Salween as the border, the treaty also sought to bring raids by Kayah in Chiang Mai territory to an end.

Provocation by the Kayah must not have ended as a result of this treaty since the Yuan and their Siamese overlords were only too happy to offer to help the British in 1888 in overcoming resistance by Sawlapaw, the chief of Kantarawady, to British efforts to annex Kantarawady to British Burma. The British, although welcoming the offer at the time, turned a deaf ear to the Yuan and Siamese claim to making the Salween the border between the Karenni district of British Burma and northern Thailand. Although the Salween does now form the border for a short distance, it does so in an area below that of Kayah State.[73]

The annexation of Karenni to British Burma in 1888 did bring to almost a complete end direct relations between the Yuan and the Kayah. Conflicts along the border were subsequently handled by representatives of British Burma and Siam, the latter having taken over the control of foreign affairs for northern Thailand by this time. Today, only a few Kayah communities remain in northern Thailand as a legacy of eighty years of relatively intense and mainly hostile relationships between the Kayah and Yuan.[74]

Although the Yuan rulers showed almost no interest in Sgaw and Pwo Karen who lived beyond their territories since, unlike the Kayah, they had developed no stable political entities,[75] they took definite interest in the Sgaw and Pwo who had settled in northern Thailand. These Karen, who had settled, or had been forced to settle, in northern Thailand in greater numbers than the Kayah[76] established their homes predominantly in the hills to the west of Chiang Mai. In these areas, they took the place of the Lua' (or Lawa) who had been the original upland inhabitants of the area but who had subsequently all but abandoned the hills and had been assimilated into Yuan society.

In a few places, however, Lua' still remained and were recognized by the Yuan rulers as having the right to stand, politically, between the Karen migrants and themselves. Peter Kunstadter, on the basis of oral histories gathered in the hills in Mae Sariang district, reports the following:

> Skaw Karens, coming [in about 1850] from the West, began moving into the territory once held exclusively by the Lua?. The Karens recognized the Lua? as lords of the land and paid them annual tribute of 10 percent of their rice crop. Each Karen village owed tribute to some particular Lua? village, within whose territory it was located. . . . [The Lua?] relayed a portion of the tribute which the Karens had paid them [to the Prince of Chiang Mai or Lampun], and in return the Prince recognized the Lua? claim to the land and their right to collect tribute from others [Kunstadter 1967: 641].

Other Karen, however, were subject directly to the Yuan rulers. In my own research in Mae Sariang in 1967–68, I gathered oral histories from several lowland Sgaw Karen villages. The headman of one village (Mae Han) reported that lowland Karen paid tribute and taxes directly to the princes of Chiang Mai and to the local governor of Muang Yuam (Mae Sariang). Cotton thread, as well as cloth and clothing (both male and female) woven by the Karen, was given annually to representatives of the prince of Chiang Mai. The Karen also paid a tax of paddy, the amount depending on the size of the fields, to the governor of Muang Yuam. A similar type of tribute relationship is reported by David Marlowe, who carried out research among upland Sgaw Karen living in the hills flanking the Mae Ping valley:

> An annual symbolic tribute was paid to the Chiang Mai authorities [by these Sgaw Karen]. This tribute consisted of representative items produced by a village or a group of villages and it included such items as hand woven blankets, shirts, skirts, pots of honey, and some produce of gardens and swiddens. These were gathered by Karen elders for presentation to the government's representatives. It is stated that when tribute was given within the boundaries of a Karen area, "the authorities were never allowed to enter the village itself but shared a ritual meal with the village elders at some place outside the village," usually at the village well or river watering point. It would appear then that the Karen were at first a semi-autonomous, tributary, dependent people under the protection of the Princes of Chiang Mai. This status apparently changed to that of an incorporated people in the latter part of the nineteenth century when symbolic tribute was replaced by the 4 rupee or old baht head tax on all males considered subjects of the Kingdom [Marlowe 1969: 54].

The Yuan records also provide further information on the structure of the relations between Sgaw (and probably some Pwo) Karen and Yuan during the nineteenth century. Under Yuan rule, there was at least one official who was given responsibility for collecting tribute and taxes from the hill people, the Karen included. The first mention of such an official in the Yuan chronicles is the story of Kǫn Kaeo, the Upparat of Chiang Mai in 1774–75. In 1831 a Siamese letter to one of the Burney missions refers to "the late chief at Wen Mien, an inhabitant of Zemmai [Chiang Mai], who was Chief over the Karyans of the District of Zemmai."[77] In the 1890s, a minor member of the house of Chiang Mai "was made responsible for collecting tribute and taxes from Karen, Meo, and Yao hill tribes. . . . It was necessary to have a [Northern Thai] native make contact [with the Karen] in order that they might be willing to pay tribute" (Prani 1963: II, 351). Even as late as the early 1960s, there was a Northern Thai who was a descendent of a Yuan official who had played an intermediary role between Karen and Yuan still serving as "moral leader" of Karen living in Ban Hong district, Lamphun province (Prani 1963: II, 36–37).

Although many of the Karen who lived in northern Thailand from the nineteenth century on had well-structured relations with the Yuan, there were some who appear to have lived in almost totally autonomous communities, recognizing neither the Yuan rulers nor any of their subjects as having any authority over them. Hinton reports that Pwo Karen living in the southern part of what is now Mae Sariang district, Mae Họng Sọn province, "have no tradition of having paid tribute to the Thai princes of Lamphun and Chiang Mai, nor did they give any form of payment to the Lua? whose former agricultural land they occupied" (Hinton 1969: 9). This isolation and autonomy of at least some Pwo contrasted with the patterns of the Sgaw in yet another way. It was the Sgaw who in the teak forests of northwestern Thailand took on distinctive roles as loggers and elephant managers.

The Karen who settled in northern Thailand maintained a religious identity distinctive from that of the Yuan. Most of the Karen in northern Thailand to this day follow an indigenous Karen religion focused on an ancestral spirit cult. Moreover, in the 1880s, Christian missionary work among the Sgaw in northern Thailand began to be carried out by Karen Christians from Burma (Truxton 1958: 110–11). In Burma, following the first conversion of a Karen by Adoniram Judson of the American Baptist Mission in 1828, missionaries had been immensely successful in converting the Karen.[78] And although the Karen Christian community in Thailand has remained small, it follows forms of Christianity that were first established among the Karen in Burma. Even the Karen who were (nominally, at least) adherents of Buddhism tended to follow Burmese rather than Yuan forms. This came about not because of the migration of Karen Buddhists from Burma such as happened in Siam but because some Karen (mainly Sgaw) adopted the religion of those with whom they worked in the teak trade. Until the 1930s, the teak trade in northern Thailand was dominated by Burmese, Mon, and Shan who followed Burmese forms of Buddhism.[79] There is little evidence regarding Karen millennial movements in northern Thailand before World War II, although given that such movements existed among the Karen communities in central Thailand from their inception (Stern 1968A) and that they emerged in northern Thailand after the war,[80] it would not be surprising if they had existed before that time.

In addition to being associated with millennialism from their very beginning, the Karen who lived in Siam proper (i.e., in Kanchanaburi and Tak provinces) also developed more organized political entities than was the case in the north. Also in contrast to the Karen of northern Thailand, a larger percentage of the Siamese Karen were lowland wet-rice cultivators rather than swidden agriculturists. Like their northern cousins, the Siamese Karen were also active in the teak trade.

Francis Mason reported in 1832 that the Siamese Karen settlers in Kanchanaburi province "live in large villages, are Boodhists, and have monasteries or kyoungs with Karen priests, where the Taling [Mon] language is taught."[81] Mason's observation regarding the religion of these Karen bespeaks the close relationship between the Karen of this area and the Mon, a relationship we have already observed was long-standing in Burma. In 1873 Pwo Karen living in Kanchanaburi province were again reported as being predominantly "professed Buddhists" (Carpenter 1873: 10–14). Again, the form of Buddhism was that of the Mon, although for some of these Karen this religion had recently been adopted as the result of contact with "timbermen" from Burma (Carpenter, p. 14).

Although some of the Siamese Karen of the 1830s were Buddhists in the Mon Buddhist tradition, others were probably followers of a very active millennial movement that had emerged in Burma near the Siamese border; this movement definitely had won support among Siamese Karen by 1848 (Stern 1968A: 306–7). This movement was the forerunner of several Karen millennial and quasi-Buddhist sects that were to emerge in the 1860s (Stern, p. 308). Two of these sects, Leke and Telakhon, acquired significant followings among the Siamese Karen (Carpenter 1873: 14) and have persisted to the present. Indeed, the present-day leader of the Telakhon, a Pwo Karen, has his headquarters in southern Tak province in Thailand (Stern 1968A: 315).

Christian missionary work among the Siamese Karen was initiated by a Sgaw missionary from Burma in the late 1860s or early 1870s (Carpenter 1873: 9). However, these initial efforts met with no success and subsequent efforts have not added many members to the Karen Christian community in Thailand.

The Siamese appear to have taken little notice of the growing Karen population in the western border region until about the middle of the nineteenth century. A Siamese document from 1844 mentions that a Siamese official had appointed two Karen as *tsokays*[82] or police under him and had provided them with letters granting them permission to settle in Tak province near the border.[83] By the time the Anglo-Siamese Border Commission set out to demarcate the border between British Burma and Siam in 1866, the Siamese had recognized three Karen vassal chiefs (whose offices were hereditary) as holding jurisdiction in border districts in upper Kanchanaburi province:

1. Phra Sisawat: chief of Sisawat district on the middle Khwae Yai above Kanchanaburi. He also served as one of the commissioners for the Siamese side (Bagge 1866: 5f.; Cao Phraya Thipakǫrawong 1962: 335; Stern 1971A: 31).
2. Phra Mae Klǫng: a Pwo Karen who was chief of the district of Mae Klǫng on the upper Khwae Yai (Bagge 1866: 15; Stern 1971A: 32).
3. Phraya Si Suwannakhiri (Pawapho or Phra Phai): chief of Phra Suwan district on the upper Khwae Nǫi (Bagge 1866: 48; Bunchuai Sisawat 1963: 104; Stern 1971A: 32–33).

The title each held—*phra* or *phraya*—was conferred by the Siamese court in recognition for services rendered and not, as Stern has suggested (1971: 32–33), as an indication of the size of domain controlled. C. H. Carpenter, who in 1872 visited the third of the Karen chiefs above, described the district and population of Phra Suwan. The ruler, the highest Siamese-appointed official this side of Kanchanaburi, was said to be a Pwo Karen and lived in a village comprising mainly Pwo.

> There is a belt of Sgaw villages to the south of them, and a larger one to the northeast, but all in this vicinity are Pwo. . . . [The] district is covered with rugged hills, and abounds in rocky fastnesses known only to the Karen themselves. . . . They have long been practically independent of the Siamese. The other races are taxed to the very limit of their endurance, but no tax or service of any kind is extracted from the Karens, except to convey occasional messengers of the King from one village to the next.
>
> The governor professes to be a Buddhist, and supports a large monastery. . . . The people pride themselves on a strict observance of the Buddhist law. . . . The Sgaw quite generally retain their primitive superstitions without adopting Buddhism [Carpenter 1873: 11].

The finding that the Karen were not required to pay taxes is confirmed by a member of the Anglo-Siamese Border Commission who visited border areas in Siam populated in part by Karen in 1866:

> His Majesty the King exempted all his border subjects from taxation, but imposed on them the duty of supplying his officials with food, etc., and otherwise assisting them when they required it during their visits to the border. This was done with a view to

prevent emigration but the people say that after all it comes to the same thing in the end, for these [officials] come rather often and they have to feed their retinues and provide elephants without recovering any compensation [Bagge 1866: 31–32; quoted in Stern 1971A: 35–36].

The distinctive place of the Karen among the subjects of the king of Siam also appears to find symbolic expression in one of the titles of the king as "King of the Karens" (Seidenfaden 1967: 14). When this title was created, I have not been able to determine.

The Siamese Karen continued to be accorded distinctive political identity well into the twentieth century. A Karen Christian evangelist, Thra Loo Shwe, reports that when he visited Sangkhlaburi district in Kanchanaburi (what previously had been Si Suwannakhiri district) in 1924, the chief, Phra Suwan, was still a Pwo Karen (Loo Shwe 1962: 68). However, this man's position was only a vestige of an older order that was rapidly being replaced throughout the kingdom of Siam. At the end of the nineteenth century, King Chulalongkorn and his advisors had devised a new scheme of local administration whereby all local hereditary rulers, down to but not including the village level, were to be replaced by officials of the Siamese crown. This scheme was implemented during the first years of the twentieth century, and by 1924 Phra Suwan must have been one of the last of the old-style officials remaining.

The reforms of King Chulalongkorn also ended the relative autonomy of northern Thailand. With the disappearance of the Yuan rulers, so too went the basis of the special tribute relationships that held for the Karen (and other tribal groups) in northern Thailand. The destruction of the traditional basis for Karen accommodation to the political order of the Yuan and Siamese resulted in leaving the Karen in something of an ambiguous position. Still today, many, if not a majority of, Karen are treated neither as full "citizens" of Thailand nor fully as "aliens."

The religious distinctiveness of the Karen vis-à-vis the Thai, whether expressed in the form of traditional religion, millennialism, or Burmese types of Buddhism, still obtains for the most part.[84] Some recent efforts, dating only from the late 1960s, have been made to spread Thai Buddhism among the Karen and other tribal groups.[85]

Most Karen in Thailand continue to live as upland swidden cultivators and, as such, are considered by the Thai as being members of a category of people—*chao khao* ("hill people")—who are a recognized minority in Thai society. Moreover, as swiddening is strongly disapproved of officially by the Thai government, which considers that it is destructive of forest resources, those who follow this mode of cultivation have only a tenuous right to their means of production. In some areas, such as in Mae Sariang district of Mae Hong Son province and in parts of Tak and Chiang Mai provinces, Karen (mainly Sgaw) continue to have distinctive roles as lumberjacks and as operators and members of elephant crews whose task it is to bring logs out of the forests.

The distinctive place that the Karen came to occupy in the Thai economy during the course of the nineteenth century and that they continue to hold to the present time has contributed to the drawing of ethnic boundaries between Karen and Thai. These boundaries have been reinforced by the fact that the Karen are also politically differentiated from other groups, although today that differentiation is predicated upon being in a limbo state between citizens and aliens—not, as in the nineteenth century, upon being organized into separate, albeit dependent, politico-administrative units. That Karen follow religious traditions other than the standardized Thai Puddhism of contemporary Thailand also marks them as being other than Thai. The recognition of Karen as a distinct ethnic group in contemporary Thailand, while based upon the structure of relationships between Thai and Karen, has been conceptualized with reference to ethnic categories which, as I have shown in this chapter, have a long history in Thai chronicles and other literature. That these categories—most usually known under the labels of *yang* and *kariang*—have a long history has also served to reinforce the idea that the Karen have a distinctive ethnic status within a world dominated by Thai.

Notes

1. In this chapter, I use the term *Siamese* to refer to the premodern kingdoms of central Thailand and to the Tai-speaking inhabitants who were politically dominant in these kingdoms. I use the term *Yuan* to refer to the Tai-speaking people who were politically dominant in northern Thailand from the end of the thirteenth century to the end of the nineteenth century. Their principalities are collectively known as Lannathai and individually known by the name of the capital city. The most important of these, and the one with which we are most concerned in this chapter, is Chiang Mai. The term *Tai* I have reserved for referring to anything pertaining to the Tai-speaking people of the present-day kingdom of Thailand. This kingdom assumed its modern form at the beginning of the twentieth century.

2. *Nyang* in the spoken language.

3. For example, the few Karen-speaking Pa-O who have come to northern Thailand primarily as traders have been and still are known as *Tongsu,* a term cognate with the Burmese word *Taungthu.*

4. Muang Yang, located in present-day Kengtung State in Burma and clearly not inhabited by any Karen-speaking people, receives occasional mention in Northern Thai chronicles. See, for example, the Chiang Mai Chronicle (Khanakamakan catphim ekkasan thang prawatsat 1971: 77, 113–14, 118, 123–25; Sanguan 1972B: 97, 148–51, 154–55, 161–63); and the Yonok Chronicle (Prachakitcakoracak 1964: 395, 469–70, 473, 480).

5. On the basis of internal evidence, this chronicle would appear to have been composed in the fifteenth or sixteenth century. It was originally written in Yuan.

6. Archaimbault's source was a published Thai version of the myth that appeared in *Warasan Sinlapakon [Journal of the (Thai) Fine Arts Department]*, 6, 9 (1953): 85–87.

7. If this Mu'ang Yong can be equated with Muang Yong of other Yuan sources, it was located north of present-day Chiang Rai province in Kengtung State, Burma. It is this area that was the base from which Tai-speaking people spread into what is present-day Thailand.

8. For a more extended discussion of this myth, see Archaimbault (1973: 131–54).

9. See, also, Harry Marshall (1922: 13–14); William Dodd (1923: 250–51); Blanchard et al. (1957: 64); and Phra Borihan Thepthani (1965: 87–88).

10. Professor Jones presented his views in a personal communication to the author.

11. Jones in personal communication cited in note 10. For more on the linguistic argument regarding the *Urheimat* of the Karen, see F. K. Lehman's chapter in this volume.

12. This type of structure of ethnic group relations did not disappear in the wake of events in the eighteenth and nineteenth centuries. However, it ceased to be the only type of structure whereby relationships between so-called civilized and tribal peoples were ordered.

13. The relevant passage of the Burmese chronicle, *Hmannan Yazawin Dawgyi*, appears in U Aung Thein's *Relationship with Burma* (Aung Thein 1959: 143–45). In the Somdet Phra Phanarat recension of the Ayutthayan Chronicles *(Phra ratchaphongsawadan krung Ayutthaya* 1962: 275), the name of the commander is given, but he is not identified as being *kariang*. It is possible that Prince Damrong's source was a Mon account or chronicle.

14. Theodore Stern (personal communication) has been able to identify Umluk as a border post and Peter Kunstadter (personal communication) has added that he would "hazard the guess that Umluk is a good Lua' [Lawa] town name." Inthara Khiri, according to Stern, "appears in the Burmese records as Eindagiri from at least 1553." A Phraya Intha Khiri is mentioned in the Chiang Mai Chronicle as having been a subordinate official under the Lord of Raheng (Tak) in the late eighteenth century (Notton 1932: 223). This would appear to place Intha(ra) Khiri on the border west of Tak. F. K. Lehman (personal communication) has offered a more elaborate interpretation of the references to Inthara Khiri and of the ethnic identification of the three *muang:*

> *Inthara Khiri* is most likely to be understood not as a *province* of northern Thailand (Lanna Thai), but as one of the surrounding more-or-less vassal or border territories in which we might properly expect the presence of foreign peoples. . . . In at least the

Burmese and Mon monarchical-cosmographical system (Shorto 1963; Spiro 1967), a Buddhist throne in the full imperial sense was located in a kingdom with a classical cosmographic name and was required to be suzerain over surrounding territories that were definable as separate countries in terms of themselves possessing classical names.

Supposing that the three principalities were, in fact, rather small, local "towns" we still need not suppose that Northern Thailand had really at that distant time incorporated Karen populations in proper provinces, but only that these outlying regions had *some* political connection with Chiang Mai and that, consequently, they were symbolically treated as classically named places if not actually administered as such. It certainly does not necessarily imply that these were anything like Karen principalities.

15. The information on Mµang Pai is drawn from the chronicle of this southern Shan state that was compiled by its *sawbwa* in 1896 and that appears in English translation in the *Gazetteer of Upper Burma and the Shan States* (Scott and Hardiman 1900: II, 440–53). Nigel Brailey (1970: 39) provides a summary of the portion of the chronicle that makes reference to the Karen.

16. These assertions regarding the Karen at the beginning of the eighteenth century are based, in part, upon the study of Saw Hanson Tadaw, "The Karens of Burma: A Study in Human Ecology" (Tadaw 1961). Saw Hanson Tadaw argues that the major movement of Karen into lowland settlement in lower Burma followed the annexation of the area by the British. The implication is that before that time, the Karen were almost exclusively a hill-dwelling people.

17. My own guess is that the label *Gwe* applied to Smin Htaw Buddhaketi designated a Mon-Khmer tribal group rather than a Karen group. For another interpretation, see Lehman's essay in this volume.

18. On Buddhist millennial ideas in Burma, see E. Sarkisyanz (1965), E. Michael Mendelson (1961A, 1961B, 1963), and Theodore Stern (1968A).

19. Smin Htaw Buddhaketi's subsequent history takes him from Pegu to Ayutthaya and then to Chiang Mai, perhaps by way of China, and then back again to Burma where he apparently died. See Brailey (1970: 34 *et passim*) for a summary of accounts regarding Smin Htaw Buddhaketi.

20. Thip Chang was associated with a monk who in the chronicles is called a *phu mi bun* (Pho Saemlamciak 1970: 59; Prachakitcakǫracak 1964: 426f.). As I have shown elsewhere, *phu mi bun* denotes a Buddhist millennial figure (Keyes 1972, 1973, 1977).

21. Stern (1968A: 299), drawing on John Cady's history of Burma (Cady 1958: 31n), has noted that "When in [1757] the resurgent Burmans under Alaungpaya dealt the death blow to the Mon Kingdom of Pegu, Mon and Karen alike passed under a heavy yoke. The Karen in particular found themselves oppressed and insecure. Like other aliens, they were subjected to a burdensome poll tax payable in forest products in lieu of the services required of ethnic Burmans." J. S. Furnivall has noted that in 1839 taxes obtained from the Karen (consisting of beeswax, cardamon, sesamum oil, and cloth) were one of the most important sources of revenues for the government of Anglo-Burma. It is likely that these taxes had originated during the period of Burmese rule (Furnivall 1956: 33, 35).

22. The support for the conclusions given here can be found primarily in Stern's study of Karen millennialism (Stern 1968A). Some additional evidence is contained in a study by Brailey (1970), although I differ from Brailey in some interpretations of the data he presents. In particular, I question his conclusion that the Karen played an important role, as Karen, in the major political changes in Burma in the eighteenth century. For further discussion of Karen millennialism see above, pp. 20–22, and Hinton's chapter below.

23. In reconstructing the following account of Kǫn Kaeo and the story of the first Karen who became subjects of the Yuan, I have used the Chiang Mai Chronicle as my major source. More specifically, I have used a version of the chronicle that was published in Thai in 1972 (Sanguan 1972B: 118, 122, 125, 129–30). The other Thai-published version of this chronicle (Khanakamakan catphim ekkasan thang prawatsat 1971) and the French translation of another recension of the same chronicle (Notton 1932) provide no additional information. Some elaboration of the story is to be found in the Yonok Chronicle (Prachakitcakǫracak 1964: 430, 443, 452–53).

24. Muang Yuam is the old name for Mae Sariang, today a district seat in Mae Hǫng Sǫn province. Thatafang is an old ferry landing on the eastern shore of the Salween opposite the landing of Dargwin on the Burmese side. Thatafang is located today in Mae Sariang district. I have not been able to locate Muang Pǫn.

25. Tha Sithǫ and Tha Sithae are ferry landings on the western side of the Salween and are located in what is today the Karen state of Burma. The name Mae Paphaku appears to be a Karen word. Muang Thalang is the Thai name for Papun, today in the Karen state of Burma.

26. This seems unlikely since Kǫn Kaeo had been dead for over four years. King Taksin, who had just finished bringing Laos under Siamese rule by force of arms, was concerned that the vassal Yuan also remain loyal. He also may have been upset by Ca Ban's notable lack of success in the war with the Burmese.

27. These revolts are briefly mentioned by Brailey (1970: 47), whose sources were James Scott and J. P. Hardiman (1900: II, 442) and G. E. Harvey (1967: 264–65). The Yuan chronicles mention nothing about Muang Pai at this time.

28. Probably refers to the fact that there were four officials who shared the power of a *muang:* the *cao,* or "lord," *upparat* or *upparatcha, ratchawong,* and *ratchabut.*

29. *Kang* is a title, probably Shan, that appears to be used for one who was the headman of a number of villages. It might be translated as "chief" (see Lehman's chapter in this volume).

30. In the Yonok Chronicle (Prachakitcakǫracak 1964: 452), it is said that this chief was "persuaded to swear fealty" to Kawila.

31. In the Yonok Chronicle (Prachakitcakǫracak 1964: 453), it is stated that "Phraya Samlan and the local nobles [*phu mi chu*] gathered a group of retainers and secretly attacked Ban Tǫngphu for the first time. Prisoners were sent to the capital."

32. An apparent reference to a series of raids made to capture people to send to settle in Chiang Mai.

33. In the Yonok Chronicle (p. 453), these two officials are not identified by title.

34. *Fa,* a Yuan word for the Shan title *sawbwa (saohpa),* sometimes

written *caofa*. This title is used only for the rulers of *mụang*. In the Yonok Chronicle (p. 453), this ruler is called Fa Nọi Muat. This name, whether Nọi Mot or Nọi Muat, is definitely Yuan (or Shan) and not Burmese or Karen. This suggests that the ruler of Papun at this time was a Shan *sawbwa*.

35. That the emissaries first called upon Kang Saen Luang is clear from the context.

36. The Yonok Chronicle (p. 453) says a "silk cloth."

37. *Saen* is a Yuan title, given to the lowest ranked official in the hierarchy of hereditary officials (Prani 1963: I, 99). *Luang*, in Yuan, means "large." *Saen luang*, thus, was a Yuan title, probably conferred by the princes of Chiang Mai on local officials who had jurisdiction over a small number of villages. It may have been the equivalent to the Shan *kang*.

38. Since the emissaries were headed towards Papun, it is likely that Kang Saen Luang was living in an area across the Salween River from territory now in Mae Sariang district of Mae Họng Sọn province. This would have him in what is today the Karen state of Burma. His domain was obviously not in what is today the Kayah state of Burma.

39. The Yonok Chronicle (p. 453) says that, "The officials took Fa Nọi Muat to Kawila at Pa Sang for one time."

40. This passage does not appear in the Yonok Chronicle.

41. Ban Thafang is probably Thatafang (see note 24).

42. *Phọ mụang*, literally "father of the mụang," is the Yuan title given to a ruler of a small *mụang*.

43. Kiti is a name associated with the history of Mae Sariang district; this suggests that this *phọ mụang* may have been living in the vicinity of Mae Sariang in present-day Mae Họng Sọn province.

44. Although all versions agree that this name is *yan*, it is possible that Mụang Yuam was actually intended. If so, the name would be that formerly given to Mae Sariang district in Mae Họng Sọn province.

45. *Acan* ("teacher") and *nan* ("former Buddhist monk") are titles connected with activities associated with the Buddhist temple. Tho was probably the leading layman of a local Buddhist congregation.

46. It is possible that all the communities referred to in this passage were located in present-day Mae Sariang district, Mae Họng Sọn province. I have elsewhere (Keyes 1970) reported on evidence of large-scale evacuation of Yuan-speaking populations from this area in the late 1700s.

47. In the period between 1774 and 1796, the capital of Chiang Mai principality was not Chiang Mai city.

48. Prani, in a collection of biographies of Northern Thai leaders, says that "among the people who were forced to settle in the new Chiang Mai kingdom under Kawila were people from Mụang Yang Daeng, Mụang Yang Suai Kabang. . . ." (Prani 1963: I, 5). He does not give his sources. The term *yang suai kabang* appears later in the Chiang Mai annals and so was a term known from the early contacts between Yuan and Karen. It is not a term used today and I have been unable to find to which Karen group it referred, although I suspect it was used for Sgaw Karen. *Suai* and *kabang* have, from their spelling, been borrowed from some non-Tai language.

49. Although the Chiang Mai Chronicle has no record of the treaty, an account is given in the Yonok Chronicle and in a document entitled "Records of Treaty Making between Chiang Mai and the Red Karen Country," published by Sanguan Chotisukkharat in his *Collected Accounts of Lannathai*

(Sanguan 1972B: 543–80). Sanguan says of this document, which is incomplete, that "I do not know who was the author of this document because I obtained it from an old notebook which was torn. It consisted of four pages of foolscap and came from 'Records of Chiang Mai History' by Phra Mahamụn Wutthiyano of Wat Họ Tham (Wat Cedi Luang) [Chiang Mai]" (Sanguan 1972B: 545). The published version employs a Siamese, rather than a Yuan, vocabulary. Since Sanguan has published records without changing the vocabulary, it would seem likely that the original version from which Sanguan made his copy was also in Siamese. Since it is stated in the document that at the time of its composition Cao Inthanon (1871–1901) was ruler of Chiang Mai, it seems quite plausible that the document was prepared in conjunction with the controversy that developed in 1888–90 over the border between British Burma and northern Thailand.

50. The reports of the work of the British members of the Anglo-Siamese Border Commission are given in a letter from the Foreign Department of the Government of India to the secretary of state for India, dated 1890 (Government of India, Foreign Department, 1890).

51. Mụang Yuam is the old name for Mae Sariang, today the seat of a district in Mae Họng Sọn province.

52. The "Records of Treaty Making" say that "Phra Cao Chiang Mai Kawila, when he was still Phraya Mangraiwichaprakan Kamphaeng Kaeo, ordered Cao Chiang Mai Chang Phụak, when he was still Phraya Upparat (Cao Tham Langka), to make an inspection of the kingdom's frontier lands which were under Chiang Mai" (Sanguan 1972A: 545).

53. The "Records" give this name as *pha phọ* (Sanguan 1972A: 541). *Fa* and *Phra* are both titles, the former being the Yuan cognate of the Shan *sawbwa* and the latter being a Siamese title (but also see Lehman in this volume). In English sources, the name of this Kayah ruler is given as Papaw and Papaw-gyi (*gyi* being a Burmese word meaning "great"). From this information, we know that Papaw, who is generally supposed to have founded Kantarawady, was the ruler of Kantarawady by at least 1809. He was still ruling in 1837 when he was visited by a British official (Brailey 1970: 39) but probably died shortly thereafter.

54. That is, "ruler," equivalent to a Shan *sawbwa*.

55. On one map consulted, I discovered a Wan (Shan for Ban, "village") Hsa-ya located on the eastern bank of the Salween at a point a few minutes north of the nineteenth meridian.

56. Since the Karenni were attempting to establish their claim to territory east of the Salween by providing the British commissioners with accounts such as this, the assertion made here must be treated with some scepticism.

57. A Burmese phrase. Scott gives its meaning as "buffalo horn hill."

58. Sawlon, the capital of Kantarawady state.

59. Kun Yuam is Khun Yuam, the seat of a district in present-day Mae Họng Sọn province; Mèhongson is Mae Họng Sọn.

60. This story is told in two places in the reports of the Anglo-Siamese Commission. The first version, obtained by Ney Elias, the chief British commissioner, from the chief *pongyi* (Buddhist monk) of Kantarawadi, is rather garbled (Government of India, Foreign Department, 1890: 1083). The second, a brief note by Scott whose source is not identified, corroborates the Thai account except in date. Scott places the event as having happened "in the

first or second decade of the present century" (p. 1057). Amusingly, Scott queries the authenticity of the story even though it provided support for the British contention that the Salween was not the western boundary of Chiang Mai. The story also appears in the Siamese-Yuan account of the "Records" (Sanguan 1972A: 546–47).

61. The Yuan-Siamese "Records" say the forests of this area had been assigned to the domains of the famous Sihing image (located at Wat Phra Sing in Chiang Mai) since the time of Mengrai, that is, since the late thirteenth century. An official in the service of the image, Phraya Thao Saen, was responsible for collecting the tax (Sanguan 1972A: 548).

62. In an unpublished history of Mae Hong Son, which appears to have been compiled in the 1930s, only passing reference is made to Karen (who are not referred to as "Red Karen") living in the vicinity of the place where the Shan were later to establish Mae Hong Son. No mention whatsoever is made of Sawlasa's settlement (Phra Phibun Borihan n.d.).

63. See Lehman's essay in this volume.

64. See footnote 48.

65. These facts appear in *The Burney Papers* (Henry Burney et al. 1910–14) and are summarized by Stern (1971: 24–25).

66. This fact appears in the Burmese "Glass Palace Chronicles" (Aung Thein 1959: 82) but not in the Siamese account of the same event.

67. Patawi is in the mountains close to the shrine of the Buddha's shadow near Saraburi.

68. See R. Halliday (1922: 41). The similarity of the Siamese and Mon words, together with the argument advanced in the paper, support strongly the etymology of the Siamese term *kariang* which I have proposed here. I disagree, then, with Erik Seidenfaden who says that the name *kariang* "may be synonymous with Riang, the Mon-Khmer people inhabiting the Shan States or part of them prior to the advent of the Thai, and by them wrongly attached to the Karens" (Seidenfaden 1967: 114–15).

69. W. A. Archer, in a report in the same source, records that Kayah had settled in the Mae Pai valley east of the Salween and west of Mae Hong Son in about 1850 (Government of India, Foreign Department, 1890: 1096). Scott found that the area north of the Mae Pai and east of the Salween had been settled in about 1856 (p. 1059).

70. Ney Elias, the chief commissioner of the Anglo-Siamese Border Commission, found that in the area south of the Mae Pai valley, Kayah had settled in small numbers in 1880 or a little earlier. This area was mainly settled by "white Karen" (Government of India, Foreign Department, 1890: 1086).

71. An English translation of this treaty, made from a Siamese copy of the Yuan original, appears in an annex to a letter from Mr. E. B. Gould, British Chargé d'Affaires and acting Consul-General in Siam to the Marquis of Salisbury (Gould 1889).

72. In the reports of the Anglo-Siamese Border Commission, this scepticism is so qualified as to make one suspect that the Kayah were trying to convince the British that the Yuan and Siamese were making a false claim. In the summary of the commission's report, the following conclusions are expressed regarding the treaty:

> Enquiries were made regarding the treaty said, by the Siamese, to have been concluded between the Karen Chief and the Chiang

authorities (Siamese) in 1882, but neither the present Karenni Chief nor any of his headmen had any knowledge of such a document. Some denied its existence; others said that if any treaty had been made, it must be with the late Chief, Sawlapaw, now deposed and in retirement [Government of India, Foreign Department, 1890: 1045].

Curiously, there is no record that anyone asked Sawlapaw about the treaty.

73. The debate between Britain and Siam over the border between northern Thailand and British Burma can be found in Gould's letter (Gould 1889), in a memorandum prepared by the Siamese Legation in London (Siamese Legation in London 1888), and in the reports of the Anglo-Siamese Border Commission (Government of India, Foreign Department, 1890). For a summary of the debate, see Sao Saimong Mangrai's study, *The Shan States and the British Annexation* (Saimong Mangrai 1965).

74. On the Kayah in Mae Hong Son, see Lehman's chapter in this volume.

75. In 1856 a Karen, who styled himself as the Minlaung and was the leader of a sizeable millennial movement in British Burma, was forced by the British to flee for refuge to Chiang Mai. From there he organized a force and went back to fight again in an area around Kawkareik in present-day Karen State, west of Tak in Siam. He was beaten and forced to flee once again, this time to Karenni (Stern 1968A: 307-8).

76. This point is somewhat misleading since if the British had agreed to the Salween border claimed by the Siamese, there would have been a sizeable Kayah population in northern Thailand.

77. Quoted in Stern (1971A: 24).

78. By 1919 there were approximately 230,000 Karen who were either communicants or children of communicants of Christian churches. The Baptists had the largest number with about 200,000; next came the Catholics with 25,000; and finally the Anglicans with 5,000. The Christian community represented about 15 percent or a little more of the total number of Karen living in Burma at the time. See Harry Marshall (1922: 300-301).

79. These observations regarding the affiliation of Karen with "Burmese" Buddhist traditions as the result of relationships developed in the context of the teak trade are based upon my own research in Mae Sariang. Also see Kunstadter's essay in this volume.

80. See Hinton's and Marlowe's chapters in this volume.

81. Quote by Stern (1971A: 21-23), who took it from "Rev. Mr. Mason's Journal" by Francis Mason, which appeared in the *Missionary Register,* 18 (1833): 321.

82. According to Lehman (personal communication), this word is "a standard Burmese title for Karen chiefs."

83. This document is contained in *The Burney Papers* (Burney 1910-14: IV, 1; 130-32) and is quoted in Stern (1971A: 28).

84. See Kunstadter's, Marlowe's, Iijima's, and Hinton's chapters in this volume.

85. See Keyes (1971). On the basis of some research carried out in 1973, I would say that the Buddhist mission program to the hill tribes *(thammacarik)* has grown rather more sophisticated than when first I encountered it in 1967-68. It has had some success, although proportionately more with groups such as the Meo than with the Karen.

A People Between:
The Pwo Karen of Western Thailand

Theodore Stern

To discuss the Pwo Karen in historical perspective is to confront the twin issues of placing the Pwo among the varieties of Karen and of subsuming the diversity that is Pwo under a spanning commonalty. In the past, a number of properties have been taken to demarcate the Pwo as a cultural entity, and if we select language from among them to serve as a marker, it is not to regress to that position, so roundly criticized by E. R. Leach (1954; see also Moerman 1965, 1968), in which "tribes" linguistically defined are seen as homogeneous and, perhaps, eternal entities: we simply find the possession of a common language a convenient measure of historical continuity.

For the Pwo, indeed, the choice of language is particularly appropriate, since it is still significant in their own definition of their ethnic group. In their view, it serves as a primary sorting criterion: no one is truly a Pwo who does not speak the tongue. For those aliens who sometimes learn it, secondary criteria of association or cultural character are easily adduced. For the Pwo, moreover, their language serves to locate them within the larger family of Karen speakers. Taken thus, the Pwo stand in immediate contrast to the Sgaw; then in ever more remote genetic relationship to Taungthu, Bwè, and the like; then to other Tibeto-Burman speakers; and beyond. The more immediate of these relationships are consciously held by the Pwo themselves when they recall their mythology, particularly when they are under the power of a millennial belief in a future kingdom of the reunited Karen.

Karen legend characterizes the Pwo as a people who were driven by the Sgaw, a somewhat more numerous branch of the Southern Karen, into the littoral lowlands of Burma, terrain that in historic times extended from the lower Sittang across deltaic Burma and down the Tenasserim coast to Mergui. Here they adopted a riverine way of life—so successfully, indeed, that Pwo crews frequently took first place in the royal boat races at Ava (Fytche 1878: I, 334). From this habitat arose the Burmese appellation, *Myitkhyin,* River Chin, by which they were sometimes known (Mason 1882–83: I, 92). In comparison to the Sgaw, the Pwo are commonly characterized by authors as coastal and lowland people, in contrast to people of an interior, upland terrain, and as dwelling in larger, more ordered villages (Mason, p. 92): indeed, one suspects that the contrast may sometimes have been read into the situation, as seems to be true with the Northern Thai who, Peter Hinton (1969: 3f.) reports, characterize the Pwo as civilized villagers and the Sgaw as jungle Karen.

In the Burmese littoral, Pwo came into contact with the Mon. The linguistic data, both phonological and lexical, show that such contact was widespread among the Karen, attested most strongly among the Pwo and Sgaw and fading away among the Northern Karen (Henderson 1965: 422–24, 430; Luce 1953: 1, 1959A: 9f.). It may well be that the Southern Karen, and in particular the Pwo, were intermediary in transmitting elements to other Karen groups.

It has usually been assumed that Mon relations with the Pwo were on the whole closest: the Burmans characterized the Pwo as "Talaing (Mon) Karen," in distinction from the Sgaw, whom they dubbed "Burmese Karen," a contrast made in corresponding terms by the Mon (Shorto 1962: 42, 70, 170). In thus categorizing the two branches, both Burmese and Mon seem to have taken them at the point of their highest distinctiveness. It seems unwarranted to assume that Mon relationships were exclusively with the Pwo, for they had much to do with other Karen peoples, such as the Taungthu. Nor does the designation signify that the Pwo had become wholly absorbed by the Mon. Rather, it is to be taken with the corresponding term for the Sgaw as an equation expressing the loose symbiotic relation linking a Karen people on one side with a major lowland civilization on the other.[1]

Although the distinction was made, it does not follow that either segment of the Southern Karen was unitary in its characteristics. At least in the days following the first Anglo-Burmese War (1824–26)—although admittedly those were unsettled times—missionaries encountered Karen villages in the Tenasserim in a continuum, interspersed at their nether end with outlying Mon villages in the lowlands, but studded as well along mountain streams as one ascended inland. It is to be suspected that upland Pwo may well have shared as much with their Sgaw neighbors as with their more acculturated lowland congeners, who already had become humble citizens of the Buddhist world.[2]

The Pwo of Thailand, with whom we are most directly concerned in the remainder of this chapter, stem largely from the Burmese Tenasserim. Although David Marlowe (1970) has asserted that Karen in northern Thailand purchased usufruct from the rulers of Chiang Mai between 200 and 400 years ago, the evidence presented by Charles Keyes in this volume favors the view that Karen settlement in this area dates from the end of the eighteenth century. One significant increment to the Karen population in Thailand came from the repeated abduction of peoples by the Lannathai states in the north and by Siam in the south.[3] In the vicinity of Moulmein, from perhaps the eighteenth century, the Pwo stronghold of Dongyan was repeatedly attacked and its inhabitants carried off by the Siamese. After gaining their freedom through labor payments, the majority returned, leaving a few scattered colonies in Siam (Smeaton 1887: 70).

The major event releasing large-scale movements of Karen across the passes into present-day Thailand dated from the middle of the eighteenth century when the resurgent Burmans, under Alaungpaya and his successors of the Konbaung dynasty, in swift campaigns extirpated the Mon kingdoms of lower Burma and sacked the Siamese capital of Ayutthaya. "The Karens," Mason heard from those in Burma in the nineteenth century, "have not been long in Siam. Many went thither when Martaban was destroyed, because they heard it was a good country; some, whom the Siamese had kidnapped, were there before, and some went when the Siamese beseiged [sic] Tavoy" (Mason 1884: 123; see Stern 1971A for discussion). In the north, Sgaw moved into lands west of the Salween vacated by a withdrawal of Northern Thai (Yuan) elements (Keyes 1970).

It seems probable that the Pwo among those northern settlers came from that limb in Burma that had been least adapted to lowland life and to Mon Buddhism, unless—which seems less likely—through readaptation they had lost all Mon-derived characteristics. A comparison of modern Sgaw and Pwo drawn by Peter Kunstadter (1970A) in a study of Mae Hong Son province shows both peoples dwelling in upland contexts as swidden farmers cultivating some wet rice as well, to which the Sgaw add wage work as loggers. In rural lowland settings, only the Sgaw appear, primarily as wet-rice farmers and loggers. In town, the Sgaw dwell in largely Karen quarters, again as paddy farmers, gardeners, wage laborers, and low-echelon government officials. The Pwo in town seem by contrast to be marginal, for they are characterized as impoverished migrants, those who have failed in upland farming, the day laborers, and the opium addicts. In all three settings, the Pwo are animists, and even in the uplands the Sgaw include some Buddhists and Christians. In this region, it is clearly the Pwo who manifest the lesser degree of acculturation.

By contrast with the northern Pwo, those who entered central Thailand seem to have borne more heavily the Mon impress and to have maintained preferential contact with Mon emigres in Thailand itself. Indeed, there is some evidence that some Karen leaders entered Thailand at Mon behest and under Mon aegis (Stern 1971A). As early as 1826, those dwelling a few miles below Three Pagodas Pass, in the headwaters region of the Maenam Khwae Noi, were already engaged, together with Mon troops in the service of Siam, in the extraction of forest products and the production of cotton and cotton cloth, which they were soon rafting to market in Bangkok (see Stern 1971A for details). Their preference for the Mon style of Therevada Buddhism was likewise reflected in a long-time loyalty towards the Mon monastery at Photharam, on the Mae Klong between Kanchanaburi and Ratburi. Yet through time, these people have continued besides to maintain contacts with the Tenasserim towns and with cities beyond in Burma, through tours that combine pilgrimage, sight seeing, and trading.

Despite their early ventures downriver, these Pwo of the headwaters region have long been isolated by distance and jungle from pervasive Thai influences. In the wake of the first Anglo-Burmese War, the upper Mae Klong was administered by Mon, initially by the military forces responsible for its defense and subsequently by officers from that army serving in quasi-civil capacity under the governor of Kanchanaburi. By 1839 their ranks included a Karen district officer, already denominated by the Siamese title Phra Si Suwannakhiri (or Phra Suwan), a name that also applied to the region this officer administered at the headwaters of the Khwae Noi (Richardson 1839 and 1840: 1027). As the Mon thereafter gravitated downriver to the Siamese plains, responsibility for the marches devolved upon the Karen. By 1866 two other Karen governors in addition to Phra Si Suwannakhiri were designated to administer areas on the other branch of the Mae Klong, the Khwae Yai. Phra Sisawat presided over the middle course of the river and was, like Phra Si Suwannakhiri, made responsible to the governor of Kanchanaburi. Phra Mae Klong, who controlled an area in what today is southern Tak province located on the upper reaches of the Khwae Yai, separated from the lower reaches by an unnavigable rapids, was attached administratively to Muang Uthai. At the time of the administrative reforms and the consolidation of central power in the 1890s, Karen governors were left in office. The line of Phra Si Suwannakhiri continued until 1924 when the last incumbent, then designated *yot nai amphoe* ("head district officer"), finally retired.

Indirect rule thus served at once to insulate the Karen and to stabilize their position within their new country. Meanwhile, they continued to receive cultural influences from their former homeland. Thus it was from Buddhist Karen behind Moulmein that there arose the millennial Telakhon movement that once extended downriver almost to the provincial capital of Kanchanaburi itself, and it was from much the same sources that their orthodox Buddhism, after the turn of the century, renewed itself and captured Karen loyalties. It is only within the past two generations that the Karen of the Khwae Noi headwaters have come under pervasive Thai influences, with direct administration by Thai officials, the opening of public schools, and the growing penetration and exploitation of their region by commercial interests.

Thus the Pwo of Thailand, and in particular those of the central regions, are far from constituting a people exposed for the first time to the impact of a lowland civilization. Rather, the central Pwo lie between two civilizational styles and are presently undergoing a readaptation toward that of the Thai. This is graphically reflected in their speech, as when two men discuss the "real" Karen words for "cup" and "table," the one adducing Mon-Burmese, the other Thai, loanwords. Indeed, the Pwo phrase for that blessing of civilization, "customs duties" (*ako' phasi*), neatly blends a term shared by Burmese and Mon with another of Sino-Thai derivation.

The Northern Pwo

A more particular comparison among four communities in Thailand will provide details of the course of culture change the Pwo have undergone there. These instances are not to be construed as points lying upon a straight line; rather, they comprise selective adaptations within diverse settings. Nor are all observed differences among communities to be attributed to their present contexts: some of those differences within the Pwo heritage, as intimated above, had already developed in Burma.

In northern Thailand lie two communities that may be taken to have built upon a Pwo tradition relatively lightly influenced by the Mon. The upland village of Dong Luang, studied by Hinton in 1968–69, lies on a plateau over 3,000 feet in elevation, over a day's walk from the nearest Thai village, between the towns of Mae Sariang and Họt (Hinton 1969: 6). East of it, near Họt, the *amphoe* (district) seat, lies the village of Ban Hong, a Karen community studied by Hamilton in 1960–61, squeezed among non-Karen settlements in the valley of the Mae Ping (Hamilton 1963, 1965).

These two northern communities share many social and ritual features that seem part of a Karen heritage. Each village has a ritual head who officiates in the cult of the village guardian spirit and whose office passes patrilineally. In both, if a new village buds off, a man patrilineally related to the ritual head becomes head of the daughter community; in Ban Hong the guardian spirit of the parent community releases a "child" to take corresponding office with the new one. Cognatic links connect the ritual head of Dong Luang with most of its households. In annual or semiannual ceremonies to the village spirit, all households must send representatives.

In both villages, several matrilineages are represented, although not necessarily restricted to a single community; and matrilineal kinsmen array their houses together, a practice that Hamilton sees as reminiscent of the Karen long house (see also Iijima 1970: 19–25 and Iijima in this volume). The matrilineage, which Hinton sees as distinguishing the Pwo from the Sgaw, is primarily ritual in function, with an ancestral cult headed by the senior woman of the lineage. In curing ceremonies, she presides as lineage priestess and all members of the lineage, and only they, must be present. Marriage is monogamous and remarriage rare. Married daughters tend in Dong Luang to establish residence in the parental village; in Ban Hong the preference is to marry within the community. There is initial uxorilocality, in addition to the residential clusters already mentioned, that comprise the households of parents and married daughters. Such units often exchange labor.

Despite the prominence of the matrilineage in both of the northern communities, it is the household that is said to be the primary unit of economic and social activity. In Dong Luang, for instance, over three-fourths of the twenty-six households comprise nuclear family units, averaging 4.8 persons; of Ban Hong's thirty-five households, 60 percent are of the same type, with a median size of 6.0 members. Associated with that residential condition is an economy in which land resources are inadequate. Both communities combine swiddening with wet-rice agriculture, although in upland Dong Luang, where the latter practice had been carried on for only a decade at the time of study, it accounted for only 3.5 percent of the area under cultivation. Swiddens in both are small, averaging only 4.9 *rai* for Dong Luang and 2.0 *rai* for Ban Hong.[4] Even at the latter village, where a Lua' (Lawa) paddy field has been reclaimed and is being farmed by several households, the wet-rice fields average but 4.0 *rai*.

In consequence of their land poverty, only four households in Dong Luang reap enough rice for their own needs; Ban Hong villagers, hedged in by other communities, produce only one-fifth to one-third of the rice they require. In both places, then, people must supplement subsistence farming by raising livestock for sale, selling surplus crops and jungle products, engaging in wage labor for Thai or Karen, and selling manufactures, including, in Ban Hong, Karen-woven articles modified to Thai tastes.

As James Hamilton (1963) makes clear, the villagers of Ban Hong are deeply engaged in a market economy. They pursue long-range trading, drawing on Thai capital to buy cattle in Burma for resale in Thailand. Other middlemen include salesmen who purvey Karen products to Thai customers, and labor bosses who manage wet-rice fields for themselves or others, Karen or Thai. It is the heads of that third of households who own or manage irrigated rice fields who incline toward Buddhism. Taken together with those who follow traditional ideals as closely as possible and those forced into inferior dependency as wage workers, Hamilton sees the Karen of this lowland community assorting into incipient classes that shift toward the status of Thai peasantry.

The Central Pwo

By contrast with the northern Pwo, those in Kanchanaburi province, in the headwater region of the Khwae Nọi, exhibit a greater continuity of Mon influence. Here we again take for comparison two communities. The rural village of Waplonkhu lies in the valley of the Bi Khi, one of three major confluents that combine to form the major river. At a distance of three hours' travel by foot, at the confluence itself, stands the administrative town of Sangkhlaburi, with a total population of some 1,600, over a quarter of them Karen.

WAPLONKHU

By comparison with those already considered, both of the central communities are well endowed with land. Waplonkhu and neighboring villages lie, like Ban Hong, in a river valley but in a region far less densely settled and preponderantly Karen. Of thirty-five households (including Waplonkhu's twenty-four), twenty in the year of study (1965) had planted irrigated rice in fields averaging 21.5 *rai,* and the other fifteen were farming swiddens averaging 12.1 *rai.* Here the total yield of rice is sufficient to meet the food requirements of almost all households and to leave a surplus, which is sometimes sold. Supplementary income is gained through selling garden and orchard crops and livestock, by rental of elephants to loggers, by logging or by other wage labor, and by selling manufactures. Among these villagers real property and its inheritance in equal shares by offspring are important considerations—probably bulking larger in their concern than in Dong Luang or even, perhaps, Ban Hong.

The Bi Khi Pwo are strongly Buddhist. A monastery has stood in Waplonkhu, it is said, since at least the turn of the century, serving a wide area, and 87 percent of the men interviewed had served at least a novitiate in the Sangha (the Buddhist monkhood). Participation in Buddhism has led to the decline of the blood brotherhood, still attested among the Pwo of northern Thailand, and which seems to have been replaced here by the bonds of common service in monastic school and in the monastery. Similarly, temple festivals and the performances of village dance troupes have replaced funeral wakes as occasions for courtship. With Buddhism have come what one man termed the "more scientific" practices of astrology and numerology to take the place of chicken leg-bone divination in forecasting the future.

In comparison with the northern Pwo, those of the Khwae Nọi headwaters have a matrilineage abbreviated to the degree that in ritual scope it resembles the condition of the Sgaw. The earlier Buddhist millennialism (Stern 1968A) in this area has left a residual opposition among the Karen to the sacrifice of domestic animals in spirit cults, including sacrifices to the ancestors. Although in Dong Luang, Northern Thai Buddhism is seemingly compatible with the lineage sacrificial cult, in the more intimate context of the plains the latter at least undergoes modification and may give way altogether (Keyes, personal communication).[5] In the Khwae Nọi region, Karen who have become Buddhist have had to foresake the ceremonies of the old lineage cult; and today there is said to be but one household in the Bi Khi drainage that still maintains it. In each Buddhist Pwo household, there is a Buddhist shrine maintained by the senior woman, the household thus becoming a ritual unit redirected toward the monastery. The ancestors are still honored annually—local Lao and Mon Buddhists also maintain such ceremonies—and on these occasions the celebrating unit is the household rather than the lineage. A similar ritual shift from lineal principles to those of locality and affiliation is found in the cult of the village guardian spirit, the local Lord (Stern 1968B; cf. Iijima 1970: 34–36; and Tambiah 1970).

In some respects, the marriage practices among Bi Khi Pwo resemble those of Pwo communities in northern Thailand. Over half the marriages surveyed in Waplonkhu and adjacent communities have been contracted within the Bi Khi drainage, although less than one-third involve parties from within the same village. In the north, Dong Luang and its neighbors taken together (Hinton 1969: 21) exhibit a comparable degree of village endogamy; Ban Hong (Hamilton 1965: table 14) shows a somewhat higher value, approximately 50 percent. Median household size on the Bi Khi, slightly in excess of five persons, is intermediate between the values for the two northern communities.

With these similarities go other features more distinctive for the Bi Khi Pwo. In marriage, for example, Dong Luang villagers include descendants of unions with other hill peoples (Hinton 1969: 15); those of Ban Hong tolerate, but generally disapprove of, unions with non-Karen (Hamilton 1965: 111, n. 3). Attitudes on the Bi Khi resemble those at Ban Hong, with perhaps a greater degree of permissiveness: almost one-fifth of all unions are with migrants from Burma, and over 8 percent are with non-Karen, primarily Lao. Again, although on religious grounds the villagers of Dong Luang frown on remarriage (Hinton 1969: 17), those at Ban Hong show on their record that 11 percent of marriages are remarriages (Hamilton 1965: table 10). The figure for Waplonkhu and its neighbors is close to that of Ban Hong, but slightly greater, amounting to some 15 percent.

Differences occur as well in residential arrangements. The matrilineage, it will be recalled, is reflected among the northern Pwo by household uxorilocality, often related to ultimogeniture, in which married daughters and their husbands live sequentially with the daughters' parents, the youngest couple remaining to inherit house and other effects and to support the aged parents. Linked with this is the formation of uxorilocal neighborhoods, as each older married daughter, moving out of the house to make way for a newly married younger sister, resettles nearby.[6] On the Bi Khi, the weakening of matrilineal ritual ties might be expected to link with a decrease in the incidence of the joint lineal household, that includes an uxorilocal junior couple. Instead, the joint lineal household is prominent on the Bi Khi, comprising no less than 42 percent of the sample, and of that type, no less than 24 percent are of uxorilocal character. Moreover, almost every couple for which such residence was possible at the time of marriage—in some instances the wife's parents were already dead—reported initial uxorilocality. By contrast to Dong Luang's 76 percent and Ban Hong's 60 percent, nuclear-family households at Waplonkhu and its neighbors stood at 56 percent of the sample. The ideal of household uxorilocality is shared alike by Pwo in the northern and central communities. However, the Bi Khi househead farms a larger field than does his counterpart in the north and needs regular help in cultivating it. The larger tract, it might be said, furnishes grounds for maintaining the institution of the resident son-in-law, who provides that assistance.

The uxorilocal neighborhoods, on the other hand, appear less frequently on the Bi Khi, and when they occur, they do not exhibit the spatial alignment described for the north. Part of this relates to the inheritance of irrigated rice fields and of fruit orchards, which pass in equal shares to the children, may derive from either parent, and often lie at some distance from the homestead (see Stern 1965 for details). The desire to live close to such property, which is ordinarily divided among heirs at the retirement of the househead, in addition to secondary claims of support by the husband's parents (an expression of the bilaterality discussed below), has weakened the occurrence of uxorilocal clustering. When a househead requires occasional assistance beyond his household, he is likely to seek it through labor exchange with a friend, rather than from kinsmen resident in such a neighborhood.

Both in Ban Hong and among the central Pwo, there exists a bilateral system of kinship nomenclature. In the north, it occurs along with matrilineal rules of exogamy. In the Khwae Nọi region, the rule is not unilineal but is applied bilaterally, involving equally relatives in the father's as well as in the mother's line; nor do the genealogies, incomplete though they are, reveal any infraction of that rule. Although, again, it cannot be attested that a unilineal rule was formerly observed in the Bi Khi region, it seems probable that the factors discussed earlier may have been conducive to a shift toward bilateral exogamy. Hamilton (1965: 123) has summarized the social structure of the Pwo of Ban Hong as Normal Nankanse; that of the Bi Khi Pwo is Matri-Eskimo in form. The two types, as George Murdock (1949: table 73) has shown, are mutually convertible by descent stages. David Marlowe (personal communication) has found bilateral exogamy among the Sgaw of Chiang Mai province, while other Sgaw seem to be matrilineal, suggestive of a parallel to the Pwo data that should reward further investigation.

The culture the Bi Khi Pwo have developed has been shaped by past Buddhist millennial experience. Although it is consciously Karen, Bi Khi villagers have not clung to traditional elements as symbols of Karenhood, but have built up an identity out of a composite of borrowed features. Their language they retain, but they have developed their own form of script from the Mon-Burmese to record it (Stern 1968C). During World War II when the Thai prime minister, Phibun Songkhram, instituted policies to encourage the adoption of Western dress, Karen dress was officially discouraged, weaving fell largely into disuse, and most of the Pwo turned to Mon-Burmese dress. Musical styles, instruments, and dance forms show pervasive borrowing from Mon-Burmese and Lao-Thai sources together with readaptation to a Karen context (Stern and Stern 1971). Even Karen names are often modelled upon, and sometimes are lexically derived from, the Burmese. The monasteries the Karen maintain that have become the focus of regional consciousness link them through pilgrimage and service with the Buddhist world in Burma and Thailand. In emulative fashion, the Bi Khi Pwo have thus developed a life-style that incorporates them distinctively into that larger world on a footing of essential parity. Although they feel somewhat rural, they sense no unbridgeable gap between them and the Burmans and Thai; perhaps that millennial legacy they seem outwardly to have forsaken still holds the promise that they are a people whose day will come.

SANGKHLABURI

It is in Sangkhlaburi that the Pwo enter into a new ecological setting, that of town life. This administrative seat of the *king* (branch) *amphoe*[7] lies less than half a day's travel from the central Bi Khi villages. Bi Khi Karen visit it every three months or more, finding lodging with relatives or friends during their stay. With its two monasteries, Karen and Mon, its shops, schools, and mission hospital, Sangkhlaburi has a population in excess of 1,600. Over a quarter of them are Pwo, with only a few Sgaw: here as in the hinterland, *kariang,* the usual Thai term for Pwo, is extended to Karen in general. If Sgaw must be distinguished, it is by the term *kalang/karang*.[8] The other townsfolk include a few Tibeto-Burman-speaking people, locally known as Lawa, and a handful of Taungthu; together with major segments of "Lao" from Laos, the Shan states, and northern Thailand; Mon, post-World War II political refugees from Burma; and Thai, largely officials from the plains on temporary station in this frontier post. Beyond the town are satellite villages of Karen, Lawa, and the camp of the Border Patrol Police.

Within this polyethnic setting, compartmentalization along ethnic lines is matched by greater openness in other spheres. Even the prominence of ethnicity in social intercourse differs among the constituent groups in town. The Thai, for example, are distinctive by virtue of their political office and their preponderantly urban background. With the exception of a few policemen, long in residence, some with Karen wives, they dwell in cantonments in the administrative quarter, not far from the house site of the last Karen governor, and when off-duty, keep their own company. Conscious of embodying the cultural identity of Thailand, here they encounter other proud, if unaggressive, traditions. When, during Songkran (the traditional New Year) the Thai mounted an elaborate costume parade, only one Karen family, that of an official, participated, although many looked on. The major part of the population was soon engrossed in carrying out its own ceremonies of lustration and pagoda building within the grounds of monasteries.

The Mon, political exiles, form another close-knit community. Segregated across the Khwae Noi for reasons of security by Thai officials, they dwell under the benevolent authority of their abbot. The only Mon in Sangkhlaburi who live apart from their fellows are a few young men who, because of drinking or gambling, have been formally ostracized. They have moved to the main portion of the town, taken Karen wives, and are gradually making a new start.

Toward that internally diverse group called the Lao, the Thai feel most closely akin, since they share much linguistically and culturally, and because they include among their number several policemen. The Lao, however, are most at home with their Karen neighbors, with whom they share a rural background. The Lawa and Taungthu (Tongsu) are each too few to constitute viable ethnic entities.

The Karen in town are prevailingly immigrant; among houseeheads, 57 percent have come from elsewhere, primarily the rural countryside. Moreover, no fewer than 49 percent of the Pwo houseeheads are married to non-Karen. Such interethnic unions are somewhat more frequent among immigrants, suggesting the lessening of restrictions when the network of kinsmen has been left behind. Karen have married with Lao most frequently (25 percent), less often with Mon (9 percent) and Thai (8 percent), and sparingly with the few Taungthu (4 percent) and Lawa (3 percent). As in the Bi Khi villages, Karen women enter into interethnic unions with greater frequency than do the men. In Sangkhlaburi, where the difference is marked, it reflects in part the preponderance of Karen women, as labor migration carries men out of town. These Karen townsmen are further marked by a degree of remarriage striking when contrasted with the other communities, particularly those of the north: even among households in which both heads are Karen, almost one in every five men and one in every three women are in at least a second marriage.

To examine the economic consequences of life in town for those Karen who live there, consider the condition of thirty-eight households headed by Karen couples. The twenty-one households that subsist principally by farming in lands near the town grow more cash crops and realize more income from them than do their Bi Khi cousins, even on somewhat smaller tracts of land. Cultivating swiddens of a median size of 5 *rai* or irrigated fields averaging but 13 *rai*, they gross perhaps twice as much as do Bi Khi farmers, on the order of 2,000 baht[9] a year, from the sale of surplus crops. Their cash crops bring returns that are also on a larger scale, for the two most affluent of these farmers, who gross 7,000 and 10,000 baht, respectively, from tobacco raised on riverside plots, far exceed the annual gross of the wealthiest Bi Khi farmer, who realizes but 2,600 baht per annum.

At the lower end of the scale below these farmers are nine households that engage in subsistence farming to supplement income from wage labor as farmhand, charcoal burner, sawyer, or as deckhand for a river launch. At the upper end in eight households are persons whose primary income derives from salary as policeman or teacher, from income as shopkeeper, from the rental of elephants for logging, or from operations as logging contractor. Such men engage in large-scale farming, cultivating cash crops with hired Mon and Karen laborers on extensive (40–50 *rai*) tracts of irrigated rice or gardens and orchards on the order of 6 *rai* apiece. For these individuals, as for their wealthier Thai and Lao counterparts, farming is a means for investing surplus income. The magnitude of primary economic activities among the Karen of the upper echelons may be suggested by the gross annual income reported by two individuals at the top of the scale: 35,000 and 55,000 baht, respectively.

Geared to a cash economy, Karen townsmen have largely forsaken the joint lineal household, which in all its forms accounts for only 16 percent of the thirty-eight households just considered. This situation, and particularly the decline in popularity of the uxorilocal household, is not to be accounted for by suggesting that immigrant Karen women have left their parents behind and so cannot reside with them after marriage; for the incidence of household types is much the same for those eighteen units in which the wife was born locally as for the twenty in which she was an immigrant. We can rule out as well the general condition of urban life or the examples of others, for a number of Lao, among others, continue to favor the joint lineal household. For those Karen who are primarily farmers, the fields cultivated are relatively small, for which the members of a nuclear household provide a sufficient work force. For wage earners and cash croppers alike, there seems as well to be a premium upon setting up one's own household, with the consequent freedom to spend one's earnings as one will.

To this condition can be added the virtual disappearance of uxorilocal neighborhood clusters, in part because they had already been on the wane in regions such as the Bi Khi from which the immigrants came, and also because they are difficult to establish in a densely settled community.

At the same time, Karen, like their fellow townsmen, report frequent exchanges of visits with local relatives, on the order of several times a week. They also visit rural kinsmen, for the most part annually; and a temple festival on the Bi Khi draws a massive exodus of Karen from Sangkhlaburi. Many Karen households in town host a visiting rural kinsman, who may be surveying the prospects before bringing in his own family to take up permanent residence.

Among such boarders are also to be counted rural children who have been sent to live with kinsmen in town to take advantage of the superior schooling Sangkhlaburi has offered for almost four decades. Karen are zealous to take advantage of education: the proportion of school children who are Karen (50 percent) is more than double the proportion of Karen (21 percent) in the school-age population in town. A comparison of adult Karen in Sangkhlaburi above and below the age of forty gives graphic evidence of the progressive advantage gained through education and the familiarity it brings with the Thai language and Thai ways: it is chiefly the younger, better educated men who are moving into mercantile and salaried positions.

In turn, the interference of schooling and the competition of other interests have somewhat weakened the degree of commitment of Karen townsmen to the monastery. This may spell a departure from Mon (and rural Karen) standards of almost obligatory service in the novitiate toward the more permissive local Lao and Thai standards. With incomplete returns, and with many failures to respond, our data for monastic service show a figure of only 47 percent for the Karen in town, with corresponding figures for Thai and Lao, respectively, of 36 percent and 26 percent. However, a comparison of Karen men above and below the age of forty shows no evidence of further decline. The village guardian spirit, the local Lord, whom the Mon honor as do the Karen and Lao, seems to be losing ground as he is shown to be powerless before the scoffing of Thai officials and the advances of Thai technology (Stern 1968B).

In Sangkhlaburi, then, as in Ban Hong in the north, so close to the *amphoe* seat, the Pwo are finding differentiation upon an economic scale that locally ranges from the level of wealthy Lao and lesser Thai officials to a limit somewhat above that of impecunious newcomers among the Mon. They have also entered upon a diversified range of roles transcending ethnic lines. In one setting, they are Karen; in another, Buddhists, Thai citizens, lumbering contractors, or the like. Under these circumstances, it might be anticipated that a sense of ethnic solidarity arising out of shared tradition would, in a Durkheimian sense, give way to affiliations recognizing status in a larger organic unity.

There has indeed been modification. As is suggested by the record of intermarriage, the sense of community has been enlarged; the boundaries have become more diffuse. Taungthu, Karen, and some Lao fraternize and regard the Karen monastery—founded, indeed, by Taungthu monks—as their own. For the Thai, Karen townsmen are difficult to characterize: these city-bred officials are more comfortable in treating Karen as if they were all the capable and somewhat exotic woodsmen of the remote hamlets. When such officials camp in the jungles, which they regard as the natural domain of the Karen, they are scrupulous in following Karen magical techniques for averting prowling tigers. With that image of the "primitive" Karen, they must reconcile, even for the Bi Khi villagers, the long tradition of their Buddhism and the record of the Karen governors. Although some Thai may differentiate Karen Buddhism from theirs by reference to the exotic features of monastic architecture and of Karen ritual gestures, and remark on the alleged unintelligibility of their Pali chants, they concede the undoubted piety of their worship. As for the governors, their memory still endures, for the last of the line retired with his Thai wife to live out his days in the provincial capital, and two of his Karen sons-in-law, both respected figures, are prominent in Sangkhlaburi. In the end, in their daily transactions, Thai officials often find ethnicity an inappropriate attribute for dealing with the variety of Karen townsmen, as other features are seen of more immediate relevance.

Do the Karen of Sangkhlaburi adumbrate conditions under which they will merge into an indeterminate populace? There are local instances in which immigrant Lao pass in public contexts as Thai and in which Taungthu and part-Karen claim to be Lao. The high degree of intermarriage can hardly fail to have its effect in blurring ethnic boundaries. Yet many townsmen, themselves the product of interethnic unions, in reporting their identity choose that of one parent—sometimes the parent of the same sex—to characterize themselves. Indeed, they may claim one identity with outsiders but accept another from their peers. They rarely assert a hyphenated identity.

The Pwo language continues to be an important element in Karen identity; yet it is by no means an exclusive property today. Not only do all Karen speak it, but so do many Lao and others who marry Karen; and Thai officials, who look upon the Karen as a group with something of that mixture of fascination and disdain that American Indians encounter in the United States, pride themselves upon learning at least a few phrases of this *lingua franca* of the hills.

Thus against the perspective of the other three Karen communities, that in Sangkhlaburi is internally diversified; for its members, the matrilineage no longer maintains a Karen boundary; neither language nor dress is any longer an exclusive marker; the Karen monastery is shared with others; and Karen children study a Thai curriculum with other children at school. Such conditions are bound to erode the distinctiveness of a Karen identity.

Yet as Barth and his associates have made clear (Barth 1969B), ethnic identities are to be seen, as they develop, in the context of larger networks. Within town, those Karen who learn the Thai language and ways do so as a matter of biculturation. The Karen elite enjoy their position and command respect in Thai eyes primarily because they continue to maintain solidarity with other Karen. The teacher is valued because she can communicate with Karen children who have yet to speak Thai; the logging contractor must marshal Karen elephants and loggers from the surrounding villages for his enterprises; and the shopkeeper, although he sells to all, has built his custom upon a mutual trust established with fellow Karen. So long as Sangkhlaburi continues to draw upon immigrants from the rural reservoirs, so long as the Pwo in town maintain their links with kinsmen in the villages, the consciousness of a common Karenhood is likely to be refreshed.

This chapter has compared four Pwo Karen communities in Thailand, conceived of as radiations into as many different contexts. Through an analysis of concomitant variation, changes have been deduced in the areas of economic adaptation, social organization, and religion. Extension of such analysis to Pwo in settings dissimilar to those considered here, and to other peoples in analogous contexts, may permit a more precise expression of the relevant processes of change and continuity.

Acknowledgments

For review of an initial draft, I offer thanks to my colleagues Vernon R. Dorjahn and Don E. Dumond as well as to Charles F. Keyes and Peter Kunstadter. The research upon which this essay rests was undertaken in

1964–65 under a grant from the National Science Foundation and under the local sponsorship of the National Research Council of Thailand, to which I make grateful acknowledgment.

Notes

1. Two other interpretations of the contrast warrant discussion. Nigel Brailey (1970: 44), speaking of the eighteenth-century "Carianners" of Lower Burma, in contrast to the "Okpo Karens" of the north, characterizes them as "probably less well-organized and more inclined to inter-marry, the modern *Pwo* being perhaps the descendants of Mon unions, and the *Sgaw,* those of Burman unions." Such an explanation of the formation of these two divisions seems highly unlikely. When Michael Symes reported on his visit to Ava in 1795, he cited Father Vincentius Sangermano on the "Carayners, or Carianers": "their villages form a select community, from which they exclude all other sects, and never reside in a city, intermingle, or marry with strangers" (Symes 1800: 207).

In discussing the earlier version of this essay after its presentation at the symposium, F. K. Lehman suggested that the equation may relate to succession, the Mon regarding the Karen as autochthones in the country they had come to dominate. This view is lent a certain plausibility by such Mon legends as that of the hero Kun Atha, the offspring of Thamala, king of Pegu, and the daughter of an aged Karen couple (Harvey 1925: 5f., quoting the *Nanda-thara*). However, I know of no corresponding view relating the Burmans and the Sgaw.

Basic similarities between Pwo and Sgaw communities today suggest that the differences may comprise no more than minor traits of dress, ritual detail, and language of symbolic importance on the order noted by Michael Moerman (1965, 1968) for the Lue.

2. For the two Pwo communities in northern Thailand treated here, some evidence is provided. Ban Hong, on the Mae Ping, stems from Pwo migrations from Burma initiated about two centuries ago (Hamilton 1965: 30), and Dong Luang, no to the west, is more recent, the oldest Pwo settlement in the vicinity being no more than 120 years old (Hinton 1969: 8f). They may thus be said to stem from approximately the same historical period as the Pwo of the central border. From a linguistic standpoint, the Pwo spoken in the vicinity of Ban Hong seems to be close to the Pwo of the Khwae Nọi headwaters (Cooke, Hudspith, and Morris 1976; Stern 1968C). This does not, of course, preclude the possibility that the northern Pwo may have incorporated individuals and cultural features from among other Karen or, indeed, from non-Karen.

3. It may be posited that it was within the period subsequent to the first Anglo-Burmese War that the Mon term *kareang* passed into Thai. Similarly, it may have been the Karen governorships that were associated with the assumption, by the Siamese monarch, of the title "King of the Karens" (Seidenfaden 1967: 117; and Keyes, this volume).

4. One *rai* equals two-fifths of an acre.

5. Keyes' recent general statement (1971: 553) for the Karen historically in northern Thailand that "What they knew of Buddhism had come from

the Shan, Mon, or Burmese who live in present-day Burma . . . rather than from the Yuan or other Tai-speaking peoples living in present-day Thailand" holds no longer for either of the two northern Pwo communities considered here. James Hamilton (1963: 214) speaks specifically of the Thai Buddhist temple as a focus of religious acculturation, and Peter Hinton (1969: 3) states that Northern Thai Buddhism has had an important effect upon the Karen in his region.

6. In David Richardson's time, Karen villages on the upper Khwae Nọi comprised from three to six long houses, each holding several families, with a separate ladder for each family (Richardson 1839 and 1840: 1032). It is possible that the long house was the residential forerunner of the uxorilocal neighborhood, as Hamilton has suggested (also see Iijima's chapter in this volume).

7. Since my field work in 1965, the town has once more attained full *amphoe* (district) status.

8. The terms *kariang* and *karang* may stem from the same alien designation taken at different times. The former echoes a form in Old Burmese in a single inscription from late Pagan (Luce 1959B: 2). Since it occurs in Mon (Shorto 1962: 70), this language may have been the source for the Burmese. Keyes has remarked (in this volume) that the corresponding form is recent in Thai. The second term reproduces the literal value of the written Burmese form now pronounced *kayin*.

9. At the time of the study, the baht was worth approximately 5 cents in American exchange.

The Karen, Millennialism, and the Politics of Accommodation to Lowland States

Peter Hinton

The upland minorities of Southeast Asia have traditionally resisted the efforts of the large, powerful lowland states to assert hegemony over them. In so doing, the minorities have used at least three strategies: first, alliance with the lowlanders; second, selective accommodation at local levels; third, armed rebellion. A group may have responded in any of these ways at various stages of its history; further, since minority populations are dispersed and political coordination is difficult, various sections of the population may, at any one time, have reacted in different ways.

The Karen, whose territory lies to the east and west of the Thailand-Burma border, face two lowland states; in this chapter, I discuss the strategies thay have adopted to deal with them. Although I am centrally concerned with the Southern Karen peoples (the Pwo and, to a lesser extent, the Sgaw), I also consider it useful to compare their response with that of the Northern Karen (the Kayah). In concluding my analysis, I dissent from the view of Theodore Stern (1968A) that frustrations and exploitation suffered at Burmese hands led the Karen to eschew political action and seek consolation in the realm of millennial fantasy.

82   Peter Hinton

Lowland Relations with the Pwo Karen

I want to begin by analyzing the relations of Pwo Karen in Mae Sariang district (located in Mae Hong Son province of northern Thailand) to the Thai government. As of 1969,[1] these Karen, unlike those in accessible areas, had little contact with government officials and one might expect they would be little concerned with their relationship to the Thai state. In fact the opposite was the case: the Pwo were wary of government intentions and through primitive diplomacy tried to reconcile their interests with those of the Thai.

The economy of the Pwo Karen around Mae Sariang was marginal and based on the subsistence production of swidden rice (see Hinton 1978). Villages were usually loose, and unstable alliances of cognatically related nuclear-family households and rough terrain impeded contact among communities and with lowland settlements. Neither conventional Buddhism nor Christianity had had any decisive influence on the religion of the area.

Government officials rarely visited hill villages; instead, representatives of Pwo Karen communities periodically journeyed to the office of the district officer in Mae Sariang to pay taxes, hear edicts relating to the Karen, and maintain general liaison with the Thai.[2] Government law-enforcement agencies did not operate extensively in the hills, and even cases of homicide were dealt with according to Karen custom. There were few government-run schools or medical institutions readily available to the Pwo Karen.

The Pwo Karen who represented their communities in dealings with the Thai agencies were normally village headmen; their role was quite central in village-state relationships. Who, then, were these headmen, and what was the scope of their authority? Conceivably, power and authority could rest in the hands of the most prosperous individuals. In practice this was not the case. Such men could not acquire dominion over land, for all arable soil was owned communally by villagers, with usufructuary rights being held by constituent households. Nor could they command a disproportionate share of the village's labor resources, for cropping was strictly on a household basis and any additional labor was recruited by reciprocal arrangements or by immediate payment in cash or kind.[3] I did encounter a few Karen who lent rice to others at high interest rates, but such practices were deplored and strong sanctions applied to persistent usurers. Generally, if rice was acquired to augment dwindling household reserves, the transaction was accompanied by immediate cash payment. Further, there was no network of trade or ceremonial exchange that a shrewd person could have exploited to his political and economic advantage.

Wealth was, in any case, entirely relative, and the only feature distinguishing one who was rich by Pwo Karen standards from a man of average means was the ownership of a few more head of livestock, a share in an elephant, or perhaps possession of a small area of irrigable land. In the Karen view, one became rich by being shrewd, industrious, by having several strong unmarried sons to help in the fields—and by being tightfisted. Those less well off generally attributed the wealth of the few to their meanness more than to any other factor, although custom did not dictate that successful farmers should share their crops with hungry relatives. Economic success was not attributed to the blessing of the spirits, even though their cooperation was necessary. All a farmer could do was make routine offerings to the spirits concerned (lavishness of sacrifices counted for little), ensure that the moral behavior of his family could cause no supernatural offense, and then, if crops faltered or beasts fell ill, make immediate and appropriate amends to the spirits.

The only hereditary offices were of ritual, not political, prominence. There were, first of all, the female heads of the Pwo matrilineages, which were usually dispersed over several villages. Their role, however, was limited to the sphere of curative ritual. More important was the role of village ritual head, which was transmitted patrilineally. The task of the ritual head was to mediate between a community and its territorial guardian spirits. Despite the importance of his office, the ritual head had little authority in secular affairs unless he met other criteria for leadership.

In political affairs, the same egalitarianism was evident as in the attitudes to wealth (cf. Marlowe and Kunstadter in this volume). Decisions involving the whole community were usually reached by consensus among all adult male members. Ostensibly all had an equal voice, but it was undoubtedly true that during these deliberations some men were more influential than others. Such influence was due not to age, or wealth, or to the fact that a speaker held the office of ritual head, but simply to the ability of some to speak convincingly, to sway the assembly with the force of their arguments.

Such men were held by the Karen to possess "clever hearts" (*sjae saa*). They were shrewd, articulate, and subtle in debate, able to sway the assembly without dominating it. These talents were widely respected. The men who possessed them were the nuclei around whom villages formed. Their abilities were highly valued not only because they could be exercised to reconcile the factions within a community, but because the men, as village representatives, could deal most effectively with the Thai officials.

It was generally possible to assess the reputation of the village leader at a glance, simply by counting the number of households comprising his community. If he could smooth the troubled waters of intravillage affairs and was shrewd in his dealings with government authorities, his village would be large, perhaps totalling as many as forty-five or fifty households. If he failed on either count, sections of his community would break away and form autonomous villages under more able leadership.[4]

There were two factors that strictly limited the following a village leader could command. First, the swidden economy demanded a large area of land, and the optimum village size was determined by the necessity for all members to have convenient access to their fields. If the village was too big, those with fields in the periphery of its territory had to spend too much time travelling between village and swidden. Second, the Thai government adhered to the principle of one headman per village, unless a number of small settlements were closely grouped. One headman represented six villages, but his position was exceptional. A village leader had no authority to negotiate with government authorities unless he was an officially recognized headman.

The effect of these limitations was to confine political authority to village level. But there was one man who was potentially in a position to lead a great number of Karen. Khae Chae Uae, known by the Thai as Khruba Khao, the White Monk, had won a large following among the Karen of Mae Sariang and surrounding districts. Defrocked as a Buddhist monk some years ago because of his unconventional teachings and methods, he continued to operate independently as an itinerant religious teacher, wearing the white garb from which his name was derived. Although he was evidently of Northern Thai origin, his major following was among the non-Buddhist hill people, particularly the Sgaw and Pwo Karen. He had been a disciple of Khruba Siwicai, a priest greatly revered by the Northern Thai, who during the 1920s helped lead resistance in the traditionally autonomous northern provinces against the assertion of centralized rule from Bangkok (see Keyes 1971: 557–58).

The White Monk spent a good deal of time during 1968–69 in the town of Mae Sariang—being too fragile to travel in the hills—where he was visited by a great many Karen from the surrounding hills. His devotees claimed he had magical powers, including invulnerability to physical harm. Personal charms he distributed were greatly treasured, and his printed scrolls were used in traditional agricultural rituals. The Pwo claimed he was head of all the Karen—Pwo and Sgaw—and discounted the importance of the small following he had among the Lua' and Northern Thai. Pwo informants said he emphasized that relations between the Karen and the Thai government would deteriorate. He urged no radical political action, but his solution—earnestly considered by many—was to lead all the Karen in Thailand back to Burma where he claimed there was ample land, and where he could maintain influence over the spirits that would be beneficial to all.

The system of leadership in the hills was thus partially but significantly related to the priority the Karen placed on stable relations with the lowland authorities. To what extent were Karen interests actually threatened by the Bangkok government? Generally speaking, the Mae Sariang area was peripheral, both geographically and politically, to the Thai nation, so authorities had little reason for intervening in Karen affairs.[5] But there was one area in which Karen and government interests clashed. This was in relation to the forests of the hills: the Karen had to clear the trees for their swiddens, and the Thai wanted to exploit the valuable timber found in some regions. There was a blanket proscription by the government on the cutting of upland timber, but the law was impossible to enforce and no Karen in my study area had been prosecuted. This law did, however, create chronic tension between Karen and state authorities, especially when unscrupulous officials exacted bribes from Karen wanting to avoid punishment.

Thai taxation requirements did not constitute a significant drain on village resources. A small house tax was levied, and licenses had to be acquired for firearms and whiskey stills. Village headmen received a small stipend for their services.

I would suggest that the concern of the Karen about their relations with the Thai body politic was disproportionate to the immediate and foreseeable threat government agents and edicts posed to their interests.[6] Yet their attitude *was* explicable in terms of the long history of oppression the Karen had suffered at Burmese hands.

Far from being peripheral to the area of Burmese interests, the Karen in Burma inhabited country adjoining the rich, Burman-populated plains. Their hills contained some of the richest and most accessible teak forests in the country. Successive regimes tried to maintain a tight monopoly over this timber, and Karen manpower was sought by Burmese monarchs needing slaves, corvée laborers, and soldiers. The history of Burmese-Karen relations seems to have taken a roughly cyclical course: when the Burmese were powerful, the Karen were oppressed; when Burmese power declined, the Karen rebelled. In fact, the eastward migration of Karen into Thailand in the mid-nineteenth century followed one of their more recent abortive revolts and defeat by the armies of the Burmese king Alaungpaya.

As a consequence of their unfortunate history, attitudes of re-sentiment and distrust are embedded in Karen folklore. These sentiments were most vividly reflected in the oft-related stories containing what I call the orphan theme. These stories concerned the dealings of an orphan with a person known as the *kho sang mang,* which roughly translates as prince or government official. Invariably the prince tried to misuse or humiliate the orphan: he might try to steal his wife, send him on a futile errand, or force him to plant his rice in an unsuitable place. Yet the orphan, because he, like the village headman, had a clever heart, was always victorious in the end: he killed the would-be wife stealer, returned from the futile errand as a rich man, or reaped a bumper crop from the stony ground.

The significance of the choice of the orphan as hero appears when one considers the status of orphans in Karen society. The nuclear family was a very important unit: children were reared almost entirely by their own parents; the nuclear-family household was an independent economic unit and was preserved by strong sanctions against divorce and infidelity. A child bereft of his parents faced a dismal prospect. Orphans were not always permanently adopted into another household, but often commuted between the homes of various aunts and cousins, sometimes located in far-flung villages. Such children had no home they could call their own and often manifested signs of insecurity and anxiety.

The Karen explicitly identified themselves as a people with the orphans of folklore. Like the orphans, they were deprived and insecure. As the orphans were forced back onto their resources of ingenuity and guile in a hostile world, so were the Karen as a people.

There are also stories that explain how the Karen people came to be like orphans in the first place. Their origin myth recounts how the Karen and the archetypal members of all other ethnic groups were created as brothers by Buddha. The Pwo Karen was the oldest and the *kho lae* ("European," "Indian") the youngest.[7] For a time, all the brothers lived in what is now Burma, but while there, they all quarrelled except the oldest and the youngest—the Pwo and the European. Sometime later Buddha bade them all pay homage to him, and when they came, he distributed gifts. To the European, he gave the gift of writing. To the Pwo, he gave a box containing gold, silver, and many other valuables, warning him not to open it until he reached his village.

The younger brother was, however, curious, and persuaded the Pwo to open his box. As a consequence, the contents spilled out and immediately turned into a vast expanse of flat land. This became the European's country. The Pwo returned to his village in the hills, empty-handed and destitute.

Other stories relate how the Karen missed out on gifts of wealth and knowledge that were handed out to mankind from time to time by benificent spirits. The Karen were always sitting in the shade, or gossiping by the track, and so received nothing.

Golden epochs, past or future, had little place in their mythology; indeed some, more pessimistic than most, claimed that even the luck of orphans had run out after a boy, the antihero of one story, killed his parents so he would be heir to the guile commonly attributed to orphans. The Karen have an acute sense of human fallibility: the notion of original sin was never far absent from their folklore.

These stories served to remind the Karen of their precarious position vis-à-vis the lowland states, while their leaders tried to smooth over differences with the Thai and the White Monk held hopeful prospects before his followers. My generalizations would also be valid for Karen living closer to the lowlands, whom the Thai government had brought under close administration (cf. Keyes 1969). My suggestion is that if the remote people are suspicious of official intentions, those within the Thai administrative orbit would be very much more wary, owing to more frequent conflict between their own and government interests, especially over the felling of timber in the hills. Under such circumstances, the latent hostility towards lowlanders expressed in the orphan stories would possibly become manifest.

The situation of the Northern Karen, the Kayah, whose territory lies about 150 miles north of Mae Sariang, was very different from that of their ethnic brothers to the south. There are insights to be gained from comparison of the two peoples.

Lowland Relations with the Kayah Karen

The Kayah are closely related to the Pwo and Sgaw in linguistic and other cultural respects (Lehman 1967B). Like most Southern Karen, they live mainly in the hills and have a swidden-based, rice-subsistence economy. Unlike the Pwo and Sgaw, they inhabit country geographically, politically, and economically peripheral to the Burmese state. Yet they do have a close relationship with another valley-dwelling people—the Shan, a Tai-speaking people who inhabit country around the edges of Kayah territory and the narrow valleys that extend into the hills.[8]

It is this close relationship that makes the position of the Kayah vis-à-vis the lowland states so different from that of the Pwo and Sgaw. To understand this, it is necessary to consider briefly the Shan political system.

The Shan, although large in population, and despite their valley habitat and Buddhist religion, were never able to produce a state civilization on the scale reached by the Burmese and Thai. Instead, Shan society was fragmented into a number of small, unstable statelets that were chronically at war with one another. Each was headed by a hereditary prince (*sawbwa*) and combined extensive trade, intermeshed with the Chinese trade network, with rice production. F. K. Lehman attributes the fragmentary nature of the Shan polity to ecological factors: "the traditional multiplicity of Shan principalities is itself largely a result of the dispersion of the Shan among often sharply separated upland valleys" (1967B: 113), circumstances very different from the vast plains of the Cao Phraya and Irrawaddy river systems that formed the bases for the Thai and Burmese states.

Despite these differences in scale, the Shan statelets adopted the ideology and apparatus of statehood directly from the Burmese model. Further, Lehman notes that "however independently powerful they may have been throughout much of Burmese history [the *sawbwa*] always claimed their authority to be in one way or another derivative from the ideally unified Burman royal establishment" (1967B: 18). Although in actuality they were often quite independent of the Burmese monarchy, they called themselves "Sawbwas . . . a title of vassalage, in this case to the Burmese monarchy though not necessarily to an incumbent monarch" (p. 18). Thus the Shan who when united could constitute a sizeable force were not constrained from toppling regimes they found objectionable.[9]

The hill habitat of the Kayah and their swidden economy caused the scattering of their settlements in a fashion similar to the pattern of Pwo and Sgaw villages. On the whole, villages were politically independent of one another; yet from time to time, forceful leaders were able to link a large number of communities in a usually reluctant and ephemeral confederation. The Kayah chiefs modelled *their* quasi-state systems on the Shan pattern, but, being pagans, "did not adopt the Buddhist ritual and cosmological model as the basis for their 'royal' political and social constitution" (Lehman 1967B: 20). They claimed to possess superhuman powers, but these were based on a syncretic mixture of Kayah religion and Buddhism. The administrative apparatus of these quasi-states was rudimentary, and the only tribute paid by villages was symbolic (Lehman, p. 22). The Kayah chief had only one sanction, the use of armed force, to keep dissident villages in his fold: "Briefly, the Kayah Sawbwas protected some Kayah villages, raided others, presided over Kayah and non-Kayah alike with an organisation whose main object seems to have been to manage their trade with the Shan or the Shan states proper" (p. 24).

The management of trade was a prime motive for a Kayah chief's ambitions, and an economic base for the existence of the Kayah statelets. The Kayah themselves do not appear to have engaged in trade to any great extent but were able to exploit the vulnerable Shan trade routes that traversed the hills. They were thus able to exact a toll on passing caravans or on timber extracted by Shan from the forests they controlled.[10] Since the Shan states were small and relatively unstable compared with the Burmese civilization, the hill people were from time to time able to exert decisive political and economic pressure on the Shan by harassing traders and raiding lowland towns from their hill sanctuaries.

The Pwo and Kayah Compared

It is now possible to attempt some systematic comparisons of the Kayah and the Pwo-Sgaw positions vis-à-vis the lowland states.

1. The Southern Karen, both Pwo and Sgaw, inhabited country the Burmese had definite political and economic reasons for wanting to control. The territory of the Kayah, on the other hand, was marginal to Burmese interests.[11] The Pwo and Sgaw in Thailand retained many of the attitudes that were appropriate to the position of their compatriots in Burma, even though the Thai, unlike the Burmese, had few motives for intervening in their affairs.

2. The Pwo and Sgaw were in direct confrontation with the Burmese, while the Shan were juxtaposed between the Kayah and the plains civilization. The Shan, although oriented towards the Burmese polity, were potentially, and sometimes actually, powerful enough to resist Burmese control.

3. The Kayah were able to influence Shan politics because their strategic position permitted them to apply economic sanctions that could dislocate the small-scale Shan polities. The Southern Karen, on the other hand, could not control the supply of any commodity of decisive importance to the Burmese or Thai states. They could, thus, exert little economic leverage to political ends.

4. Similarly, although the Kayah quasi-states were of small scale, their leaders needed wealth beyond the productive capacity of their subsistence economy to maintain supralocal power. These additional resources were obtained through their control of trade routes and timber supplies. Because Burmese intervention was thoroughgoing, but also because no important trade routes appear to have crossed their country, the Southern Karen were denied these additional sources of income. There was thus no economic basis for Sgaw and Pwo leaders to extend their domain.

5. The Shan, by adapting the Burmese model of monarchy for their own small-scale purposes, unintentionally placed before the Kayah an ideology of statehood that could be further adapted to the even smaller scale hill context. The Pwo and Sgaw, on the other hand, knew only the model of the large plains monarchy.

Several writers (e.g., Kunstadter 1969A; Marlowe 1969) have drawn attention to the symbiosis between Thai lowlanders and upland Sgaw Karen in the north of Thailand. It is necessary to emphasize, however, that this symbiosis was local—usually taking the form of trade partnerships between individuals in hill and valley villages—and of limited cultural and economic consequence. Unlike the context of Shan-Kayah interaction, it was of no great *political* consequence in regulating relationships between uplanders and lowlanders.

The Role of Millennial Movements

Theodore Stern (1968A) has written a fascinating account of two millennial movements—known as the Ywa and Telakhon cults—that occurred among Karen about 300 miles south of Mae Sariang. His material is relevant to the present essay, but his interpretations are very different from my own. Thus, while relating the Ywa and Telakhon movements to the foregoing discussion, I highlight my conclusions by emphasizing my divergences from Stern's analysis.

The Ywa movement, which flourished throughout the nineteenth century, had its origins in a myth of creation similar to the one I have outlined above. According to this myth, Ywa (in Mae Sariang, Yuae), the creating deity of Pwo mythology, made the Karen and all other ethnic groups as brothers, the youngest being a white man, who, shortly after the act of creation, went travelling away, taking with him a golden book containing all the secrets of literacy, wealth, and power, which were thus denied to the Karen, who consequently remained poor and politically impotent. The myth contained the prophecy that the white brother would one day return with the golden book, revealing its contents to the Karen who would then become wealthy and powerful (Stern 1968A: 303).[12]

The arrival of American Baptist missionaries in the early nineteenth century seemed, to many Karen, to be a fulfillment of this prophecy, for the foreigners were white and brought a book they claimed to be the key to enlightenment. The missionaries won a great many converts, primarily among the Sgaw, but at the same time some Karen leaders claimed they alone would be able to interpret the contents of the book and lead the Karen in the overthrow of Burmese hegemony. Large numbers of Karen united behind these prophets in abortive rebellion against the Burmese (Stern, p. 305).

The Telakhon sect was a successor to the Ywa movement, and, Stern notes, has adherents to the present day, mostly in more isolated regions. Its leaders still promised the overthrow of Burmese authority in the hills, but despite similar references to the Karen origin myth, saw Christianity as a rival to the millennial faith.

In his interpretation of the cults, Stern draws heavily on the relative deprivation hypothesis developed by David Aberle. Relative deprivation occurs when "a negative discrepancy occurs between legitimate expectation and actuality" (Aberle 1962: 209). When a group's efforts to correct such a "negative discrepancy" by conventional means are consistently frustrated, his argument runs, the people will compensate by recourse to supernaturalism. Under such circumstances, millennial prophecies predicting a sudden and dramatic upheaval of the world order to the advantage of the "relatively deprived" achieve large followings. Stern asserts that the Ywa and Telakhon movements "gave unambiguous voice to political aspirations. The day of the Mon kings, of the Burman kings, and of the Siamese kings are past . . . and the day of the Karen king is yet to come, when the Karen will dwell within the great town, the high city, the golden palace" (Stern 1968A: 304). The movements were motivated by "both the envy toward the superior civilizations of their neighbors—a factor in that relative deprivation of which Aberle speaks—and the bitterness of their lot when those neighbors became oppressors combined to drive them to seek redress in religion" (Stern, p. 299).

The appropriateness of this explanatory framework can be seriously questioned on theoretical grounds. Mary Douglas, for example, has pointed out that the argument rests on untested psychological assumptions about the way people react when they are deprived and oppressed (1970: xvii). Further, in practice, the relative deprivation hypothesis has proved of little predictive value: on the one hand, not all groups that are relatively deprived seek religious compensation, and, on the other, some groups that are *well off* in relation to other reference groups are galvanized by millennial ardor.

In any case, were the cults Stern describes really so novel? Both occurred after contact with Europeans. There is no reason to suppose there were not similar movements before the visitations of Baptist missionaries. Whether or not there were, I suggest the cults were not prompted by frustration and they were not a symptom of withdrawal; on the contrary—and this is crucial—they were attempts to unite many, if not all, Karen behind a common banner against an external threat.

There was, on the one hand, the fact that Karen villages were isolated, scattered, and self-contained; on the other hand, there was the reality of Burmese power, directed against the Karen. Villages may not have been able to resist the Burmese forces, but the Karen as a bloc may have been able to resist. The cult leaders realized this, however imperfectly—for their perceptions of the extent of Karen population and territory were limited—and understood that the hiatus had to be overcome if resistance was to be at all effective. Consequently, their appeal was to the Karen people *as a whole*.

In this respect, the White Monk fit into the same mold as the Ywa and Telakhon leaders, even though he made no millennial predictions. Similarly, the Kayah chieftains claimed magical powers and sometimes messianic qualities; yet their intentions were to achieve immediate and short-term political advantages and economic goals through an amalgam of pure charisma and naked coercion. They were confronted by no outside intruder of great power; consequently their political energies were spent in internecine struggles for power and wealth.

Significantly, the Southern Karen leaders did not use coercion to win or maintain their followings. The one model for authority transcending village and locality that was available to the Pwo and Sgaw was that of charismatic Buddhist monarchy—the ideology of power in the lowland states. This Stern clearly recognizes: "For the Karen a major source of their millenarianism can be found in the Buddhist kingdoms which surrounded them, each organised to provide a magical counterpart of the cosmic order. In such a kingdom the ruler is cosmocrator, linking his realm and the world order as a ritualist, drawing waters down to fructify the earth, presiding as the earthly analogue of Indra in the city of the gods" (1968A: 300). This notion is so prevalent in Southeast Asia that it would have been worthy of note if the Karen leaders had *not* tried to adapt it for their purposes. The fact that they did was scarcely exceptional and the embroidery of Christian elements in the postmissionary era incidental.

My interpretation, that the Karen prophets were groping towards pan-Karen solidarity, gains credence from consideration of the activities of the Karen National Defense Organisation (KNDO), which has been operating in Burma since the conclusion of World War II. Its objective is to achieve an independent Karen state, carved out of Burmese territory, and its leadership consists of a sophisticated British-trained military and civilian elite.[13] Although it has yet to achieve its primary aims, the KNDO has at least been able to deny the Burmese government access to the Karen-inhabited hills west of the Thai frontier. The KNDO represents an effort to harness pan-Karen sentiment in the support of a modern political movement. Just as the old-style Buddhist monarch's day has passed, so has the time of the charismatic prophet among the Karen. This is not to say that such leaders do not still arise in primitive areas—the Telakhon movement and the White Monk's large following indicate that they do. But the initiative in Karen affairs has passed to modern political organizers. Both types of leaders are similar in one important respect: both seek Karen unity against outside threat.

Notes

1. My field work was carried out during 1968–69 under the auspices of the Tribal Research Centre, Chiang Mai, Thailand.

2. Each district officer (*nai amphoe*) was directly responsible to a provincial governor (*phuwarachakhan cangwat*). Most districts were divided into subdistricts (*tambon*), each headed by a *kamnan* who was a local peasant, not a civil servant. Mae Sariang district, even though it was one of the largest districts in Thailand, had not been divided into *tambon*, because of its remoteness and the fact that government administrative structures had not been fully developed there.

Officials attached to specialist agencies of the government—educational, police, medical, and agricultural—were also located in Mae Sariang.

The Karen had little understanding of the workings of the Thai bureaucracy above district level. They were surprised when I told them the district officer was not directly appointed by the king and when I explained there was an elaborate hierarchy of authority.

3. There were few occasions that involved coordinated effort by all households; in fact, collaboration was only necessary during the annual burning of the swiddens, when fires had to be carefully controlled.

4. With the proviso that the breakaway section included a man patrilineally related to the ritual head of the parent village; this would permit the performance of rites to the territorial guardian spirit of the new village.

5. The picture was different in some other parts of the northern hills; adjacent to the Laotian frontier, government forces were in conflict with Communist-affiliated Meo. Similarly, antinarcotics agencies were active in opium-producing areas. But the Karen neither grew opium nor were in any way involved in the Indo-Chinese War.

6. This situation may have been different in regions where the law against cutting forest was more strictly enforced.

7. The Pwo term *kho lae* is a grab-bag category that includes Europeans, Indians, and any person with a dark skin; in fact it means any non-Oriental foreigner from a far-off land.

8. All ethnographic material on the Kayah and Shan is drawn from F. K. Lehman's accounts (1967A, 1967B).

9. The Shan have in fact brought about the fall of several monarchs through the use of force, particularly during the rule of the kings of Ava (Saimong Mangrai 1965: 49).

10. E. R. Leach (1954: 21) mentions similar exploitation by Kachin and

other peoples in Burma. It is also interesting to note that in northern Thailand, remnants of Chiang Kai-shek's armies for some years exercised power disproportionate to their numbers by both engaging in opium trading and levying a toll on independent merchants whose caravans had to pass through the hills.

11. The Burmese and subsequently the British regarded Kayah territory as a neutral buffer zone between themselves and rival powers to the east (see Saimong Mangrai 1965).

12. This myth is similar in essence to some I recorded in Mae Sariang district.

13. The Karen were actually granted a partially autonomous territory in Burma under the 1948 constitution. It did not, however, include lands in the Salween district that would have made it a viable economic entity. The Karen leaders were bitterly disappointed with the arrangement that was made, feeling that the British government had let them down after they had made a notable contribution to the defeat of the Japanese during World War II (Tinker 1957: 23–25). Moreover, the 1948 constitution itself was abrogated after Ne Win took power in the military coup of 1962.

Sgaw Karen man using elephant to move teak logs near Mae Sariang, northern Thailand

Sgaw Karen from hill village at shop in lowland Thai village near Mae Sariang

ABOVE: *Sgaw women and children in lowland village near Mae Sariang.* FACING PAGE, top: *Sgaw Karen participating in a ritual dedication of a Buddhist* cetiya *in a lowland village near Mae Sariang.* FACING PAGE, BOTTOM: *Pwo Karen from a hill village who have come to a Buddhist temple in Mae Sariang to beg on a Buddhist feast day.*

Pwo Karen men from hill village near Mae Sariang

Ethnic Identity and Sociocultural Change Among Sgaw Karen in Northern Thailand

Shigeru Iijima

Sociocultural Change in Hill and Plains Karen Villages

This essay concerns the persistence and change of ethnic identity among Sgaw Karen peoples living in Mae Sariang district, Mae Họng Sọn province, in northern Thailand. The field work on which this study is based involved research in two Sgaw Karen villages in Mae Sariang district. Initial research was in the upland village of Mae Ha Ki, located on the western fringes of the Bọ Luang Plateau. Mae Ha Ki is about two kilometers from Mae Họ, a small marketplace on the Họt-Mae Sariang Road, and approximately twenty kilometers from the township of Mae Sariang, the main local administrative and commercial center in the area.

For comparative purposes, research was also undertaken in the lowland-plains Sgaw Karen village of Phamalọ. This village is located on the outskirts of Mae Sariang township on the western bank of the Yuam River. Through work in both an upland and a lowland village, it was possible to obtain a picture of different stages of social and cultural change among the Sgaw Karen of Mae Sariang district. It is only within the context of the changing sociocultural situation that Karen identity can be adequately understood.

DISORGANIZATION OF THE LONG HOUSE AMONG THE HILL KAREN

The history of the hill village of Mae Ha Ki is obscure, but it appears likely that it was settled as part of an expansion of the Karen population in what is now Mae Sariang district in the middle of the nineteenth century. Although Karen may have begun migrating into northwestern Thailand about 200 years ago,[1] in the area of Mae Sariang district in which Mae Ha Ki is located, Karen settlement would appear to have occurred about 120 years ago. During this period, Karen, including both Sgaw and Pwo, began settling in areas vacated by the original hill population of the area, the Lua'.

> About 120 years ago Skaw Karens, coming from the west, began moving into the territory once held exclusively by the Luaʔ. At first they settled only on mountain tops, in the areas which the Luaʔ had abandoned when they were consolidating their villages [Kunstadter 1967: 641].

Peter Hinton, who has studied Pwo Karen in the same area, thinks "the oldest village in the study area is Mae Cang established about 120 years ago" (Hinton 1969: 9). Although Mae Ha Ki may not be among the oldest villages in the area, it does seem likely it has existed in the vicinity of its present site for at least a little over a century.

From its beginnings, Mae Ha Ki has consisted of a community of people whose primary occupation is slash-and-burn or swidden cultivation. In the early years of its history, it appears that the village consisted of a single long house. According to old R, who is the *sapga* or religious leader of the village, when he was a boy (about seventy or eighty years ago) "many villagers got together and ate food at the meeting place [*blǫ*] of our long house [*hi*]. At that time I was about ten years old. Therefore everything of that time is in memory as if it were a dream."

The existence of long houses in Karen villages in this area in the past is confirmed by the report of J. P. Anderson who travelled across the Bǫ Luang Plateau in the early 1920s.

> The [Karen] villages are mostly built high up on the mountain sides, and the houses are built entirely of bamboo, with roofs of leaves. As a rule each family has its own house, generally containing only one room. . . . I have, however, seen two villages where the houses were long buildings, each divided into several rooms, and inhabited by several families, all related to each other. The floor is raised about 4 or 5 feet from the ground, and the space under it is the residence of pigs and fowls. There are no

gardens, and seldom any fence in a Karen village, the houses being just scattered about in a clearing on fairly open hill side [Anderson 1923: 54–55].

Further evidence of Karen long-house villages has been given by Harry I. Marshall for the Pegu Hills area of Burma:

> In the Pegu Hills we find the single-structure village, which seems to have been the characteristic Karen dwelling from early times. It might be described as a bamboo apartment-house on stilts, accommodating on the average from twenty to thirty families. It is spread out on one floor, and each family occupies not one "flat" but a room, called in Karen "deu," which faces a central corridor running the length of the barrack [1922: 56].
>
> At best the Karen village-house is habitable only for a year or two, was built by the combined efforts of the men of the little community from material of which the supply is abundant, and can be replaced quickly. When, therefore, disease begins to spread among the adjacent families, they scatter to the four winds with their most necessary belongings. Soon they gather and build another village on a new site and, having removed the last of their possessions from the old infected structure, leave it to decay or set it on fire [1922: 63].
>
> Such a village, a "th'waw,"[2] is usually rebuilt on a new site each year. The new location is sought by the local chief during the hot season, after conference with the elders and after the crops have been brought in. The place selected by the chief is fairly level, adjacent to the area to be cut over the coming year, and near a spring or stream that will not dry up during the hot weather. In the old days it was also necessary to choose a site that would be high and easily defended against raids. Before the decision is finally made, the chief must consult the auspices in the form of chicken bones, and if these are propitious and no laughing-bird (Lanius) calls "chet chet," the men begin to cut bamboo with which to construct the village [1922: 56].

Finally, regarding the Karen long house, Marshall concludes:

> I do not say "home," for the Karen language has no word for home. The house is, however, something more than the eating and sleeping place of the village families; it is the center of their domestic life and worship and as such possesses a certain amount of sanctity [1922: 64].

Whether or not Marshall is correct about the long-house community being the original form of Karen settlement, the fact is that it was probably the characteristic community of only a small percentage of even the earliest settlements in the Mae Sariang area. In the 1880s, Holt Hallet, an Englishman who visited Mae Sariang, reported that the "wild" or "timid" Karen, that is, the upland-dwelling, swidden-cultivating Karen, lived in villages with separate houses in which the average number of inhabitants was about seven (Hallet 1890: 37). It is possible that the defense function Marshall noted the long house provided may explain the existence of long-house villages such as Mae Ha Ki on the Bọ Luang Plateau. At the time when the Karen were first moving into this area, the district was very unsettled and subject to periodic raids by roving bands of Kayah, also known as Karenni (cf. Hallet 1890: 30–31; Keyes 1969, 1970).

Whether they were long-house villages or villages with separate houses, the original upland Sgaw Karen hill villages in the Mae Sariang area were, because of the adaptation of the villagers to long-fallow swiddening, not permanent settlements. Marshall's observation that the long-house village is "habitable only for a year or two" (Marshall 1922: 63) is matched by Hallet's observation that the upland villages with separate homesteads "are temporary erections, only occupied for a year or two at a time" (Hallet 1890: 37).

Given the present-day emphasis of villagers on cognatic kin ties, it seems probable that the long-house community of Mae Ha Ki consisted of a core of cognatic kinsmen who were descendants of a common ancestor plus another group that had been recruited through marriage. It is likely, again on the basis of present-day population figures, that the Karen long-house community accommodated a considerably smaller population than is to be found in the long houses of such other Southeast Asian peoples as the Iban of Borneo (Freeman 1964: 8–10).

The chief of the early village of Mae Ha Ki, like the chief of the Karen long-house villages discussed by Marshall, had both secular and religious functions. His role was defined entirely in terms of Karen custom, since the administration of the court of Chiang Mai, to say nothing of the administration stemming from Bangkok, had not penetrated into the hill areas in which Mae Ha Ki was located.[3] The extent of the authority of such a chief appears to have depended less on the institutional features of his role than on his personal influence. Such is evident in the case of the most famous of the customary socioreligious leaders of Mae Ha Ki—Pomohe. Pomohe, who was grandfather to R, the present *sapga* and a former village headman, and the great-grandfather of the present village headman, exercised influence not only in the Mae Ha Ki long house but also over several others in the vicinity through his performance of traditional rituals.

On his death, however, this supravillage unity collapsed. According to his eldest grandson, "Everyone of this village has become childish since the death of Pomohe." In larger perspective, the fact that the village alliance wrought by Pomohe collapsed after his death may reflect the inherent instability of authoritarian political structures among the tribal peoples of northern mainland Southeast Asia (cf. Marshall 1945: 29; and, especially, Leach 1954).

At what time Mae Ha Ki was transformed from a long-house community, which shifted location every few years or so, to a settled community comprising separate homesteads is not clear. This transformation appears to have happened about a half-century ago and about the same time the long-house communities Marshall had found in Burma also disappeared (cf. Lewis 1924: 40–41). The reasons for the transformation of Mae Ha Ki, however, are more clear. From about the beginning of the twentieth century, the Thai government began to exert its control over the Mae Sariang area (cf. Keyes 1969). As a consequence, the area became more peaceful and secure. Of greater importance, perhaps, has been the demographic change in the hills that has resulted in a contraction of land available for long-fallow swiddening (cf. Kunstadter 1971). The people in Mae Ha Ki have had to shorten their swidden cycles, using the same land more often. Moreover, they also began to cultivate wet rice on permanent fields.

At present, no Karen long-house villages can be found in this area. Even in the deep forests of the western borderland of Mae Sariang district where Karen villages, such as Mae Saku, Mae Kongka, Mae Te, and Mae Ge, still follow the older long-fallow patterns, long-house villages do not appear to exist. A vestige of the long-house community may exist in the northeastern part of Mae Họng Sọn province, near Mụang Pai, where Keiji Iwata found villages in the late 1950s in which each household "had a larger than usual structure and more members than the typical nuclear family which is to be found inhabiting the households of most upland Karen villages today."[4] Such exceptions notwithstanding, the older type of upland community, whether with a long house or separate homesteads, which was adapted exclusively to long-fallow swidden agriculture, has rapidly ceased to exist in the Mae Sariang area.

INTRODUCTION OF WET-RICE CULTIVATION AND ITS EFFECTS

According to the villagers' own statements, swidden farming in the hill village of Mae Ha Ki has been in decay for several decades. The main reason seems to be the overexploitation of their fields because of increasing population in the whole hill area. Without new fields that could be brought under swidden cultivation, the fallow period on the fields belonging to the villagers of Mae Ha Ki has been reduced by several years from the former cycle of ten or more years. A reduced fallow cycle leads to poorer yields for the increasing population. In addition to reduced fallowing, soil sickness[5] is another probable cause of decreasing fertility.

Because the agriculture of Mae Ha Ki was decaying, a villager named Siki went (fifty or sixty years ago) to the plains in the valley of Mae Sariang and learned how to cultivate wet rice from the Yuan or Northern Thai and the Lua' living there. He brought this knowledge back to Mae Ha Ki and attempted, with the aid of other villagers, to introduce wet-rice cultivation into the village. In the beginning, the villagers worked mainly by trial and error. Although they did build foot paths between wet-rice fields, in contrast to the practice in swiddening, they did not appreciate the need for proper water control. The water thus leaked through the unstamped beds of the fields. Given such experience, the hill Karen became aware that their knowledge of the wet-rice technology was insufficient; again they sent some of the villagers to the plains to relearn how to prepare a wet-rice field before starting cultivation. With their lessons better learned, some villagers have now become wet-rice as well as swidden cultivators. Still only six out of the twenty-five households of the village are engaged in wet-rice cultivation. That more villagers have not adopted wet-rice cultivation is, in part, a result of their passive and indifferent attitude to the "new" technology and to their perception that there is a shortage of land that could be brought under wet-rice cultivation.*

Although the introduction of wet-rice cultivation in Mae Ha Ki is still limited, its effects have been far-reaching. First, wet-rice cultivation has permitted an increased degree of stability in village agriculture. Rather than depend upon a land-use pattern that requires fields to lie fallow for a number of years, the villagers now generate part of their rice supply by cultivating the same fields year after year. Together with the reduced fallow cycle for swiddening, the cultivation of wet rice has had as a concomitant the disappearance of the seminomadic way of life in the village. The village is now a permanent settlement.

Second, villagers are now aware of an alternative mode of adaptation in striking contrast to the mode they knew formerly. Unlike swidden agriculture (particularly on the shortened fallow cycle), wet-

---

Editor's Note: The perception by swidden cultivators that land suitable for wet-rice cultivation is in short supply is perhaps illusory as the case of Java illustrates (cf. Geertz 1966A; also cf. Boserup 1965). However, the work involved in transforming swiddens into terraced wet-rice fields is considerable.

rice cultivation does not always require the use of manure or fertilizers to maintain the standard of the yield. Rather, the irrigation water itself brings important chemical elements for plant nutrition, such as potassium, calcium, and magnesium. In addition, inundation promotes the supply of nitrogen to wet rice through accelerating the nitrogen fixation and the decomposition of organic matter in the soil of the wet field. Moreover, the sequence of inundation and desiccation of the fields enhances the effectiveness of phosphorus.[6] Irrigation water also eliminates soil sickness.

The introduction of wet-rice cultivation has also involved the introduction of animal husbandry on a larger scale than previously known, since water buffaloes are used in the new agriculture. In swidden cultivation, the digging stick used by men is the main tool for preparing the fields. In wet-rice cultivation, however, water buffaloes pull the plows and harrows and are deemed to be indispensable.

Associated with the new mode of adaptation has been a change in land-tenure patterns that are coming to be applied to swidden as well as wet-rice fields. Under wet-rice cultivation, some hill Karen found it necessary to employ labor-intensive techniques to bring the fields under cultivation for the first time. Eventually, a land-ownership system began to emerge under which wet-rice fields have come under private ownership. A concomitant shift in tenure has also begun in the swidden fields as well. The significance of the shift in tenure patterns can be conveyed by the counterposing of the following attitudes expressed by a father and his son. P, one of the oldest villagers and a former village headman, observed that "All the villagers are entitled to till the surrounding hills. It is not always necessary for the children to cultivate the same swidden fields as their parents." In contrast to this traditional conception, K, P's son and the present headman, cultivates the swidden fields of old P and treats these fields as though they were his "own." I questioned K about this and the middle-aged man replied that "The swidden field, like the wet field, has been inherited from my father. Thus, it will be given to my son and daughter when I get old."

As this shift in attitude between generations suggests, a tendency towards individualization among Mae Ha Ki villagers has begun that even affects the families of swidden cultivators. The basic social and cultural order obtaining among the hill Karen has begun to be reorganized as a consequence of the introduction of wet-rice cultivation.

SOCIAL AND CULTURAL CHANGE IN A PLAINS KAREN VILLAGE

Phamalo̜, the plains Karen village studied, was established by Pablo̜, a Karen from the hill village of Mae To̜p, about three generations ago. When he came to the Mae Sariang area from the northern village, small bamboo houses belonging to peoples of several ethnic groups were already scattered over the western bank of the Yuam River near the present town of Mae Sariang. Pablǫ was joined by other Karen from villages such as Mae Et Ki and Hue Pu, and together they formed a small hamlet.

In its initial stages, these "plains" Karen engaged in swidden agriculture because there was ample land available to them. In the meantime, two Indian Muslim merchants called Sutek and Alimot started to open some wet-rice fields in the vicinity of present-day Phamalǫ with the help of Northern Thai laborers. Shortly afterwards, the Karen settlers bought the as yet unfinished wet-rice fields from the Indian merchants and began cultivating them according to methods they learned from the Northern Thai, Shan, and Lua' living in the area.

The Phamalǫ Karen, having become familiar with wet-rice culture in this way, not only gradually developed the typical plains methods of producing wet rice but also adopted associated agricultural rituals. In contrast, the hill Karen villagers of Mae Ha Ki, like the villagers in other hill Karen villages, have not adopted the ritual activities associated with plains wet-rice cultivation.

As the villagers of Phamalǫ shifted from swidden to wet-rice cultivation, the elaborate cooperative work involving the whole community, which is peculiar to swidden agriculture, began to disappear. Moreover, the kinship and territorial basis of upland Karen social structure was undermined by the adaptation of the Phamalǫ villagers to the plains social environment. This trend has been accelerated as a consequence of intermarriage of plains Karen with non-Karen. Insofar as I can trace the pedigree of Phamalǫ, it includes Northern Thai, Central Thai, Lua', Khamu, Burmese, and Cambodian elements.

This absorption of "foreign elements," which is characteristic of the plains Karen village, is not common among the hill Karen. In fact, I could not find a single interethnic marriage in the genealogies of Mae Ha Ki villagers. Moreover, recruitment of outsiders into the plains Karen villages is not, in theory at least, limited to affinal contracts. Even I was strongly encouraged "to be a Karen" by many villagers of Phamalǫ while conducting field work there. When I asked how "to become a Karen," the villagers replied simply that I should participate in *talutaphadu*, the great village rite every year, by sacrificing a pig for *hti k'cha kǫ k'cha*, the Lord of Water and Land. Technically, to be a Karen, it is still indispensable for one to have a *bgha* or ancestral spirit. To acquire a *bgha*, it is essential that at least one parent be Karen since one inherits a *bgha* from one's parents.

However, it is noteworthy that outsiders are not considered automatically excluded from "becoming Karen" in the plains village.

This openness of the plains village contrasts markedly with the closed character of the hill village. But although the trend towards individualization has begun in plains Karen villages, one's identity is still determined primarily by descent from village members.

The plains Karen are but one people, and a significant minority people at that, among the various peoples who inhabit the plains. In contrast, the hill Karen comprise the overwhelming majority of the population of the upland areas surrounding Mae Sariang. Given these facts and the associated "openness" and "closedness" of the plains and upland villagers, respectively, the character of Karen identity in the two villages is quite different.

The Religious Basis of Ethnic Identity

In the process of social and cultural change of the Karen, religion has played an important role in preserving the sense of ethnic identity. In Karen animism, although there are many other spirits and deities, the part taken by *bgha* or the ancestor spirit is especially important. Therefore we must begin our discussion of the relationship between Karen religion and Karen ethnic identity with a description and analysis of the belief in the *bgha* and the associated *oxe* rite.

BELIEF IN BGHA AND ASSOCIATED OXE RITES

Karen ethnic identity has not disappeared despite the rapidity of sociocultural change the Karen have experienced. Peter Kunstadter has observed that in comparison with the Lua', the Karen stick to their identity much more, no matter whether they live in hill or valley villages (Kunstadter 1969B: 3). I believe the essence of Karen self-identity derives mainly from the Karen belief in *bgha* and in their practice of the associated *oxe* rites.[7] Since I have described and analyzed the belief in the *bgha* and *oxe* rites elsewhere (Iijima 1967, 1971), I will discuss here only those characteristics that function to maintain Karen identity.

The *bgha* are ancestral spirits of kin groups called *dopuweh;* these groups perform the *oxe* rites propitiating the *bgha*. As can be seen from the figure on page 108, the *dopuweh* is matrilineally based. At marriage, a man remains in the *dopuweh* in which he was born. However, once his own wife becomes the head of a *dopuweh* on the death of her mother, he ceases to belong to the *dopuweh* in

A Dopuweh, *a Ritual Group of the* Oxe *Rite*
(An arrow shows a man leaving or entering the group. Dashed lines indicate the group's extension or contraction as this movement occurs.)

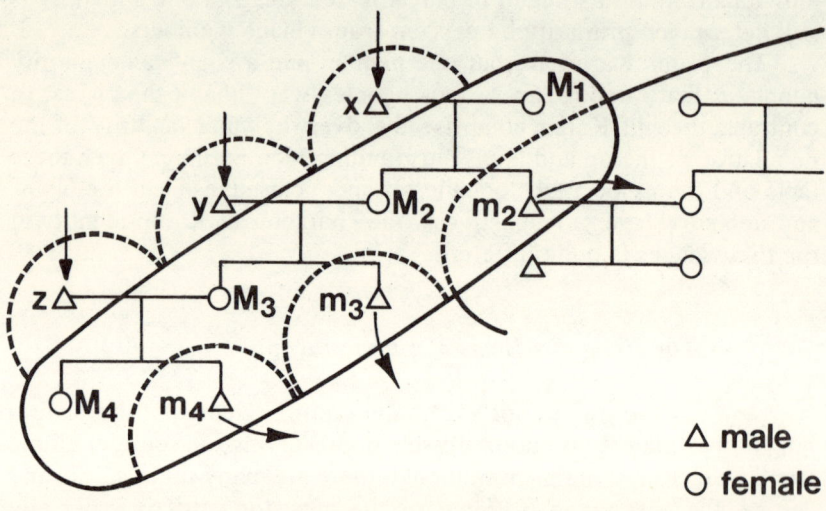

△ male
○ female

which he was born and becomes a member of the *dopuweh* his wife now heads.

The *oxe* is performed for the *bgha,* an ancestral spirit who is believed to be the most closely related to the eldest living female in the group. When this woman dies, the *dopuweh* fissions, with new *dopuweh* forming around women of the next generation. Although most *dopuweh* consist of the co-residents of single households, this is not always the case. So long as the woman of the senior generation remains alive, her descendants, no matter what households they live in and even if they have moved away from the village, remain members of the same *dopuweh*.

The *bgha* presides over all activities of the members of a *dopuweh*. Individual members of the *dopuweh* may propitiate the spirit through the sacrifice of a pig and/or some chickens to obtain a favor. If some member of the *dopuweh* commits an act that angers the *bgha,* all members must perform the *oxe* rite since all stand in danger of suffering misfortune or sickness in retribution for the offensive act. Even if no members of the *dopuweh* suffer misfortune or sickness, the *dopuweh* will perform the *oxe* rite at least once a year.

Oxe, which means, literally, "feeding the *xe* (*bgha*)," is practiced among both hill and plains Sgaw Karen and among Pwo Karen as well. Roughly speaking, there are two ways of performing the *oxe* rite among the Sgaw: the *oxe chuko* (*oxe* rite à la Sgaw) and *oxe pgo* (*oxe* rite à la Pwo).

When the date of an *oxe* rite, whether *oxe chuko* or *oxe pgo*, is decided upon by divining from chicken bones, messages are sent to all members of the *dopuweh*. All members of the *dopuweh* are required to participate in the *oxe chuko* offering regardless of the circumstances. Marshall has explained why:

> Unless all the members of the family are present at such a ceremony, except those excluded from the feast, the offerings are thought to be objectionable to the "Bgha." If a person absents himself from a feast that is being held to promote the recovery of a sick relative, he is suspected of desiring the continued illness or the death of the sick one. Or his absence may be interpreted as an effort to bring calamity upon some member of the family. Such charges are made against the member of a family who becomes a Christian and remains away from the ceremony. The others allege that he no longer retains his affection for his kindred and is willing to bring illness and disaster upon them by his absence, which angers the "Bgha" [Marshall 1922: 257].

For those who follow the *oxe chuko* rite, it is difficult to move far away to such a distant place as Chiang Mai, Mae Hong Son, or Chiang Rai to take a job. The rite of *oxe pgo*, however, is more flexible than that of *oxe chuko*. Although all those who follow *oxe pgo* are expected and urged to attend the rite, it is not impossible to perform the *oxe pgo* rite with a *dopuweh* that lacks some of its members. In such cases, some curried rice with some chicken and/or pork from the sacrifice are dried in the sun and given to the absent member when he or she next returns to the house.

All of the participants are expected to arrive the night before the performance of the rite and to spend the night in the house where the rite will be performed. The participants are also required to put on Karen dress lest they be "eaten by the *bgha*" (*bgha o*) and become mad. Full Karen dress is strictly observed by the members of *oxe chuko* groups, while an abbreviated costume, such as a Karen "longie" (a sarong or tubular cloth for the lower part of the body), is permissible for the male members of the *oxe pgo* groups. Members of the *oxe pgo* groups believe that males have less close relations with the *bgha* than do females.

On the morning of the ritual, all the members of the *dopuweh* assemble in the living room of the house. Thereafter no other language but Karen is permitted. The ritual leader recites some prayers, and a pig and/or a few chickens are sacrificed to the *bgha*. This leader, *xeko*, is always the eldest female of the *dopuweh* in *oxe chuko* rites. However, although it is desirable for the members of the *oxe pgo* groups to elect a female leader, the eldest male in a *dopuweh* is also permitted to perform this function if his wife has died and he either has very young unmarried daughters or no daughters. After the ritual leader has made the sacrifice, a rice porridge is prepared to which meat of the sacrificial animal is added. This food is presented to the *bgha* and the participants then "dine with" the spirit.

The *oxe pgo* rite differs from the *oxe chuko* in the manner of sacrificing a pig. Although in an orthodox *oxe chuko* rite, the pig must be sacrificed in the room of the house in which the offering is made, in *oxe pgo* rites the pig can be killed outside the house. It is probable that this difference between the two rites has been important in the process of sociocultural change among the Sgaw Karen. Some of the villagers of Phamalọ told me they were unable to become true Buddhists so long as they continued to sacrifice four-legged creatures such as pigs in their houses. The blood from such sacrificed animals contaminates the house, and no image of the Buddha can be placed on the *dapo* or altar shelf[8] in a contaminated house. Thus, the Lord Buddha could not be worshipped in the authentic way of plains-dwelling Tai.

As can be seen from the accompanying table, there would seem to be little difference in religious affiliation between the hill village of Mae Ha Ki and the lowland village of Phamalọ. Twenty-four percent of the hill village households follow the *oxe chuko* rite as compared with 33 percent of the lowland village households; 56 percent of the households in Mae Ha Ki follow the *oxe pgo* rite as compared with 50 percent of the lowland plains households. In sum, 80 percent of the hill village households and 83 percent of the plains village households continue to preserve the belief in *bgha* and the associated *oxe* rite.

Religious Affiliations of Two Villages, Expressed in Number of Households Practicing Each Rite

Religious Rite	Mae Ha Ki (hill village)	Phamalọ (plains village)
Oxe chuko	6 (24%)	16 (33%)
Oxe pgo	14 (56%)	24 (50%)
Chakasi	3 (12%)	7 (15%)
Christian (Catholic)*	2 (8%)	1 (2%)

*Christian households do not have *bgha*.

The apparent lack of religious difference between the hill and plains villages suggested by these figures is misleading. In the plains villages, the practice of both *oxe chuko* and *oxe pgo* tends to be a "compromise" form that makes even the rite of those who follow the *oxe chuko* similar to that here described as *oxe pgo*. These "compromise" forms are called *chuko goma* and *pgo goma*, where *goma* means "middle way" or "medium." In contrast, the hill villagers tend to be stricter even in following *oxe pgo*. Although it was difficult to obtain exact statistics, because of the reluctance of informants to talk about such matters, on how many households follow "compromise" or "strict" forms, it would appear that although many plains villagers practice compromise rites, their hill cousins continue to stick closer to the tradition.

In spite of the differences between *oxe pgo* and *oxe chuko* and between compromise and strict forms of each,[9] there remains a common cultural denominator in all *oxe* rites that plays an important role in preserving the ethnic identity of the Karen, even those Karen in the process of change.

This common denominator can be summarized as follows:

1. The *dopuweh* or the matrilineal group is both the smallest and largest corporate group of Karen society. The belief in *bgha* and the *oxe* rite function to strengthen the cohesiveness of the *dopuweh*.
2. Unless a member of a *dopuweh* gives up the *oxe* rite, he is required to be ready to participate in the ritual whenever held. One's freedom of movement (e.g., migrating to a geographically or socially distant place) is limited, although it is greater if one follows the *oxe pgo* rather than the *oxe chuko* rite.
3. "Karenness" can be preserved well so long as the *oxe* rite is performed since it is indispensable for participants to speak Karen and to wear Karen costumes during the ritual.

Although the common denominator of all *oxe* rites is important in preservation of "Karenness," the differences between the rites are also significant in determining how Karen adapt to changed circumstances. Given the greater freedom of action permitted followers of *oxe pgo* or of the compromise form of *oxe chuko*, it is possible for such Karen to adopt some economic or religious changes that make them more similar to the Tai-speaking Buddhist peasants who are their neighbors. On the other hand, followers of the strict forms of either type of *oxe* rite are less "detribalized" and preserve more of their ethnic identity as Karen.

NEW RELIGIOUS ELEMENTS AND ABANDONMENT OF *OXE* RITES

Beginning about fifty years ago, some lowland Buddhist elements were adopted by the villagers in Phamalọ. Most important of these was the construction of a *cetiya* or stupa, which symbolizes the Buddha, on a hill above Phamalọ. Ritual observance of such major Buddhist ceremonies as the "Beginning of Lent," the "End of Lent," and Visakha-puja (commemoration of the birth, enlightenment, and death of the Buddha), as well as *songkran*, the traditional Thai New Year, are held at the *cetiya*. The inclusion of Buddhist elements in the religion of the Phamalọ villagers appears to have caused little change in traditional Sgaw religious practice. This situation contrasts markedly with those cases in which Sgaw have adopted the *chakasi* rite or Christianity.

The *chakasi* rite* serves to terminate responsibility to the *bgha* and, thus, to eliminate the necessity for performing *oxe* rites. Conversion to Christianity also terminates the obligations to the *bgha*. Elimination of the *oxe* rites is considered to be a positive move by some Karen since their daily routine and many trading transactions are perceived to be hindered when they continue to perform these rites.

The *chakasi* rite is performed in front of a withered tree on the outskirts of a village. In both Mae Ha Ki and Phamalọ, this is a simple rite presided over by a Shan hermit, Pusala (called Pusasa by the Karen). Those who participate in the rite, who may be members of the same *dopuweh*, roast the seeds of cultivated plants such as chili, rice, kidney beans, soya beans, maize, cucumbers, and sesame to terminate their germination potential. They sacrifice a chicken and make a curry from it that, along with rice and fried fish, is offered to the *bgha* at the dead tree. Generally, the participating members of a *dopuweh* recite formulae in Shan and chant some Buddhist verses in Burmese.

After this offering at the dead tree, the Shan hermit takes some cotton thread and performs *kichu* (or *kisu*, i.e., *mat mụ* in Northern Thai), "tying of the wrists," on all the participants; he then tattooes small spots on each hand of all those involved. The members of a *dopuweh* need to perform this simple rite only twice a year thereafter; after three generations the descendants will be liberated completely from the troublesome rite of *oxe*.

Although both Protestant (American Baptist Mission) and Catholic missionaries have had success in converting a significant number of Sgaw in other villages, very few people in either Mae Ha Ki or

---

*Editor's Note: For further discussion of the *chakasi* rite as performed among Karen in Mae Sariang district, see Kunstadter's chapter, pp. 132–134.

Phamalǫ had become Christian. In Mae Ha Ki, there were two Catholic households; in Phamalǫ, there was only one Christian, also a Catholic. The little data gathered do not permit any proper analysis of the impact of Christian missionary work among the Sgaw Karen of Thailand.

There is a social cost paid by those villagers who try to terminate belief in the *bgha* by performing the *chakasi* rite or by converting to Christianity. Whoever ceases to perform the *oxe* rite is thereafter tabooed from interdining with members of his *dopuweh* when they are eating pork and chicken. The pig and chicken are indispensable to the Karen in both their religious and their secular life. Exclusion from interdining with those who eat pork and chicken serves to deter those who would give up their ethnic identity.

TALUTAPHADU, AN EMERGING VILLAGE RITE IN THE PLAINS

The Sgaw Karen living in the Mae Sariang valley, like Pwo Karen who have been plains dwellers for some generations, perform a rite called *talutaphadu* ("great rite") at least once a year to propitiate *hti k'cha kǫ k'cha* (sometimes written in other works as *hti k'sa kaw k'sa*), the "Lord of Water and Land." Sgaw Karen living in hill villages, in contrast to their lowland cousins, apparently do not perform this village ritual.

In the hill village, *hti k'cha kǫ k'cha* is considered to be a supernatural being who hangs in the air like ether. In the Sgaw villages in the Mae Sariang lowlands, such as Phamalǫ and Mae Han, this spirit appears similar to the *phi caothi caodin caomųang,* the Northern Thai "Deity of the Land." Moreover, the ritual of *talutaphadu* resembles somewhat the rites found in Northern Thai and Shan villages called *liang phi caothi caodin caomųang,* the "Rite of the Deity of the Land" (cf. Stern 1968B).

Let me summarize the *talutaphadu* rite in Phamalǫ village as I observed it on May 28, 1966. In the early morning, women and children from each household brought two small bunches of leaves called *suedok*,[10] two chickens, and a pair of candles to the house of the *sapga* or religious leader. In addition, eleven bottles of liquor were purchased with money contributed by all the households of Phamalǫ. Although home-made liquor is preferable to factory-manufactured liquor, the villagers of Phamalǫ abide by Thai law that forbids the distilling of liquor by anyone except those who are licensed. In buying their factory-made liquor from a shop in Mae Sariang, the lowland Karen thus differ from their hill cousins who continue to make their own liquor.

At nine o'clock almost all of the male villagers came to the shrine (literally, the "house," the *talutaphadu-da*) of *hti k'cha ko k'cha*. The shrine is made mainly of bamboo and is located at the foot of the hill on which the village *cetiya* is located. Once there, no one is permitted to return to the village from the shrine until the *talutaphadu* rite is over. The villagers then fetched water and repaired the deity house and cleaned the surroundings. Hot water was prepared for cooking.

As soon as the arrangements were made, the *sapga* called all the participants together in front of the deity house. He chanted prayers in Karen while holding a bundle of *sue-dok* leaves in his hands. These he directed towards the deity house and towards a simple altar to the left of the shrine. Four bottles of liquor were dedicated to the deity house and three to the altar. The *sapga* again repeated prayers in which the names of nine absent villagers were mentioned and protection for them from calamities and misfortune was requested.

Then one of three village elders, who was called *dosuda*, "sacrifice-leader," began killing chickens by beating them with a stick. While the other two elders did not do so, other participants followed him in killing chickens and the pig. The *dosuda* also struck a sacrificial pig with a bamboo stick and his assistant stabbed the pig in the throat. The chickens and pig were dismembered and cooked under the supervision of the *alochino,* or "cooking leader," who is also one of the three elders. A washbasin full of curried chicken and pork and of the rice brought from each house was offered to the deity house and to the altar to the left of the shrine.

The *sapga* lit a huge candle made out of many small ones that had been twisted together. He recited another prayer and then picked up some popped rice that had been offered to the deity house. This he discarded and picked up another handful until he succeeded in having an even number of kernels of popped rice. This was thought to be a sign of the arrival of *hti k'cha ko k'cha* at the deity house from *doi kham* (a Tai name), the Golden Mountain, which is believed, according to Tai legend, to exist in the east. After confirming the arrival of *hti k'cha ko k'cha* at the deity house, the *sapga* sprinkled some liquor over the house and the altar. The three village elders who were officiating partook of the food together with the deity just as Tai monks do in many Buddhist ceremonies. When the three old men finished eating, the other villagers began. While the others were eating, two of the elders (the *sapga* excepted) distributed liquor to all participants regardless of age. Chants called *uta* (or *hta*) were repeated again and again in a monotonous tone by the participants. With the chanting, the main part of the *talutaphadu* ritual was over and the participants started on their way home. They gathered again at the house of the *sapga* where a drinking party continued for hours.

Ethnic identity and consanguinity were not emphasized at the *talutaphadu* rite. Unlike the *oxe* rites, any male villager is entitled to participate in *talutaphadu* irrespective of his ethnic background. Moreover, there is no requirement that participants speak only Karen or that they wear only Karen clothing. Participants are related as fellow villagers and not as kinsmen. In contrast to the *oxe* rite, the *talutaphadu* ritual does not function to reinforce kin group membership or to underscore "Karenness." This ritual links the Karen villagers to a lowland culture common to the Northern Thai and the Shan. It is noteworthy that the rite is performed only among the Karen of the plains and not among their hill cousins who preserve more of a tribal flavor to their culture. The Karen plainsmen have made a selection from lowland rituals dedicated to territorial spirits and have combined these with distinctively Karen elements.

Sociocultural Change and Ethnic Identity

Sgaw Karen culture developed in relatively autonomous hill villages adapted to swidden cultivating. Although in the past, some of these villages were organized into long houses, the basic units of hill Karen society are the kin groups known as *dopuweh*. Membership in these groups is reinforced by periodic performance of the *oxe* rites, dedicated to the *bgha* or ancestral spirit. In a traditional sense, to be a (Sgaw) Karen was to be a member of some *dopuweh* and a participant in the *oxe* rites.

This traditional culture has been challenged by the stagnation of swidden cultivation, the introduction of wet-rice cultivation, the migration of some Karen from the hills to the lowlands, the invasion of a monetary economy, the extension of Thai administration over Karen-inhabited areas, and the spread of Buddhist and Christian religion and the *chakasi* rite. These challenges have resulted in sociocultural change in Karen society, change that can be said to be transforming a "tribal," consanguineally based society to a "peasant," territorially based society. Such changes have not been uniform for all Sgaw Karen, as can be seen from our contrasting pictures of a hill village and a lowland village in Mae Sariang district.

Kinship still remains important as the basis for organization of Karen life even in the lowland villages. In lowland as well as upland villages, the belief in *bgha* and the practice of the *oxe* rites continue to be important for most Karen and to be significant for the definition of "Karenness." However, there is a difference between lowland and upland Karen in that the plains Karen generally follow compromise versions of the *oxe* rites and their hill cousins continue to follow more strict versions.

The shift from an exclusively consanguineally based social organization to one that also employs territorial criteria is evident in the performance of the *talutaphadu* ritual, which involves the followers in worshipping a "Lord of Water and Land." Although this ritual is found in lowland Karen villages, it appears to be unknown in the upland villages.

In the lowlands, the Karen have had to associate with their neighbors, irrespective of their ethnic background, to organize paddy field irrigation. Many lowland Karen have also come to participate in important Buddhist rituals such as those marking the beginning and end of Buddhist Lent and the ceremony of ordination into the Buddhist clergy. Some lowland Karen also join in the observance of such important Thai ceremonies as *songkran* (the traditional Thai New Year) and *loi krathong* (a festival at which offerings are floated on the water).

Yet, despite the trend towards becoming peasant and the participation in some aspects of Thai culture, even the lowland Karen cannot be said to be assimilating to lowland Thai culture. The *talutaphadu* ritual itself seems to play an important role in preventing the Karen from losing their identity. The deity *hti k'cha ko k'cha*, however much he may resemble a Tai counterpart, is a Karen spirit addressed in Karen. Those who worship *hti k'cha ko k'cha* are thus set apart from those other plains dwellers whose territorial spirit is called by another name.

The apparent openness of the lowland Karen villages, in contrast to the closedness of the upland villages, may also represent an adaptation that has permitted the Karen to retain their identity in changed circumstances. Christoph von Fürer-Haimendorf's analysis of the Chetri caste in Nepal (1960: 12–32) is suggestive in this regard. The Chetri, the second highest ranking caste in the Hindu caste system of Nepal, permit intermarriage between Chetri and non-Chetri (even including the lower castes) in violation of the orthodox Hindu tradition. Von Fürer-Haimendorf has explained this by observing that in such a marginal area of Hinduism as Nepal where the Hindu minority is in danger of absorption by such groups as the Tibeto-Burman Sherpas, Gurungs, Magars, and Tamangs, the Hindus have safeguarded their identity by defining it in terms of culture rather than in terms of descent. Similarly, in Mae Sariang where the Karen are a majority, as they are in the hills, they can afford to maintain "purity of blood" by not intermarrying with other people. In contrast, in the lowlands the plains Karen are a distinct minority vis-à-vis the Tai groups. Hence, the plains Karen, like the Chetri of Nepal, maintain themselves as a "cultural" rather than a "pure-blood" group and accept intermarriage with neighboring non-Karen peoples.

Sgaw Karen culture and society in Mae Sariang today thus falls along a continuum from tribal to peasant, with the hill dwellers being more tribal and the plains Karen more peasant. Although the lowland Karen villages have opened up to influences from non-Karen sources and have adopted some non-Karen practices, even the lowland Karen have remained distinctively Karen.

Acknowledgments

The field work on which this essay is based was conducted over a period of twenty-one months from 1963 through 1965. I am grateful for the generous support of this research afforded by the Center for Southeast Asian Studies, Kyoto University, the Ford Foundation, and the Asia Foundation and for the assistance provided by the National Research Council of Thailand and the Department of Public Welfare of the Royal Thai Government. I am also grateful for the opportunity of being able to write this essay while at the School of Oriental and African Studies of the University of London during 1970-71. I am indebted to Barbara Ward, Bill Epstein, and Charles Keyes for their kind criticisms and comments on the essay. However, all of the errors, as well as the opinions, found in this essay are the sole responsibility of the author.

Notes

1. Compare Keyes (1970) and see his chapter on "The Karen in Thai History and the History of the Karen in Thailand" in this volume. A Thai source (Khanakammakan prachasamphan lae ekkasan kancatngan chalǫng 25 phutthasatwat 1957) states that Thai officials came across Karen in the eastern part of Mae Hǫng Sǫn province about 140 years ago.

2. *Th'waw* refers to village in the Sgaw Karen language.

3. Villagers did send, as annual tribute to the prince (*cao*) of Chiang Mai or Lamphun, two cotton blankets (*yadoti*).

4. Personal communication from Professor Keiji Iwata, Tokyo Institute of Technology, September 1971.

5. Soil sickness is considered to be caused by a chemical substance secreted from the roots of upland rice as well as the nematoda living in the roots.

6. The author owes this analysis to Professor Hayao Fukui of Kyoto University.

7. The author owes much to Dr. D. H. Marlowe for his kind suggestions regarding the *oxe* rite.

8. The *dapo*, literally "flower place," is a shelf located above the normal level of people's heads on which offerings to the Buddha are placed.

9. There are also some differences in the *oxe* rite as practiced by the Pwo. A Pwo from Hot district, Chiang Mai province, living in Phamalo said that Pwo in Hot and Lamphun sometimes offer small fish called *nya-pla*, instead of more expensive animals, to the house spirit. It was also said that Pwo Karen in Lamphun can offer bamboo rats to the *bgha* at the time of the *oxe pgo* rite.

10. F. K. Lehman thinks that these leaves are a kind of *Eugenia* that figure in Buddhist rituals (cf. Lehman's chapter in this volume).

Ethnic Group, Category, and Identity: Karen in Northern Thailand

Peter Kunstadter

In discussions of ethnicity, distinctions should be made among the concepts of ethnic group, ethnic identity, and ethnic category. By *ethnic group* I mean a set of individuals with similar consciousness and mutual interests centered on some shared understandings or common values. Such groups often organize some of their behavior to maintain their perceived mutual interests. Just how much must be shared and how much may differ is a matter for further discussion. By *ethnic identification* I mean the process of assigning an individual (including oneself) to a group or category, and thus implicitly recognizing boundaries of community of interests and predicting a set of behavioral traits appropriate to members of the group or category, which may influence relationships within or outside the group or category. An individual may aspire to identify himself with a group to enjoy prestige or other attributes attached to that group and may modify his behavior to achieve this end. By *ethnic category* I mean a class of people or groups, based on real or presumed cultural characteristics, with the implication that a categorization is a more or less systematic application of some kinds of rules to the variety of known individuals or groups, and that behavior toward members of a category will tend to be similar under some circumstances. An ethnic category need not correspond to the ethnic group with which it may share a name, depending on who is making the categorization and on the context in which the categorization is applied. It should be understood from these definitions that ethnic groups (or their boundaries), identities, and categorizations are not necessarily permanent, and that their applications may depend on social context.

Studies in Southeast Asia have contributed several generalizations to theories of ethnic groups, categories, and identities. E. R. Leach (1954) demonstrated that ethnic groups or ethnic categorizations are not necessarily synonymous with a culture or a social system. What Leach showed for the category "Kachin" is also true for the category "Karen." In Burma the range of cultural and social structural variation among people labeled Karen encompasses swiddeners in the hills, wet-rice cultivators in the valleys, and sophisticated town and city dwellers who subscribe to a variety of animist, Buddhist, and Christian philosophies, speak a number of sometimes mutually unintelligible dialects, and organize their lives in their communities in different ways. In Thailand this variability is only slightly reduced. At least at the lower levels of description it is clear we must speak of "Karen social structures" rather than of "the social structure of the Karen," just as we must speak of "Karen dialects" rather than of "the Karen language."

As we study varieties of ethnicity in Southeast Asia, we begin to understand that ethnicity, at least in part, depends on reference to some other group; the reference is often phrased in terms of confrontation, opposition, or contrast (cf. Lehman 1967A), and thus in part depends on context. People define themselves (as distinct from others) and are defined by others (as distinct from themselves). The defining principles are not necessarily the same on both sides, and consequently the groups encompassed by the definitions do not necessarily coincide. It follows that neither ethnic identity nor ethnic categorization is immutable or uniquely determined for any individual or group, and that identity, for example, may vary depending on whether self-ascription or identification by someone else is used. Examples in this chapter suggest how ethnicity may function similarly to many other kinds of social categorizations, including local group or community, social class, religion, and nationality, each of which may imply some feeling of identity, adherence to some common values, and, under conditions such as Fredrik Barth (1969B) suggests for ethnic groups, some boundary defining and maintaining mechanisms.

Barth (1969B: esp. 13–15) feels that ethnic groups contain people who are "playing the same game," and thus may expand or diversify their social relations "to cover eventually all different sectors and domains of activity." I do not believe this distinguishes ethnic groups from many other kinds of social categorizations. My differences with Barth are two-fold. First, role ascription in no society is based exclusively on ethnicity but always involves things such as age, sex, marital status, kinship, and their associated patterns of interaction, which may limit the degree to which all "domains of activity" may be covered. Second, it is clear that individuals and groups may play different games in different contexts. This involves a change from time to time in their ascription of identity to themselves and to others, their categorizations, and their definitions of group inclusiveness.

In the case of Karen identities, there has usually been good congruence between the point of view of those who consider themselves to be Karen and the point of view of those who consider themselves to be something else. In other words, Karen and non-Karen have generally agreed about the boundaries and identifying features that define "Karen." But this situation may not persist, because the drawing of boundaries is dynamic and responds to change both within the defined group and in external conditions.

Geographic dispersal has had little effect in modifying Karen consciousness of kind, probably because Karen subpopulations have not been completely isolated from each other. Local cultural variations have developed within major dialect groups in response to ecological or social conditions but have not obscured the identity of Karen within these groups. Demographic interchange (intermarriage and migration) persists at least between nearby local groups in spite of variation of ecology, religion, or village social structure.* None of the subsystems with which I am familiar has developed social processes that would lead to sharp differentiation from or exclusion of other parts of populations defining themselves as Karen. When change

---

*Demographic surveys in Mae Sariang district lead to the following generalizations. Migration is relatively common among upland Karen villages and hamlets, and among lowland Karen villages. There is much more migration from upland to lowland Karen villages and to mixed ethnic communities around Mae Sariang town than in the opposite direction. Karen may come from or go to other Karen communities several hundred kilometers away, but there is little movement to non-Karen communities outside Mae Sariang district. In the current generation (as compared with the past, when intermarriage with Lua' was more common) there is no movement of non-Karen into Karen upland communities. A few upland Karen have married and moved to upland Lua' communities in recent years. A few Northern Thai have married and moved into lowland Karen communities. The amount of intermarriage in lowland Karen communities and in the mixed ethnic communities has increased in recent years, but the rate of ethnic intermarriage is lower for Karen than among Lua' living in the mixed ethnic communities, and Karen are more conservative than Lua' in the ethnic variety of their marriage partners. It is less common for children with one Karen parent to assume non-Karen identity than for children with one Lua' parent to become non-Lua'. For further details see Kunstadter (1979).

comes in the definition of Karen identity, it seems likely that it will be a change on the part of the outside definition. I believe this will be in the form of a merging of Karen with other non-Thai rural minority peoples into a single category: hill tribe.*

The situation of Karen vis-à-vis Thai has changed in the twentieth century and especially in the past twenty-five years. Both the categorizations (including the characteristics attributed by Thai to Karen, and the other people with whom the Karen may be categorized) and the contexts of interactions have been changing very rapidly, while there has been little change in the boundary of the Karen population or in the behavior of the Karen amongst themselves. I believe modernization leads to homogenization and amalgamation of groups through their categorization into the same class by outsiders or vis-à-vis outsiders who are perceived as treating the amalgamated group all in the same fashion. The style of administration of minority groups, both within and among nations, has changed from one of divide and rule to a preference for dealing with a single (although amalgamated) adversary through a uniform set of policies. Localized differences, which used to be the basis for feudal-like relationships—whether they were grants from Northern Thai princes to Lua' or Karen upland villages or treaties between the United States and "sovereign" Indian tribes—are not tolerated in an era of centralized administration.

Studies of Thai relationships with minorities have suggested the great ease with which some non-Thai people have been incorporated into Thai society. The absorption of a large portion of the Chinese minority is an outstanding example of this phenomenon (e.g., Boonsanong Punyodyana 1971; Skinner 1957, 1958, 1964), as is the absorption of numbers of Mon-Khmer-speaking peoples such as the Lua' (Kunstadter 1967, 1969A, 1969B) and the Khamu (LeBar 1967). Many other groups that have not been systematically studied to date have also been absorbed into Thai society with relatively little conflict (Mon, Portuguese) while some groups (Malay, "Indian," and certain "hill tribes") have tended to retain their separate identity. An examination of the patterns of Thai-Karen relations should help us understand the processes of Thai society; an examination of Karen relations with non-Karen should help us understand Karen social processes.

In what follows, it will be seen that Karen people act like Karen not only because of the cultural characteristics they or outside observers recognize as belonging to the category Karen, and not just

*In common speech the term *Meo* (the Thai designation for people who refer to themselves as Hmong), rather than *chao khao* (people of the mountains), is now frequently used to refer to all upland minority people, regardless of ethnicity.

because they identify themselves as members of a Karen group, but also because Karen have patterned, somewhat self-perpetuating relationships with non-Karen. Assuming the category Karen can be defined meaningfully, many related questions come to mind:

(a) Is there an overall pattern of adaptation of Karen to non-Karen societies? Was this basic pattern set in Burma, as a result of many centuries of Karen-Burman (or Karen-Shan or Karen-Mon) confrontation, and then transferred to the Karen-Thai (or Karen-Lua', Karen-Meo, and so on) situation?

(b) What accounts for the apparently very rapid expansion in space and numbers of Karen in northern Thailand within the past four or five generations, as compared, for example, with the relatively stable population size and distribution of the Lua' with whom the Karen have shared the hills?

(c) How can we understand the apparent paradox of the readiness of some Karen to accept religious innovation in animist, Buddhist, and Christian traditions, incorporate these changes fully and rapidly, and yet, despite these major changes in ideology, retain identity as Karen?

(d) What have been the self-conceptions, the views of others, and the realities of the situations in which Karen find themselves and in which their identity is defined?

(e) In view of the great geographic and ecological ranges (about 1,000 kilometers north and south and at least 500 kilometers east and west, in hills and valleys, isolated hamlets and cities) and considerable social and cultural differentiation (from illiterate to college educated, from traditional to Westernized, animist, Buddhist, Protestant, and Catholic) of people who are identified as Karen, what is a Karen?

(f) Under what circumstances do people identify themselves as Karen, and when do they consider themselves to be something else?

In the following pages I try to offer the beginnings of answers to these questions. Unless otherwise specified, the generalizations apply to Sgaw-speaking Karen who live in Mae Sariang district in northwestern Thailand.

Methods and Evidence

The information reported in this chapter was gathered during several years of ethnographic field work in Thailand, including residence for about a year in one upland Sgaw Karen village. Information was gathered by observation and by interviews with informants belonging to a variety of ethnic categories in addition to Karen.

The research was aimed primarily at problems of ethnography of Lua' and Karen villages, the ecology of upland agriculture, and demographic differentials between ecologically and ethnically differentiated subpopulations. Topics relevant to ethnic definitions and ethnic confrontations arose frequently, for example, with regard to competition between Lua' and Karen over land resources, intermarriage and migration, and religion.

I preferred to rely on spontaneously occurring situations or "cases" rather than posing hypothetical questions. For the most part, I deliberately avoided asking direct questions about ethnic identity or ethnic contrasts, although questions about intermarriage and religion were included in a scheduled questionnaire administered late in the field work period. The question of relationships with other ethnic categories occurred spontaneously in a variety of contexts, for example, in folk tales or in explaining apparently aberrant behavior. In what follows, I have tried to make a coherent picture from the statements and anecdotes, together with an analysis of how I think some aspects of Karen and other social systems work. An ideal study of relationships between ethnic categories would include a more detailed analysis of history, plus systematic observations of Karen and non-Karen attitudes toward ethnic identity and toward Karen identity, as well as quantified statements of the anecdotal impressions given below.

Actual behavior is perhaps more valuable than expressions of attitudes in understanding the nature of relationships between groups, but cases of conflict do not always occur under comparable conditions, so it is not always easy to make comparisons at all levels of ethnic contrast. An example indicates the type of analysis I have followed.

What is the role of violence in Karen interpersonal and intergroup relations in Thailand? The data summarized in the next few paragraphs lead me to conclude that Karen in general are not physically violent. They act as if physical (or supernatural) conflicts between individuals are individual matters, not ethnic disputes or matters provoking or requiring village-wide or ethnic solidarity or collective action even when disputes involve nonrelatives, nonvillagers, or non-Karen.

The only fight I have seen between Karen was when both individuals (father-in-law and son-in-law) were drunk. The balance of the villagers were amused spectators and made no attempt to intervene. When sober, the old man treated the whole thing as a joke and asked why I had not come to take pictures.

Two men from different villages "almost came to blows" (I did not see the incident) when one began cutting a swidden within the territory claimed by another village. His claim was based on the existence of relatives living in the other village, but was not backed up by his relatives nor by the village elders of his own village of residence.

A woman died shortly after childbirth. The symptoms of her death were understood to be those resulting from sorcery. The reputed sorcerers were Karen from another village. No action was taken by the victim's relatives or other villagers against the sorcerers or their village.

A Lua' villager shot a Karen who was breaking into his house. When I inquired about the reactions of Karen in a nearby village, they told me the man was a well-known opium addict and thief. They said it was just as well that someone had shot him, since he had been shot at and missed by a Karen in his home village. The fact that the victim was Karen and his assailant Lua' was not considered important in the discussion or evaluation of the case.

In a lowland Karen village I saw a Karen hitting another man at a wedding. When I asked about the case, I was told the man being hit was drunk and misbehaving. His ethnic affiliation (Northern Thai) was not referred to in explaining his behavior, nor was the ethnic affiliation of his Karen assailant considered remarkable. There were no repercussions after this incident from Thai authorities. Karen in this area have attempted to reduce conflicts of this sort by restricting the amount of liquor publicly available, not by excluding Thai from their celebrations (see footnote 11).

The Karen at Home, or Who Are the Karen?

From the standpoint of Karen, a Karen must speak the Karen language, should know Karen folk tales, eat like a Karen, dress like a Karen, and act like a Karen to his fellow Karen. The language seems to be the most important criterion: no one who does not speak Karen is considered to be Karen (regardless of genetic origin); anyone who speaks Karen and can and does live like a Karen would be considered by others to be a Karen and probably considers himself to be one, unless he has some obviously distinguishing social identity, like a missionary.

"Eating like a Karen" seems to refer to a condition where there is little variety in the basic rice-chilis-salt diet. Karen use of pounded fish-paste is not terribly distinctive, and Karen cuisine is not considered by the Karen to be an item of pride or propriety. Food taboos exist but not as markers of ethnic distinctiveness (as, for example, pork is for Moslems). They may be applied to pregnant women not because they are Karen, but because they are pregnant. Taboos against eating certain kinds of wild game (monkeys, some kinds of large snakes) are justified with folk tales, but are ignored as often as they are observed.

Karen have many small variations in dress within a general pattern. Nowadays Sgaw men usually wear purchased Shan pants (cut, pieced, and sewn, drawn together at the top with a rope or belt) and a purchased shirt or homespun red and white blouse. Pants are a relatively new feature. In the past, they wore only the blouse in a knee-length version. A man should wear a Karen shirt on ceremonial occasions, but he can still be a Karen without it. The unmarried girl's garment is a single-piece blouse, reaching almost to the ground, usually predominantly white with some red decoration. The married woman's dress is two-piece, with a tubular skirt and a hip-length overblouse, and predominantly black. Both skirt and blouse may have elaborate woven decoration in a variety of colors. The design of the decorations varies from one locality to another, transmitted from mother to daughter or among peers. A woman may retain her natal village's style when she moves into a new village. Designs do not necessarily indicate socially significant boundaries between Karen subgroups, although there are fairly consistent differences between Sgaw and Pwo designs. Karen blouses have become popular market items among Thai and foreign tourists, but dress alone does not make a Karen.

Karen recognize the existence of a large category, "Karen," within which subcategories are encompassed. They see two bases for these subcategories, dialect and geography; they distinguish, for example, hill from valley Sgaw Karen and all Sgaw from all Pwo. Such Thai labels as Red vs. White Karen (*nyang daeng* vs. *nyang khao*), referring to dress style, or Town vs. Forest Karen (*nyang ban* vs. *nyang pa*), referring to presumed degree of civilization, or more accurately to degree of familiarity with the speaker, are not meaningful to Karen. They are applied, but not consistently, by Northern Thai. Dialect differences, for example, between Sgaw and Pwo, are well known and appear as symbolic elements in folk tales by the Sgaw, but are not consistently recognized by non-Karen.

Locality terms may be applied (people of such and such place) but the geographical, social, and demographic boundaries are not consistently applied or recognized by the Karen in the area in which I worked.

Karen in Mae Sariang District[1]

Mae Sariang district lies to the west of the divide between the Mae Ping (which after entering the Cao Phraya River flows into the

Gulf of Siam) and the Salween River (which drains into the Andaman Sea). It is a frontier area between Thailand, Burma, and the Karen and Shan states. It has been crossed and recrossed during the Thai-Burmese wars. For generations, trade has passed both east to the Ping valley and west into Burma. Thai commercial dominance in the area is relatively recent. Indian (British) coinage was the dominant currency until World War II and persists in ceremonial use; cloth, knives, and many other essentials came from Burma in exchange for kerosene, and salt came in from Thailand. An all-weather road connecting the district with Chiang Mai and the national road network was completed in 1965, and other developments have followed rapidly. For the most part, these have been concentrated in the town of Mae Sariang, but their influences have been felt in rural areas as well.

Karen are found in all parts of Mae Sariang district, both in the hills and in the lowlands. To the south of the new highway, in the hills to the south and east of town, there are mostly Pwo Karen; in the other quarters of the district, most of the Karen are Sgaw. Lua' villages are scattered in the hills to the east of the Yuam valley. There were formerly Lua' villages in the valley, but these have now become Northern Thai in ethnic identity. From Mae La Nọi to the north, the valley contains Karen villages and Shan villages; south of Mae La Nọi, the valley contains Northern Thai and Karen villages. The only town of major importance is Mae Sariang, containing the district administrative offices and the major market of the district. The population of the town and its adjacent "suburbs" includes Karen as well as Lua', Northern Thai, Central Thai, Chinese, Shan, and "Indians" (mostly Moslems from the Noakhali area of Bangladesh).

Although exact figures are not available, Mae Sariang district probably has as high a proportion of Karen to Thai as any other district in Thailand, at least 40 percent.[2]

In the hills of Mae Sariang district, Karen are clearly dominant numerically and territorially, although village histories indicate that the first settlements in the then Lua'-controlled hills were no more than five or six generations ago. Karen settlement in the valley of the Yuam seems older than this, and although the valley Karen are not numerically dominant, they have managed to maintain their land holdings and Karen identity in spite of increased population pressure from Northern Thai and Shan.*

**Editor's Note:* The earliest firsthand report of Karen in what is today Mae Sariang district comes from the journals of Dr. D. Richardson, who was sent on several investigative trips to northern Thailand and the Shan states in the late 1820s and the 1830s. In December 1829 and January 1830, Richardson found Karen in the hills from the confluence of the Moei and Yuam rivers (which then was, and is still today, at the border

When Karen first settled in the hills of Mae Sariang district, they did so at the pleasure of the Lua', from whom they begged use of swidden land and to whom they paid an annual tribute of one-tenth of their rice crop. Space was made available to the Karen by Lua' who had consolidated their dispersed hamlets into fortified villages at a time when raiders (possibly Kayah) from Burma were common.[3] Some Karen moved into Lua' villages within which they intermarried, but maintained their separate identity in their own houses. Their descendants still live in some of the Lua' villages in the northeast corner of the district; but they have moved out of some of the other Lua' villages to establish their own hamlets. Still other Lua' villages have apparently converted entirely to Karen identity, incorporating Lua' members as well as descendants of Karen.

The speed of the growth of Karen populations is illustrated by the chart on the facing page, which shows the history of one village cluster known in Thai as Ban Huai Phung. The circumstances of this village's growth and subdivision appear to be typical for the area. Founders came in very small numbers "from the west," established relationships with Lua' for land, in some cases intermarried with Lua' women, and gradually enlarged their land holdings as they increased in numbers.

A change in administrative patterns probably assisted the Karen in their competition with the Lua'. The titles to Lua' land, and thus the rights of the Lua' to collect rent, were granted by the Northern Thai princes, in return for small tribute payments (Kraisri Nimmanhaeminda 1965B). The Karen, when they moved onto Lua' land, paid tribute, indirectly through the Lua' who were their "lords" and also directly to the prince, in the form of specially woven cloth. But when the Bangkok government took over administration of northern Thailand around the turn of the century, it abolished the northern princes' rights to collect tribute and allocate land. The Bangkok government

---

between Thailand and Burma) to the vicinity of Mae Sariang town itself (Blundell 1836: 607–11). On his second visit to Mae Sariang in December 1836 and January 1837, Richardson also found Karen living in the hills north of Mae Sariang town all the way to the border with the Kayah State (Richardson 1869: 104–7). But he makes mention only of Lua' (Lawa) living in the hills to the east of Mae Sariang along the route to Chiang Mai, which he travelled in 1830 (Blundell 1836: 612–13). It would appear, then, that the areas west of the Yuam River in Mae Sariang district had been settled by Karen sometime before 1829, but that the movement of the Karen eastward into the hill area in which Kunstadter carried out his field work did not occur until after the 1830s. This is consistent with Kunstadter's reconstruction based on village histories (see page 129). Richardson also made several references to Karen being directly under Northern Thai officials appointed by Chiang Mai. The subordinate relationship of Karen to Lua', here described by Kunstadter, would appear to have begun sometime after 1836–37. To this analysis Kunstadter adds that this subordinate relationship of Karen to Lua' may have been characteristic only of the hill area north of the route travelled by Richardson.

The Growth of the Village Cluster Ban Huai Phụng

Time	Hamlets (number of households)					Total Households
c. 1860			kenaypekey (2)			2
c. 1925	swaylawkeythakho (9)		kenaypekey (5)			14
1944–45	swaylawkeyla (6)	swaylawkeytha (8)	klokwaykey (4)	kenaypekey (1)		19
1967–68	(16)	(32)	(8)	(5)		61

Time	Event
c. 1860	Village founded by mother's father of present headman, who married a Lua' woman, plus another Karen household.
c. 1925	Village split after present headman was married, to allow more convenient access to field and larger areas for cultivation.
1944–45	Further village division as result of smallpox epidemic at the end of the Japanese war.
1967–68	Census.

took for itself the title to the hill lands, subjecting Lua' and Karen alike to head taxes. They gave no special recognition to the Lua' as original owners of the land; they neither recognized titles to hill fields (including boundaries of traditionally recognized village territories), nor allowed the Lua' to continue to collect rent. Since that time, Karen seem to have taken over increasing amounts of hill land, in part by sheer weight of numbers. In recent years, the lack of definition of traditional land rights has turned out to be a double-edged sword, as Karen have come into competition with Meo.

Ethnic Stability and Cultural Change

People who consider themselves Karen have demonstrated great flexibility in adapting themselves to different or changing conditions, while maintaining Karen self-identification. Social structural variability is one example of this. In the lowlands of Mae Sariang district, where irrigable agricultural land has been scarce, Karen villages have apparently been long-established and relatively stable. In the hills, where opportunities for settlement have, until recently, been plentiful but scattered, village socioreligious structure has been inherently unstable. The result of the instability and frequent fission of hill villages has been wide and rapid dispersal of the upland Karen population. This dispersion has apparently been advantageous to Karen in competition with the Lua' for swidden land resources.

One mechanism by which village social structure instability has been created in the hill villages has been the adherence to the principle that in religious matters one cannot accept the religious authority of a real or classificatory younger brother, and the failure to establish an unambiguous principle by which authority can be established in the absence of an ideal heir. The ideal heir of the village religious leader (*thipokawkesa*) is his eldest son. If the eldest surviving child is a female, neither she nor her husband nor their descendants can accept the authority of her younger brother; if the leader has no sons, there is no clear agreement about the primacy of his younger brother or younger brother's children, or his sister's husband or children (especially if she were an elder sister). Postmarital residence is usually determined by availability of irrigated land or access to swiddens. Hill Karen marriages are frequently village-exogamous for males, so even if the leader has a proper heir, he may have married out of the village by the time his father dies. If no one has ultimate authority, factions are formed, which may split apart if land is available for a new settlement.

The contrast in authority structure between hill and valley Karen villages is analogous to what E. R. Leach (1954) described between *gumsa* and *gumlao* Kachin in highland Burma. Upland Lua' share with hill Karen the same environment and technology, but the Lua' have strong village leadership, especially with regard to control of village swidden-land resources. This suggests that the difference between upland and lowland Karen is not simply a direct social response to the differences in control of resources implied between swiddening in the hills and irrigated agriculture.* Moreover, the authority of Lua' leaders in the hills has actually been eroded by the introduction of irrigated agriculture (Kunstadter 1966; in press).

The explanation of variation in Karen social structure seems more likely to be found in the Karen's relationship with the natural and social environment external to their villages. The lack of central authority in Karen hill villages and the associated rapid dispersal of Karen population have helped the Karen succeed in their demographic and geographic competition with upland Lua' in a situation where the use of overt force was discouraged by the dominant Thai political force, and claims based on traditional use were not recognized by the Thai legal system (Kunstadter 1969B).

In contrast with what Leach reports for the Kachin in Burma, there seems to be no tendency on the part of the Karen to associate changes in political structure, economic-technical changes, or changes in religion with changes in ethnic identity. Karen in both the hills and the valleys seem to consider their ethnic identity to be quite satisfactory, although they recognize behavioral differences between themselves and others with similar identity and they frequently modify their traditions to suit the local natural, technical, or social environment as well as sometimes for personal convenience.

These generalizations can be exemplified by major changes in religious affiliation in recent years in Karen of Mae Sariang district. There is no single Karen religion. Some people have substituted a tattooing ritual for ancestral worship; some have converted to Christianity as a substitute for animism; others avow Buddhism as a supplement to animism. Feeding ancestral spirits (*awkre*) is predominant among Karen in the Mae Sariang lowlands and also, according to

---

*Swiddening involves low capital investment, no permanent improvements of the land, and no scarce resource such as water that can easily be controlled. Irrigated agriculture involves high initial investment of capital or labor, semi-permanent improvements of the land—leveling, diking, digging of ditches—and control over the water.

David Marlowe, in the hills of western Chiang Mai province. In the Mae Sariang Hills, it has been replaced by tattooing (*cekosi*).*

The personal history of the principal tattooer of the Mae Sariang hills, a man born about 1900, illustrates attitudes toward religious change:

> I went to Burma as a youth of ten or twelve, to go to school. My parents were too poor to pay to feed me if I went to school in the Buddhist temple in Mae Sariang, so they sent me to the American Baptist Mission school in Burma. I was baptized and trained for seven or eight years, and came back to Thailand as an evangelist for two years. I lost interest in Christianity, and went back to Burma for a couple of years, working as a clerk in a plantation, and then worked three years as a pharmacist's helper for a Karen doctor in a Burmese hospital in Papun. He taught me medicines to drive out spirits. I had to give up most of that when I returned to Thailand because I could not get the proper ingredients, but I still use some of the prescriptions, along with what I learned from a book I bought in Burma, which tells how to do away with these ancestor spirits.

The Burmese text contains instructions on the ritual to satisfy permanently the demands of ancestral spirits by making an offering of roasted seeds and pledging to renew sacrifices when the seeds bear fruit. Following this, tattoo marks are made on the participants to signify that they have undertaken this rite. The practice has apparently been followed by the majority of the hill Karen in Mae Sariang district, but has been rejected by most of the valley-dwelling Karen on empirical grounds: "After all, it's such a useless thing, you still have to do wrist-binding, and it costs you pigs and chickens just the same." "He is a crook, a fake. . . . He tattooed me about five years ago, and within three years four of my children died, so I went back to feeding the ancestor spirits, and everything has been all right since then."

In the hills, practical reasons are given *for* undertaking the *cekosi* rite. "After my husband died, it was just too much trouble. We were supposed to raise some chickens and pigs just for the spirits, and another set for the people to eat or sell. I just could not keep those special animals separate, and I did not have time to run all over searching for a special pig when one of my children was sick."

**Editor's Note:* This tattooing is performed ritually and is the same as the kind discussed above by Iijima (pp. 112–113) as the *chakasi* rite. Iijima says that the main tattooer, a man named Pusala (Pusasa in Karen), was a Shan. Apparently the man discussed by Kunstadter in the next paragraph, a Karen, is a different person.

Ethnic Group, Category, and Identity 133

Underlying some conversions to Christianity there may also be a desire to affiliate with a powerful organization, to gain an education, or to get medical care. Conversion to Christianity and subsequent reconversion to animism may both be rationalized in terms of greater convenience in dealing with obligations to spirits, and on the basis of social relationships. For instance, one man told me:

> I was tattooed many years ago when my children were young, to avoid all that trouble with special pigs and chickens. Before that, when the children were sick and we divined the cause, it used to show that we had to feed the spirits from my mother's family. I'd go back to my mother's mother's home . . . but she kept putting me off saying she had no chickens. So I had my family tattooed to get rid of these spirits. After that I became a Christian to try to get rid of more spirits—but then I went back to tattooing again when some of the elders were converted to Christianity and tried to tell me what to do.

Another man reported:

> I was originally tattooed when I was a very young boy, at the time my father was tattooed. I was baptized about 20 years ago [apparently early in the 1940s], before I got married, because my wife was a Christian and I had to be a Christian to marry her. I went back to feeding the spirits again because all the Christian leaders moved back down to the valley, and I did not know what to do when people got sick. There was no one here to lead Christian prayers, so I went back to praying the way I knew.

Still another reported:

> I had been tattooed when my father was tattooed, when I was very young. After I was married, my father-in-law was *awkre,* and my father was already *cekosi*—my wife had gone home several times to perform the *awkre* rites, but I hadn't done so. I was fed up with feeding the spirits. So about eight years ago I was baptized.

In contrast with Christianity, Buddhism does not require a decision not to be animist. In the valley, where contact has been sustained for a long time between Karen and Buddhist Northern Thai, Buddhism may be considered normal behavior:

> It [our religion] is a combination—we still hold on to our tradition of wrist-binding, even those who have been tattooed do this, and we offer the first rice and first water every day to the Origin and

> the Truth, the parents who have created us, take care of us, protect us on our journeys, care for our children and our village, keep away disaster and disease, and make us prosper. This isn't just for the spirits of our parents, this is for the Origin and the Truth in heaven. When we go to the Buddhist temple, we take offerings to the priest to make merit. The priest teaches us and represents the voice of the Creator and the Origin. When we come home we pray by ourselves, directly to the Creator.

This level of sophistication has not been reached by hill dwellers:

> I was tattooed when I got married, because my wife was tattooed. I consider myself to be a Buddhist because a priest told me, "It is good to do good and get merit and be blessed, and it will help you against falling ill, because you people in the hills do not know how to worship." I went to worship the priests last year, after they invited us through the headman. I have done this two or three times.

An old woman says: "I stick to *awkre* for my own health, but I make merit [with the priests] so I will prosper."

These examples suggest the variety of responses by Karen to external influences in the realm of religion. At this level of discourse, the explanations given by informants for their behavior are largely personal ones having to do with their immediate convenience (not faith or belief) or with their immediate pattern of social relations. In addition to problems dealing with hostile spirits, conversion to Buddhism or Christianity has implied contact or affiliation with a larger and more powerful society and better access to the perceived benefits of civilization, such as literacy, steady wage labor, and more effective medical care.

Karen informants are familiar with the Thai Buddhist ideology— "do good, get good"—but they do not necessarily believe evil deeds lead to misfortune, at least in this life. Nor are they necessarily convinced of reincarnation in higher or lower forms of life, depending on the accumulation of merit or demerit in this life.

Karen Economic Status and Ethnic Identity

Within Karen hill villages, the doctrine of shared poverty is adhered to for public image but is not followed in reality. The range of wealth in terms of net worth, including both consumer goods and productive resources, may be extreme, from a household that owns only its house and a small garden patch, plus a few chickens and perhaps a pig, to a household owning one and a half elephants, seven buffaloes, seventy-five chickens, two dogs, and two irrigated fields in the hills and one in the plains (rented out). Between the two examples, there is surprisingly little difference in life-style: dress is virtually identical, houses appear as well made, food is about the same. The wealthy family has not indulged in plural marriages, servants, jewelry, radios, expensive religious objects or ceremonies, or stylish store-bought clothing. There is a strong desire to accumulate, but not for display, not for redistribution, not particularly to enjoy, not to improve position within Karen society or to earn access to Thai society, but rather, apparently, to control productive resources and thus to ensure one's own economic security. Ability to redistribute may indicate the blessing of the spirits is upon an individual ("if X were a real leader the spirits would favor him with good fortune and bountiful harvests, but he is just as poor as anyone in this village"). But by itself (without a proper claim to ancestral sanction), wealth may not be an indication of spiritual propriety or ability to lead men.

In this connection, Karen have considerable ambivalence about their children, who are depicted as ungrateful in folk tales, anecdotes, and daily conversation. Accumulation of property to found a family dynasty seems not to be an important motive, even if such a concept were realistic in terms of the sorts of investment opportunities that have been available.

Some Karen think their economic condition is a mark of ethnic identity. They recognize that Thai may be richer and more powerful than they. They believe individual ethnic transformation, although possible, may be undesirable. A Karen widower implied these ideas in speaking of his infant daughter:

> I want my daughter to go to the valley and go to school. . . . With an education you can become a teacher, and the work would be easier than weeding and working under the conditions we work under now. I would want my daughter to live in the plains because it is an easier life than in the mountains. . . . It is only that working conditions are easier down there. A Karen is a Karen—she should not become Thai. A child who has been in the plains and studied is better off. When hill people go to town they don't know how to sit or stand or bargain. But a child brought up in town is better off for knowing these things. . . . When my wife died [shortly after childbirth] there were Thai who offered to adopt my daughter but I wouldn't let them even if she starved, because I knew that if they did she would become Thai. I have only this little girl as a descendant, and whether she lives or dies,

> I would rather she grows up bearing the likeness of her origin. The seed was a Karen, and the plant should be a Karen. I want to have a descendant who is a Karen. If she were adopted and not a Karen, it would be like a seed that grew up and died without flowering.

This man seems to believe (but not completely consistently) that ethnic identity is not genetically inherited but is a matter of early childhood training. It is evident that Karen think of themselves as a cultural group (in the anthropological technical sense):

> If a Thai baby were adopted by Karen from the age of my daughter, it would surely grow up to be a Karen. He would be regarded and treated just like the Karen. . . . PP, a Thai, married a Karen woman, and stays at T village. That man cannot speak good Karen, but he lives like a Karen, eats what we eat, and works hard—he must have been a Karen born in the wrong race.[4]

The consequence of the beliefs and the conditions with which the Karen live has been (at least in this area) to develop an undifferentiated, unstratified, fluid society, with few self-perpetuating social groupings (even villages may split). In short, although there are individual economic differences and although economic gain is a strong personal motive, there is little or no lasting economic differentiation. Although there are opportunities for individual geographic mobility and economic change, and many changes of fashion in styles of Karen religion, there seems to be no tendency for fundamental socioeconomic transformation of Karen society.

Karen populations have taken an interstitial position (in Lehman's terms) vis-à-vis other village-based agricultural societies, as well as vis-à-vis more powerful, more highly organized societies such as Thai, Shan, and Burman. They have occupied incompletely filled space within ecological niches also occupied by other people. They have been able to retain their identity while doing essentially what the other occupants have been doing, not by specializing or filling a role (like those of Chinese or "Indian" merchants) that fits into the total (national) social system but was not being filled by anyone else. Role differentiation occurs within Karen societies to produce political mediators and economic middlemen, but these are not a characteristically Karen specialty. Whether they will be able to maintain this pattern of interstitial adaptation in the modernizing world and the rapidly changing national society of Thailand is not yet clear.

Extra-Village Relationships

KAREN AND OTHER KAREN

Karen frequently talk of their relations with others in terms of kinship, which may be a reference to the real facts of marriage or descent, may refer to a myth, or may refer to closeness of social relationship regardless of genealogical connections. This clearly applies to relationships between individuals in the same or nearby communities, and may also apply to relationships with people belonging to other ethnic categories. These relationships may be justified on the basis of two kinds of myths: those that roughly correspond to historical ethnographic reality with regard to linguistically related groups (e.g., kinship with Sgaw, Pwo, Taungthu, Kayah, and other "Karens"), and those that have no ethnographic reality (e.g., kinship with Europeans and Americans). Such myths are an important and commonly reiterated portion of Karen oral tradition. They may set the initial conditions for a relationship between individuals from one or another of the categories, and may be referred to as rationalizations or explanations for behavior, but they do not thereafter determine all behavior regardless of individual characteristics or the nature of the particular context of the interaction. A Taungthu trader will be treated by a Sgaw rural villager as a trader or as an old friend, not just as a mythically linked relative, and as such the content of the relationship may be no different than that with Thai, Chinese, or Indian traders. A Sgaw Karen speaker may consider another speaker of the same dialect, regardless of "real" ethnic category, to be more Karen than a Taungthu whose Karen dialect is not mutually intelligible with Sgaw.

With this introduction to some Karen feelings about themselves and others, we can begin to examine systematically relationships between Karen villagers and the world beyond in demographic, territorial, legal-political, and religious-symbolic contexts. We begin with Karen relationships with other Karen villages, which will serve as a basis of comparison for Karen relationships with non-Karen groups.

Karen hamlets and even large villages are not demographically independent. Karen marriages are up to 30 percent village exogamous, the ideal pattern being that the groom moves to the house of his bride's father; eventually he may establish a new household within the bride's father's village. In fact, postmarital residence depends as much on availability of agricultural land resources as on the ideal uxorilocal pattern. Analysis of census materials plus informants' statements on motives for migration suggest that marriage exchanges between villages do not follow any necessary pattern. The governing factors seem to be propinquity plus familiarity and chance of contact between eligible bachelors and maidens, and between their elders who may arrange their marriage. Thus there is a star-shaped pattern of distribution of relatives around each village, binding villages to one another in a far-reaching web of relationships. By virtue of such relationships, an individual who has limited access to land in his own village may claim access to land through relatives in several other villages. The networks are not confined to the distinctive hill and valley environments, but cross from one to the other, although there is net migration from hills to valley (see the map on the facing page).

The impression of complete flexibility in land-use rights that may have been given in the preceding paragraph must be amended. Ordinarily only the resident descendants of founders of a village (or hamlet) may have a *clear* claim on land within that village's territory, but descent need not be unilineal. Claims abandoned by emigrants may sometimes be reasserted if they return to their natal villages.

Aside from claims of free access to swidden land within the village territory, Karen have no necessary attachment to a particular village, and their Karen identity seems in no way to be bound to a place of residence. Generalized or transportable spirits are much more important than localized ones. An apparent exception to these general rules is with respect to the ancestral spirits, which are important in the *awkre* form of animistic religion. Performance of the curing rites of this system requires the presence of all the descendants of the individual for whom the ceremony is being conducted, regardless of whether they reside in the same hamlet or village. Thus distant children must be summoned to participate, and the ceremony may be delayed until they arrive, or if they are too distant, a piece of the sacrificial animal is set aside for them to eat when they return. Although the ceremony requires assembly of the descendants, it is *not their bond to a locality* that is important; *rather it is their attachment to the person* of their parent or grandparent wherever he or she may be. In the hills of Mae Sariang district, many families have abandoned this particular ceremony in part because of the nuisance of summoning distant relatives; others still practice it, and it remains the predominant form in the lowland Karen villages.[5]

The boundaries between Karen village lands in the Mae Sariang hills may be unclear and subject to dispute. In the area with which I am familiar, government intervention has not been requested as it has in Karen-Meo confrontations over land. Resolutions through negotiations between elders or headmen of the villages are sought, and appeals are made to the disputing individuals (who seem not to have solid backing from their villages) to treat each other as relatives.

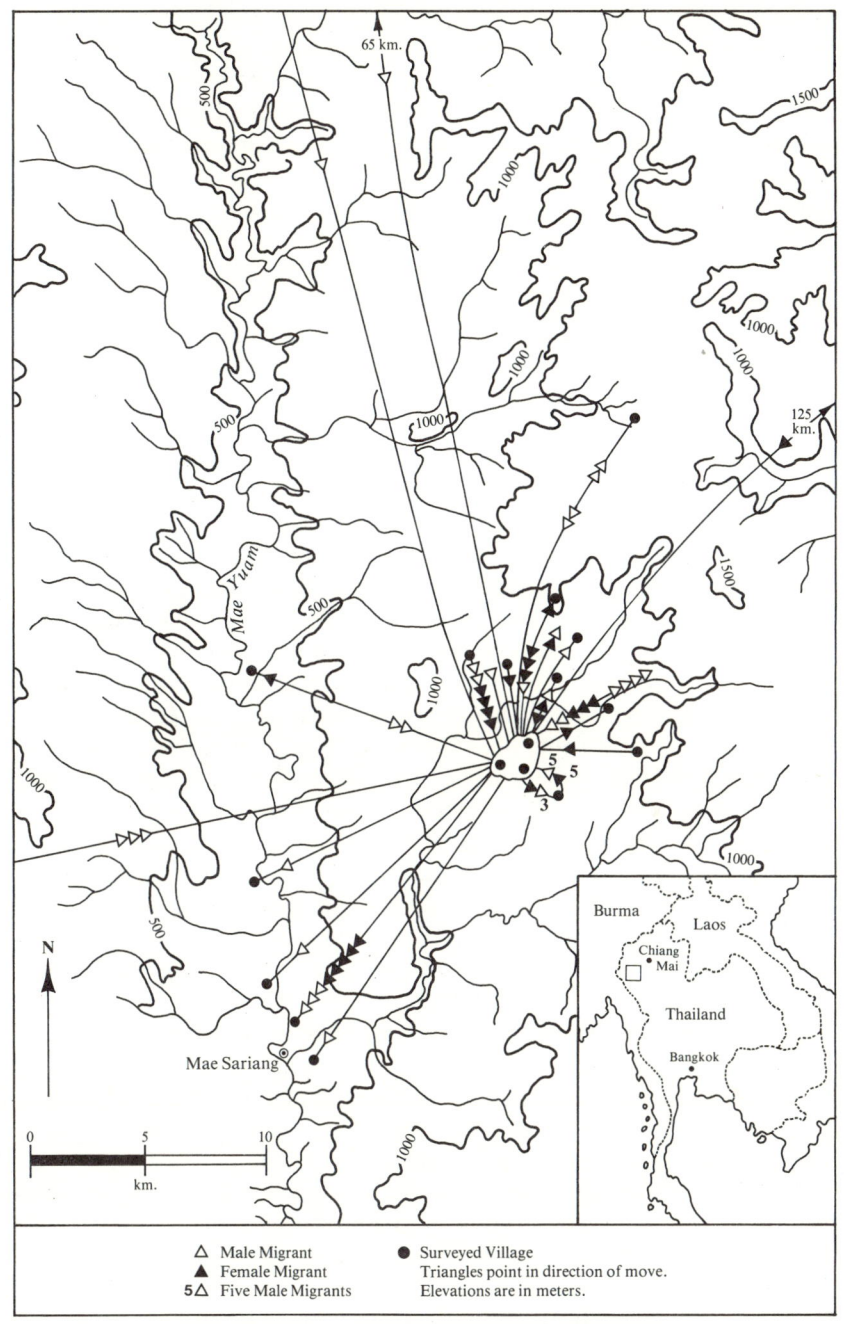

Migration to and from Three Karen Hamlets

Villages in this region seem *not* to act as corporate groups in land disputes with other Karen villages.

Within Thailand (or at least within the area of Mae Sariang district with which I am familiar), there is no legal or political organization of Karen above the level of the village. Headmen or elders may be relatively unsuccessful in governing the behavior of their villagers within the village; they can do little or nothing to enforce their will beyond the limits of the village and are not well able to coordinate activities of two or more villages in items of mutual interest such as burning swiddens.

There is no essential pattern of economic relationship between Karen villages. Although Karen may prefer to deal with other Karen in buying or trading agricultural goods or animals, they will also deal with Thai, Lua', Meo, or whoever happens to be around. Similarly, Karen wage laborers will work for other ethnic groups, but Karen networks of wage-labor recruitment do exist within the lumber business, for which the forest labor is largely Karen. Karen often exchange agricultural labor (e.g., during planting and harvesting and more rarely during weeding) with families or relatives in nearby villages. This is one of the chief opportunities, along with major life-crisis ceremonies (marriages, funerals), for courting between villages.

Special Karen patterns of interaction appear in the symbolic context; it is here, apparently, that one is defined as a Karen. It should be clear at this point that this definition is not in terms of *formal* religion. The Karen recognize many varieties of religious practice as valid for themselves or other Karen. Proper Karenness, then, seems to lie in the observance of proper Karen etiquette, such as the obligation to speak the Karen language, to offer hospitality (in the form of a newly cooked pot of rice and a place to sleep), as well as common knowledge of traditional Karen folk tales and songs. The hospitality should really be offered to *any* visitors; the obligation to speak Karen, and in general not to try to define yourself as superior to another Karen, seems to be the essence of a proper relationship with another Karen, and this applies within villages as well as between them.

Karen folk tales frequently discuss relations with other ethnic categories. One example is a tale regarding the separation of Sgaw Karen from the Taungthu, who speak a related language and are regarded as "brothers." They became estranged after Sgaw, in the absence of the Taungthu, killed a porcupine. When the Taungthu returned and received a share of meat, they complained that their brothers were cheating them: "the animal must have been bigger than an elephant, judging from the size of its hair—why didn't you save any meat for your Taungthu brothers?"

KAREN AND LUA'

Both Lua' and Karen in the Mae Sariang hills may refer to individuals of the other group, or to the other group as a whole, as "relatives." Thereby they express the idea that they have lived alongside each other for so long that they are used to each other; they feel they share the same natural environment (in fact, Karen in this area may refer to themselves as "Karen of Lua' country"). They know they use the same technology with a mutually understandable work organization, that their supernatural environments, if not identical, are largely governed by similar rules and populated by similar beings, and that, as relatively poor, powerless peasants, their patterns of relationships to the rest of the world are essentially the same. In other words, for some purposes, they have a strong feeling of identity and mutual interest and include one another within their group boundaries regardless of the facts of "real" kinship. Of course there are also differences.

Typically, Karen and Lua' upland villages are separate, but we have already indicated this is not always the case. Mates are occasionally chosen from each other's villages; both sexes may move in either direction. The spouse who moves (as an individual) into the other's village usually assumes the ethnic identity of the village into which he or she has moved. This means changing dress style, speaking the language of the host village, and accepting the assumption that children will belong to the ethnic group of the village into which they are born.

In recent generations, cross-ethnic marriage seems to be less frequent than it was three or four generations ago. In the past, it seems likely that Karen sought Lua' wives because of the relative scarcity of Karen who could serve as marriage partners. Lua' villagers report that their grandfathers or great-grandfathers journeyed to the west, perhaps to Burma, to get Karen wives—the reason for this is unclear, although Karen wives may have been less expensive than Lua' wives, for whom a substantial bride price must be paid. Those Lua' who have taken Karen spouses in recent years have been relatively poor and apparently unable to arrange marriage in any other way. Bringing Karen women into Lua' territory may have been the stimulus for Karen settlement in the region.

Another pattern of demographic interchange is cultural transformation of Lua' families who in past generations were unable to make a success in a Lua' village. The families about whom I know moved into Karen villages and became Karen to escape the crushing expenses of animal sacrifices to Lua' spirits in the case of chronic illness. Karen families do not transform themselves into Lua' in similar fashion. Few if any Karen speak Lua' and the idea of becoming *culturally* Lua' (although they recognize real and fictive genealogical ties) seems ludicrous to most Karen. Marriage with Lua' may be accepted, but it definitely is not preferred.

Lua' identity and culture seems much more bound to particular places than does Karen identity; localized ancestral spirits and named individual village guardian spirits are important to them. For a Lua', moving away from the village into which he was born implies much more of a break with his identity than it does for a Karen. Thus Lua' families that move to Karen villages or to the lowlands tend to lose their identity as Lua'. The net effect of this, combined with the more rapid growth rate of the Karen population, has been to make the Karen numerically and territorially dominant in the hills where the Lua' were the only occupants around 150 years ago when the Karen first arrived.

Part of the process by which Karen have acquired land from the Lua' has already been described: in general, swidden land for which rent has once been paid has become Karen land. In recent years, increasing numbers of irrigated fields have been transferred from Lua' to Karen hands as Karen have loaned rice or money and then foreclosed the mortgages when the Lua' land owners were unable to repay the high interest rates. One indication of ethnic differences is that such transactions seem to have been much more common between Lua' and Karen than among the Karen themselves or among the Lua'. The greater ability of Karen to accumulate capital and convert it to beneficial or productive use is also seen in their success in purchasing elephants. Lua' fortunes seem to be declining, while Karen fortunes are increasing. In part this may be because the Lua' have a much more expensive community religious system and more expensive curing systems than the Karen; in part it may be because Karen are less likely than Lua' to spend money for nonproductive goods (like wooden rather than bamboo houses) or for prestige possessions (silver coins for bride price).

The government does not intervene in disputes between upland villages; elders of neighboring Lua' and Karen villages may meet to discuss matters of mutual interest (boundaries of adjacent village swidden lands, timing of swidden fires), but neither can enforce his will on the other. Past history of use, first claimant in the current year, and force of numbers (without violence, which they feel *would* probably bring government intervention, to everyone's detriment) seem the ultimate principles of political action between Lua' and Karen villages, although again there may be a constraint to act as relatives since they consider they have lived alongside one another for such a long time that they are "like" relatives in spite of their ethnic distinctiveness. No reference is made in such discussions to the fact that the people actually may be *real* genealogical relatives because of past intermarriage.

Karen and Lua' will occasionally hire each other as wage workers. Lua' working for Karen ordinarily do things such as levelling irrigated fields, on cash contract; Karen working for Lua' are more likely to be children of very poor families who work for assigned periods assisting in agricultural labor in return for room and board and a small payment in rice. Karen and Lua' may work side-by-side in wage work for Thai employers, for example, in mines. Lowland Karen lumber contractors in Mae Sariang, however, prefer not to hire Lua', but they maintain widespread contracts with Karen.

Karen and Lua' occasionally trade in each other's villages. In the villages with which I am familiar, this may be done with anyone. Although casual visiting and trading are often done with friends, there is no fixed pattern of "trading partners" (*sahai*) as Marlowe has reported for Karen in Chiang Mai province. If vegetables, forest products, fruit, or crafts are involved, trade between nearby villages seems to be largely barter. Usually trade is for cash if large domestic animals are involved. Payment for rice may be in cash or kind. Interest is charged for credit when rice or money is borrowed. There seems to be no standard cross-ethnic differential of interest rates for cross-ethnic loans. Rates seem fixed by supply and demand, reputation of the borrower, and past dealings with the lender. The general rule appears to be: the more distant the person, the higher the interest will be. Immediate relatives occasionally loan without charging interest, but this is rarely if ever done between individuals from different villages, regardless of ethnic identity.

Karen and Lua' recognize clearly the religious and symbolic differences between their cultures and point to these as well as basic personality differences as the things that set them apart from one another. Karen believe that Lua have "sharp ears" and Karen have "thick ears": Lua' are clever at learning new languages, and many of them in the Mae Sariang hills speak Karen as well as Northern Thai and Lua'. In contrast, few hill Karen can speak intelligible Northern Thai, and those who speak it do so grudgingly. Karen do not use Northern Thai as a joking and courting language as do the Lua'. Almost no hill Karen know any Lua'; they prefer to have their Lua' friends speak with them in Karen. Lua' appear to view language as a means of expanding their interpersonal relations while Karen view language as a mark of their identity. Valley Karen, however, have expressed pride in their ability to speak Thai and think this is proper because they are living in Thailand.

Lua' consider Karen to be dirty, and Karen think the same of Lua'. Nonetheless they visit one another and eat and drink together on occasion. Lua', who normally invite anyone who is going by to "come, eat," feel the Karen are a bit too forward in accepting the invitation whenever they are in the village, and unless they are particularly close friends avoid ceremonies such as weddings in Karen villages to avoid being unwanted guests.

Karen consider Lua' to be much better organized than they, for example, in the matter of cooperating in fighting forest fires that threaten swidden lands used by the village.

Karen and Lua' agree that the Lua' have many more spirits than do the Karen; both agree that the Karen are favored in this and both refer to the widely known tale in northern Thailand that describes how the Northern Thai lost almost all of their spirits by carrying them in a loosely woven basket, the Karen allowed many of their spirits to escape from the top of an uncovered basket, but the Lua' carried their spirits in a tightly woven, tightly tied, and covered basket. To this day the Lua' must feed a much greater number and variety of spirits than either Northern Thai or Karen. The story also suggests the characterization of the Lua' as careful, meticulous, and almost compulsive, and the Karen as somewhat sloppy, careless, and lazy. Systematic behavior differences along these lines are observed and recognized by both groups: Lua' swiddens are neatly bounded by rows of sorghum on their sides, and fenced top and bottom with carefully trimmed and bound horizontal and vertical poles; Karen swiddens have sorghum planted almost anywhere; fences are often made of brush piled against a crude framework. Lua' build sturdy stiles or ladders where main trails cross the fields and fences must be erected to restrain buffaloes; Karen often leave it to each traveller to get through the fields as best he can.

The social structure of religion is another contrast between Lua' and Karen. Lua' frequently have village-wide ceremonies, but this is much more rare among Karen whose ceremonies are almost always for individuals or families or perhaps sets of related families within the hamlet.[6] Karen recognize clearly that they do not organize themselves for religious activities in the same degree as do the Lua'; but Karen self-deprecation in reporting these facts is often followed immediately by a remark indicating how pitiful the Lua' are because they have to be bothered with so many expensive rituals.

The overall patterns of curing rituals, which involve similar processes of divination to detect the spirit cause of an illness, summoning the spirit, feeding it an animal sacrifice, and urging it to leave its victim, are common between Lua' and Karen, and specialists of either ethnic group may be sought by the other in case of an intractable illness. Religious consultation between Lua' and Karen is not sought by either group for village-wide ceremonies, nor for ceremonies directed at spirits believed to be peculiar to either group.

In sum, hill Karen in Mae Sariang district align themselves with their Lua' neighbors as fellow rural minority people having mutual interests in a common social and natural environment, and thus they feel "like relatives." They compete for land within a framework set by Thai society, and they differentiate themselves by virtue of language and cultural differences recognized by both. They recognize the possibility of change from one to the other identity, but neither thinks this is ordinarily a desirable change.

KAREN, NORTHERN THAI, AND THAI

Karen consider themselves more distinct from Northern Thai and Thai than from Lua'. There is very little demographic interchange between Karen and Northern Thai or Thai populations. Unlike Lua', Karen who move to town do not do so with the understanding that they or their children or grandchildren will become Thai. There are few Karen who pass as Thai, and those who show tendencies to act like Thai are often deprecated by their friends and neighbors. When intermarriage, which is very rare, takes place between Thai and Karen, it tends to follow the Thai pattern and is likely to be less stable than Karen marriages with Karen. Marriages between Karen women and Northern Thai men are usually thought to be short-lived and thus potentially disgraceful for the Karen, who do not believe in divorce. Lowland Karen have told me that one reason they want their daughters to marry at an early age is to be sure they are married before they have a chance to have an affair with one of the Northern Thai who may be wandering through the village.[7]

There are major contrasts between traditional Northern Thai and contemporary Thai governmental categorizations of Karen and other rural minorities. One illustration of the importance of this difference is with regard to changes in land-ownership customs already alluded to. Karen are not the masters of their own destiny in the sense of controlling access to land resources essential to their livelihood. Both Karen and Lua', and to some extent rural Northern Thai, remember the tributary or feudal relations between themselves and the Northern Thai princes. At least for the Lua' there is historical evidence that the relationship was conceived of as a direct one between leaders of Lua' communities and representatives of the prince. One aspect of this relationship was the possibility of simultaneous recognition of the rights of several claimants to benefits from the land, including individual-use owners, the community (or community leaders), and the prince, roughly paralleled by symbolic recognition of ancestral and other kinds of spirit owners.

In the nineteenth century, the prince recognized land-tenure claims of communities and evidently considered Lua' claims as prior (and superior) to Karen claims. Thus Lua' communities collected rent from Karen using land customarily claimed by Lua' communities, and both Lua' and Karen communities paid tribute to the prince, while Lua' and Karen individuals paid at least symbolic tribute to their community leaders and to the spirit owners of the land. The prince apparently reserved the right to settle disputes between communities but granted to village leaders the right to settle disputes within their villages.

The Thai central government has a different theory of land ownership based on the premise that ultimate ownership of all land in the kingdom resides with the king (i.e., the state) and use rights, including rights of development, sale, extraction of minerals and timber, and so on, are granted to individuals (not communities) for certain classes of land and for certain uses. This theory was applied to northern Thailand, along with the extension of central government power beginning around 1900, and has profoundly affected relationships between communities and ethnic groups, especially in the hills, since communal land claims and traditional patterns of use for swiddening are no longer recognized as legitimate. Thus Lua' communities can no longer be the landlords of Karen communities, and there is no longer legal or political recourse for violations of customary use of boundaries. In cases of dispute over swidden land in the hills, when government authorities have been asked to intervene (especially vis-à-vis Meo), they reportedly have taken the position that "hill people should settle those disputes among themselves." Apparently all claims to swidden land, no matter how well established historically, are regarded as equally illegitimate, and all hill people are regarded as equivalent before the law; hill communities no longer have a direct contractual relationship with the paramount political authority.

Karen generally still recognize the prior claims of Lua' to swidden land Lua' farmers have used recently, and tend to offer payment for use rights to such land, but they consider long-unused land as a relatively free good and may attempt to establish claims to it by cutting trees first, asking permission or offering payment only if challenged. Rather than pay the village leaders, the new user pays the previous user directly; thus, de facto, land-use rights are becoming individualized, although Lua' still retain a stronger sense of community swidden-land ownership than do the Karen.

Karen in Mae Sariang district clearly recognize Thai hegemony over the territory of Thailand and accept the legitimacy of paying taxes for use of the land.[8] In the hills, their contact with the Thai with regard to land has been limited to tax and irrigated-land registration requirements and, occasionally, the claim of "eminent domain" over subsurface minerals or for highway construction. Another area of contact and conflict of interests with somewhat similar effects is the government claim to ownership of and control over the disposition of teak and other valuable tree species.[9] As already indicated, the government has not recognized and will not enforce traditional claims to land except land used as house or village sites or as irrigated fields.[10] This places all upland agricultural areas in jeopardy. To date this has been a relatively minor factor, but as roads are built, more upland areas are opened for homesteading and settlement by Thai or for mining or commercial use. Thus, swidden rights are being increasingly challenged. Undoubtedly this type of conflict will increase in the future and will color and complicate Thai-Karen relationships.

Thai laws and Karen customs with regard to land use in the lowlands are much more congruent. Irrigated fields are real property, titles to which can be and are obtained by Karen as well as by Northern Thai. In general, Karen have managed to maintain control of fields in the lowlands on which they were the original developers in spite of an increasing Northern Thai population, except in special circumstances, for example, where highway construction has passed through the fields or where construction has brought workers to reside in the Karen villages.

Karen living in rural villages recognize they live under Thai law, but Thai law has touched them at relatively few points. Karen born in Thailand are considered locally to be citizens of Thailand. Because Karen have lived in Thailand for many generations, and because many of them have irrigated fields, they have *traditionally* been considered to be "Thai people" as contrasted to "hill people" such as the Meo, Yao, Akha, and Lahu who are more recent arrivals and who are often opium growers. The Border Patrol Police may give special attention to some Karen villages as they do to "hill people" villages, but this was done originally not because the Karen were considered to be recent migrants and thus non-Thai, but rather because they lived in the hills and border regions where normal lowland administrative and social services had been slow to reach. As suggested below, the ethnic categorization of Thai is changing and Karen at present may find themselves placed in the hill people category regardless of past patterns of administrative relationships and present patterns of behavior. In recent years, a stereotype of hill people has seemed to be developing among some Thai, based on presumed characteristics of the Meo. The Meo have gotten by far the most publicity of all hill minority groups, and their presumed attributes dominate the stereotypes applied to hill people much as the presumed characteristics of the Plains Indians set the stereotype for all Indians in the United States. An equation tends to be drawn in which "hill people" equals Meo, that is, recently immigrant, opium-growing, nomadic swiddeners who are possibly Communist. In the future, these presumed attributes (generally inapplicable to Karen) may increasingly affect Thai-Karen relations to the extent that Karen are considered by Thai to be hill people rather than people of Thailand or traditional tributaries of the Northern Thai princes. Eventually this may result in increased feelings by Karen of consciousness of kind with other upland minority peoples with whom they have little in common other than being placed in the same category by Thai. This process may be reinforced by sending Karen children to special schools for hill people, rather than building schools in their own villages or sending them to the nearest Thai schools.

Formal procedures for proof of citizenship (birth certification in Thailand, etc.) or for immigration (passports, visas, and the slow process of naturalization) seem not to be required for Karen farmers who live near the Burma border, and who may have been born on either side and may move back and forth to their fields. Such requirements are enforced more vigorously in the cases of Karen political refugees from Burma, who tend to be better educated town dwellers, or for Karen, regardless of their birthplace, who wish to become civil servants.

Because of the closing of the Burma border due to political activities on the Burma side, travel across the border has diminished. This in turn has greatly restricted trading and wage-labor opportunities that used to be important to people on the Thai side. But enough contact remains to increase the awareness among the Karen in the border regions of the differences of political and economic realities in Burma and Thailand, comparisons the Karen feel favor the Thai side.

Legal requirements may prove to be barriers or hurdles to Karen seeking to enter into the mainstream of the urbanizing Thai social and economic system. Karen feel that they may be discriminated against, especially at the local level, by overly zealous enforcement of civil service requirements for proper birth registration. Names and dates of birth of Karen born in hill villages were often incorrectly recorded in district office records in the early days of registration, and this or some other similar legal argument may hold up the appointments of Karen as teachers. It seems clear that the regulations are not designed to discriminate against Karen as such (they are more likely to have been directed against Chinese or other foreigners). Their application against Karen may be a result of the fact that almost all educated Karen are Christians or of the unofficial position (also applied to Thai of Chinese descent) that civil service jobs require Thai ethnic identification, not just citizenship.

Such problems do not occur in the normal life of agricultural villagers. For them, the chief mediator of government relations is the village headman, usually chosen by the villagers and recognized by the district officer. Headmen are paid a small salary to attend monthly meetings at the district office, to carry announcements back to the villages, to urge villagers to conform to government registration and tax rules, and to act as an official host for touring government officials. Official headmen seem to be a variable lot. Often they have been chosen because they know enough Thai to deal with government officials, rather than because they are the true leaders of their village. Some occupy neither a religious office nor a position of real authority and thus feel very uncomfortable.

The Karen seem to have worked out a variety of compromises in adapting to Thai laws they view as onerous. For example, each household that brews liquor is supposed to pay an annual license fee. Often, however, the headman or the heads of each "lineage" will pay the fee, perhaps in recognition of both their own and the government's position of authority. In this case, they calculate that the brewing (for religious purposes) is done in their honor. The religious head is supposed to get the first drink of the liquor from each household in any ceremony, after a little has been offered to the spirits. In the lowlands, perhaps only the religious official will take out a license to brew liquor, and he brews only the amount necessary for a small portion of the ceremony, while his followers simply buy liquor from a government-licensed distillery.[11] Regulations against slaughtering buffaloes may be avoided if the buffalo has died a natural death, so the "accidental" death of a buffalo will be reported to the headman, whose word, as a governmental official, would not be doubted. This sort of accommodation allows life to proceed in the village without much disturbance from government regulations, unless an individual headman sees benefit in government programs and is strong enough to convince his villagers to go along with the scheme.

Karen are considered sufficiently important in local politics that their votes are actively sought in government elections. During the

1969 elections of province representatives to the national parliament, election workers were active in both lowland and hill Karen villages, a process that has occurred in previous elections. Candidates or their backers distributed campaign posters, some of which were translated into Karen, and made political speeches (in Thai).

Karen attitudes toward the election process ranged from interest to cynicism, much as one would find in an American election, and with many of the same rationales given. As one informant told me:

> The headman tells you to vote for N. . . . The headman would naturally say vote for N because he works lumber with him—but that's for the headman's good, not mine, so why should I vote for N? . . . Big elephant owners who have connections with N's company, like T [a Karen] and X—he's a Thai who marks trees for the company—came up to tell us how to vote. How can that Thai guy ever get the votes of the Karen? He is so domineering, he shouts so. . . . The politicians come tell us to vote for them or their friends. "If you are in need," they say, "blankets, clothing, and rice will be given to you." Those big elephant owners [Karen] who wanted their man elected as representative, some got 100 baht, some got 200 for voting, but we didn't get anything. . . . Everything they said amounted to the same thing. But after they're elected, where do you see them? You never see them again. So you just put your vote in the box of someone else.

The quotation implies that there is no Karen voting bloc. It also suggests that concern about personal gain takes precedence over the ethnic identity of the candidate or his spokesman, and that the response to the spokesman depends on the perception of his personal qualities, not his ethnic identity. Despite their activity in politics, the economic context seems to be the most important one in defining relationships between Karen and Northern Thai or Thai.

Economic relationships include sale and purchase of agricultural commodities and manufactured goods, wage labor, rental of services and land, credit relationships, and contractual arrangements. Karen in both the hills and the valley have generally been subsistence farmers. They have produced small surpluses of rice, pigs, and other domestic animals, which they have sold or traded either in the market or to purchasers who come looking for a particular item. The tradition of trading partners, mentioned by Marlowe for Karen-Northern Thai relations in Chiang Mai province (Marlowe 1969 and below, pp. 183–186), seems not to have developed in Mae Sariang district. Karen are liable to buy and sell or perhaps even borrow with particular traders in town whom they have gotten to know and trust, but the relationship does not go beyond this. These are not large-scale commercial operations, and they have not to date involved much mortgaging of crops in advance of harvest, as has been the case in the Chiang Mai area.

The category of "Thai trader" is not a precise one, and a distinction might more properly be made between town and market people (who may be ethnically Northern Thai, Shan, Taungthu, Chinese, or "Indian") and rural Karen. The relationships between these categories does not seem to be a function of the ethnic categories involved, but is more a function of the ecological and economic situation. The traders usually have some advantage in the situation, since commodities brought to town for sale will almost never be returned home. Transportation costs are too high (in terms of time and potential loss). The producer must sell his goods, and there are limits to his ability to bargain in this situation. The balance of advantages seems not to be entirely with the merchants, however, and gouging is not institutionalized as has been reported, for example, in Indian-Ladino relations in Central America. Rice prices are reasonably standard, pigs are usually readily salable, and neither has to be sold to a trader, since they can be sold directly to town-dwelling consumers for cash.

In this immediate area, most trade in town is done with cash, rather than with credit, although credit sales seem to be increasing and have been reported to be extensive in the Mae La Noi subdistrict. Such credit as is extended to Karen farmers in Mae Sariang town is on a small scale, usually based on the good reputation and long-standing relationship between trader and villager, and does not involve mortgaging fields (Karen fields in Mae La Noi subdistrict have been reported mortgaged and lost to merchants). Mortgaging arrangements seem more likely to be *among* Karen and Lua', with the credit going in either direction.

Karen have for several generations participated in wage-labor (or cash-contract labor) arrangements with town-dwelling employers. The chief industry in which Karen in Mae Sariang district are employed is lumbering. Most legal lumbering is done by very large (national-scale) companies that are the successful bidders for government permits to cut the lumber in particular areas. These companies in turn negotiate with subcontractors who agree to a specific job for a specific price, usually to cut and deliver the logs to a particular point where they can be picked up for processing.

Subcontractors are usually Karen and employ Karen workers almost exclusively. A few of these operate on a large scale, recruiting labor and elephants from many different villages over a fifty-kilometer radius. The business is becoming increasingly complicated as it becomes increasingly regulated. Successful bidding on a subcontract requires intimate knowledge of regulations and close estimates of the time and labor needed to do the job. A few hill-dwelling Karen are sufficiently experienced to bid on subcontracts (or sub-subcontracts), employing their own elephants and recruiting their own labor, but for the most part the hill Karen work for lowland-dwelling Karen subcontractors. Thus most of them are shielded from direct contact with their ultimate non-Karen employers.

Relationships between subcontractors and their non-Karen employers seem to be relatively stable. The Karen are not at a disadvantage in this context, since they possess the elephants and the skills necessary for this kind of work. No machines have yet been developed to replace elephants in dragging logs out of the woods to points where they can be loaded for road transport.

Work in lumbering conflicts in part with the subsistence agricultural cycle (work with elephants must be done in the rainy and cool seasons, the time of weeding and harvesting), but loss of agricultural labor is apparently compensated for by gain of cash income and lack of drain on the village family rice supply during the season when lumbermen are working in the woods.

Although there has been considerable construction work undertaken in Mae Sariang in the past decade or so, the Karen do not appear to have benefited from the employment opportunities created by construction. In part, this is a function of the concentration of construction in Mae Sariang town where new roads, sewers, a water system, schools, a courthouse, and housing for government officials have been built. In part, it may be a function of the close relationship between politics and construction in Mae Sariang. Construction projects are almost entirely initiated by some segment of the government. In 1969 the chief highway contractor was elected to be the provincial representative to the national parliament. As we have seen, Karen are only marginal to Thai politics; they may suffer from their lack of political cohesion in the allocation of jobs in the politically dominated construction sector of the economy.

Rural Karen have been employed in increasing numbers as casual laborers in agricultural jobs offered by non-Karen, mainly Northern Thai and Thai, employers. Many of those who take such jobs are desperately poor, recent migrants from the hills; some are opium addicts, willing to work for just enough money to keep them supplied with food and drugs. With the increase of population in the hills, the decrease in productivity of hill agriculture, and the increase in number of addicts, the supply of casual labor has increased radically, and the price of day labor has declined (from 10–12 baht to as low as 5–6 baht per day in 1970), despite the increase in employment opportunities in Mae Sariang town since the late 1960s. Again, this seems not to be a function of institutionalized discrimination by non-Karen against Karen, but instead results from an increasing oversupply of untrained labor. Temporary or permanent Karen migrants from the hills seem willing to take jobs elsewhere, but do not have the money for transportation or the knowledge or connections to know where to seek employment.

In general, the economic position of rural people seems to be declining relative to that of city people. Commodity prices paid to the farmers and agricultural wages have remained relatively stable and low (in part as a result of deliberate government policy to keep the rice price low), while opportunities and salaries for skilled labor have increased rapidly. Thailand is participating in the "consumer revolution," and manufactured goods of great variety are penetrating even the most remote rural markets. Karen are like other farmers in experiencing a decline in economic position compared to urban peoples; their poor position has little or nothing to do with the fact they are Karen.

Karen are most apt to phrase their comments concerning relationships with Northern Thai and Thai in symbolic terms, although we have seen that these relationships are usually determined in other contexts. Karen mythology reflects a long-term recognition of the existence of other ethnic groups with higher levels of sociopolitical integration than the Karen. Karen usually attribute their low relative position in the hierarchy to the foolishness or laziness of the Karen, for example, in the well-known Golden Book myth, which indicates that Karen lost the opportunity to get literacy, knowledge, and power in general by neglect of their duties.[12] Thai do not figure in these stories nearly so much as do Burmans or whites, but the symbolic association of wealth, power, and literacy seems to have been transferred to the Thai as rulers of the locality within which the Mae Sariang Karen now live.

In the context of religion, Karen recognize that Buddhism is the religion of the Thai (or, in Burma, of the Burmans), and although Karen also may practice Buddhism, those who do so apparently consciously consider that they are adding something to traditional Karen religion. Lowland Karen in Mae Sariang district, for example, say that they mix the two traditions. They feed ancestral and other spirits, and they also go to the Buddhist temple, honor the Buddhist monks, and make merit. Many seem to have a fairly clear idea of the major tenets of Buddhism, some of them enter the Buddhist order, and many of them participate in the important annual Buddhist ceremonies. Some of the lowland Karen villages have built pagodas that are visited by Thai monks, but few villages have resident monks.*

Hill Karen recognize the concept of merit, but few consider themselves Buddhists; they may attend a ceremony at a *wat* or seek the aid of a priest, but usually this is for some specific purpose (making merit for a dead relative, curing opium addiction, etc.). In doing so, they understand they are entering a non-Karen world, but they seek to do so where there is a Karen, or Karen-speaking, monk.

Only sporadic efforts have been made by the lowland Thai Buddhist officials to missionize in the Karen hill villages. A few temples were built in hill villages before World War II, but they were soon abandoned and have not been revived in the more recent missionary programs, sponsored by the Bangkok hierarchy, which have been implemented to a limited extent in this district. Occasionally Thai priests pass through Karen hill villages and assist in *khọ*-sending ceremonies (for removal of malevolent spirits). Aside from the few missionary monks, none stay in Karen villages for any length of time.†

Khruba Khao (now deceased), a defrocked Buddhist priest, apparently of Northern Thai descent, proclaimed himself as the Buddhist priest of Karen and Lua' and was accepted as such by the hill people and by many of the valley Karen. For many years, he organized (together with his Northern Thai or Thai managers or assistants) merit-making occasions, associated with building temples and other good works, and summoned Karen and Lua' villagers to attend. His proclamations made it clear that these were occasions for the Karen and Lua' people, not for the Northern Thai, so even the tutelage Karen got in Buddhism on these occasions was done in a social setting that removed them from much direct contact with Thai.

Karen-Thai social boundaries may be taught to and reinforced in Karen children by using Thai as bogeymen ("the Thai will take you away if you don't stop crying"). Such expressions seem not to be directed specifically against Thai because they are Thai. They are used to frighten children, and any handy outsider (anthropologist, policeman, Thai trader) may be labeled as the potential abductor. Informants tell me that in Burma, Karen parents threaten their chil-

---

*Editor's Note: In 1968 only one Karen village in Mae Sariang had a permanently established temple-monastery (*wat*). One other village had a *cetiya* (pagoda) at which a non-Karen monk was a permanent resident. In Mae Sariang town, the abbot of one temple monastery was a (Pwo) Karen.

†*Editor's Note:* For a description of the Buddhist missionary program among the tribal people of Thailand, including information on the program as carried out among Karen in Mae Sariang district, see Keyes (1971).

dren with abduction by Burman Buddhist priests. Similarly, Thai parents may threaten their children with abduction by Karen.

Language seems to be the most important item by which Karen set themselves apart from Thai. Some of them, especially valley Karen, learn to speak Thai, which they recognize they need in dealing with government officials, and which may be unavoidable in the market. Nonetheless, they are clear that the proper language for Karen to speak is Karen, and that when one Karen speaks to another in Thai he must be doing so only to assert his superiority. People who speak Karen, who live with Karen, and who do not attempt by their actions and attitudes to place themselves above Karen may be Karen; people who do not speak Karen cannot be Karen regardless of who their parents are.[13]

KAREN AND MEO

A description of Karen relations with Meo and with foreigners, two groups with which they have much more limited contexts of contact, will illustrate further the nature and the dynamics of Karen ethnicity.

Karen-Meo contact in Mae Sariang district has been relatively recent. Karen have little accurate information about Meo and appear not to have incorporated the Meo into their mythology. Meo first founded settlements in the district in about 1960 (Geddes 1970, 1976) and have established only two major villages to date. The focus of the Karen-Meo relationship seems largely commercial, based on the Meo opium economy. In their southward movement, some Meo have found suitable soil for cultivation of opium in areas occupied by Karen. These Meo have sometimes offered to purchase cultivation rights from the villages within whose territory the suitable soil was located, and sometimes have merely occupied and taken control of land customarily reserved for watershed protection. Karen reactions have been mixed: sometimes they have sold out, sometimes they have attempted to resist, and sometimes they have appealed to Thai authorities for assistance in protecting traditional village land claims.

It is clearly understood by Karen that Meo are able to move into Karen territory because Meo are more powerful, and because territorial rights in the hills are not legally enforced. Karen attempting to protect their land have been shot, and, although police have investigated, the Meo remain. Thai officials to whom appeals have been made for protection of traditional boundaries and swidden land-use patterns are reported to have said the Meo have just as much right to cultivate in the hills as anyone else.

There is little demographic interchange between Karen and Meo. There is no intermarriage, but a few Karen children may have been adopted by Meo (no specific cases in Mae Sariang are known to me, but this follows the pattern reported for Meo elsewhere). Karen servants sometimes become attached to Meo families; often these are opium addicts who become hangers-on in Meo villages, hoping to earn enough to support their habit. Meo recruit Karen and Lua' laborers to work in their opium fields, paying either in cash or in opium. The effects are sometimes to addict the workers, with the result that they may become detached from their home villages. Meo never work for Karen employers.

Meo villagers in this area depend on the existence of Karen and Lua' villages nearby for a supply of agricultural labor and for rice. They do not grow sufficient rice here for their own subsistence, as they are reported to do elsewhere (e.g., Keen 1978).

Thus the overall pattern of relationship between Karen and Meo is one of mutual dependency, but the balance of power is with the Meo, given the present administrative situation in the hills in which traditional use rights to land are not protected by the governmental authorities.

We have suggested that there is now a tendency for some Thai to lump Karen in the same category with Meo. This seems to foretell a general change in the Thai posture with respect to the Karen, and implies that the Karen will find themselves placed in the general "hill tribe" category by the Thai regardless of past patterns of relationship.

KAREN AND FOREIGNERS*

The importance of Karen-foreigner relationships far outweighs the number of foreigners involved. It lies in the contexts of self-conception of the Karen and in the changing context of relationship between Karen and Thai. Foreigners are considered to be the younger brothers of Karen in Karen mythology, but they are thought to be blessed with the ability to read and write, and thus have the key to knowledge, material wealth, and power. This belief has been used to justify the actions of foreign missionaries in teaching literacy together with Christian religion (the Word from the Golden Book), but it also has established a conceptual association between white men (missionaries) and power and wealth. In Burma it was precisely the appearance of an alliance of Karen and foreigners that widened the

---

Editor's Note: "Foreigner" is here used as a gloss for the Sgaw Karen word *koloa*, which mainly designates white Europeans or Americans.

split between Karen and Burmans along the lines of Karen, Christian, foreigner vs. Burman, Buddhist, "native." Of course not all Karen in Burma are Christians, and it is not just Christian Karen who have participated in the Karen independence movements. Nonetheless, the presumption of sympathy between the foreign missionaries and Karen is one that may influence the relationship between Thai and Karen much as it colors the relationship between Burmans and Karen.

Until very recently, when a few public schools have been opened in Karen villages, missionaries have been the source of most education (or at least have assisted in the education) for Karen in Thailand. This means that almost all educated Karen in Thailand are Christian. Missionaries have also been the major source of medical care, economic development, and welfare assistance to Karen. Such services seem clearly identified in the minds of Karen and probably in the minds of Thai with foreign missionaries. Thus it seems possible that Karen using the missionary's path to upward mobility will thereby separate themselves from Thai society. This tendency may be supported by the existing feeling that Karen do not want to lose their identity as Karen, and by the missionary interest in maintaining their investment in Karen literacy and Karen identity. For the missionaries, Thai equals Buddhist; Karen who "become Thai" are likely to fall away from the church as well.

I speak here of what appear to be structural oppositions within the system, not necessarily conscious motivations on the parts of the actors or even the legal realities of the situation. Religious toleration is the law of the land. Thai laws have been designed to make the Christian churches Thai churches. Church property is held by Thai citizens, the formal organization is staffed by Thai citizens, and foreigners are allowed by immigration laws to understand that their position in Thailand may not be secure. Nonetheless, the identification of foreign interests with Christian Karen seems likely to remain.

Conclusions

The descriptions above suggest several conclusions in regard to Karen identity, group, and category in northern Thailand. There is a set of people who, under some circumstances, apply a term meaning "Karen" to themselves and to others who would similarly label themselves. There is a consciousness of kind among these people, although such identity labels might not be consistently applied to them by others with whom they are in contact. The set of people calling themselves Karen corresponds fairly well to a group sharing some basic values, beliefs, and behavioral characteristics, but within which there are major behavioral differences. There is no overriding social organization within the group. Given the diversity of Karen and their lack of supra-village organization, Karen systems of categorizing ethnic groups, including their own, are probably not uniform, and under many circumstances do not correspond to the categorizations of Thai who lump them with other hill people.

Under what conditions is Karen identity invoked by people who identify themselves as Karen? Seemingly in situations where there is something to be explained or rationalized in terms of recognized or presumed differences between two ethnic categories. Ordinarily Karen believe they should look after the physical well-being of their children to the greatest extent possible, but a father rejects for his infant daughter the advantages of growing up in the valley and explains it by reference to Karen identity. Ordinarily Karen are not Lua', but in some circumstances (e.g., vis-à-vis the Meo, in regard to land-use customs, in assisting at curing ceremonies, or in drinking at a ritual), they consider themselves to be sufficiently "like relatives" to act in concert. Ordinarily Karen are not Thai, but a Thai may be a Karen if he lives, eats, and works like a Karen, and, although Karen are expected to speak Karen, a Karen may speak Thai because he is after all a citizen of Thailand. Buddhism is the religion of the Thai (and the Burmans), but a Karen may wish to make merit in the Thai Buddhist way to gain some reward or benefit. Karen characterize themselves as lazy and careless and believe the white man is powerful and wise, but white men cannot work as hard as Karen and would have difficulty in subsisting on the meager Karen diet of rice and chilis.

The shifting of ethnic references to suit contexts is illustrated by my conversation with an adolescent girl in a Karen swidden when I noticed her chewing on a piece of red soil.

"Why are you eating soil?"

"Because I am Lua'."

"What do you mean by that? I thought you and your parents were Karen."

"We are, but I have Lua' relatives, and Lua' women eat soil like medicine, and so do I."

"Do Karen women do that?"

"No, only Lua' women."[14]

"Would you like to marry a Lua' boy?"

"No!"

"Why not?"

"They're too dirty, and I don't want to get married!"

Apparently a series of values or ideals may be invoked to explain behavior or establish identity with an individual or group, but the identity need not be consistent from one instant to the next.

Patterns of Karen-non-Karen relations seem to be determined both by the Karen's self-conception of what it means to be a Karen and the value in being a Karen, and by the conditions that govern the relationship, instead of by any stereotypes or systematic discrimination related to ethnic identity. Karen deprecate themselves with respect to other ethnic groups, and yet they consider themselves to be superior to them, an opposition repeated in most folk tales or myths that mention any other ethnic group plus the commentary they inevitably provoke. The Thai social system is relatively open, and many members of other ethnic groups (especially Lua') have been absorbed in a process going on for hundreds of years. Despite the permeability of the boundaries of Thai society, few Karen have made the change. Instead they have frequently opted for paths to modernity that have maintained their separate identity, even while trying to increase their participation in Thai institutions. Perhaps following a pattern first established in Burma in the early 1800s, they have used mission-related schools as a means of obtaining the education required for entry into modern urban occupations. Even in their participation in the Thai-dominated economic system, only a few Karen interact with the Thai managers. Most have their relations with their Thai employers mediated by the few Karen subcontractors. Instead of participating directly in Thai Buddhism, many have used Khruba Khao as their mediator for entering into Buddhist religious practices.

I have implied that the reason for this pattern may be the prior development of the Karen-Burman relationship in Burma. The Burmans were apparently much less tolerant of cultural differences, much more militant in their conflicts, and much more exclusivistic in restricting absorption of non-Burmans than have been the Thai. Beyond this, there was a much clearer and longer "divide and rule" policy by which the British colonialists allied themselves with Karen and other minorities in opposition to the Burmans. Karen in Thailand may be reacting to what they presume are the intentions of the dominant society based on the history of Karen-Burman relations.

Unlike Lua', whose myths relate that they once were superior to all others, Karen have few such illusions; still, they accept the "nation of nationalities" model rather than the "melting pot" model as the ideal national structure. They will accept Lua' neighbors and even Lua' ancestry, but not Lua' identity; they will accept Thai dominance, but reject Thai identity. For Karen, ethnic identity is cultural and social rather than biological or racial. They have reached this conclusion even after having been in contact with people of markedly different cultural *and* physical characteristics, such as white foreigners. People may be relatives even though they are not really Karen; people may become Karen even though they are not genetically Karen. In many contexts, Karen maintain the ability to act toward non-Karen as individuals, not in terms of ethnic categories or stereotypes, but the overall pattern of behavior in all the varieties of Karen social structure in Thailand seems well adapted to maintaining Karen identity within their interstitial position.

Contrary to Barth's assertion that members of an ethnic group are all "playing the same game," there are many aspects to the identity of any person and they are called forth under different conditions. The ethnic aspect of the individual's identity and even the definition of the ethnic aspect will be an important determinant of behavior vis-à-vis some other individual only in certain situations. In addition to being a Karen (in contrast to being Lua' or Thai), a man is also an individual governing his actions in response to the actions of anyone else; he is a member of a particular household and village, in contrast to all other households or villages; he has relatives, in contrast to people he considers not to be relatives, and he lives in Thailand, in contrast to some other nation.

In defined contexts, Karen have characteristic patterns of ethnic categorization, characteristic attitudes toward other ethnic groups, and consistent patterns of self-identification. Many of the conditions of relationships within Karen groups and between ethnic categories are now being set in terms of national economic, demographic, and political developments, which are beyond the level of attitudes and which are insensitive to Karen control. It seems likely these conditions will determine the ethnic categorizations invoked in northern Thailand and the patterns of Karen-non-Karen relations to an increasing extent in the future.

A common, and probably generally inaccurate, stereotype of nonliterate societies is that they have homogeneous cultures and standard patterns of relationships with other societies. The descriptions of Karen cultural variations and the varieties of relationships between Karen and non-Karen in this chapter should suggest the heterogeneity of such relationships, especially in the past. Present trends suggest that with modernization, there may be a homogenization of the patterns of relationship, especially as regards Karen vis-à-vis Thai society. Large, centralized bureaucratic systems seem unable to cope with local cultural and ecological variations except through use of standardized, uniform policies. As these policies are applied uniformly throughout the nation, old patterns of relationship between communities established in a period of decentralized administration are being obliterated.

Such institutions as hill-tribe schools (bringing together Meo, Yao, Karen, Lua', Lahu, Akha, and other minority-group students), the multigroup tribal villages on display for tourists, and, perhaps, the Tribal Research Centre are examples of governmental institutions and their commercial analogs of the centralized, homogenizing sort, even if the avowed intention of such institutions is to document and preserve ethnic variations. With such institutions, hill tribes are set apart from Thai. By virtue of this categorization, hill tribes, which may have little in common other than their distinction from the Thai, may be treated in a relatively uniform fashion, despite the fact that many Thai people may occupy the same environment (foothills and hills) and use similar technologies (swidden agriculture). Within this situation, it is likely that the presumed characteristics of the most notorious of the hill tribes will be attributed to all peoples who are encompassed by the same label. This was the history of American Indian affairs and seems likely to be the future of hill-tribe affairs in Thailand. In the Thai context, this means that presumed characteristics of the Meo (often incorrect) will be applied to such very different people as Karen.

Acknowledgments

This chapter is a revised version of a paper presented at a symposium entitled "A Pivotal or Marginal People: The Place of the Karens in Southeast Asia," held at the Annual Meeting of the Association for Asian Studies, Washington, D.C., 29 March 1971. It presents data collected primarily in Mae Sariang district, Mae Hong Son province, northwestern Thailand, between 1963 and 1970. The research was supported by the National Science Foundation, National Institute of General Medical Sciences, National Geographic Society, Princeton University, and the University of Washington. Field research in Thailand was sponsored by the National Research Council of Thailand. The research could not have proceeded without the aid of many individuals, especially the Karen villagers of Laykawkey. Their help and hospitality is hereby gratefully acknowledged.

Notes

1. See Peter Kunstadter (1967, 1969A, 1969B, 1970A, 1970B, 1972, 1978, 1979) for ethnographic and demographic background. See David Marlowe (1969) for a description of ethnic relations of Karen in Chiang Mai province.

2. Census figures do not distinguish Karen from Thai. This estimate is based on the figures from the 1960 census of Mae Hong Son province, Table 7, "Ability of Population 5 Years and Over to Speak Thai." The estimate assumes that most of the non-Thai speakers are Karen; that the numerous hill-dwelling Karen are less likely to have been counted than valley-dwelling Thai speakers; and that the Shan and Northern Thai (who may not speak standard Central Thai) were probably counted as Thai speakers in the census. The actual proportion of Karen is probably higher than this estimate based on language ability, because Karen appear to be reproducing faster than other segments of the population and thus would have grown more rapidly since the 1960 census, and also because their rapid growth implies a larger proportion of under-five-year-olds than the other segments of the population.

3. Peter Hinton reports that where he worked, Pwo Karen moving into the southern part of Mae Sariang district in the mid-1800s found the Lua' had withdrawn from sufficient land to allow space for Pwo Karen settlement without payment of tithes, and that there was little intermarriage between Lua' and Pwo Karen. My informants from the same area report Pwo Karen there still honor Lua' ancestral spirits, although not all of them still recognize the source of these spirits.

4. The point, that in acting like a Karen, one is a Karen—as in acting like a Thai, one is a Thai—is further elaborated upon in Marlowe's essay in this volume.

5. Marlowe (personal communication) has found evidence that indicates that *awkre* religion predominates in west-central Chiang Mai province, immediately to the east of Mae Sariang district. His historical and land-tenure information suggests he is dealing with an older and more stable settlement pattern than that found in the Mae Sariang district hills. The unpopularity of *awkre* in these hills may be due to the recent widespread dispersal of the Karen populations in the Mae Sariang hills, which has left relatives widely scattered.

6. This statement refers to upland Karen in Mae Sariang district at the present time. Lowland Karen at present have communal Buddhist ceremonies, for example, for New Year. Both upland and lowland Karen villages in Mae Sariang are reported to have had communal men's houses (*blaw*) and associated communal ceremonies in the past (cf. Iijima 1970 and Iijima in this volume).

7. A major exception known to me to the general rule of little or no change in ethnic identity from Karen to Northern Thai is that of several small villages in the Chiang Mai valley. These villages, located near Sanpatong district, Chiang Mai province, were settled several generations ago by Karen prisoners of war from Burma. Their descendants have now become Thai, to the extent of having given up Karen language, religion, and dress style.

8. In response to a question about the history of taxation, the headman of a lowland Karen village in Mae Sariang district told me that his parents had told him of sending specially woven blankets to the prince of Chiang Mai, via a Northern Thai official in Mae Sariang. Then he added, "We Karen used to govern and collect dues from everyone. Our administration was so oppressive and the taxes were so heavy that the tumplines of the carrying baskets rang like guitar strings when the people were bringing in their tribute. We were so oppressive that everyone got disgusted and chased us out. Now we pay taxes to the Thai, just like everyone else."

9. In this there is no difference in Thai policy vis-à-vis upland Thai or upland Karen.

10. According to Thai law, upland areas are classified as "waste" land. On this land, the state reserves for itself rights to all lumber and minerals, which can be exploited only by concession. Upland land can also be claimed by private developers who use it for irrigated agriculture or for house sites, but swidden cultivation is not an acceptable or legitimate use of such land (Sophon Ratanakorn 1978). Thus, the law clearly favors commercial agriculture, industrial development, and sophisticated lowlanders over hill dwellers, regardless of their ethnic identity.

11. According to Karen custom, the spirits must be the first to partake of the liquor, and payment of tax on distilling was interpreted by some as giving the government a portion before giving liquor to the spirits. Communal ceremonies at the men's house (*blaw*) are reported to have died out but not because of this cultural conflict or because of complications in obtaining licenses to brew the necessary liquor. The explanation given by lowland Karen for stopping the communal ceremonies was that the free flow of liquor on these occasions attracted Thai, and drunken fights occasionally resulted.

12. A local version of this tale is as follows: "In olden days God was visiting His two sons, the White Man and the Karen. He asked the Karen to take Him home, and the Karen replied, 'I am too busy—I have to weed my fields,' so God left a leather book for the Karen on a tree stump. He asked the White Man to take Him home. The White Man went with his Father and returned with the Golden Book. For his faithfulness the White Man got all the skills and knowledge of the Golden Book. The Karen brother was too dumb. He even forgot to collect the leather book from the tree stump. Finally when he remembered it, it had fallen on the ground and the hens had gone after it, scratching it so badly he could not read it."

13. A Karen woman living in Mae Sariang town says "people tell me I should speak Thai with my younger children so they will learn it. I prefer to speak Karen with them. They understand Northern Thai because they hear so much of it. They will learn Central Thai when they start school. That's soon enough."

14. So far as I could determine, her ethnographic and genealogical information was correct.

In the Mosaic: The Cognitive and Structural Aspects of Karen-Other Relationships

David H. Marlowe

In many senses, mainland Southeast Asia has been a forcing ground of sociological theory, a laboratory of human social relations that serves as both the generator and graveyard of the most fruitful models designed to account for the structuring of human social behavior. One need only note the central role played by this area in the work of Claude Lévi-Strauss (1949), E. R. Leach (1954, 1960), and J. S. Furnivall (1956) to see the truth of such an assertion. One may also add that there is much that is contradictory and confused when one tries to abstract a common sociology or social anthropology from the works of all three. Most particularly the "Burma" of Leach and the "Burma" of Furnivall appear to be entities that loom up in an awesome disparity from a commonly named ground but that possess few other common characteristics. It is not my purpose to attempt to harmonize these disparities but rather to use them and to offer qualifications to both in attempting to draw a more extended model of the structural and cognitive bases of certain key relationships between Karen and other peoples in the region. It is my contention that "social reality" can be understood only when it is dealt with as a stratified set of sets of possible and existentially real relationships coexisting in social space and differentially evoked in time. Furthermore, this reality is one that undergoes constant transformations applicable to both the individual and the group.

In the light of these contentions I propose a status for the Karen as "central." By central, as I hope to make clear, I do not mean centrality to the political, social, economic, or military domains that have risen and fallen in Southeast Asia—the universe of princeling, dominion, and walled city. I do aver that they are central to the understanding of those wider social processes and relationships that have characterized the region. For the wide geographic area of "Burma," the Karen have occupied a set of medial positions between domains, between political dominions, and between the ecological niches of the "hill" and the "valley." They serve as a defining point for a hierarchy of relationships that without them is seemingly a set of polar opposites, and they serve as well to demonstrate the relative nature of social identity and the process of transformation of identity.

It has been usual for anthropological commentators to describe the social topography of mainland Southeast Asia by two mutually exclusive sets, those of the "hills" and the "valleys." The basic distinctions between these groups are usually considered to be: modes of subsistence, that is, swidden farming vs. wet-rice culture; religion, animist vs. Buddhist; kinship structure, unilineal vs. bilateral systems; and polity, the decentralized, essentially egalitarian, "tribal" systems vs. the "centralized" city-state or nation-state. Valley people are found in large, homogeneous blocks and hill people are characterized as forming a diversified ethnic or cultural mosaic (Burling 1965; Leach 1960). Robbins Burling quite flatly asserts that "until the last century [the hill people] have never had more than tenuous political ties with the plains" (Burling 1965: 2). Leach, on the other hand, has quite correctly characterized the long-standing high degree of political, if not cultural, interconnectedness between the two (Leach 1954, 1960). In addition to the fundamental differences between hill and valley based on the occupation of differing ecological niches, Leach also proposes a fundamental metacultural differentiation between the two, describing the hills as following a basically Sinitic cultural pattern and the plains, a fundamentally Indian pattern (Leach 1960).

Burling describes a pattern of group organization in the hills that is essentially one of long-term boundaries existing between discrete groups but points out that such boundaries are permeable, rather than absolute, at least in the diffusion of cultural traits and attributes. Leach has described the relativistic, dynamic, and transformational nature of categories and groups for the Kachin in *Political Systems of*

High Burma (Leach 1954). In this work, he explored both the mechanisms involved in the sociological allocation of groups to ethnic categories other than their "culturally" defined ones, for example, "Lisu" or "Chinese" to Kachin, and the transformation of groups from one category to another on the basis of economic and ecological criteria, that is, the transformation of Kachin to Shan and vice versa. Leach's implicit model is, however, that of a two-category system in which a hill tribesman may be transformed into a valley dweller and vice versa with no significant medial steps.

It is difficult to find a construct that aptly describes the structure of group relationships in "Burma." Viewing it in the context of the twentieth-century colonial situation, Furnivall coined the term *plural society* to describe the system in Burma wherein a coherent polity and integrated society could be maintained out of disparate culturally and socially differentiated units. As Furnivall describes the plural society:

> It is . . . a medley [of peoples], for they mix but do not combine. Each group holds by its own religion, its own culture and language, its own ideas and ways. As individuals they meet, but only in the market place, in buying and selling. There is a plural society, with different sections of the community living side by side, but separately, within the same political unit. Even in the economic sphere there is a division of labor along the racial lines. Natives, Chinese, Indians and Europeans all have different functions, and within each major group sub sections have particular occupations. There is, as it were, a caste system but without the religious basis that incorporates caste in social life as in India [Furnivall 1956: 304–5].

The essential features that characterize the plural society are diversity, cleavage, conflict, dissensus, and political domination of the whole by one of its parts, more often than not a colonial minority group. Leo Kuper and M. G. Smith have further refined the concept of pluralism as "the differential incorporation of two or more collectivities within the same society. It has been argued that such differential incorporation generally presumes significant antecedent differences or institutions, culture, and ethnicity between the collectivities concerned; and further, that it restricts assimilations by preserving or promoting the institutional distinctness of these structurally segregated collectivities" (1969: 91). It is readily apparent that the "plural" model of Furnivall, M. G. Smith, Kuper (Furnivall 1956; Kuper and Smith 1969; Smith 1960, 1965), and others, and the relativistic transformational model presented by Leach, represent different models of the social order, particularly as applied to the Indo-Chinese situation. In part, these are differences involving historical change, that is, traditional vs. colonial relationships (see Leach 1960), and differences in domain, the "center" vs. the "frontier." In part, they involve the criteria for and the construction of social categories (Leach 1954).

F. K. Lehman, dealing with the Chin, takes note of the relativistic and transformational nature of social or ethnic categories in Burma and cautions against the application to Southeast Asia of Western constructs of the "group" and its relationships (Lehman 1967A). Even during the height of the colonial era, participants in the Burmese plural system had conflicting views of the nature of the relationships between ethnic categories. In testimony given before the Burma Reforms Committee on the question of communal representation, for example, a Burmese district magistrate testified that "I do not think that the Karens should have communal representation, because the Karens as far as I know are just like the Burmans in their mode of living." He went on to note, in response to a question from Dr. San C. Po, a noted Christian Karen nationalist leader, that he did favor communal representation for Indians and Anglo-Indians because "These people are after all alien to this country; the Karens are our own brothers, they belong to this country and it will be highly desirable to put them in the general electorate. . . ." (Burma Reforms Committee 1922: 22). An Indian spokesman supporting communal representation for the Indian community asserted that he objected to the Karen having communal representation since "There is no very serious difference between the Burman and the Karen" (Burma Reforms Committee 1922: 126). At the same time, numerous Karen Christians protested that the Karen *did* form a separate community.

At the end of this chapter, we will return to the model of a plural society and evaluate its applicability to the Karen and their neighbors. In the intervening sections, the transformational model of Leach will form a basis for much of the analysis. We can now begin to examine Karen-other relationships by asking: what does it mean to say that one is a Karen and what are the implications of being a Karen? The material presented here is based primarily on research among the Karen of Chiang Mai province in northern Thailand.

The Behavioral Basis of Ethnic Categorical Usage

In the context of Southeast Asia, the important diacriticals related to group classification are almost entirely behavioral, that is, language, dress, ritual, and so forth. Physical and ascriptive differences exist and are used and seen as such, but they exist primarily in terms of the diversity among groups. Given such a basis of group definition, it follows that individuals can move freely from one category to another depending upon the behaviors exhibited at any given time. There is no question of "passing" or "deception," no social sense of "being other than what one is" when such transformations are effected. If I behave like an X than I am an X and will be treated like an X rather than as a Y masquerading as an X.

This understanding of human relations presupposes a recognition of the common humanity—a fundamental sameness—of all men. In Southeast Asia, there is widespread ideological underpinning for this understanding in the legends and myths of the creation of "men" following the coming into being of the founding genitor and genitrix. For example, there is a Chin tale, given by Lehman, which is much like the most widespread origin myth of the Karen:

> All mankind, they say, is descended from a woman called Hlinyu who laid 101 eggs, from the last laid of which sprang the Chins. Hlinyu loved the youngest best, but he had gone away, and before she found him again the whole world except bleak mountain ranges had been partitioned out among her children. So the first Chin man got the hills as compensation [Lehman 1963: 32].

The Karen myth I recorded in Chiang Mai in 1967 went as follows:

> At the beginning there were two people. The grandparents did not tell me who they were or where they came from, only that there were two people who were the father and mother. One day, in the mud of their one paddy field they found 101 crabs and ate them. Then it followed that first woman gave birth to 101 children. Each of these children had his own language. They were the Karen, the Lua', the Northern Thai, the Shan, the Burmese, and so on. That is how it was at the beginning. Now I have always heard it said by my parents and in the words of the grandparents that all people everywhere were from the same parents. They are all children of the same parents [*daw bu vhwe ti sa*].

Human equivalence, the commonality and sameness of men, and their common origin are here expressed in the deepest and most profound symbolic arena of unity known to Karen—their status as children of the same parents. Despite behavioral differences among men, this ideological position is part of the foundation of the Karen system of viewing the social world. Shway Yoe (Scott) quotes a Burmese Karen tale of the creation that accounts for Karen oppression by the Burmese:

> The Karens account for their wrongs in the following way. When Yuwa created the world he took three handfuls of earth and threw them round him. From one sprang the Burmans, from another the Karens, and from the third the Kalas, the foreigners. The Karens were very talkative and made more noise than all the others, and so the creator believed that there were too many of them, and he threw another half handful to the Burmans, who thus gained such a supremacy that they soon overcame the Karens and have oppressed them ever since [Shway Yoe 1963: 443].

Another variation on the same theme is given by A. R. MacMahon, who relates the following Sgaw Karen version of origins:

> In ancient times there were seven brothers, whose parents divided a bamboo bucket into seven pieces and giving a piece to each of them told them that they would become the representatives of different peoples and clans, and after having been estranged from each other for a season, would eventually come together again, and living in peace and friendship, would bring with them their portions of the bucket, and restore the latter to its original shape [MacMahon 1876].

The co-equal status we share as men as well as our coevality and interrelatedness to each other in time and place are further emphasized by the Karen myths that cover that most critical event, the nonacquisition of writing on the part of the Karen as opposed to its acquisition by their neighbors. Since the Karen define themselves as "children of the same parents" with the other groups in their environment—in strict point of fact, the named groups that are usually cited are the lowland groups—the absence of writing, that *sine qua non* of the diacriticals of the "civilized" or the "sown," is of major importance to them. It is one of those factors that bear upon the ultimate position of the Karen as a category which is part of the "sown," but not *of* the sown in their status as Karen. The following myth was also gathered from Sgaw in Chiang Mai:

> Once upon a time the Great Lord called all the people to him, the Thai, the Burman, the Shan, the Karen, the European to come and get the book of learning which he was to grant them in order that they might be able to read and write. The Karen at this time were busy cutting grass in the foothills in order to feed the water buffaloes of all the people and so said to the others, the Shan, the Thai, the Burman, the European, "We must cut the grass to feed the water buffaloes, you go first and we will go get it later."
> The others went and got their books of learning and then came

back. The Karen were still at work cutting grass on the hill. They called out to the Karen, "Come get your book." The Karen said, "Brothers, we have not yet finished cutting enough grass to feed the water buffaloes. Will one of you get it for us?" Some of the others went back to the place where the Great Lord was distributing the books and got it. They brought the Karen their book. The Karen were still busy cutting the grass on the side of the hill and had not yet cut enough so they could come down and get the book. They called out and said, "Put it in a tree." The others put the book in a tree for them. In a while it fell out and it was eaten by the animals. That is why we do not read or write.

The lack of literacy is one of the commoner themes of Sgaw Karen songs, particularly the *utah* or courting songs. Thus in Chiang Mai, a boy or girl who could read, taught either in the Thai schools or by an itinerant Karen Christian, would respond to the *utah* of one without knowledge with the following taunting song as a put-down (all translations by the author):

> The heel of the foot is colored red [referring to dawn].
> Write a letter to the Priest.
> The heel of the foot is colored green [referring to evening].
> Write a letter to the Abbot.

Another self-deprecating song goes:

> Book, little chicken scratches in the earth, chicken scratches.
> Can't read, can't read at all.
> Book, little chicken scratches, chicken scratches.
> Can't read, can't read at all.

Other songs are touched with longing, as the following:

> Book, you hang on a long hook
> From the roof top, from the tip of a tree.
> Let the finger touch the paper.
> It looks but can't see.
> Book, you hang on a long hook
> In the middle of the heart.
> I let the finger touch you
> But nothing comes out.
> You live far on the way of the tree.
> You know books of both large and small kinds.
> You live far, you who live under the tree.
> You know books of the large road and the small road.

Yet others, like the following, are rejecting of books and the ways that literacy implies:

> Oh yellowest leaves of the tree.
> I don't know books and I don't believe in them.
> Carry on the shoulder the whitest leaves of the tree.
> I don't know books and I don't believe you.

And finally some, like this last song quoted, are extremely specific to the Karen-other situation:

> The book goes down to the trunk of the tree.
> Man, if not a Khon Myang, cannot read it.
> The book goes down the tree trunk.
> For a man, if not a Khon Muang, to read is not easy here.

Critical as it is, literacy or its lack is the product of an event. It is not that the Karen are different or unneedful of literacy. They, like the others, the lowlanders of the "sown," were equally entitled to it and offered it as equals. They did not achieve it, in part fortuitously, in part because of a status that decreed they had to finish cutting the grass on the hills that would feed the water buffaloes belonging both to themselves and to all the others. The "Great Lord" did not single them out to be nonliterate, nor did he grant literacy to the Thai, the Shan, the Burmans, as a special mark of their inherent status. The event specified no fundamental differences between the Karen and the others. Only the different behaviors of each subsequent to the event specified the differences.

The equivalence as "children of the same parents," that is, the fundamental sameness that lies behind the masks of nominative differences in which men and groups are clothed, is not just expressed in myth and legend. It is a norm of perception. Man is a natural occurrence in a natural world. Being such, men cannot fundamentally differ from each other save in nominative ways. Man is born, perhaps vitalized by the spirit of an ancestor, perhaps not, but he is part of the natural order of things; he has an age and he dies. "What is a man and why does he die?" Said a Sgaw villager in answer to my question, "He is flesh and water, he is no different in that than a buffalo, an elephant, a lizard, or a tiger. If you are flesh and water, you die. I do not know why. There is no reason that I know of, but you must die like the elephant or the dog." Another put it this way, "We die because we are alive. We are the same as a tree, we are born, we grow old and we die as a tree or animal does. Men are the same thing.

Me, you, the Thai, the others, we are all made of the same thing, we are all made the same way."

Since we are the same, it is not surprising that Karen villagers see human disabilities as operating within the boundary of this commonality. The invariable response to my question about whether Karen or Thai get sick in the same way, from the same sources, was an inevitable "exactly the same." I found no villager in any of the places in which I worked who could conceive of an alternative pattern. Yet in terms of external appearances, this, perhaps, should not have been so. Illness is central to the Sgaw Karen ritual and religious system. It is the signal system through which the spirits, the *da muxha* of places, and the spirits of the ancestors, the *sii kho muu xha*, signify either their displeasure or their desire to be fed. In a survey of 505 Karen households carried out in 1967, 75 percent claimed that the *sii kho muu xha* had brought them one or more illnesses during the previous year. In response to questioning about this, one villager said to me, "Look, we and the Khon Muang get sick for exactly the same reasons for there is no difference between us. We think that the spirits bring disease. If they bring these diseases to us then they bring them to the Khon Muang exactly the same way. They have the same illnesses. We serve the spirits so we don't have to use a lot of medicine. The Khon Muang don't serve the spirits so that's why they have so many medicines and why they use a lot of medicine." His thoughts were underlined by the response I got from the ritual leader of the village to the equivalent set of questions. He looked at me as if I, the questioner, were more than a little dotty for asking about such self-evident things. "We get sick exactly the same," he said. "We are both the same blood and bone. We are all children of the same parents. We may call the spirit by different names, for some people are Karen and some are Khon Muang; the illnesses are identical. The reasons are the same thing."

The common identity of the substantive is underscored by the acquired nature of the nominative. I might cite a young Karen father who turned to me as I played with his infant son and stated, "You know, if you were to take my baby to America with you he would be an American. If he were to come back when he was an adult, he would speak and think just like you. He would know nothing of the Karen." Equally, in the course of many discussions about inappropriate or deviant behavior, I can rarely recall a "genetic" argument invoked against a wrongdoer. People were assumed to behave "the way they did" because it was the way they had been taught to behave. Parents and kinsmen had failed to teach them the right ways to behave. They had fallen in with bad companions and it was assumed that no matter how exemplary the parents and the upbringing, one would perforce do the sorts of things that one's associates did. Young opium addicts were not "bad people" but people who had been taught "bad ways" by others—Meo, Haw, or Karen opium addicts. When a middle-aged Karen villager fantasized about living in the city, he did not phrase it in terms of wishing he had been born an urbanite but rather in terms of the lack of mastery and the potential for acquisition of urban skills:

"I don't like to go to town; I don't know how to. I wouldn't know how to earn rice in a town."

Me: "Do you think that's just the way the Karen people are, that they can't live in a town?"

"Oh, no. You have to learn how to live in a town. If there were a school here I'd go to it, I think, to learn. I think sometimes I'd like to learn how to live in a town just to see if I could" (Marlowe 1969: 61).

In the scheme of things as seen by Karen, "behavior" and "category" form an inseparable dyad. If one's behavior is appropriate to a category, one is not subject to the rules of the category of origin. That is, a Karen who behaves as a Thai within a Thai setting transgresses no rules for Karen when doing so. Acts that would be outrageous amongst Karen but appropriate to the other setting are considered legitimate behavior since they take place within the Thai category. One's parents may deplore such behavior but no feasible punishment is entailed within the Karen cultural unit nor can any Karen furies be invoked against the perpetrator. The appropriateness of the behavior is always relative to the category in which it is enacted and the category is never assumed to set standards that substantively constrain the individual as a Karen when he is nominatively a Thai—such substantive constraints in that situation must be Thai. My favorite example of the acceptance of this view is one presented by a former research assistant of mine. This young man, who was raised as a Karen Baptist and had become a moderately successful prize fighter, smuggler, and swinger, had been married four times and had innumerable mistresses. Two of the few truly rigorous rules of "Karendom," no matter what religious persuasion one be, specify that one marries once and forever, or at least until the death of one partner, and that the only legitimate sexual intercourse that can take place must take place within the framework of that one indissoluble marital union. My assistant noted that all of his wives had been either Northern Thai or Thai as had all of his friends and lovers. I once asked why he had never married a Karen, and I received a heartfelt response that on the surface might have appeared improbable, given his espousal of something very much akin to the *"Playboy* philosophy."

"Look," he said, "as long as I marry Thai girls and sleep with Thai girls it's all right [he married and divorced them at the district registry office, not in church]. I can divorce them or leave them. It doesn't matter. Now one day when I am ready to settle down I will marry a Karen girl in church. But you must understand, when I do that, that's it. I can't ever get divorced, or leave her, or play around again. That's why I keep away from Karen girls. Someday I will marry one and that will be it, but not yet. I'm not ready for it yet. . . ."

This same fundamental organization in terms of the dyad of behavior and category or domain is also illustrated in a conversation I had with a headman's wife whose father had been a Khon Muang. We had been discussing her kin and had been going through and listing her known kinsmen of her mother's side, categorizing them in terms of sex, residence, and relationship. When we came to her father's people, she began with the phrase *dze phiinawngana ba,* "my kinsmen of my father," in which the word for "kinsmen" was Northern Thai, not Karen. She proceeded to list the kinsmen, using their Northern Thai kinship titles.

Perhaps the best assertion of the behavior-domain dyad is one that was given to me in the course of characterizing a Sgaw settlement's relationships with the supernatural. The villagers in this settlement, in addition to keeping the full round of services for the spirits great and small, were also members of the congregation of the local Buddhist temple. One day, as we walked along together on our way to a merit-making ceremony, I asked the headman if there were any conflicts between serving the spirits and serving the Lord Buddha. "No," he said, "they are both for the same thing, to ensure that there is food and clothing and a life for all of us." "But," I went on, "do the spirits ever show anger at your serving the Lord Buddha as well as serving them or does the Lord Buddha ever show anger at your serving the spirits?" He looked at me uncomprehendingly, smiled in embarrassment, and scratched his head. "Ever anger? No. The Buddha eats sweets and flowers and the spirits eat flesh and rice. That is the difference between them. How could there be anger?" A hillman put it more pithily when he said, "If you are smart in the ways of the spirits you do not have to go to make merit at the temple. If you are not smart in serving the spirits then you must go to the temple to ensure those things."

This model, which links behavior to category, is not unique to the Karen; rather, we see it emergent in them as part of the general mode of cognition of the groups with whom they form a common set. In contemporary Thailand, for example, one often hears the statement, "His parents are Chinese—but he is a Thai." What is meant is that if an individual's behaviors and associates are Thai, he is *prima facie* a part of the Thai category.[1] On the local level, one hears these kinds of assertions almost continuously from Khon Mụang rice farmers who live contiguously to Karen settlements. The Khon Mụang farmer whose paddy rest house was just behind the Karen village in which I resided simply asserted that "These *yang* are just like us; they are paddy farmers just like us; we are the same people." The *acan wat*, the secular leader of a nearby Buddhist temple, said, "The only difference between the *yang* who live in this village and the Khon Mụang who live in my village are the spirits. The names we call them are different. Other than that we are exactly the same. The same people." Theodore Stern has reported an almost identical situation regarding the Pwo Karen of Kanchanaburi (Stern 1968C: 8).

Karen Social Structure in Comparison to Northern Thai

In the above description, we have seen that members of groups such as Karen and Khon Mụang share fundamental constructs, with the possibility of transformation from membership in any one group within a set to any other group based on the co-identity of the "substance" of the members of the various groups. According to this model, any *a* from category *A* can be transformed into a *b* from category *B* if he is able to exhibit the behaviors appropriate to category *B*. There is an important caveat that must be entered here: Although individual members of the set are equivalent and can be equivalently transformed from one domain to another and subsets of the categories are also equivalent on the local level, the categories are not. History and ecology have established the basic rules for determining the categories, and although transformations take place, at times in a seemingly egalitarian manner, these basic rules are hierarchical. At moments in time, certain categories can and do subsume other categories that cannot in turn subsume them within the same historical duration. We will return to this latter.

The primary term that Sgaw Karen use to describe those whom they consider to be their structural equivalents is the phrase "people of one place." *People of one place* are those who are seen to share enough commonalities with Karen so they conceive of having the same kinds of interactions and relationships with them as they would or could have with members of other Karen villages. The latter are often also referred to with the same term. To the Sgaw Karen of Chiang Mai, a person of the same place would be a resident of a neighboring Khon Mụang, Thai Lue, Shan, or Lua' village, that is, a farmer of fixed abode and little political power. These are the people with whom Karen often have regular social, personal, and commercial ties. Karen work jointly on the irrigation ditches with them, exchange labor with them, invite them and are invited to weddings and funerals, and Karen bless or are blessed by them during participation in ritual events such as the Buddhist New Year and the Karen postharvest festival. When Karen in Chiang Mai speak of marriage possibilities other than with other Karen, the people they mention are Khon Muang, Thai Lue, Shan, and Lua' who live in nearby communities.

Given this assertion of commonality, what then of cultural differences and cultural boundaries? Are these not basic barriers to such a system of cognition and such possibilities of alliance? The answer, I believe, is an only modestly qualified no.

Certainly the ability to operate in a "correct" fashion with other than one's own kind is facilitated by the commonalities: a common ecology and economic system; a common agricultural technology and diet; universal common concerns about weather, crops, children, illness, death, and politics; and also, importantly, a common *lingua franca*, Northern Thai, through which all exchanges can be made. Polycultural knowing, however, goes beyond the bounds of the obvious or of those things that are the same within both domains. Karen know and exhibit the customary behaviors of their neighbors when they are with them. The money tree made by the Karen villagers for a local temple festival will be interchangeable with those made by their Thai neighbors. Their behavior at the bathing of the priest or the Buddha images or at a Khon Muang funeral is indistinguishable, save for the costumes of the participants, from that of the Khon Muang. Even if one is not skilled, one lives with a perpetual awareness of what the differences are and of what they signify. In 1965, at a wedding in a village in western Chiang Mai, the brother of the bride gave a comparatively sophisticated performance of Thai sword dancing. A year later in Cọm Thọng, one of my friends performed a devastating set of caricatures of Khon Muang, Lua', Meo, and Pwo Karen eating, interspersed with remarkably accurate bits of dialogue and miming of their behavior. The group of Karen on the porch with me laughed at his accuracy and applauded his humor.[2]

With only a few minor variations, the Karen kinship system is structurally identical to those of the Tai-speaking people—Khon Muang, Lao, Thai, Shan, etc.—and those of the Burmese and Mon. The Sgaw Karen kinship system is a bilateral one, basically of Eskimo type (Murdock 1949: 223), with special attention paid to the differentiation of juniors and seniors in the lines of descent. No unilineal descent groups are to be found among the Sgaw; this distinguishes them from the majority of hill peoples. The only descent group of consequence is a three-generation-deep, bilateral one, the group for which exogamy and marital regulations are defined. This comprises those who share enough of the common substance of the ancestral spirits, the *sii kho muu xha,* to be "truly" related kin.

The basic structures of the Karen and Khon Mμang systems follow identical rules; ascending and descending generational fusion with junior-senior line differentiation is the critical element. As with the Karen, the Khon Mμang system is extended, as a system of address, in the same intergenerational manner to nonkin, using age differentiation as its criterion for categorical inclusion. Both Karen and Khon Mμang exhibit the same kinds of patterns of behavior in any given transaction that requires the use of these terms. An operational knowledge of one such structure enables the individual to transform his system into its homologue with ease. The nominative aspects of the systems differ, but structurally, for each ego and alter, the relationships and expectations are very much the same.

In many of their particulars, the rules for the governance of marriage are equally similar; so, too, is the role of the ancestral or house spirit, the *sii kho muu kha* of the Sgaw Karen and the *phi punya* of the Khon Mμang. The marital regulations of the Sgaw Karen, at least the jural or nominally prescriptive ones, can be summed up as follows:

1. Marriage is forbidden between first cousins.
2. Marriage is forbidden between second cousins if the woman is from a line of descent senior to that of the man.
3. Marriages between parent's sibling and parent's child are forbidden.
4. More than one marriage by the children of one family with those of another is forbidden; in this context the "family" is considered to extend to first cousins.

Khon Mμang, according to Gertrude W. Marlowe (G. W. Marlowe 1965–68), do not express these rules as prescriptions as the Karen do; but they justify comparable behavior on the basis of the shame or embarrassment that would follow if one behaved differently, or with statements that something would "not be right" or would be "terrible" to imagine. For both Karen and Khon Mμang, marriage is, at least to some degree, governed by the ancestral spirits of the family. In the case of the Sgaw Karen, the *sii kho muu xha* is the controlling authority, the guardian of the jural rules, and the dispenser of punishment for their infringement. In the case of the Khon Mμang, according to Gertrude W. Marlowe, the *phi punya* who are the generalized ancestors inherited through the matriline have as their primary function the regulation of sexual intercourse and they will visit illness upon the family for acts of illicit sexual intercourse or if they are not informed of a marriage within the family. In fact, the formal wedding ceremony in a Khon Mụang village consists of informing the *phi punya* of the houses of both bride and groom of the marriage (G. W. Marlowe 1965–68). Although there are differences in emphasis, the structural elements relating to these spirits are remarkably similar. An equivalent case can be made for other significant structural orderings of each group's universe, for example, patterns of postmarital residence, the hierarchy and responsibilities of non-Buddhist supernatural deities, and so forth.[3]

The freedom of intermarriage between Karen and others has impressed many contemporary observers of the Karen. In one village in which I worked, five of sixteen households had members or children who had been married to either Khon Mụang or Khamu migrant miners (a number of Khamu have settled in Karen areas in Mae Caem district as well) and six remembered ancestors who were not Karen. In another village, four households had children married to Khon Mụang and four remembered ancestors who were not Karen. The ancestors in all these cases were either fathers or grandfathers. The structure of the *sii kho muu xha* terminates genealogical history beyond three ascending generations, and all ancestors beyond that are simply assumed to be Karen. Several non-Karen men who had married Karen wives and settled in their wives' villages for a long period were simply assumed to be Karen. It was pointed out to me that A had been a Khon Mụang but was now a real Karen (*bu kun yo no no*). He spoke Karen, served the various "lords" properly, and served the *au xhre* to the *sii kho muu xha* exactly as any other Karen would feed ancestral spirits. In other cases, Karen men who had married Khon Mụang women had become typical Khon Mụang rice farmers, pillars of the temple congregation, and members of all the usual associations. Residence in most cases was determined by land; a significant marital bias of both Khon Mụang and Karen is to "go to where the land is." In the Karen case, the "rightness" of the transformations of Khon Mụang to Karen and Karen to Khon Mụang is defined by the ideological assertion that "you follow the path of the woman." That is, the house is the woman's domain and one does things in her manner. I did observe several cases in which Khon Mụang wives came to live in Karen villages with their Karen husbands; they tended to conform to Karen behaviors.

My findings, together with those of Stern in Sangkhlaburi, Kanchanaburi province,[4] give one pause then in dealing with the assertion of earlier commentators that Karen rarely intermarried. I consider that the number of affinal ties has in most cases been governed by a series of practical factors rather than by ideological considerations about the nature of intergroup relationships.

Karen-Other Group Relationships

Thus far we have focused upon the cognitive and structural processes within the social categories at hand, attending primarily to the common ideological and structural features that characterize the Sgaw Karen and the other groups who comprise the "sown." Let us turn next to the system of ties and relationships between groups, as they interact on the local level, that reinforce the community of perception found within them.

The "real" world of Karen, Northern Thai, Thai Lue, and so forth is only occasionally a world in which ethnic categories are salient. Usually it is a world of local links and local arrangements. In a recent paper, Lucien Hanks has characterized northern Thailand as a universe of villages in the sense that the village is the nexus of a web of patron-client relationships that serve as the essential or fundamental social units into which people are organized (Hanks 1972). Gertrude W. Marlowe has characterized the local social system somewhat differently as a set of differentially inclusive networks, each organized around a common locus—kinship, work groups, commerce, religion, patron-client, and so forth—that make the village a residence unit but not the essential social unit, either for its members or for the comprehension of the system (G. W. Marlowe 1972). There is no substantial disagreement between these viewpoints except as to whether or not a given network represents centrality to comprehension of the system. Both agree that the physical existence of a given territorially bounded residence unit, the village, by no means implies that that unit exhibits fundamental properties as a social unit as well. In fact, the social system may not be referable to a single central unit of analysis but may well be the product of multifold units that must be taken together to provide a unit of analysis.

The Sgaw Karen village is "a sometime thing" just as the Khon Muang village is. There are intermittent moments of corporate behavior and a sense of normative corporateness based upon the use of a kin idiom and a model for one's fellow villagers. But the discrete moments of collectivity for the village are counterbalanced by those other discrete moments for various members of the village when they operate as members of collectivities for which the village has no essential meaning.

Superficially the Karen village would appear to fit Leach's description of the "democratic" hill village (Leach 1960: 64); however, the Karen village is not particularly different from a Northern Thai village. The ritual leader of the Karen village, the *sapwaa zii kho,* has political authority precisely in those realms that are not the province of central authority: setting the dates of rituals in the course of the annual round, dealing with sexual transgression of a nonfelonious nature, and arranging affairs concerning the health and welfare of the village as part of its relationship with the spiritual world. Other affairs, those of the secular domain, lie in the hands of the village headman, the *kae ban* (as he is called in Northern Thai) or *phu yai ban* (Thai). The same individual often, but not always, fills both roles.

When the offices are held by different individuals, there is sometimes conflict about the extent of authority that may be exercised in either realm. For instance, the headman and ritual leader of a village in Cọm Thọng often bickered with each other about the setting of dates in the ritual calendar. The former would assert that as *kae ban,* it was his responsibility as an agent of the government to determine when the people should be called together for corporate functions; the ritual leader always firmly asserted that this was his function since he was the proper authority in spiritual matters. In a village in Bọkeo, the headman was also ritual leader but interestingly, or perhaps predictably, would be referred to differentially by the villagers as either *pati sapwaa* ("uncle," ritual leader) or *kae ban* depending upon which domain was involved.

The distinction between the two domains of ritual leaders and headmen is loosely that of the "sacred" and the "profane," that which is jurally proper in man's relationship to the spiritual world as opposed to that which is jurally proper in man's relationship to the polity of which he is a part. This differentiation goes far in unravelling the subtleties of the Karen relationship to land. The "Great Lords" *ta mu xha pado* and *ka ja pado* reign over the land and govern the success or failure of those men who are their human co-participants in the joint system that describes the supernatural and natural worlds. The Great Lords hold the land, the paddies, the jungle, the hillsides, the waters, the rivers and the rains, and the irrigation ditches as "essences." The villagers' rights to land as members of one of the village congregations in a river valley are rights to the use of land as land, of waters as waters. They have the right to till the soil and use the waters in return for properly serving and attending to the needs and rules of the Great Lords. There is no right of ownership involved in the contract between men and the Great Lords; the right that is involved is that of being a participant in a relationship, as a member of the village congregation, that allows the village agriculturalist to use land for production without incurring the devastating retaliations he would otherwise incur for operating in the spiritual domain without sanction. These retaliations—crop failure, epidemic and individual illness, and the like—are the semiotic system through which the Lords make known the status of their relationship with men. If the Great Lords turn their faces, nature can, and will, wreck harsh devastation upon the villagers. If they are properly served and their rights properly observed, the worst of the assaults of the natural world, such as a smallpox epidemic, may be turned away before it enters the village.

The land as such—the river valley, its named streams and their tributaries, the paths and roads that transect it—is also part of the physical political and secular domain of the state—the prince of Chiang Mai, then his successor, the Royal Thai government. Rights to use and hold the land as an "actual place" are rights contractually derived from the prince or state that is the nexus of the social and political order. These rights are not held by the ritual leader or the village as a collectivity, but by individuals. In this sense, the Karen differ markedly from groups such as the Kachin where "Chiefs and village headmen on the other hand own the land (*madu*) or rule it (*up*)" (Leach 1954: 155). The Karen villager holds rights of usufruct in the land. These rights, which enable him to eat (*au*) of the land, derive originally from contracts made by the "founding families" of the river valley with the prince who granted them to Karen settlers. The prince's claim to ultimate title was recognized through the symbolic meal and taxes in kind, the *au ga ti*. Through these, the Karen and the prince's representative, the *phanya,* reaffirmed each year Chiang Mai's secular overlordship and the Karen settlers' status as dependents or clients.

Today, agricultural land, in the form of paddy fields, is considered by the individual Karen proprietor to belong safely to him insofar as he possesses a clear title to it that was granted by the government. Much attention is paid to the transfer of land upon death or when elderly parents reapportion it among their children. The paramountcy of the government's proprietary rights to the land is such that parents will often delay the transfer of land to children if they have any premonition of future stress in their relationships. In such cases, as it is put, once the transfer is made, the parent is bereft of legal rights to the produce of the paddy field. His child's obligations are those of sentiment and the ideal obligations prescribed by kinship relationships. At best, the parents can count on the disapproval of other members of the community in respect to untoward acts on the part of the children. No jural authority can be invoked against them, however. I know of a number of cases in which villagers sold their land either to Khon Muang or other Sgaw Karen over the outraged protests of parents who had given it to them some years before. In one case, the widowed daughter-in-law of a ritual leader sold her deceased husband's land, the title to which had been transferred to her after his death. The ritual leader, I was told, opposed her violently, and five years later when I was there he was still grumbling about it whenever we discussed matters pertaining to land holding. However, he had had no recourse. The dichotomy between the appropriate regulations of the spiritual and secular domains was brilliantly illuminated by the fact that her actions in no way affected her participation as a member of the village congregation. She had offended her father-in-law but not the Great Lords; she had transgressed against her kinsmen but not against the community.

Equivalently there were no ways in which members of the community could legitimately intervene whenever village members decided to sell land to others, particularly to Khon Muang. The village had no control other than that of sentiment over the proprietary interest of the villager in "his" land since such interest was a matter of the relationship of the villager to the state. In like manner, as I have pointed out in other contexts (Marlowe 1969: 62–63; 1973), villagers had no power to control the usurpation or alienation of swidden lands by outsiders, such as the Meo or Khon Muang or Chinese market gardeners, other than to request intervention by the state. Such requests represented attempts to get the state, in the person of the district officer or one of his staff, to declare the legitimacy or nonlegitimacy of use of its lands by the villagers and others in terms of long-standing patterns of use and relationship—that is, to have the state make an affirmation of secondary rights of usufruct rather than of primary rights of tenure.[5]

The government-appointed headman, the *phu yai ban*, possesses an authority that is essentially lineal in terms of its sources and derivations. The Karen *phu yai ban* is usually responsible for from two to five settlements, each being an independent ritual congregation. These settlements collectively comprise the official Thai government village (*muban*), the smallest unit of administration. Usually, the headman appoints an aide (*phu chuai*) as his, and therefore the government's, representative in settlements other than that in which he resides. The political authority of the aide derives from his position as a representative of the government. The headman is responsible to the subdistrict or commune officer (*kamnan*) who, in turn, is responsible to the district officer (*nai amphoe*). This is the standard Thai system of local administration and the network of authority derives from the village's position in the Thai administrative system. Unlike the situation of the Red Lahu of northern Thailand, described by Anthony Walker (1969: 44–45), where the headman must at times be guided by the wishes of other Lahu headmen who had wide inter-village authority, there is no secular political authority that has its basis in a wider Karen order.

The Karen village headman cannot rule capriciously and arbitrarily. Decisions, in responding to or in implementing government policy, are taken by him in consultation with the elders and mature male householders of the village. It is the view of such villagers that he represents to those about him in the chain of administration. In acting in this fashion, he operates differently from any Khon Mųang headman. In addition, the headman also serves as local magistrate. As such, he may impose fines on villagers for failing to comply with governmental orders, particularly those involving levied labor for projects such as road maintenance. He is also partly responsible for maintaining the peace of the village and for fining people, as one headman put it, for "custom breaking." By this, he meant such things as disputes between households, drunken behavior, destruction of the property of neighbors, and petty thefts. The legitimacy of his role as magistrate lies again in the network of authority of the state. He may, if the case justifies it, refer local disputes to higher authorities. For example, if two households within a village have a dispute over control of land or water, the headman will be appealed to first. If he fails to effect a compromise to the dispute informally, it is anticipated that he will bring the dispute and its participants either to the *kamnan* or to the district office. Such incidents are rare since Sgaw Karen, like Khon Mųang, prefer to solve disputes within the confines of the village. Nonetheless, felonies, serious assaults, and major accidents are all reported immediately to the district office, as is the presence of suspicious strangers in the environs of the village.

It is important to point out that the headman sees his authority not only as representing the state at the local level but also as representing the people to the authorities. In one case, when the government wanted village labor levied to build a new road into the hills, the Karen headmen, along with some neighboring Khon Mųang headmen, responded, after consultation with the villagers, that they would not participate since the road brought them no benefits whereas one that they were already working on under the auspices of the abbot of a nearby temple would indeed benefit them. The road scheme was dropped. In another case, a group of headmen, from an area heavily dependent on swidden culture, came to the district office to protest the potential deleterious effects of new forestry regulations on the economics of their villages. The Karen headmen who came to represent their villages' needs to higher authorities acted as the structural equals of Khon Mµang headmen.

In addition to the political network there are other semiformal networks that the Karen share with the Khon Mµang. Over 50 percent of the Sgaw Karen families I surveyed in Chiang Mai in 1967 claimed to have a *si-so* (Karen) or *sahai* (Thai). A *sahai* is a non-Karen lowlander, usually a farmer or farmer-trader, with whose family a Karen family is informally allied. There are elements of the patron-client relationship operative on both sides. Khon Mµang often have a number of Karen families as their *sahai* and vice versa. The lowlander provides food, shelter, and hospitality to his Karen counterparts when they come to market, to attend temple festivals, or to carry out business of any sort in the environment of the lowlanders. The Karen reciprocates when the Khon Mµang's trade, business, or work takes him into the high valleys or the hills. The relationships involved are warm and intimate ones; long hours will be spent in gossiping, drinking tea and whiskey, and the women will often aid in food preparation and service. Gifts of tobacco, produce, and other things will often be made. In one walking trip I made in the hills of northwestern Cǫm Thǫng, when I was seeking a second field work site in 1966, my two Khon Mµang porters seemed surprised that I had brought food with me. The elder, who was a woodcutter who went to the hills often, pointed out that he had a *sahai* in each village we would visit. These were friends of long standing and as a matter of course would provide food as well as shelter to us.

The Karen, in turn, often first turn to their Khon Mµang *sahai*, often in preference to their Karen kinsmen, to borrow rice at times of need. In some areas, relationships are of significant temporal depth, sometimes involving the third and fourth generations of the same families. In Cǫm Thǫng district, where distances are short between Karen and Khon Mµang settlements, Karen often take the opportunity of visits to the market to make a round of courtesy calls upon townsmen and nearby villagers with whom they have such relationships. Many of the cases of intermarriage I have recorded have taken place between individuals whose families were allied in the *sahai* relationship. The extent and intensity of *sahai* relationships are, of course, governed by proximity and the cultural composition of the market center most used by the Karen of a given area. Most Karen using markets in Cǫm Thǫng district or Samoeng district tend to have *sahai* both in the market center and in the Khon Mµang and Thai Lue villages between them and the market. Karen in western Mae Caem district and in Mae Sariang district tend not to have Khon Mµang *sahai* but rather seek hospitality from the lowland Karen of the market towns. Such individuals are simply friends (*t's'skaw*) and not *sahai* since the latter specifically implies a relationship between two individuals or households of different cultures (Marlowe 1969: 58–59).

Villagers are tied, as well, into wider systems of patronage involving Khon Muang and others. A number of large-scale Khon Muang traders and merchants have wide circles of Karen clients to whom they stand in the position of patron in the "classical" Thai patron-client relationship described by Lucien Hanks and others. Many Karen are economic and local political dependents of such patrons, who are normally located in the main market towns they use. Often a Karen will be the client of more than one such *pho liang*. The patron extends credit, advances money on future rice crops, provides hospitality, gives advice, and aids his Karen clients in time of difficulty. One hill trader, prominent in the opium business, refused to purchase opium from Karen cultivators because of his position as a patron to large numbers of Karen. This status, he felt, made it incumbent upon him to discourage poppy cultivation because of its possible attendant destructive consequences. He felt no such compunctions, however, about purchasing opium from the Meo (Marlowe 1973). In times of difficulty, the patron will often intervene on behalf of the client, as when his Karen clients are involved in a situation in which they stand in marked structural asymmetry in relation to those individuals or institutions with which they are in contention. In the mid-1960s, when a group of tin miners were attempting to force the sale of Karen paddy lands for hydraulic mining, a trader, with a large circle of Karen clients in the area, arranged at the request of the proprietors for the transfer of title of a number of small holdings to his own name. All parties agreed that the "sales" were pro forma. It was felt that the trader, by virtue of his economic and political position and connections, would be more effective in blocking further alienation of the land.

There are equally important patron-client ties in the realm of religion. Six hundred twenty-seven (56%) of 1,112 non-Christian Karen families I surveyed in 1967 reported to have gone to at least one festival or service in the past year, most often at a Buddhist temple at the New Year or end of Buddhist Lent. In most cases, the people involved felt they stood in a special relationship to either the abbot or another monk in the *wat* involved. Such relationships were often long standing and it was regularly offered that a given abbot or monk was "one" who was "especially concerned" for their welfare and to whom they had special ties. In a wider arena, many Karen of northern Thailand felt they had a special relationship with the *khruba khao,* an unfrocked monk and the leader of a cult widespread in northern Thailand (Marlowe 1969).[6]

These examples demonstrate that the Karen of Chiang Mai see themselves as intricately tied to their local, non-Karen neighbors in myriad ways. As much as he is a part of the village, the individual Sgaw Karen is, as well, a part of other networks—political, affinal, economic, patron-client—in which he participates without specific reference to the village itself. His categorical identity, as opposed to his cultural identity, depends upon the relationship and event that mark the moment at which one chooses to express such an identity. When a group of Sgaw Karen and Khon Muang elders sit together talking and one of the latter observes that "these *yang* are just another kind of hill Thai," the Karen nod in agreement.

Another context that symbolizes the essential elements of Karen-other relations at the local level is a ritual one observed in Cọm Thọng district. One of the more important local ceremonies in Cọm Thọng is the *hae mai kham,* the carrying of supports for Bodhi trees found in the courtyards of temples, which takes place in the course of Buddhist New Year. Until a few years before my field tour (1965–68), Karen villagers in the nearby foothills always participated in the rites within the town of Cọm Thọng itself, bringing their supports to Wat Dio Kaeo, one of the oldest temples in the town.[7] A few years ago, the Karen began participating in the ceremony at Wat Mae Tia, a small temple located nearer the Karen villages and at which Karen women, along with Khon Muang women, offer food to the monks on a regular basis. This change was explained by the Karen as being a function of the growth of Cọm Thọng town: Formerly, "everyone in Cọm Thọng knew us and we knew them. Now it has become very big, there are many strangers, people who do not know us. They drink, and when they drink, they fight. If we were to fight, they are so many and we are few. So now we go to Wat Mae Tia where we all know each other."

Each of the two Karen villages in the foothills near Cọm Thọng town manufactured a support for the Bodhi tree. These are long, curved, and painted beams with one end cut out in the shape of a "U" to prop up the heavy hanging branches of the tree. On the morning of the ceremony, the support was mounted on an ox cart and festooned with Thai national flags and red, white, and blue streamers. A representative of each household then bathed the support with lustral water (called *nam sompọi* by the Khon Muang) acquired the day previously at Wat Luang—the main temple in Cọm Thọng. The villagers all dressed in their finest traditional Karen costumes—the men mostly in their red home-woven shirts and white head coverings;

the women and girls in their usual traditional dress with all their jewelry. The older unmarried girls dusted their faces with rice powder as they do on other festive occasions. The procession set out, with young men of each village yoked to the ox cart carrying the support, others playing gongs and drums, and others dancing.

The Karen headman led the parade of the two villages. "Before," he told me, "the procession was led by the ritual leader, but he can no longer come." The ritual leader was eighty-three, suffered from severe rheumatoid arthritis, and no longer traveled much beyond the confines of the village. "I lead the procession," the headman went on, "as headman, and as the ritual leader's assistant." The object of the ceremony, the headman said, was "to ensure health, prosperity, and a good agricultural year for the people of the Mae Tia river plain." This view of the ceremony was also enunciated by the Khon Mụang.

As the procession arrived at the temple, the Karen villagers were met by householders of the Khon Mụang villages that share the paddy lands of the Mae Tia with them. The chief monk and his novice also met the procession in the courtyard. The support of the Bodhi tree was then raised, while the Karen headman and the chief monk shared a mat upon which they prayed together and the other Karen and the local Khon Mụang were seated elsewhere in the attitude of prayer. Cheers went up as each post was wrestled into place and there was much discussion of the hopes for success of the ceremony. One Khon Mụang villager explained to me that "this was something that the Karen, as the original settlers, often did for all the people. It was their role to put up the supports since they were the first people of this place, and the first to live upon this land. The Khon Mụang villagers," he went on, "did not have to bring 'supports' as the Karen did it for all." The first part of the ceremony ended with more prayers led by the chief monk and the Karen headman.

The second part of the ceremony consisted of a ritual bathing of the chief monk with lustral waters, a ceremony known in Northern Thai as *dam hua*. For the Khon Mụang, *dam hua* is both a demonstration of respect and a way of repaying another for a service rendered when the other is structurally superior. The act is usually performed at New Year for important status superiors, worthy elders, patrons, and so on. On this occasion, the Karen also participated. After the *dam hua* of the chief monk, the entire congregation, including the Karen, went to ritually wash the Buddha images in the temple. Then a festive meal was eaten by all participants.

Following the meal, the Karen returned to their own villages to prepare for the afternoon and evening. The previous day, in the course of their visit to Cọm Thọng's Wat Luang, representatives of the Karen village had made the rounds to *dam hua* various Khon Muang leaders and elders in the surrounding villages. In turn, that afternoon and evening, the young people and many of the elders of the surrounding villages, and some from Cọm Thọng itself, came to *dam hua* the elders of the Karen villages. For some hours, there was a constant stream of Khon Muang young people as well as numbers of elderly men and women who came, as representatives of their families, to show such respect. Although, as in most such affairs in northern Thailand, there was more fun and jollity than high solemnity, one was impressed as elderly Khon Muang, heads bowed, hands together in prayer, received the blessings and prayers that they might "live well" in the coming year from elderly Karen men and women.

The actions described in this brief portrayal of the ceremony of the *hae mai kham* are, I believe, a paradigmatic model of the local relationships between Karen and Khon Muang. In essence, we have two groups in which participation in the domain of each by the other is symbolically critical to the survival of the other. The ritual presentations of respect, passing from Karen to Khon Muang and then back again, are the semiotes of their joint participation in the category "people of one place" as well as of the necessary relationship between them as differentiated separate groups, Karen and Northern Thai, in their relationship to the spiritual world. Each defines for the other the legitimacy of their place in the Karen-Northern Thai dyad, the necessary minimal unit of meaning for both.

Hierarchy of Social Relationships Involving Karen

At this point, we must make some important distinctions about the actual relationships of the elements in the *local* social system—individuals, groups, and categories—and try to order the relationships between elements as they operate as differentiated subsystems at various hierarchical levels. For the purposes of analysis at the local level, and by local in this context I mean all of Chiang Mai province, we can take our three fundamental elements—the individual, the territorial group (i.e., village clusters), and the category—as operating in somewhat different ways within several hierarchical systems. Not all of these systems are included within the dominant hierarchical system within which the ordering of categories is primary and groups and individuals, forming the lower level of the hierarchy, are secondary.

The individual, the minimal element of the system, is defined, following a behavioral model of perception, as plastic. Both he and others see him as "being the way he is because of the way in which he was brought up"; that is, he is what he is because of what he has learned. Everyone in the local system accepts the essential equivalence of individuals per se, no matter what nominative cultural tag they originate under. An individual can shift membership from one cultural group to another by being able to play by the rules of the game, that is, by wearing certain clothes, speaking a given language, performing certain rituals, and so on. The variability of the rules is vast but the criteria for membership are limited in the sense that there are no intricate inner mysteries to master. Rather there is a fairly limited set of behaviors required for one to assert and be accepted in an identity.

Both Karen and Khon Mµang almost make a fetish of the variability that exists between village clusters and settlement areas of the same cultural group. As one Karen put it to me when we discussed the extreme variations between river valleys, "Each river valley does things in the way that the grandparents who settled it said things should be done [*pi pu a lu a la*]. Why should the grandparents think the same way or do things the same way? They were all different. After all, you had four grandparents and eight great-grandparents. Now, did they all think alike? Of course not. Why would you think that our grandparents thought alike?" Khon Mµang in Chiang Mai continually point out, whenever asked about "ways" in which things are done, that one cannot generalize from settlement to settlement. The most often-heard phrase I can recall was: "For us, no two villages have the same customs." At this level, the individual is an element in a single set, "men." Their common identity is established by their biological sameness, their original equivalent status as children of the same parents, and the knowledge that the systematic likenesses and differences between groups are acquired rather than ascribed characteristics. Individuals, however, do not exist *in vacuo* but rather exist as social persons defined in reference to a position in a transaction. Here we enter the crux of the matter insofar as the relationships of the ordering of the elements are concerned at the local level.[8]

The question involved is that of the identity of the group in the context of its local network of relationships. We may and should ask the question: if all men are basically the same, and if cultural similarities are as great as we have indicated on the local level, why are groups distinguished and what is the significance of distinguishing between them? Here we must look closely at the ordering of the systems of hierarchy and the relational complexes that define them, with the events of incorporation, contrast, and opposition in which the varying relational complexes are operative. Nominative differences, we must recognize, are, despite their plasticity, "real" differences. Despite all the cultural convergences involved, the groups involved remain "real" groups, when taken as cultural units speaking different languages and referring to themselves and each other by terms that imply these differences. One of the problems we seem to create, however, is that of focusing exclusively upon those criteria that differentiate by ethnic category groups or roles in a system of intergroup relationships, thereby ignoring those alternative criteria that define group or role relationships in nonethnic hierarchies. Ethnicity involves an oppositional or contrastive set of relationships. F. K. Lehman (this volume) and Fredrik Barth (1969B) have in this sense defined ethnicity as the social organization of cultural differences. But the ethnic domain is only one of those domains that account for the organized behavior of men. It is in this poly-domainal sense that we view certain of the events and construct our models of relationships at the local level. The kind of relationship we observe between the Sgaw Karen and Khon Muang in the ceremony of the *hae mai kham* is not an interethnic relationship in that structurally it has nothing to do with the Karen as "Karen" and the Khon Muang as "Khon Muang." What is significant, in terms of underlying structure, are two things: the sharing by local groups of a common territory and the fact of precedence among these groups in that one is recognized as having spiritually legitimized man's relationship to the land before the arrival of the other. The hierarchy, then, is ordered in terms of:

People of One Place

Seniors   Juniors

The hierarchy is ordered not in terms of *who,* ethnically defined, but in terms of *when* and *where,* defined in terms of settlement of the area by local groups.[9] Other relational complexes—friendship, patron-client, employer-employee, and so on—are similar in that they comprise ordered relationships and hierarchical systems focused around transactional events rather than around ethnic and cultural criteria.

It is the existence of local hierarchies defined by criteria such as "when" and "where" that impresses me as being fundamentally responsible for the collapsing of ethnic categories at moments when locality is contrasted against a wider world order. They serve, because of the commonalities of the "where" and "when," to present the observer and commentator with what we might call a metacultural description of the local group—that is, not a description of the elements of the separate cultures that are held in common, but a description referable to the common culture, that is, the shared events, of the groups or networks as such. In these terms, the upper bound of the hierarchy is the local group or network and is not defined by wider encompassing terms such as Khon Muang, Karen, or Thai. The upper bound of the hierarchy at the *hae mai kham,* for example, is the paddy plain of the Mae Tia. At that moment, it is not really subsumed in any wider human system. It is with this kind of system of reference that my Khon Muang neighbors would make the statement that the *yang* are another kind of hill Thai, or my Karen friends that "we and the Khon Muang are exactly the same, people of one place." Let me illustrate this with another example.

One of the more important minor ceremonies of the Sgaw Karen is that of the *surr do ta,* the chasing out of the minor illness entities of the village. For the Karen community of Mae Tia Glo in Com Thong, the *surr do ta* was a "closed" ceremony—that is, it had ethnic significance as a boundary-maintaining device against others. No nonpermanent resident of the village was allowed to be present in the village during its performance. In fact, I was asked to leave the village on the day of its performance. In Bokeo subdistrict of Samoeng district, the *surr do ta,* on the other hand, was structurally one of the nonethnic events; it was involved in the hierarchy of local rather than ethnic relationships. In the Bokeo scheme of things the ceremony of the *surr do ta,* rather than being a confirmation of ritual difference, symbolically represented for the Karen their equivalent status as Buddhists, that is, as a unit in the ecumene of the "sown." The ritual leader while making *talai,* the bamboo stars hung on the doorways of the houses to keep the illness entities from entering, kept pointing out to me that these were not "a Karen thing." He went on to state that this was a Buddhist thing, a thing of the Khon Muang, and that he had learned it from them and from his father, who knew it very well. "In the old days [before the Japanese war]," he said, "we had our own *wat* in Bokeo and my father was always at the *wat.*" The ceremony itself was performed by two Khon Muang woodcutters who used a palm leaf book from which they read the service. The headman explained to me that it was very important that the words come from the book since the power of the book, being of Buddhism, was so much greater than the power of words alone. "The ceremony," he went on, had always "been performed by a Khon Muang." The present practitioners were two woodcutters who were working on his new home. Normally, it was done by Uncle G, an elder of the village of Ha Sompoi in northern Bokeo. He, however, had not been able to come. Ha Sompoi shared paddy lands with the northern Bokeo villages.

Although the emphases of the *surr do ta* are somewhat different from those of the *hae mai kham* in that there appears to be no Karen reciprocity, we can model it equivalently. In this case we have another group of "people of one place." The villages operate as separate elements. Their "equivalent" status in Buddhism is affirmed by the literate *surr do ta* practitioner, who represented the senior line in our example. The nonliterate members of the village were the junior line. Once again, the ethnic statuses of the groups as Karen and Khon Muang are not those that are germane to the event; rather their statuses as more and less proficient Buddhists are what are important.

We can see that such nonethnic hierarchies are double-edged in their functions. On the one hand, they erase ethnic distinctions in favor of local ones. On the other, through such "noncultural" constructs as "junior" and "senior" or "more" and "less proficient," they also operate to maintain and preserve the boundaries between the groups. In the very act of defining cultural and ethnic differences out of transacting groups operating as either a real or symbolic collectivity, the structural differences between the groups are reaffirmed. The moment of solidarity is, at the same time, a moment of differentiation and division. The moment of union has consequences of tension since that which is being proclaimed is not cultural but structural differentiation as an aspect of the ordering of the universe. If one leaves one's village, if one moves to another valley, one can cease to be a Karen. As long as one remains in place, as part of the Karen category, one cannot cease to be a Karen since one cannot change one's necessary temporal or ritual juniority or seniority to the others who share the place. In this sense, the endurance of difference certainly appears to be more a function of subtle structural rather than overt cultural differences.

Beyond the hierarchies subsumed in nonethnic first terms, there are others that involve groups as "named" categories. In certain of these hierarchies, cultural difference, as such, begins to play a role of some importance. That is, the groups are not, as in our above examples, subsumed under a culturally neutral term like "people of one place." Let us take the example of the "sown" and the "wild" as seen on the local level. We often separate the hills, the jungle, and the plains in terms that are far too sweeping. We oppose the one against the other and, because of the apparent evidence of human social and ecological difference in the wider society of mainland Southeast Asia, tend to forget that neither the "wild" nor the "sown" is a bounded entity. We superimpose the view of an escarpment, a critical discontinuity, that divides the plainsman from the hills. In doing this, we forget that the hills begin with low rolling foothills, that gardens and swiddens lie beyond the paddies and the terraces, and that many plainsmen spend the better part of their working lives timbering on the high valleys and slopes. Above all, we can lose sight of the fact that the hills lie between the plains. The pathways and drainages of the hills are the high roads of the plainsmen. They are trade routes of east to west local commerce. Thus, the hills are an extension of the plains for the lowlander, in that they are and have been a domain in which a fair amount of his behavior must take place, just as the plains are in many senses an extension of the hills to the hillman. The Karen with their network of kin reaching back into the hills are the human part of the Khon Muang's perception of the hills as part of *their* world. To the Khon Muang laborer, forager, trader, or peddler moving in the hills or across them, the Karen are that extension of *their* system which provides the traveler with food, shelter, and guidance. The domain of the Karen is, thus, part of the domain of the Khon Muang and not an alien or alternate one. In a very real sense, the *yang*—the Karen—are those who hold the "wild" for the "sown" and thus are encompassed by the "sown."

The last hierarchy we shall attend to is that of the political system. Within the fabric of the polity, Karen like Khon Muang exist as one of a number of local "named groups"—Khon Muang, Lua', Shan, Thai Lue—all of whose political identity is Thai. As such, the Karen see themselves as part of an overall Thai political system run by the Central Thai, the *da djay,* which encompasses them, the local Tai-speaking people of the north, called *zo,* and others who are seen as part of the "sown." Within this hierarchy, an interesting bifurcation takes place. Although the Central Thai provide the category that encompasses the elements constituted of the local named groups, they are not themselves encompassed by the category as it is applied locally. They are the foreign authority, the power source of the polity, and, as such, are classified as extra-systemic at this local level of operation. To the Karen, a *zo* is not a foreigner, but a *da djay* is.[10] One sees here, then, that rule of the hierarchy of named categories according to which members of the encompassing category can never be members of the category encompassed so long as they maintain their higher-level identity. Categorical incorporation is unidirectional and proceeds from the element to that which encompasses it. The converse does not hold, in that anything which belongs to the ascending category of the hierarchy cannot be translated into the category below it, representing as it does a different level. Karen can be incorporated as a kind of Thai into the Khon Muang category above since it carries the same unique first-term or relational complex as being part of a hierarchy of Thai. However, the Khon Muang element in the category carries no term by which it can be ordered as Karen. Each level of the hierarchy possesses dual attributes, in that there is one set of elements, such as Khon Mųang or Thai, that define the level as well as other elements, such as Karen, Lue, or Khon Mųang, with which the first set co-exists on the level below. The fundamental logic of the system itself provides for incorporation in one direction but boundary maintenance in the other.

The ordering of named categories is fixed only insofar as the distribution of power between the named groups remains stable. The highest encompassing category of all is that authority which holds overall political dominion. Each descending level encompasses those whose political dominion is, theoretically, derived from the power on the ascendant level above them. If there were to be a rearrangement of the power relationships, the positions of the various named groups in the hierarchy would change, as would the ordering of possible transformations of groups in the hierarchy from one named category to another. The upper-lower boundaries that maintain the ordering of the groups would change correspondingly as, indeed, has happened historically with the Mon vis-à-vis Thai and Burmans. For any lowland group, the maintenance of one's identity as a member of a named group appears to be an epiphenomenon grounded in the regularities of structure rather than in the inhering attributes or qualities of the group. We may sum up the structure of such relationships by categorizing it as a hierarchical system with bounded levels but open movement and recruitment from the bottom to the top, the openness provided by the ideology of behavior and equivalence.

I have heretofore referred to what I would call the "classical set" of social relations in mainland Southeast Asia as polydomainal. That is, rather than any single domain, such as culture, ecology, or polity, operating as the central construct controlling relationships between categories and groups, there are a series of domains, some exclusive, some interpenetrating, some inclusive, with which the position of any category is defined for self and others. Like E. R. Leach, F. K. Lehman, Michael Moerman, and others, I see the key elements and others in the paradigm as those of "hill" and "valley," or the "wild" and "sown," but I do not see these as simple contrast sets. For the purposes of establishing an analytical model we may assert a rough tripartite order taken from the point of view of the valley dweller—the "sown," the hills as distinct from the "sown," and the hills as an extension of the "sown."

The hills of the "hillmen" are typified by groups such as the Meo, Yao, Akha, and Lisu. These are the alien hills, that is, the hills taken as a more or less separate ecological niche exploited in ways not germane to the lowland. From the point of view of these uplanders, small segments of the lowland system—markets, traders, and so forth—represent the extensions of the hills into the valleys. However, the peoples involved hold the hills for themselves. Their concourse with the valleys takes place between representatives of differing domains that maintain qualities of uniqueness vis-à-vis each other.

The hills of the hillmen, however, are not the only hills or wild areas the valley dweller deals with either realistically or cognitively. There is, as I have pointed out in the case of Karen in Chiang Mai province, the "wild" as an extension of the "sown," that is, the hills that are a necessary component of the lowlander's total ecosystem. The valley merchant must cross them to get from one valley to another. Armies had to move through them with confidence, emissaries depended upon regular access across them, and travelers needed assurance of safety within them. It is in this aspect of the hills that we come to grips with the Karen as the holders of the "wild" for the "sown." They are the "marchmen" of the civilized who hold the hills as part of the dominion of the valley.

In other essays (1969, 1970, 1973) I have remarked upon the negative relationships that Karen have with other hillmen, as has Peter Kunstadter (1969A; and in this volume). The Karen have no feeling of kinship with the true uplanders like the Meo. Meo, Lisu, Lahu, and so forth are aliens; they are of the domain of the "hills," qua "hills," not of the domain of the "hills" as an extension of the "sown." The profound commonalities, despite local territorial disputes, that Karen and Lua' feel about each other underlines this. Each sees the other as sharing the same position in the general scheme of things. Each sees itself as an extension of the civilized into the hills; each sees itself as equally deeply invested in the universe of the paddy farmer and the universe of the swidden cultivator.[11]

In the Karen terms used for classifying people ethnically, a distinction is made between those to which the term *keh* is prefixed and those to which it is not. Although the Karen call themselves *bu kin yo*, Tai-speakers *zo*, the Lua' *gowah*, Europeans *gola*, and so forth, they refer to other hill peoples as *keh meo* (Meo), *keh lissaw* (Lisu), and so on. This term *keh*, which is cognate with the Shan *ka*, designates "people of the wild." All *keh* are swiddeners, in contrast to the Karen, some of whom are swidden cultivators but all of whom could or would be paddy farmers if the opportunity presented itself. This pattern in which the world is divided into the "sown," the "hills" as an extension of the "sown," and the "hills" as a contrastive domain is an old one.

There are elements of class differentiation involved in the position of the Karen or in the determination of the category Karen. Certainly, in Burma one can safely assert that "Karen" was, in many senses, the hierarchically lowest category encompassed by the kingdom itself not as a matter of alliance but of incorporation. The class attributes of the Karen category are underlined today by the Khon Muang view of the Karen that is often expressed in Chiang Mai province: the Karen are perceived as a species of "hillbilly"—a poorer, less effectual, backward kind of Thai—like the "back-hollow Appalachians" of North America rather than the distinct and alien "red Indian." There is a provocative message in W. C. McLeod's "Journal of 1836–37" that lends strength to this supposition. On the eighth of March, McLeod and his party passed a group of Chinese porters on the road between Kengtung (Chiang Tung) and Kenghung (Chiang Hung) and he described them in the following passage:

> A number of Chinese porters carrying cloth and cotton to China, and some trading from village to village with dried fish and radishes passed us; when traveling homewards they go the same distance, each day, as the mules. The load is carried on the back, supported by a rope running under the bottom of the back, and fastened to a flat wooden collar resting on the back of the neck, to which it is fitted, and which is supported by both shoulders; a rope is passed round the forehead and the upper part of the pack, this balances it and prevents it falling backward. These porters though stout bodied, are not such fine looking fellows as the men who accompany the mules and who call the others the Karengs of China [McLeod 1869: 68].

The situation in Burma at the beginning of the nineteenth century had, from G. E. Harvey's description (Harvey 1967), aspects of caste developing within it and, indeed, the portrait we have of Karen endogamy from the early Burmese commentators may be a reflection of the generalized rules of class endogamy within the kingdom. There appears to have been a real fixity to the positions of occupational categories and ethnic categories such as that of the Karen. As Harvey put it, "The various classes were clans, with rights accruing from a certain office which it was their hereditary duty to fill; marriage outside the clan entailed loss of status, and the King could degrade a man from one clan to another, for instance, from the *sadawchet-asu,* fish cooks, to the *hsindaing-asu,* elephant scavengers" (Harvey 1967: 351). As in India, here the early British administrators did not recognize the nonlocal nature of the system of social and political relations that characterized the Burmese situation and redefined its operations in terms of locality and ethnicity, thus distorting the "class-caste" model to a "bounded village–bounded ethnic group" one.

The underlying structural considerations with their aspects of class lead me to agree with Stern rather than Lehman (this volume) about the significance of the terms "Talaing Karen" and "Burma Karen." The first notice I find of these terms is an article published by Francis Buchanan in 1792 in which he states that "By the Burmans they are said to be of two kinds; Burma and Taline [Mon] Karayn" (Buchanan 1792: 233). Buchanan's selected vocabulary list of the former is essentially Sgaw; of the latter, Pwo. Buchanan notes that those who called themselves or understood these terms were those who "seemed to be conversant with the Burma ideas." Given the structure of society and the underlying principles that appear to have guided it, it would seem to be evident that the terms Talaing (Mon) Karen and Burma Karen referred, for the participants, to their hierarchical incorporation in one of the two domains, Burmese or Mon. The term *yang thai* as it is now used in Chiang Mai is an equivalent term. The reasoning for this view is based on the fact that Karen exists as a category only as part of a lowland political domain and not in and of itself. Commenting on the status of the Karen to Michael Symes, Father Sangermano indicated something of the incorporated status of the Karen when he noted that they "are the most industrious subjects of the state," and that "a great part of the provisions used in the country is raised by the Carianers, and they particularly excel in gardening" (Symes 1800: 207). Although the structural relationships between Karen and Shan and Thai were not as formally organized by the kinds of rules and regulations that characterize the Burmese class-ordered system, the fundamental categorical structure of relationships appears to have been very much the same throughout the nineteenth century.

The Karen oral tradition asserts long residence in the lands that are present-day Thailand. In Chiang Mai, it is claimed that the founding families of the river valleys of upland Mae Caem and Cọm Thọng migrated to their present locations some 250 years ago from their original homes in the valley of the Yuam. Rights of usufruct were purchased from the prince of Chiang Mai and symbolic taxes in kind paid annually to the *phanya,* the prince's representative. By the early part of the nineteenth century, when we have our first records of the Karen in Chiang Mai province, they are seen as an integral part of the prince's dominions, subject to him and operating as an extension of his polity in the hills and on the trade routes between Chiang Mai and Burma. The Karen settlement area was one chronically subject to the oscillations of the almost perpetual warfare between the Tai and the Burmese, and was over the centuries a region in which suzerainty passed regularly from one domain to the other. In 1830 Dr. Richardson had counted upon the Karen of the Yuam, that is, of Mein Lun Ghee (the present Mai Sariang), to facilitate his journey to the Karenni (Kayah). In 1837, on his next mission to treat with the Karenni, he described the Karen territory as stretching northward from Mein Lun Ghee and extending two or three days east of the Salween, a distance that would readily encompass the eastern tributaries of the Mae Caem. During this period, the area of present western Chiang Mai and Mae Hong Son provinces was thinly populated, presumably as a result of the slave raids of the Kayah. Richardson and McLeod both comment upon the sparsity of people. In January 1830, Richardson described the town of Mein Lun Ghee as a collection of about 200 huts scattered over the entire plain of the Yuam, which at that point covers an area of about forty square miles. He also noted that the governor of the town, an official under the jurisdiction of Labong (Lamphun) "levied contributions from the Karen tribes in the neighborhood" (Blundell 1836). McLeod counted twenty-five Karen households in the first three districts he walked through after crossing from Burma until he reached the Lua' settlements at Bo Luang on his way across the hills to Hot (then a village of twenty-five households) in the Mae Ping valley.

Despite the sparseness of its population, the area was in no sense an unknown one. Both McLeod and Richardson constantly note the number of trade caravans—Shan, Lao, Chinese, Burmese, Indian— which they met on their journeys. The Karen lay athwart the centuries-old major trade route between the port cities of lower Burma on the Andaman Sea and Chiang Mai and the Shan states and China. The journey was considered a normal one for traders.[12]

In a list of names of inhabitants of the neighboring states compiled in 1832 by McLeod (1869), the Karen appear under the Northern Thai rubric *niang*. The list is an interesting one, for it demonstrates the extensive relationships and knowledge of others held by the inhabitants of the trade-route cities and includes the Tai names for peoples ranging from the Burmese to the Cochin Chinese.[13] The use of the term *yang* was widespread in the Shan states, in northern Thailand, and even in China as one of those specifying terms involving a category and a set of relationships that were important in the operation of the trade routes between the sea and China.

In addition to this extensive international trade that ensured the boundaries of the state did not bound one's knowledge of the human ecology of the region, there was much local trade between the Khon Muang and the Karen and Karenni:

> They [Khon Muang] carry out to the Kareng villages iron, (procured from the Lawas) salt hatchets, &c., which they barter for

cloths, onions, chillies, wax, and cotton. To the Red Kareng country they export cattle, and procure in return slaves, ponies, and stick lac [McLeod 1869: 36].

Karen cloth was so highly prized that the Chou Raja Wun of Chiang Mai gave McLeod a three-ruppee bolt of it as a gift in return for a musket that the latter had presented him with.

The role of the Karen in Chiang Mai once again can be seen as falling into the structural category "holders of the wild and facilitators of the border" for the domain of the valley princes. As Richardson put it in 1829:

> The only hard rice that can be obtained is from the Careens, who left us today, and by whom we have been accompanied from the neighborhood of one village to that of another since leaving the Thalween. They are a fair, well limbed, athletic race, superior in appearance generally to the Talines and Burmans, but have been oppressed from them immemorial by Talines, Burmans, and Shans, whoever happen to have the ascendance. They have been obliged to furnish provisions, erect huts, cut the jungle from the edges of the path, and furnish guides to all travellers crossing the hills, the latter of which services they performed for us, and were much surprised at being paid for whatever they furnished us [Blundell 1836: 610].

Both Richardson and McLeod noted that their movements were reported to the Chiang Mai representatives by the Karen and that at times they were delayed in their travels by Karen headmen under orders of the Chiang Mai authorities. This role of representing the political authorities and reporting and helping to control the movements of strangers in the hills in response to governmental directives is one that is noted in a number of nineteenth-century accounts. D. McGilvray, for example, reported that in 1870 Karen evangelists from Burma whom he had sent to a Chiang Mai village did not even receive "common civility" from the inhabitants; he went on to state that "At last they learned the reason. The Jow Uppalat [the second ranking official in Chiang Mai] had secretly dispatched a special messenger with a letter under his own seal forbidding any Karen subject to embrace the new religion. All who did so were to be reported to him. What that meant, or what he wished them to infer that it meant, was well understood. . . ." (McGilvray 1912: 143).

The Karen position as holders of the wild for the state in the nineteenth century is indicated for central Siam as well as for the north. Dr. Collins, an American missionary, reported in the 1860s about a trip from Bangkok to Burma: " . . . after four days of waiting the long looked for quadrupeds arrived. The elephants in this part of Siam belong chiefly to the Karens, a migratory race who change every few seasons from one to another of the rich mountain valleys. From the fact that they occupy Siamese territory they are bound to furnish food, elephants, and guides to any who can bear an order from the Prime Minister of Siam. . . ." (Bacon 1873). In addition to such duties, the Karen of central Siam, along with Mon, both indigenous and refugee, served in the outpost garrisons of the kingdom.

The folk history of the Karen and their neighbors serves to elucidate and detail further the central model of group relationships we have delineated. For Tai, Burmese, and Mon, the Karen are seen as that category that both participates in the "sown" and "holds the hills and the jungles" as part of the "sown." They are in a sense the boundaries between the political domains of the lowlands as they are equally the denial of the hills and the jungles as actual physical boundaries of the state. In each case, they are the final level of the hierarchy of the state, an extension of it but not of the "sown" itself. In this sense, the Karen are central to the model of the society of Burma in that they have provided the necessary link between hill and valley in the scheme through which lowland polities have been able to incorporate the hills as a functional part of their domain. As we have also seen, the processes of hierarchical incorporation are double-edged in that as they operate to incorporate the Karen they also serve to maintain their separate status as a named category. This status was one we can presume to have been dictated by the conceptual difference between the hill and the valley. As long as the two were seen as different, although articulated parts of the same eco-system by the valley dweller, the category Karen must of necessity have remained a category apart. Karen could change; the category could not. This enduring societal model, however, could exist only as long as two fundamental conditions were met: (1) the maintenance of a differentiation of use of the hills and the valleys by the valley dwellers, and (2) the continued organization of polities in terms of the kinds of hierarchical considerations we have been discussing. As ecological zones, as well as aspects of the polity, the highlands have been undergoing transformations during the past sixty years that have tended to undermine the traditional structural differentiation between hill and valley. At the same time, the polities of Thailand and Burma have been, as a result of colonial activities and the development of Western models of the state and the group, undergoing transformation from a hierarchical to a nonhierarchical model. It is to these transformations and their consequences that we turn next.

Transformation of Hierarchical to Pluralistic Society

In Burma and Thailand within the past 150 years, the system that had been open, allowing status equivalent transformations of individuals and, through the network of local ties, ensuring incorporation of all into the wider polity, became subject to conceptions and operations that tended to close it and create closed boundaries within it. At its best, the governing hierarchical process was never in a state other than that of dynamic equilibrium. Ambivalence was consistently present in relationships between, and perceptions of, those in alternative social categories. Although many of the nineteenth-century Western accounts (e.g., McLeod 1869; Richardson 1839 and 1840, 1869; Sangermano 1885) as well as Mon histories and legends portray the Karen as an "incorporated" people, other accounts speak of the Karen as lying beyond the boundaries of civilization. For example, in 1740 Father Narini said of the Karen of Burma that "they had been settled in the country for generations but were looked on as savages" (Stewart 1909). In Buchanan's account, the Karen are spoken of as "Another rude nation, which shelters itself in the recesses of the hills and woods, from the violence of its insolent neighbors" (Buchanan 1792). The assertions of many of the missionaries and their apologists (Judson 1883; Mason 1843, 1852, 1860; Smeaton 1887; Wayland 1853) also picture the Karen as savages. We can logically hypothesize that such views of periods of "bounded" exclusion from the system were real and were intensified by proximate and comparatively short-lived responses to political events such as Alaungpaya's conquest of lower Burma, the Mon-Karen resistance against the Burmese, and the intensification of the Burmese class-categorical system attendant upon the conquest. In this sense, we may speak of episodes of strong apparent ethnicity within the overall hierarchical system. In such episodes, in Fredrik Barth's terms, ascribed membership to groups demarcated by specific cultural diacriticals was, indeed, treated in terms of the presumed existence of exclusivistic boundaries (Barth 1969B). At such moments, as G. E. Harvey has indicated, ascription and membership were deemed to be frozen, unless changes were dictated by the central political authority for either occupational or ethnic groups. If, as I believe, these events had not coincided with the irruption of the West into Southeast Asia, it appears probable that the system would have, in return oscillation, moved back to the basic hierarchical, polydomainal pattern of the metasociety, involving continuous incorporations of all of those within or allied to the "sown." As in India, however, Westerners introduced here a much different view of the nature of cultural groupings than that which already existed. To the Western administrator, boundaries were defined by considerations of locality and culture. There was little comprehension of the function of the hierarchical incorporating network that characterized so much of the social system at all levels (Dumont 1970A; Harvey 1967).

The pattern of transformation of Burma from hierarchical state to plural society has been well described by J. S. Furnivall (Furnivall 1956). As in many such cases, the apparent contradictions between the model proposed by E. R. Leach (Leach 1954, 1960) and that of Furnivall are most readily resolved by viewing differences such as those between the center—the British-administered Burman-dominated areas—and the periphery—involving local maintenance of the hierarchical patterns on the part of dyads such as the Shan and Kachin. The process of governance of the colonial power was, in a very real sense, founded upon an attempt to pursue an egalitarian view of differing cultural groups. In many instances, such as those of the Karen and the Kachin, special esteem was granted to the members of these groups. On the one hand, this tended to preserve local relationships longer than in the center, but on the other, it also ultimately served to develop more rigorously fixed group boundaries on the national level by emphasizing that a special value existed in the ascription to a given group identity. Such ethnic attribution, as in the cases of the Karen and Kachin, carried with it preferential treatment, particularly in terms of recruitment into the armed forces and police. This was a part of the usual policy of "divide and rule" in respect of developing nonsympathetic, non-Burman forces to deal with the politically restive Burmans. The net result, in the long run, as Lehman has pointed out, was the creation of a set of bounded minority groups, newly cognizant of their status as such and of their rights as independent ethnic minorities (Lehman 1967A). The model that was created is one that culminates in "pluralism." That is, a group of linguistic and cultural units was developed out of the hierarchical order with diminished ties between them and with limited possibilities for the subsuming of any one level of grouping by another. Once groups and categories achieve an independent existence and independent identity, the basic logic of relationships necessarily differs from that involved in a multilevel hierarchy. There is no such thing, in this sense, as a "Burmese" since there is no structural incorporation of the separate entities—Burmans, Kachin, Karen, Chin, and so forth. The act of defining a group as a minority, for example, to say there is a Burman majority and a series of cultural minorities, establishes a boundary that precludes the incorporation of the minority within the majority (see Burma Reforms Committee 1922). The Karen is not a Burmese; he is a separate entity, coeval with the Burman.

The plural or ethnic separatist model, applicable to the Austro-Hungarian and Ottoman empires and to numerous colonial states (Kuper and Smith 1969; Smith 1965), is a horizontal model, unified mechanically through an overriding, often quasi-abstract or alien political locus. It can perhaps most simply be characterized as the nation of strangers ruled through imposed alliances. The nation, insofar as it exists, is a conception of a governing elite that operates to maintain mechanical cohesion, that is, to see that each segment contributes its share, as a segment, to enable national administrative, political, and economic needs to be fulfilled. There is no organic or sociological integration to the plural system; there are no vertical sets that provide for incorporation of the ethnic groups or categories within each other as the same people or the same kind of people. The plural society is founded, as well, upon territorially segregated or quasi-segregated blocs of people aware and concerned about their existence as cultural entities.

Between pluralism and the incorporating hierarchy stands the *pluralistic society* (Kuper and Smith 1969; Smith 1965). The pluralistic society as seen in the United States or Australia is quasi-hierarchical, built on incorporated processes directed to differential levels of allowable public behavior. Within the pluralistic society, one may ethnically differentiate himself, or be so differentiated, by a series of "safe" behaviors—that is, those not threatening to the dominant categorical identity defined for the society as its incorporative device. If one is an Italian-American, Polish-American, or a Chinese-American, one may safely possess a language, use a cuisine, observe certain festive and ritual occasions, adhere to a religion, and have certain interests in history and historic roots that are not those of the national polity. These diacriticals, however, must be restricted to private occasions or those public events wherein such behavior is deemed structurally appropriate by the society at large. In most public behavior, one is required to behave in accordance with the public norms of the wider society as enunciated at the moment. Thus, one may celebrate Columbus Day, Kosciusko's birthday, or the Chinese New Year by donning national dress. One would go to work daily in such dress at the risk of hospitalization or loss of one's job. Equivalently, one's politics must align themselves in terms of the choices provided by the American electoral system. It would be ill met, for example, if a group of Austrian-Americans were to start a movement to establish the House of Hapsburg as their central political institution. The pluralistic model, then, involves a bifurcation in the behavior of its participants, who may behave at one set of times like members of one group, provided they behave at another set of times like Americans. That is, they must exhibit those standards that are the relational complex of the next higher level of the hierarchy of behavior, in which they, in effect, subsume themselves through their "American" behavior.

This model of the pluralistic society differs from the incorporating hierarchical model in that actual groups are not subsumed or encompassed by other actual groups, but one's own behavior is subsumed by other aspects of one's own behavior. The other essential difference lies in the amount of "public" common behavior that must be exhibited. The pluralistic society, with its demand that one set of behaviors be used to subsume another, also demands far more adherence to public sumptuary and transactional norms. One cannot be an Italian and be an American at the same time in the same sense in which one can be a Karen and be part of the Khon Mụang, and thence part of the Thai, at the same time. The pluralistic system in its regard for commonality is as little ambivalent as the plural society is in its regard for the existence of hard-edged groups. The incorporating hierarchical system, on the other hand, is in a very real sense ambivalent to its core. In terms of the Karen, much of this ambivalence appears to have been founded in the constraints that are implicit in the duality of the relationships. As the Karen were incorporated as an extension of the "sown," so also did they have to be distinguished as alien. They were not of the "sown" alone, but the guardians and facilitators of those places the sown used but did not occupy. Conceptually, they were the known that extended into the unknown, people like us but still different. It is, as history has demonstrated over and over again, he who is too close to be too different, whose differences and capacities we know, and the limits of whose power we can comprehend, that we most often turn upon, rather than the real alien whose potentialities we cannot foretell. The Karen of Chiang Mai, for example, are considered by many to have great occult powers based on their intimate relationships with the "spirits of the wild." A passage illustrating the paradigm of intimacy and distance in terms of such occult accreditation appears in a nineteenth-century missionary compendium entitled *Siam and Laos as Seen by Our American Missionaries:*

> Among the Lao, it is supposed that a sorcerer can command a spear to assume the shape of an insect, which, flying against the person whose destruction is intended, enters him and is transformed, usually into a buffalo hide, or it may assume in the body of the victim any form, according to the will of the sorcerer. The Siamese very generally believe that the Laos possess this occult power, and the Laos knowing little concerning it, credit the Karens and other mountain tribes with it. About two years ago, two Karens were brought to the city of Chiang Mai by some of their

> neighbors, charged with having caused the death of a young man by enchantment. The case was very clear against the accused. The young man had musical instruments which these Karens wished to purchase; the owner refused to sell and a short time afterward he became ill and died, I believe on the fourteenth date of his illness. At his cremation a portion of his body would not burn and was a shape similar to the musical instrument. Thus, it was clear that his death had been caused by a spirit entering his body and taking the form of the coveted musical instrument. The Karens were beheaded, protesting that they were innocent of the crimes charged against them, and threatening that their spirits should wreck vengeance for their unjust punishment. It is but just to add that cases of this kind are not of frequent occurrence [Backus 1884: 510].

Here we see, as a normal continuum of operation, the Siamese crediting the Khon Myang with great magical powers and the Khon Myang in turn crediting these powers to the Karen. Karen today either credit such powers to other distant Karen or complete the loop by crediting them to the Khon Myang. Although I came across no Khon Myang accusations of witchcraft against Karen during my field work, I did come across other like accusations and anticipations from neighbors of Sgaw groups with whom I worked. In one place, a Karen neighbor of mine recounted that her husband had been murdered some ten years before by two local Haw Chinese merchants because they believed he had killed their brother by witchcraft. The case involved an argument over a business transaction, anger, and the pronouncement of curses. When the Haw trader died, his brothers were apparently convinced of the guilt of my friend's husband. In this case, as in the one of the previous century, there was no anticipation of a negative response by the Karen as such. The political powerlessness of the Karen was known then, in the 1950s as well as it was in the 1880s, as was the Karen inability to act beyond the village or local network—a factor I refer to as the "vertical" nature of the polity in which the Karen participate.

At the same time, as we have seen, the Karen credit the Khon Myang with far greater powers than they themselves have in dealing with the spiritual world, because of the latter's possession of written texts upon which to base their formulations and transactions. In fact, the Karen have no spirit mediums. Their modes of dealing with the unknown are algorithmic; one divines a cause and makes an offering until the common denominator of "right spirit" and "right offering" is reached. If substantive knowledge of the unknown is required, Karen often avail themselves of Khon Myang spirit doctors who have actual communication with the invisible world. Many Sgaw go to Khon Muang spirit doctors and astrologers in preference to using Karen divining techniques (*ka do*).

In Thailand the group-maintaining ambivalence, based upon the dyad of intimacy and distance, has been giving way to a more profound ambivalence. Changes in the state's conception and use of its domain, as well as the growth and new ordering of populations, threaten to overwhelm the local system of relationships upon which the incorporating hierarchical system rested. It seems probable that these changes will result in replacement of the old system by either a pluralistic model with its assimilative demands upon public behavior, or, and the probabilities appear equal at this point, a plural model, at least for cultural minorities. In this latter case, integration will shift from being premised upon social relationships and a model of ecological completion and complementarity to the mechanical model premised upon the bounded cultural unit as a unique body participating in the state as itself.

The freezing of frontiers, following upon the various Anglo-Siamese treaties of the latter part of the nineteenth century, and the development of regular trade routes with border points staffed by customs officials and patrolled by troops and police, have served to vitiate the role played by the Karen as facilitators of the trade routes between domains. The set of relationships was further changed when the Siamese government assumed direct governance of northern Thailand at the end of the nineteenth century. The advent of the British in Burma had ended the oscillating power system, which, through continual redistributions of power, had ensured the ethnic fluidity apparently necessary to maintain the open system of the incorporating hierarchy. Similarly, the advent of total Siamese supremacy in Thailand terminated the formal system of incorporative alliances within the dominions of the princes that had also operated to maintain the structure of hierarchy. To the local syntagms of the hierarchical paradigm was now opposed the new paradigm of the nation-state.

The state has promoted a more or less pluralistic model of society, at least in its formal aspects, in which the "empty-set" category of Siamese or Thai citizen has replaced, at a national level, the incorporative processes of the actual groups. The state's conception of its domain, evolving more and more rapidly throughout the twentieth century, has been one in which all areas of the state are seen as arenas of actual exploitation for the nation and its populations. The hills and the jungle have ceased to be extensions of the "sown"; they are now considered areas of critical resources, as necessary to the eco-system of the nation as the paddy lands of the plains. Unlike the domains of the princes, the state does not permit differentiation of populations with respect to ecological niches since the state's ecological niche is its entire territory.

Many of these developments were slow in their flowering and World War II is the watershed between the ascendancy of the old model and that of the new. As a national model, the incorporative hierarchy is fast disappearing, a fact often perceived by the participants. As a local model, it endures, but in a much more marked state of tension and ambivalence than ever before. This tension and ambivalence have been exacerbated by the rapid growth of populations, the end of epidemic diseases and of malaria, particularly in the foothills, and the ever-quickening exploitation of the natural resources of the north. As we saw in the portrait of the ceremony of the *hae mai kham*, recent years have brought an involution or encapsulation of the hierarchical ties of localism. This has occurred in the face of the ever-expanding deluge of that "nation" of strangers oriented to a pluralistic view, who assert an equivalence of cultural behavior with political identity as a requisite for being seen as "people of one place." Brought up in an alternative system, the new population accepts the transformational aspects of the older model—that is, if one acts like a Thai, one is a Thai—but not the hierarchical aspects of it—that is, even when one is not acting like a Thai, one is still a Thai.

For the Karen, this has meant a serious schism in the continuum of the hierarchy. Whereas it once extended to include one's status as part of the dominion of Chiang Mai, it now extends, beyond oneself, to one's known Khon Mųang neighbors alone. There has been a boundary drawn between these and others, the peoples of the town and cities. These latter are now members of a Khon Mųang or Thai category that coexists with the incorporated one, but that is dominated by people who are alien both in a real sense, like Chinese and Indians, and in a symbolic sense, like urbanized Thai. They are to be feared for their power. There is little power the Karen have to counterbalance it. The loss of their status as the holders of the wild for the "sown" has taken away one of the few functions from which the Karen derived any political power. The Karen are cognizant of their powerlessness and the fragility of their position as an ethnic category allied to and derived from a position in a polydomainal system. They know they have lost their structural rights to that position, in that the hills and the jungles now also belong to many others. Thus, beyond the local level, Thai and Northern Thai are seen as threatening, somewhat assaultive, rather dislikable, and of questionable morals.

It is commonplace for Sgaw villagers to note that robbery and most other forms of criminal activity were "nonexistent before the

Thai came into this area." Or that "Karen always helped each other in time of need until even brothers and sisters learned, from the Thai, to ask each other for payment for rice." Or that "We cannot send our children to school; if we do the other children make fun of them because they do not speak Thai." The same speakers must also proclaim the limits of such hostility in the face of sociological, economic, and political necessity. This bind and its varying limits are set forth rather neatly in the following conversation with the headman of a lowland Karen village in Cọm Thọng district. We had been discussing a particularly virulent form of Karen spirit, the *tayuu* or *tayzuu*. *Tayuu* are usually brought into being through a combination of violated marital regulations and improper service to the ancestral spirits. However, another person present, whom I will call XX, noted that "there are two kinds of *tayuu*, the one from wrong marriage and the other who lives in a plant."

Headman: Really? I never heard of the second kind.

XX: Yes, it's the one that lives in the plant that the Khon Mụang call *fak wan*.[14] And the *tayuu* in it can destroy anyone who comes into the field it is in, just the same way that the other can destroy everyone in the village in which there is a wrong marriage.

H.M.: Oh, I wish I had one of those plants. (He chuckled to himself.)

Myself: What would you do with it?

H.M.: I would plant it in my garden. Then, when those Thai come to steal my fruit and vegetables it would kill them all.

Myself: Which Thai?

H.M.: The ones who come and steal my bananas and vegetables as they go along the trail up into the hills.

Myself: You mean from the villages of A and B? (I referred to the Northern Thai villages that share the same garden swidden as well as paddy and terrace areas with the Karen village.)

H.M.: No, not them. We are all people of the same place. They would not steal from me. No, the people who walk from Cọm Thọng town into the hills, those are the ones. I really don't want to kill them, just scare them really good. I wish I had one of those plants.

The headman was not indulging in fantasies about the robbery of his garden. Karen gardens were regularly pilfered. Neither limits nor defense are conceived of in terms of the abstract assault of "culture" by "culture," but in terms of remembered and anticipated real personal assaults. The old man whose son is married to a Khon Mụang girl in the next village remembers being taunted by chants of "roll the Karen out to fix the road with his oil" from town children engaged in a punning play upon the Northern Thai term for Karen *yang* and the tree *Dipterocarpus alatus,* also *yang*. Although he had as great a love and passion for punning and the game of double entendre as the Thai children, his response was based not on appreciation of the humor, but on fear and anxiety that at some point the punning insult would be the prelude to physical assault.

Even though the incidence of physical assaults on the part of northerners against Karen is low and psychological assault has not been extensive or encouraged, both sides operate in terms of the fear that such assaults potentially lurk in any number of situations. Despite the joint proclamations of sameness, both are aware that the differences remain. Thus, although one may speak of Karen as "Hill Thai," they still really remain Karen who speak an alien tongue and who are powerless and so not to be feared, although perhaps to be despised or made fun of.

Constant ambivalence is one measure of this combination of closeness and distance in the structural design of the relationship. A conversation with the chief monk of a large local *wat* underlines this from the Northern Thai point of view. The chief monk, perhaps the leading social activist of his district, had initiated the building of a road to tie together a number of villages connected only by footpaths. The labor was being contributed by the villages involved. When I accompanied the crew from the Karen villages, I noted that only Karen had come. My discussion of this with the chief monk went as follows:

Myself: Why aren't there any Khon Muang here?

Abbot: Oh, I can't have them here when the Karen are here to work.

Myself: Why not?

Abbot: There might be trouble with the young men.

Myself: What kind of trouble?

Abbot: Well, the young men might say things to the Karen girls, or talk about the way the Karen boys are working. They might make jokes about how they work, or their clothes. Then we might have a fight.

Myself: A fight?

Abbot: Yes, between the boys and the Karen.

Myself: Then this has happened before.

Abbot: No, it's never happened.

Myself: There's never been a fight?

Abbot: No, I don't know of a fight, but I'm afraid it might happen because the Karen are different and the boys might make fun of them.

Myself: But it's never happened?

Abbot: No, it's never happened.

To round out this passage and its contrast of fearful "mights" solicitous of the Karen and their powerlessness, I should point out that the abbot attempted to ensure Karen participation in all *wat* ceremonials, including *wat* fairs, with no thought of potential Karen-Northern Thai violence in those arenas of chronic personal assault. The Karen who, in fear of fights, always left a *wat* fair as soon as the serious drinking and gambling began, wondered why no Khon Muang ever worked on the road with them on the days they contributed labor.

The rapid growth of population in the north has been an essential factor in the reformation of relationships. In 1837 McLeod gave the following estimate for Chiang Mai: 704 houses in the city and a total population of 50,000 for the province (McLeod 1869: 38). This can be compared with the census of 1960: 65,736 people in the city of Chiang Mai and 798,483 in the province. To this latter we would have to add an additional 80,807, the population of the Mae Hong Son province, which in McLeod's time was accounted a part of Chiang Mai. This seventeen-and-a-half-fold increase and the growing urbanization (the population of Chiang Mai city increased from 38,211 to 65,736 in the period 1947–60 and was estimated to be above 100,000 by the late 1960s) have contributed to the reordering of relationships. A new population, new in the sense that it is urban oriented and educated in the ideas of the nation-state, is counterposed to the older but surviving localism. The cognitive set that supported the polydomainal notions of the incorporative hierarchy is as alien to this ascending and growing group as it is to the average American. To the newly educated urbanite and townsman, the concept of nationality has cultural as well as political boundaries. For him, the Karen have been transformed into a national minority within his borders, little different from the Meo, Yao, Akha, Lisu, and others firmly rooted in the hills. As I have pointed out in another essay (Marlowe 1973), the development of a hill-tribe category as a matter of governmental policy has contributed to this redefinition of the Karen and of those social relationships the concept of the "state" can encompass.

The expansion of population, particularly in the period since World War II, has also led to a rapid conceptual and actual incorporation of the hills and wild into the domain used by the lowlander. Programs for controlling malaria and other diseases have made the foothills inviting for exploitation by the lowlander. Extractive industries, developing rapidly since the middle 1950s, have been converting the high valleys of Karen occupation into highly prized segments of the lowland's total eco-system. At the same time, mass migrations of Meo, Yao, and other hillmen into northern Thailand have challenged the Karen's position in the hills. These mass migrations have affirmed an upland system in opposition to the "lowland" system and in contradistinction to the "medial" model of the hills so necessary to the existence of the Karen category in the life of the wider domain of the "sown."

In the past, the assertion of one's identity as a Karen was contrastive and partial, appropriate only to certain times and places. For most of the major areas of life, Karen and their neighbors saw themselves as interdependent participants, co-members of the same local and wider hierarchies, the one incorporated in the other. On the local level, this model has remained viable, but today it is no longer isomorphic with the metasociety's notion of "order." A transformation to pluralism with the alternatives of assimilation or encapsulation is under way. Change is sweeping away the older social, ecological, and economic bases of the incorporative hierarchy. On the local level, when a Karen begins to walk along a trail, he is almost always joined by a Khon Mụang, Thai Lue, or Shan who will walk with him side by side. He may not want the other with him at that particular moment but there is no way in which he can command him to vanish. If his journey is to a market, a curer, a ritual, a job, or to any resting place outside of a Karen village, the odds are that he will find a lowlander awaiting him at journey's end. His niche has been extending the "sown" into the hills, but the hills are now within the "sown" itself. Locally the Karen and the others have made the unknown known to each other and have found some measure of completion, each in the others' way of life and fact of existence. Nationally, this interdependence has been preempted as the earlier paradigm fades. A Karen friend once said to me, after walking from Cọm Thọng to Mae Sariang, "I walked all that way, and everywhere there were Karen and Karen villages. You know, if there are so many of us maybe we should have a province or a country of our own." He laughed nervously when he finished the thought. He was embarrassed to have voiced such a sentiment. He said it was just a thought and that he was not serious, because "No one has ever heard of such a thing as a Karen country, and we are Thai." He was thirty-eight at the time. Times and systems change and men respond.

Acknowledgments

The ethnographic data reported in this essay were gathered during field studies in 1965–68 of the social and cultural factors involved in disease epidemiology among the Karen of Chiang Mai province carried out by the author as research anthropologist, Department of Psychiatry, U.S. Medical Component, Southeast Asia Treaty Organization Medical Research Laboratory. The views expressed here are those of the author and in no way represent an official position of the Walter Reed Army Institute of Research or the Department of the Army.

Many friends and colleagues have had roles in the formulation of the ideas and the expedition and facilitation of the research drawn upon for this essay. I would particularly like to note the discussions I have had over the years, in places ranging from paddy fields to hotel bars, with the anthropologists F. K. Lehman, Charles F. Keyes, Peter Kunstadter, Clark E. Cunningham, and, above all, my wife, Gertrude W. Marlowe. A special note of thanks is owed to Harry C. Holloway, M.D., presently director of the Division of Neuro-Psychiatry, Walter Reed Army Institute of Research, for his support and for the almost infinite number of discussions and arguments we have had about the nature of human groups. This essay is dedicated to Dr. David McK. Rioch, without whose support and encouragement it, and the research on which it is based, would have never been. The essay reflects, I hope, to some small extent the comprehensive vision of human behavior that Dr. Rioch has transmitted and that has helped to illuminate the darkness of an often unreasoning age to those of us who have had the fortune to be associated with him.

Notes

1. Compare Nicolas Gervaise's seventeenth-century account of the transformation of Lao and Mon into Siamese (Gervaise 1928: 25). Leach has also pointed out similar patterns with regard to the categories Burman and Shan (Leach 1960: 143–44; Leach 1954).

2. Such awareness by Karen of behavior appropriate to those of other categories is not recent. Richardson, who travelled from Moulmein to Bangkok in 1829, wrote in his journal that "one of our Karen companions is at this moment giving most ludicrous and savage imitations of the dances of the Siamese, Taline [Mon], Burmans, and Lawas by firelight" (Richardson 1839 and 1840).

3. These commonalities speak as structural evidence to the question of the location of the Karen in the hill-valley system of socioecological division devised by E. R. Leach (Leach 1960: 64). Certainly in terms of kinship system, marital arrangements, and so forth, the Karen are plainly allied to the valley side of the dichotomy. The Karen are not, for example, characterized by exogamy to a much greater degree than are the Northern Thai. The structure of the ancestral spirits is alineal, perhaps less so than its valley Khon Muang equivalent. Other diacriticals such as bride wealth are also not to be found in the Karen context. Marriage, for Karen, as for the Khon Muang, represents a free contractual choice of the partners. It allies families and small kindreds, not groups.

4. Theodore Stern (in his chapter in this volume) reports that in Sangkhlaburi 49 percent of Pwo Karen marriages were with non-Karen.

5. The situation involved is analogous to that dealt with by Louis Dumont in his brilliant dissection of the notion of the village as a corporate

entity in India. He shows how, in the Indian case, the secondary corporate proprietorship of the village may confound the actual noncorporate structure of the individual proprietor's primary rights in land that exist as functions of his relationships within the wider polity of which he is a part (Dumont 1970B: 112–32).

6. Also see Peter Hinton's chapter in this volume.

7. Karen informants say that they began this practice at least "three lifetimes of men ago." At that time, Cọm Thọng town was only a small place. In the 1830s, McLeod counted 15 houses there (McLeod 1869: 19). By 1883 the town, then called Nan Long, had prospered and had 300 households (Colquhoun 1885).

8. Some of these matters are dealt with by Lehman in his discussion of the applications of lattice theory and hierarchical constructs in his chapter in this volume and others have been discussed by Michael Moerman in relation to that Thai-Lue of Chiang Kham (Moerman 1968: 153ff).

9. The situtation is structurally equivalent to that described for the relationship of the Khamu, as the original owners of the land, to the Lao (LeBar, Hickey, and Musgrave 1964: 113) and to that of the Lua' to the Khon Mụang in many parts of the northern Thailand.

10. Gertrude W. Marlowe has pointed out that much the same system operates on the local level in the Khon Mụang village she studied. She notes the incorporation, for example, of a Chinese, but the nonincorporation of the Central Thai (G. W. Marlowe 1965–68).

11. Such similarities might also explain the high rates of Khamu-Karen intermarriage since the Khamu appear traditionally to have occupied much the same position in Laos.

12. In 1586 Ralph Finch, an English merchant-adventurer, travelled to Chiang Mai in "five and twenty days journey northeast from Pegu. In which journey I passed many fruitful and pleasant countries" (Ryley 1899). Two hundred and fifty years later, McLeod's party spent thirty days traversing the same distance.

13. McLeod, in fact, discovered extensive knowledge of the Karen throughout the Shan states as he travelled along the great trade route from Pegu to Chiang Mai to Keng Tung (Chiang Tung), Keng Hung (Chiang Hung), and thence to China (McLeod 1869: 58).

14. *Melientha suavis,* a forest shrub. The leaves and young shoots can be eaten as a vegetable, but it may contain abnormal shoots and ears, poisoned by parasitical larvae, which, if eaten, bring about collapse and death.

Who Are the Karen, and If So, Why?
Karen Ethnohistory and
a Formal Theory of Ethnicity

F. K. Lehman

It seems there is an overriding theme for the present volume: we are trying to work out just what the ethnolinguistic category "Karen" amounts to. It is again and again pointed out, even in the title of this volume, that ethnic identity has a great deal to do with the way peoples adapt, especially to their sociopolitical environment, that is, to other peoples. If, then, we can make clear what has been and what now is the nature of the system of intergroup relations that characterizes the category Karen—and perhaps something about the historical context of intergroup relations in which this ethnolinguistic category came into being and developed—we may be able to understand the way the Karen have come to fit into the ethnological picture in Thailand. This latter I take to be a more particular focal problem of the present volume. The answer to the latter question depends upon our knowing what part Thailand and the Tai-speaking peoples play and have played in the network of intergroup relations that is the defining context of Karen. Hence, the question about Thailand and the Tai turns out to be just a particular part of the overriding theme identified at the start of this paragraph.

The present chapter is largely concerned with a semiformal theory of ethnicity as applied to this theme. The theory of ethnicity, more especially the idea that ethnic categories are the conceptual means by which peoples adapt to their social (and natural) environment, is again and again alluded to in various other chapters of this book. However, it remains for this chapter to spell out this theory systematically as it bears on the Karen. I have tried to accomplish this from the particular perspectives of my own work as both a linguist and an anthropologist, concerned in both my professions with formal theory on the one hand and with the region of Burma on the other. More narrowly still, I have gone about this task by focusing upon that part of the Karen group among whom I have worked at some length both in Burma and in Thailand: the Kayah or Red Karen (Karenni, in the older literature).

Fortunately, my work with the Kayah has had largely to do with just this problem of ethnic identity, and even with ethnogenesis, with the fairly recent origins of the Kayah as a distinct people. Moreover, the Kayah work has been carried out in the explicit context of my research among the Shan (a Tai-speaking people of the Burma-Thailand border region) and the Burmans. I began this work by seeing the identity and ethnogenesis of the Kayah as largely determined by and in this context, both historically and synchronically. In this chapter, I attempt to extend this view to the larger Karen picture.

As I have indicated, the general question of the nature of ethnicity has two aspects to it: the historical and the structural or formal and synchronic. It has hitherto been assumed that somehow the historical aspect is ultimately the more fundamental—that an ethnic category, or rather the people comprising it, are to be defined in terms of their participation in a particular historical cultural tradition. Thus it has often been held that the characterization of the ethnicity of a people or group of peoples depends in a uniquely crucial way upon the identification of the common historical tradition and therefore of the origins of that tradition and of the peoples bearing it. I shall ultimately argue against this viewpoint. Ethnicity, I will contend, is a matter of the conceptual organization of intergroup relations, and concentrating upon defining a common historical cultural tradition leads to a certain circularity of argument.

Nevertheless, historical questions and historical evidence are of genuine importance for characterizing ethnicity—not, perhaps, by way of defining a common history of some set of people but rather by way of defining the context of ethnogenesis itself, the context of the virtual invention of an ethnic category. Therefore, I will start off by dealing with questions about the historical origins of the Karen, again from the standpoint of my studies of Kayah in the Shan-Burma context and my studies in the linguistics of the Tibeto-Burman family of languages.[1] These initial sections will lead to comments on the formal theory of ethnic category systems (cf. Lehman 1975) and then to my central task, the *relational* answer to the question, "Who are the Karen, and what part has Thailand played in the intergroup context of their identity?" My own ethnographic material derives from field work among the Red Karen and the Shan, conducted in Thailand during 1967 and 1968, under a grant from the U.S. Army Medical Corps.

For the reader with only a sound anthropological background and an informed general interest in Southeast Asia, much of the present chapter may seem abstruse. There is, here, a broad spectrum of fine detail—linguistic, ethnological, and historical—much of it concerned with non-Karen but all bearing upon Karen and Kayah. The general reader can probably skim over it without losing the thread of the overall argument of the chapter. However, because I have set myself the task of constructing a rather formal theoretical argument about the nature of ethnicity in general and of Karen ethnicity in particular, this spectrum of minutiae cannot be omitted. The value of an explicit and structural argument is largely measured by the number and the empirical range of the facts it draws together in a coherent way. We need to know exactly what kinds of empirical evidence bear upon such a theory; we need to know exactly what kinds of empirical claims such a theory makes. Broad and generalized empirical treatments will not support such a theoretical argument. In the last century, Henry Maitland said that sooner or later anthropology would have the choice of "being history or nothing." My own view is that sooner or later anthropology must make the choice of being theoretically and empirically explicit or being nothing.

Karen Origins: Ethnolinguistic and Historical Evidence

Who are the Karen related to? More particularly, what is known about their origins as a distinguishable group of peoples? Since, whatever else is the case, they form a linguistic family of some kind, we may begin conveniently by examining how their linguistic affiliations bear upon this question.

It is often supposed that the present region of a language family's greatest internal diversity is a good clue to its place of origin or, at least, the place from which its present branches and members were dispersed. The area of greatest internal diversity means the area where we find the greatest number of distinct branches of the family represented.

The Larger Setting of the Kayah and Shan

I agree with the proposition first suggested by G. H. Luce (1959A) and supported by R. B. Jones (1975) that we must look to the Karen Hills—those of the southern Shan State of Burma and the immediately adjacent ones on the west of the Kayah State—when we look for the area of the greatest internal diversity of historically known Karen languages. However, we must be wary of a simplistic inference from this, for it does not necessarily tell us anything about an *Urheimat,* an original homeland, for the Karen. I know of no evidence suggesting that many different kinds of Karen languages may have been at one time more widely found outside the Karen Hills, so Jones's and Luce's conjectures about the center of dispersal are plausible inferences from present distributions, although hardly inescapable (see Lehman 1963, for a counterexample in the case of the Chin). But although the present distribution probably indicates the region of dispersal of the present array of Karen linguistic subgroups, it cannot tell us anything about where the ancestors of the Karen may have been before the time when the subgroups began to split up.

Jones (1975) points out that Luce's current inclination is to connect Karen genetically with Tai rather than with Sino-Tibetan languages. Without adhering to this radical suggestion, Jones does question the relation of Karen to Tibeto-Burman (T-B) or Sino-Tibetan (S-T), referring to the apparently relatively small number of Sino-Tibetan cognates in Karen. Many of these, he says, are Burmese loan words. The rest, he asserts, show no systematic tonal correspondences with their apparent Sino-Tibetan cognates. However, the relative number of *clear* Sino-Tibetan or Tibeto-Burman cognates is hard to judge. First, utterly transparent and unproblematical cognate etymologies are not all that easily come by even in the more developed area of comparative Indo-European linguistics. Second, it is not obvious what a *relatively* small number might be. If Karen is a Sino-Tibetan language, it is likely to be a remote branch of the family, as has long been assumed. This, in itself, would tend to obscure cognate correspondences.

There are certain features of the Karen grammar that seem to mark it as S-T, in particular the rather extensive complement of reduced-stress, open-syllable prefixes (their profusion is most marked in Kayah and hill Karen), which, from very preliminary observation, seem to represent old noun-class prefixes, which we know are an old feature of T-B morphology (see Benedict 1972; Jordan 1969; Maran 1971; and almost any treatment of classical Tibetan). On the other hand, the tonal system is indeed of a different variety from the Tibeto-Burman one. It is clearly, as the research of Jones (1961A, 1961B), Haudricourt (1945), and Luce (1959A) has shown, a two-register system derivable from an ancient bifurcation of syllable initials into opposed classes characterized by a voicing or a laryngealized distinction. This is characteristic of Thai, and also of other families outside Tibeto-Burman in southeastern and eastern Asia (Maran 1970; Purtle 1970), including Chinese as well as Austroasiatic. In T-B tonal systems, on the contrary, the main effect upon the vocalic pitch phenomena generally comes from distinctions in the postvocalic position of the syllable (Maran 1971; Matisoff 1972). However, T-B languages have also developed (e.g., in Tibetan and Jinghpaw) a low tone in association with syllable-initial voiced consonants, and this too has led in effect to a systematic register distinction. Meanwhile, Paul Benedict (1973) has gone a long way towards showing, *contra* Jones, a fairly systematic correspondence between Karen *basic* tonal categories or oppositions and the basic Sino-Tibetan ones.

Moreover, especially using the aforementioned prefixes as evidence, the number of cognates seems greater than Jones allows. Also, some at least of the Karen etyma that he says have no cognates in Tibeto-Burman appear to correspond with items in Luce's list of non-Tibeto-Burman "mystery" items in the Chin languages (Luce 1959C), and the effect of this is surely to cast some doubt on Jones's and Luce's position, since now these items indeed have Tibeto-Burman cognates, that is, in the Chin branch of Tibeto-Burman. All of this I treat in some detail, in the course of a critique of Jones's comparative work on Karen, in a forthcoming review of Sino-Tibetan comparative linguistics, and I argue there that his methods—relying too heavily on the idea that phonological segment types and tones in complementary distribution in a language must be reconstructed as coming from a single ancestral segment or tone category—are bound to obscure systematic tonal correspondences. The upshot of all this is that we have no present reason to doubt that Karen is in the Sino-Tibetan group, although whether within, or coordinate with, the Tibeto-Burman branch, it is not yet possible to say.

Nevertheless, Karen's pervasive register distinction as well as its verb-final word order—Tibeto-Burman is universally verb-medial and Chinese seems to have been in transition as to word order (Li 1975)—suggests at least a profound influence from Thai upon Karen. If this be borne out, it could mean that the ancestors of the Karen were in what is now part of Thailand at least as early as in the Karen Hills, or that they may have been in Thailand *as well as* in the present Karen Hills at some conveniently remote period of history, say, before the time of major Mon, and then Tai, expansion in Thailand, and even during the earliest years of the latter expansion. The expansion, if as thorough as we may assume it to have been, probably would have eliminated all direct evidence for the earlier Karen presence, along the lines of my reconstruction in the Chin case.

There are some data, in addition to Jones's linguistic conjecture, that suggest early Karen habitation in northwestern Thailand, specifically in what is now northern Mae Họng Sọn province. My own investigations in the northern third of the province, among both Shan and Red Karen, brought to light a curious situation. The present Shan population in this area came in starting not much more than a century ago, certainly less than two. The Kayah of the area (see Lehman 1967A) certainly came there first only well after the end of the eighteenth century, a far-flung remnant of the earliest expansion of the Kantarawady Kayah eastward to and across the Salween at the beginning of the nineteenth century; comparisons of Thailand Kayah dialects with Luce's (1959A) tables make this abundantly clear. It would seem reasonable to expect, then, that this area, like much of the rest of northern Thailand, was originally previously inhabited by the Lawa (Lua'). However, there is among neither the Shan nor the Kayah of northern Mae Họng Sọn province even the remotest hint of any tradition that these lands were, at the time of their intrusion, occupied by Lawa.

On the contrary, the Shan record, which is to some degree verifiable from documentary sources from the early nineteenth century (see Keyes 1970 and Penth 1977), indicates strongly that when they began arriving, these uplands were unoccupied. It is particularly certain that there were no Lawa there at that time. Although the Kayah have preserved little explicit tradition bearing on this point and, except among the most southerly of these Kayah, there is not even a clear idea of the existence of people such as Lawa, those who know of the Lawa are unanimous, for whatever it is worth, in denying vigorously any suggestion that Lawa were present.

This tradition notwithstanding, we do know that at some more remote historical period these hills were occupied, and presumably not by Tai. I base this judgment upon the report, as yet unpublished, by Chester Gorman from his excavations in caves in this region (cf. Gorman 1969). The uppermost layer of occupation in the caves contains clear evidence of a people who left, among other things, some sort of large, boat-shaped, wooden receptacles, presumptively coffins, and these remains, although still unstudied and unidentified, are not definitive in their resemblance to ethnographically known Lawa hollowed-log coffins. Nor do they even remotely suggest Shan. If they suggest any people at all—and I do not know whether they do, not having seen them—it may be a kind of Karen. That is, although the present Eastern Kayah of Thailand do not practice anything re-

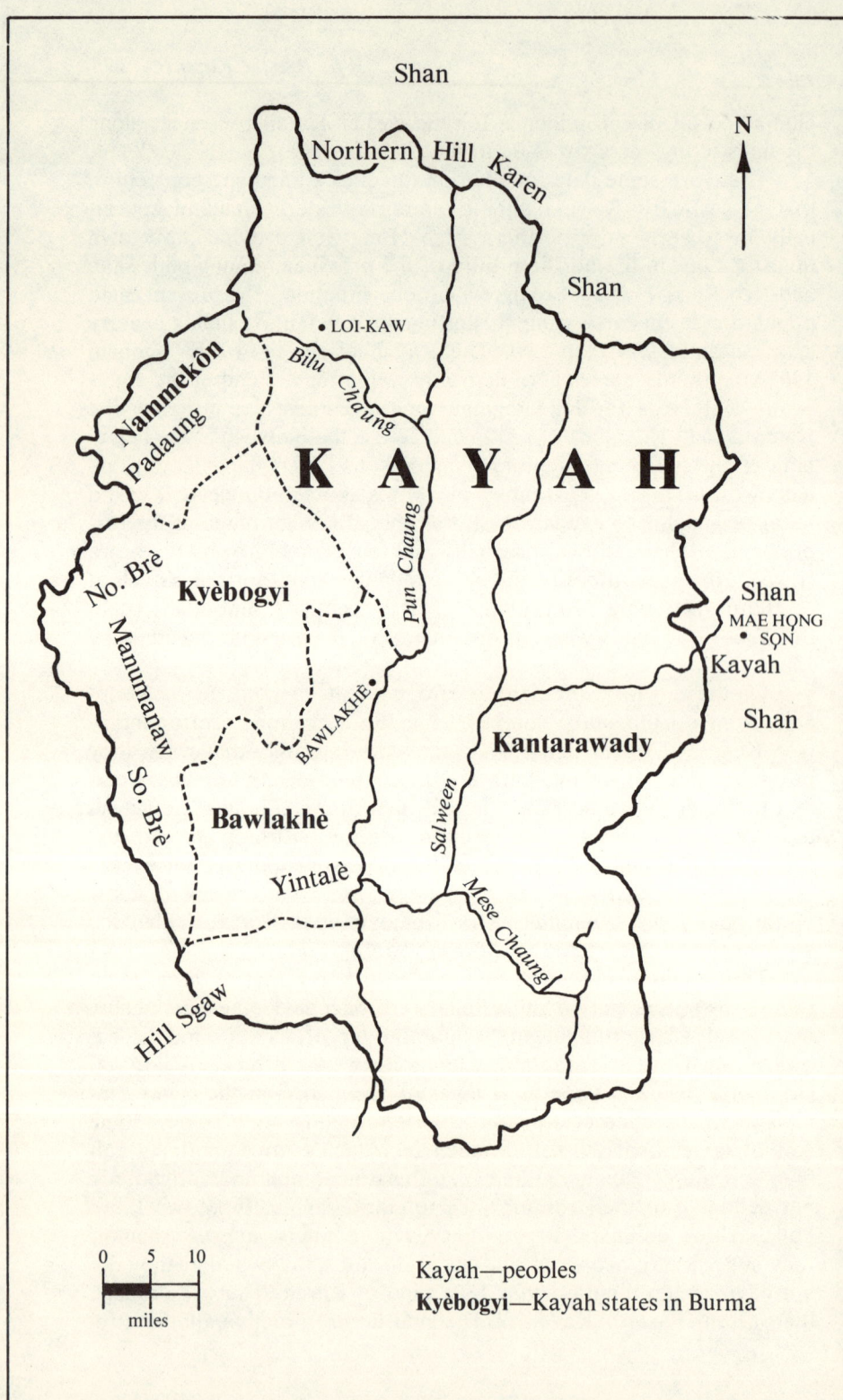

Kayah and Their Neighbors in Burma and Northwestern Thailand

sembling this sort of burial or preserve any tradition of having done so or even of having known about such a practice, some Central and Northern Karen do, among them the Western Kayah of Kyèbogyi in the Burmese Kayah State (see Lehman 1967A). It is, then, at least possible that Karen did occupy a part of what is now northern Thailand at some early historical period, and that the connections of any such Thailand Karen may have been, even then, with the present Karen of the hill country immediately on the west of the Kayah State in Burma, to whom the Kayah are most closely related (Lehman 1967A). This, if correct—and I am not asserting that it is, but only setting up a hypothesis—would not have to be taken as evidence that the Karen "came from" what is now Thailand, but only that possibly, at a time before the eighteenth century, Karen groups of the hill country just on the west of Kayah proper today, among whom we have seen that we ought to look for the most likely center of dispersion of historically known Karen groupings, may have extended more widely to include at least a part of what is now Thailand.

This would put very early Karen in some kind of plausible contact or connection with early Tai. That is a plausible situation for explaining any ancient Tai linguistic influence. But consider what this speculation can mean and what it cannot. It means that earlier in history a good part of the present range of Kayah distribution was occupied by Karen, probably rather closely related to Kayah in terms of linguistic subgrouping. It would almost certainly not mean that those Karen were the Kayah as such.

This brings me to another consideration, the historical conjecture of Nigel Brailey (1970) that the Kayah *themselves* first came to occupy their present range, including perhaps also part of the southernmost Shan states, in the eighteenth century or possibly before that. I want to look at Brailey's idea from three points of view: linguistic evidence, historical and ethnographic evidence, including a small part of the evidence he himself adduces, and the evidence, if it is that, from my own hypothesis put forward above (the apparent absence of Lawa from northern Mae Họng Sọn and the possible meaning of the late remains in the caves there).[2]

The linguistic evidence is perhaps the most formidable against Brailey's conjecture, and I have spelled it out earlier (Lehman 1967A, 1967B). Briefly, the present Kayah or Red Karen dialects form a continuous chain of mutually intelligible neighbors stretching from the isolated little group (about 1,200) in Thailand westward to Kyèbogyi, and the latter dialect is virtually identical with that of the Manumanaw,[3] a group of hill Karen at the western border of Kyèbogyi. Indeed, there are villages in these low foothills that are indifferently identified by both sides as either Manumanaw or Kayah, and traditional Kayah costume is a variant of Manumanaw, or vice versa. The Manumanaw language is mutually intelligible with so-called Southern Brè of the farther hills, and at least some Northern Kayah seems to be part of a related dialect chain with Northern Brè (see also Emmons 1966). The dialect divisions referred to are so continuous, and represent such a small degree of historical separation, that we can hardly suppose with Brailey either that Karen (namely Kayah) came to the present Kayah territory only about the last quarter of the eighteenth century, or that they in some sense returned here after a long, migratory separation. There must have been Karen in this area at an earlier date—although, as we said before, they would not have been Kayah.

What I pointed out in 1967 is still substantially correct: all evidence indicates that the Kayah established themselves politically in most of their present habitat at the expense of a previous Shan economic domination of the Nam Pilu plain sometime about the beginning of the nineteenth century. The evidence further indicates that they did this largely under the stimulus of the rising importance of the trade in teak that was taken from the western hills and ultimately floated down to British territory on the Nam Pilu and other tributaries of the Salween and, ultimately, the Salween itself. This expansion, in the light of linguistic connections, could have come from nowhere but these hills at the western edge of the Kayah State. In fact, if one looks carefully and critically at Brailey's extended quotation (on page 42) from O'Riley's 1856 report, one notices the admission that movement out of the western hills of Kayah State is clearly referred to.

Although this movement seems clear, it leaves a problem that has long disturbed me. In 1967 I was able to argue that the Kayah ethnic-political system was based in some direct sense upon ideological influences from the south, more specifically from the Buddhist millennial movements of Lower Burma of the period around the end of the eighteenth and the start of the nineteenth century (Lehman 1967A; cf. Stern 1968A and Stern's chapter in this volume). I cannot recapitulate here the argument for that conclusion, but what we know of the history of the two major Kayah states of Bawlahkè and Kantarawady clearly indicates that their respective founders both came out of the south and that they were, typically, charismatic personages, capitalizing upon their knowledge of the outside world. They founded a religious cult, on which the Kayah polity was explicitly based, strikingly reminiscent of the millennial ideology adduced by Theodore Stern among Mon and Burman Buddhists and plains Karen, both Buddhist and animist, during just this era. However, additional field work among the Shan and Kayah of western Thailand in 1968–69 made it increasingly clear to me that an overwhelmingly large portion of the ritual symbolism of this cult, as well as much of the political structure, was borrowed in the most direct and explicit manner not from Burmans or Mon but from the Shan of the southern Shan states. Why should this have been the case if the catalyst for the rise of a definitive Kayah polity came out of the south?

I can now suggest a plausible solution in the light of some part of Brailey's evidence. It seems more than likely that for some time before the late eighteenth century there had been in existence, or developing, a sort of mixed Shan-Karen political order in the general region extending from the east of the southern Shan states south through the eastern and central parts of what is now the Kayah State of Burma. It is also likely that some, perhaps many, elements of the hill Karen peoples mainly occupying the hills on the west of the Nam Pilu valley were involved in this setup, and likewise it may even be guessed that some elements of what eventually became the distinctive Kayah entity found their way to the eastern part of this region somewhat before the rise of the latter polity.

This would perhaps account for a puzzling fact. The easternmost Kayah, those of the Thailand side of the border whom I worked with in 1965 and during 1967–68, clearly recognize that they are of one ethnic category with the Kayah of eastern Kantarawady on the other side of the border, on both sides of the Salween. Eastern Kantarawady dialects differ from those of western Kantarawady (cf. Luce 1959A), and the Kayah in Thailand speak one or the other of the two major eastern Kantarawady subdialects, depending upon whether they live north or south of a line running east and west through Mae Họng Sọn town. These Kayah have from time to time intermarried and visited with the Kantarawady Kayah nearest them. However, the Thailand Kayah have no tradition that they have ever been part of the old Kantarawady Kayah state—in fact with few exceptions they currently claim no knowledge of or connection with any of the Kayah political entities. This is the case despite the fact that, in the middle of the nineteenth century, Sawlapaw of Kantarawady is well known to have raided the Shan territories around Mae Họng Sọn and south to Khun Yuam and to have settled some Kayah in at least the southern part of this range (see Keyes 1970: 230–34). Moreover, it is generally held (see Lehman 1967A) that it is the development of the state of Kantarawady, well after the start of the nineteenth century, that largely accounts for the spread of what are now the Kayah into the eastern parts of the Kayah State, at the expense of what previous population, if any, is not understood.

I suggest, but cannot argue very strongly yet, that the northernmost of the eastern Kayah on both sides of the border may have been there before the rise of Kantarawady or of the Kayah political system but were absorbed, at least on the Burma side, into the Kayah political system later on. This is consistent with the foregoing observations and alone makes sense of the persistent tradition[4] among the Mae Hong Son Kayah of their having "long ago" been associated politically with Chiang Mai—rather in the sense of the facts adduced by Brailey. Moreover, it is interesting that the cult associated throughout the Kayah State, both institutionally and in mythology, with the political system and with the legends surrounding the founders of the several Kayah states—I mean the *iylùw* ritual cycle (Lehman 1967A)—is found here in extremely attenuated form and with quite different and nonpolitically oriented mythological associations.

As I have shown elsewhere, the physical paraphernalia of the ritual are, without any question, of Shan-Burmese Buddhist origin. Indeed they are associated mostly with the fact that the semilegendary political founders of Kayah came as charismatic figures from the outside, with knowledge of the Burmese-Buddhist world, and on that basis were able to organize the Kayah into a political force. Moreover, as I said above, although I cannot set forth the facts here, the source of most of the physical symbols is clearly Shan.

It is true that the impetus under which the Kayah as such were welded into a political-ethnic entity came from the south, from the messianic Buddhist movements in which the Shan seem for the most part not to have been involved. But I submit that what they were motivated toward was the taking over of an already existing Shan-oriented political setup, in which, furthermore, elements of the very people out of which the Kayah as a people arose must already have been participant. This all was confined to the present Kayah State. When, therefore, the Kyèbogyi Kayah are represented as driving out the Shan from economic domination of the western Nam Pilu plain and of the teak trade, and replacing them there, we ought to understand rather the capture of a Shan-dominated and Shan-oriented social and economic system by one of its own internal elements (cf. Lehman 1967A).

Brailey and his sources provide various kinds of evidence for the foregoing conjecture. On page 42 he quotes O'Riley on the tradition that, say, in the middle of the eighteenth century a mixed group of Karen established a Shan-based social and political system in what later became Northern Karenni, and that this group of people were substantially swelled by people from the western hills. In fact, as he points out, it was only then that Kyèbogyi came into existence.[5] Indeed, the uncertainty about whether Kyèbogyi or the more southerly Yangtalai state of Bawlahkè was the first "Kayah" state is almost certainly a function in part of the fact that, on the one hand, the sources of charismatic authority for the movement came out of the south, first to the Yangtalai, and on the other, the motivation for the actual form of the political system came from the north, from the Shan-oriented system, probably through what became Kyèbogyi and Nyaungpalè (a former substate of Kayah in Nammekôn).

Brailey (1970: 41) makes a good deal of the fact, cited imperfectly from Camille Notton, that about the middle of the eighteenth century the ruler of Chiang Mai was supported in part by people whom Brailey construes as Kayah. Now, my conjecture would account for this fact without supposing that the people were Kayah in the sense in which we now understand that category term. Moreover, Notton (1926: 214) mentions merely "têtes rouges," which presents some difficulties of identification, since Kayah *men* did not in general wear red *headcloths* while some of the other Northern Karen men did. Moreover, the support was given by, or in the name of, a chief west of the Salween whose title and name are given as *k'ang sên luang "(de race) yang (Kharen)."* Now the title *k'ang* is a specifically Shan title for a headman, or something a bit grander, of a subordinated non-Shan hill folk. Under the Kayah State system the headman did *not* bear this title, nor did higher officers, while the chiefs bore, in Shan, much higher ones. In any case (see Keyes's historical chapter herein) these *têtes rouges* (*hua daeng*) were much too far south to be Kayah.

Brailey (1970: 43) also notes the version of Kayah traditional history that has the founder of Kyèbogyi descended from (in Francis Mason's Sgaw-transmitted text) *thau-krie,* and Brailey concludes that this is the Tso-Sha mentioned by O'Riley as the founder of Kyèbogyi village (or /kéy (ta) ljà/, in the text Brailey cites called "Kay-la-tset") eight generations before O'Riley's informant, Kéy Phow-Duw, the charismatic old man who gave his name (in Burmese Kyèbogyi) to the village and state. But here O'Riley, who is notoriously unreliable for detail, is badly confused. Kéy Phow-Duw (Lehman 1967A: 51) was himself born Sha(re) (i.e., /cja-re-/), from which, by the prefixation of the Shan ruler's title *cau* in customary Kayah fashion, one gets Tso-Sha. As for *thau-krie* (/thɔ kriə/), there is some likelihood that it is a (Sgaw-derived) rendering for the Kayah /sɔ̃ phrja/, which is, of course, the Shan for "Lord."[6] Thus, again, Brailey is misusing evidence to advance his thesis as to early dates for Kayah.

I have suggested here, as in earlier writings, that the Kayah were a subordinate component of a Shan-Karen polity before the end of the eighteenth century. This makes it necessary for me to deal with a piece of apparent counterevidence. G. E. Harvey (1967: 123–24) speaks of the early rulers of Toungoo (1280–1531) as suffering raids from Karenni and securing tribute from Karenni. This is taken to imply the existence of the Kayah political entity in that ancient period. However, as far as I can make out Harvey is unintentionally playing upon the ambiguity of the Burmese expression *Karenni*. It can mean the Kayah people proper and it can also mean the Kayah and hill Karen generally who live east of the Toungoo region. Furthermore, at least following British usage, it can be used as the name of a specific political entity. In saying "from Karenni" instead of something like "from *the* Karenni" Harvey assuredly overinterprets his evidence and flies in the face of all other historical and ethnological evidence that the distinctive Kayah polity is quite a recent affair.

What we are left with, after the foregoing assessment of linguistic and historical evidence bearing upon the Kayah and their connections and antecedents, is that probably a very few centuries ago, perhaps as recently as the eighteenth and certainly earlier, the region of greatest Karen linguistic diversity was, as it is now, the hills surrounding the present Kayah State on the west (and north), but with the peoples in question, more especially the immediate forebears of the present Kayah, probably extending east into what is now northwestern Thailand. The rise of the Kayah polity—and presumably of a distinct Kayah ethnic category—has tended to reduce the apparent geographical range of this region of central diversity to its western edge, but this is a comparatively recent phenomenon, dating from perhaps the end of the eighteenth century. If it is assumed that the region of greatest internal linguistic diversity betokens the region of dispersal of the present range of a language (sub-) family, then my interpretation gives us an account of the basis for the presumed long-standing Tai influence upon Karen languages without our having to suppose that Karen is genetically related to Tai.

But exactly how long ago the ancestors of the Karen may have come to this linguistic "dispersal" region in the Karen Hills—if indeed they came there from somewhere else at all—is a question that seems still to be wide open. We may suppose that this is part of the larger question of the place of Karen within Sino-Tibetan and of anything that we may in the future be able to say about the geographical homeland of proto-Sino-Tibetan itself or about the dispersal of the ancestral languages of the branches of the Sino-Tibetan family. On this larger question I have nothing concrete to offer, save that the region of greatest internal diversity of Sino-Tibetan as such seems to be the Sino-Tibetan borderland, and historical evidence indicates a long-term tendency for at least Tibeto-Burman speakers to move south from there, into Southeastern Asia. If Karen is a quite distinct branch of Sino-Tibetan, and especially if it was an offshoot from early Sino-Tibetan before the separation of the other branches of that family (cf. Benedict 1973: 127ff.), it may have been in the Burma-Thailand area sometime long before the rest of the branches of Sino-Tibetan. Beyond these suggestions, we cannot at present speculate intelligently.

Ethnic Category Words and Their Shifting Application: Did "Karen" Always Mean the People It Means Now?

Keyes, in his chapter on ethnohistory, argues that *yang* (*nyāng*), the current Yuan word for Karen, comes to that language from Shan, and that it came to be used so in Northern Thai because in the nineteenth century there arose for the first time in a long while the need to make the distinction between Shan and Karen. Keyes believes that the Shan term for Karen was borrowed (or reborrowed) to make the distinction. There is no question that the Shan use the word and use it in this way, just for Karen speakers; but they use it only marginally for the Taungthu (*tọng sū*), a Karenic-speaking people for whom it seems the Northern Thai also never use the term *yang*. Nonetheless, the words seem ultimately to derive from Karen usage itself (see Lehman 1967A; Luce 1959A: 8). One has to reconstruct something like /nyaŋ/ for the word that appears (but not in Jones 1961A) in many Karen languages for person, as in /(kə)yà/ (Kayah) and in /(pya)kə/ nyɔ/ and similar forms (Sgaw and Pwo) (Iijima 1970; Marlowe in this volume; Blackwell 1954: 283, under "man").

As for *kariang*, again Keyes is probably correct in supposing that this term for Karen has been taken into Siamese from the Mon. He further assumes that it is a term making sense at first only in the context of Mon-Karen relations, for which a parallel in Siam arose only in the eighteenth century. We shall have occasion later to examine how far this is true. In any event, the word is of fundamental interest. On the one hand, if we pay attention to the Mon linguistic development that derives broken or falling-diphthongized vowels from original plain ones, we can reconstruct something like /*kərang/ from Mon *kareang*. This looks suspiciously like the /(kə)yang/ above, the more so if we are influenced by the Modern Burmese pronunciation in which original /r/ has fallen together with /y/.

However, unfortunately, there is no obvious *Karen* source for that /r/, nor any particular reason within Middle Mon why medial /r/ and /y/ should have been confused. Stern (in this volume) makes the observation that in Kanchanaburi district the term *kariang* is applied to both Sgaw and Pwo, but when a distinction is needed, the Sgaw are called *karang* or *kalang*. This sort of thing clouds the issue further, but it serves also to support the postulated connection between the diphthongized and plain-vowel versions of the term, although exactly how modern Mon speakers or Siamese speakers might have arrived at the equation is wholly unclear.

It has from time to time been suggested, of course, that the *riang* of *kariang* and even the *yang* might be derived not from an original term of self-reference of the Karen but rather from a term of self-reference of some of the Austroasiatic-speaking peoples of the southernmost Shan states, the term being /(rə)yaŋ/, that is, *riang* or, in at least one variety without the prefix, *yang* (Luce 1965). Moreover, as Luce indicates, the initial /r-/ of the prefix becomes /l-/ in some dialects. There are, nevertheless, difficulties in supposing that the Mon word in some direct sense "comes from" the Danaw word, since, among other things, it is not documented that the Mon ever had anything directly to do with the Danaw, although we shall see how much they had to do with the (Pwo) Karen. It is, however, vaguely possible that the words in the Austroasiatic Danaw and in Karen have some common origin due to borrowing one way or another.

But this fails to satisfy. The initial /r-/ remains a mystery in Karen reference. After all, indications are that the /r/ or /l/ in the Danaw self-reference word is some kind of prefixal element, just as in Karen the /kə-/ seems to be, and the two, if that is how the situation lies, are mutually exclusive usages. Furthermore, indications are (Luce 1959A) that even in very ancient Burmese inscriptions the /r/ was there, namely, in references to *karyan* in the thirteenth century. Remember that in Old Burmese and Middle Burmese the /r/ had not disappeared and so we have to guess that the inscriptions showed an actual *r* followed by a *y*. Modern Burmese, of course, has simply *karang,* pronounced /kəyiN/. Finally, the situation is further beclouded by the fact that the root, if it is that, in Karen probably reconstructs as /*nyaŋ/ and this brings us back to the Yuan pronunciation today!

I present these observations not because they clear up the question, but, on the contrary, because the situation is, if anything, even more complicated and suggestive of intellectual problems of importance than Keyes or Stern might lead one to think. What may really be involved is an extension of Keyes's major thesis about these names. It seems likely, in view of the above, that the general spread of these words as used by Mon, Shan, and Burmese goes back ultimately not to a specific ethnic reference but rather to a reference for hill folk in the region between Mon and Shan, hill folk who were in some kind of symbiotic relationship with one or both of these more civilized peoples. It is probably at least this complicated, in view of the overriding fact that the terms serve as native self-reference words in both Karen and Danaw. In fact, at least in Karen, the word means simply "man": e.g., /kəjà təphrè/ (noun plus numeral plus classifier for human beings) and /kəjà li-/ (Red Karen), where the first expression, for example, can be used for any kind of person, say an Englishman or a Burman.

I should like to suggest that Keyes in his ethnohistorical chapter rather underplays the possibility of seventeenth-century (and earlier) instances of Karen population in Thailand. The recurrent wars between Thai and Burmese kingdoms must, from time immemorial, have resulted in elements of Karen being brought into Thailand. Stern's recent work admirably documents the crucial fact of population raiding as a motive in old Southeast Asian warfare (1971: 10). Given the undoubted fact that Mon from the Burma borderlands were brought into Thailand this way from time to time, it is almost impossible that some Karen did not come with them. However, it is probable that few such Karen or Mon established permanent settlements in Thailand before the end of the eighteenth century since the Burmese were in the habit of forcing border populations to resettle in lower Burma each time they invaded Thailand (cf. Hall 1950: 47). Only after the end of the Thai-Burman wars were Mon and Karen able to establish communities that remained.

Thus we have to separate two issues that Keyes unintentionally confuses. The first is the question whether a *category* Karen (or *yang* or *kariang*)—whomever it may formerly have referred to—is of old standing in Thailand, and the second is whether the present Karen *population* has ancient roots in the country. A tentative yes to the first question need in no way require the affirmative to the second, and, more importantly, a negative to the second question has simply no bearing upon the first. The real puzzle then is, if in fact Karen populations were in some close relationship to Tai from time to time, why does the term *kariang* referring to them seem to appear so late in Thai documents? No one seems to have an answer.

Keyes in his introduction to this volume has observed that ethnic labels may be used for different ethnic categories at different times. The significant point here is that ethnic labels have no a priori systematic connection at all with the usual dimensions of ethnic differentiation. There is no reason why, for instance, the referrent of a word such as *yang* has to coincide *at any given time* with a genetic-linguistic grouping. I have suggested above that to begin with it probably did not. It may mean simply any set of local populations that relate to the primary user of the label in a certain ecological and political way. Thus, for instance, the Burmese word "Chin" was traditionally used indiscriminately for most of what we now refer to as Naga, too, although Chin call themselves *zo,* a word never used for themselves by any Naga group—evidence of an ethnic distinction. Moreover, "Chin" (in the expression "river Chin") seems to have been used also, at the opposite side of Burma, for one group of Pwo Karen (Stern 1971: 7). The connection is simply that the word is an archaic Burmese expression for "opposite number" in some symbiotic relation (e.g., ally; but see Lehman 1979). I have demonstrated likewise (1967B) that "Kachin"[7] is an ethnic category corresponding to no immediate linguistic family and to no homogeneous grouping. Some Kachin are also, when occasion demands, Lisu, and Lisu is simply a separate category from Kachin, not a variety of the latter; many Lisu are in no way Kachin. I make this point here to establish that Keyes need not be understood as claiming that because, perhaps, the Siamese before the eighteenth century used the same category label for Karen as for Mon, they did not notice that the two were different kinds of people.

A General Theory of Ethnicity

Most of the chapters in this book have to grapple with how one may best demarcate an ethnic group: the Karen as a whole or else some subgroup of Karen. For instance, Theodore Stern's essay addresses itself to the problem of demarcating the Pwo as a category and placing it in the wider domain of Karen ethnic categories. Stern avoids having to set out a theory about ethnicity, because it happens to be convenient to define Pwo in terms of the obvious marker of the Pwo language. He and Keyes (in his introduction to this volume) argue against a naive view by which a people is seen somehow as an objective, immutable entity, necessarily culturally bounded—or, as in Fredrik Barth's (1969A) view, possessing a homogeneous set of cultural markers as a way of protecting its objective boundaries. I want to spell out a theory based on this idea, so I can use it later to explore the Karen system of ethnic categories more extensively.[8]

We must make a distinction among three different ideas about constellations of cultural traits supposedly associated with ethnic categories. According to the first idea, there is some constellation of cultural traits unique to a group or category and such that at least some members (or communities) within the category exhibit it. For instance, Jinghpaw is clearly the legal-ritual language unique to the Kachin system, although not all Kachin speak Jinghpaw; it is not only a unique possession but a jurally defined reference element for the category and its members as well.

Second, there is the unique constellation of traits that supposedly *every* member exhibits. Note that, not quite trivially, one such constellation or trait always exists by definition. I mean the fact of claiming membership in the given category and everything that may go with that explicit claim. As Michael Moerman (1965) has shown, it is not necessary that any other obvious constellation be unique in this universal sense, even though we all recognize that most likely, in most instances, there is one. If the category is, to start with, largely a political growth, as for instance is the case with the category "American," the likelihood of there being such a constellation recedes. I should be seriously embarrassed to try to prove its existence in this case.

A third idea is that of the unique intersection, or union, of the cultural inventories of the several members of a category. But again, as in the case of the Jinghpaw-language example, what is really important is not the fact that any such category has a common denominator of shared inventory but the fact that the membership may recognize some trait as at least a common reference point of membership. In American anthropology the whole enterprise of culture-area studies came a cropper over just the preoccupation with irrelevant common denominator inventories. There is, in short, a difference, at least intuitively, between what we may call a culturally significant and a culturally nonsignificant unique common categorial constellation. Since at least the latter kind, that is, the mere common denominator, can hardly be thought of as a *natural class* or proper subset of the cultural inventory of a group or of the cognitive universe of someone as a member of the category, it can in no way be used uncritically to infer that "unique common cultural history" that traditional ethnology takes as implicit in the idea of an ethnic category. I can summarize these introductory comments by saying that what counts in the cultural definition of an ethnic category is not possession of a unique common cultural "heritage" but the use of a set of cultural elements (language included, possibly) in a claim to membership of the category.

Consider again the Lisu case. Only the Kachin and the Lisu contain the intersection of Lisu and Jinghpaw-Maru traits and languages. It is contained in the Lisu-speaking Kachin group. Yet, so far as the arbitrary Lisu-speaking Kachin community is concerned, the Lisu part of this set of traits is referred to their Lisu identity, and the Jinghpaw elements are referred to their Jinghpaw identity. A community, *A,* may be in some category, *C,* but not exclusively in *C.* If this community exhibits the cultural constellation *X,* this does not necessarily allow us to say anything about "the culture of *C*" or even "the culture of the *A*-variant of *C.*"

Consider, as an even more homely example, the United States. The habit of eating pizza (see Bharati 1970: 273) and spaghetti is certainly in some sense a part of American culture—borrowed from Italy without question, thus precluding its being part of the common historical heritage of Americans not of Italian extraction. For many Italian-Americans, however, the eating of these things is explicitly part of their Italian heritage and not at all part of their adopted American identity. When Italian-Americans eat pizza I suggest that they are being members, however marginal, of the Italian, not the American, category. This is certainly true of the Chinese-restaurant cultural complex in America vis-à-vis Chinese in America.

Taking the United States again, who is to say that just because some complex of traits included *in* a *unique* common denominator of American culture, say the use of male tailored clothing, the necktie, and so on, is not itself unique to America that it is not part therefore of the definition of being American? It would be absurd to take such a stance. The whole business of insisting that there must be an objectively unique definition for a true ethnic category is vain. It is grounded in the romanticist tradition of associating a cultural inventory with something vaguely and mystically thought of as unique historical experience, properly attached to racelike populations. The set of traits mentioned are in fact used by Americans as important to their identity, but I suspect that some other things equally objectively characteristic of America, such as, say, sitting upon chairs, are more thought of as aspects of being part of the cultural tradition of European civilization, under which the American category is subsumed.

The very idea of *ascribing* aspects of cultural inventory to membership in such a low-level entity as an ethnic category, when it is objectively so much more widely distributed among historically related groups, is itself worthy of further investigation. It seems to be a cognitive universal for human beings to do this kind of thing, even though there are, as seen above, obvious inconsistencies in the way this usage is applied. Thus, for instance, Americans will in some contexts ascribe the dress mentioned to American culture; recognizing explicitly a higher level social-cultural system of European-American society, they will also ascribe the traits to *this* entity. Similarly, Burmans on one level think of Buddhism as a fundamental possession of Burman society. They even go to the length (cf. Spiro 1971) of seeming to deny that Burmese Christians are true Burmans, while denying that these people are any kind of foreigner either. At another level, they not only recognize explicitly that many of their neighbors are also Buddhists—that would be itself of no interest—but also that there is a wider *social system* encompassing the Theravāda countries of mainland Southeast Asia (plus Ceylon), and that their religion is in fact a sign of their membership in that social system. The proof that this is a proper cognitive category in the system of intergroup relations, even though it has no particular name, is easily found. Elsewhere (see note 14 to Keyes's ethnohistorical chapter) I point out that ideology requires political entities in that system to be mutually connected through a system of Pāli-Sanskrit classical names.[9]

Many of the classical names of major thrones are explicitly derived by grant from an earlier major throne to which the present one considers itself in part a successor state. Thus (see, e.g., Andaya 1971) Siam, in its original state of Sukhothai, was given a title for itself and its rulers by the Khmer, to whom, it appears, Sukhothai came to consider itself, within its territorial boundaries, successor. Similarly, Lanna Thai, the traditional Northern Thai kingdom, considered itself in part as both incorporating and succeeding the old Mon of Haripuñjaya. The Shan states, roughly speaking, derive the legitimacy of their princedoms, with the exception, of course, of the princedoms of the *(tai)Khün,* from the major throne of Burma; and that not in a simple way, but rather because (see Saimong Mangrai 1965) the ancient Shan kingdom of Pong, itself something of a successor state to the even older Nan Chao (the latter not in fact a Tai-based state), became, as it were, the throne of Burma when the Shan took Pagan in 1299. It can be seen, then, that explicit recognition is traditionally given to a wider social system and structure encompassing at least the Theravāda countries. Ceylon comes into the picture because the common institutional network for this system involves Buddhism prominently and Ceylon is overtly recognized as the place from which original ordination traditions are taken and from which primary Buddhist relics are got historically.

Why then the anthropologists' peculiar fixation upon the so-called ethnic category? I mean why is it that we so often, both as members of some social group and as scholars, ascribe cultural traits to the peculiar heritage of ethnically labelled groupings when in fact they can often be shown to be most relevant to higher order social structures than these? The problem is not trivial, because it cannot be assumed that we simply tend to ascribe cultural traits to the lowest levels of group organization in which we participate.

For instance, even though it is often taken for granted that a local community or some other functionally omnibus, so-called primary or face-to-face grouping is the true context of everyday life for most domains of behavior in preindustrial societies, a culture is often not ascribed to *these* entities but rather to collections of them. I think I can suggest a formal analogue to an answer to these questions, and since formal relational representation or computation seems to be a feature of cognition, I would claim that what I shall now say is possibly something of a cognitive universal for man, based upon his natural employment for relational representations of certain kinds of mathematical relations.

Suppose that we think of the network of groupings to which any *local population* belongs as an indefinitely deep hierarchy. In that case we can, somewhat naively, imagine something like a downward-branching tree, whose terminal nodes are, say, communities. But that is typically a so-called "upper semi-lattice" (Witz n.d.: ch. 5). Now each terminal node, or each community, has, say, an indefinite number of nodes directly dominating it, and the higher the *branching* node the more other terminals it dominates. Thus we can say, in some sense, that each community, C_1, is a proper member of ever more encompassing groupings in this hierarchy. But clearly it cannot even contemplate all these relations at once and it cannot, given ecological differences, geographical distances, and the facts of competition, simply and once and for all think of itself as of the same kind as *all* other terminal communities in the network. How then must it classify itself?

The answer can be suggested by reference to a fundamental theorem about upper semilattices. It says, approximately, that for any such entity, if there is an upper bound there is a *least upper bound*. Thus, roughly, every such community may be expected to have some lowest node that immediately dominates it and some other communities. Or rather, each such community will choose some relatively small range of communities with which it conceives itself as having something socially in common of importance, and will represent the situation to itself as one where this set of communities is, as it were, linked at the lowest level of branching. To say the same thing in other words, people tend to represent the more complex web of intergroup relations as straightforward upper lattices (joined semilattices), and under such a representation the least upper bound theorem automatically applies. Hence, representations will always exist in which some lowest level of intergroup linkage is outstandingly prominent, and this corresponds to the intuition underlying the universal notion of the ethnic category and its primacy for local group classification.

Local groups, then, tend to classify themselves according to precisely the strict taxonomic constraints that ethnoscientists have devoted so much attention to recently (see, most relevantly, Berlin

1971). In the first place, people have a tendency to collapse, as it were, the hierarchy of cultural relations in which they stand to various other groups. They tend to talk and think about the cultural elements they share at many higher levels of relationship in terms of the lowest of these taxonomic levels.

For example, suppose that group A shares a small inventory of cultural or dialectal traits uniquely with just a few immediately present groups who form a cohesive social network of role identification with A in the larger system of intergroup relations. Let A also share much more of its inventory of traits over successively wider regions of interrelationship. A will tend to think of its entire range of cultural inventory in terms of the first, most intimate level of interconnections. In the second place, suppose that there is a group B with which A sees itself as sharing at least some symbolically significant traits in common, and suppose that in reality this set of elements is shared very widely, relevant to some rather remote level of the hierarchy of cultural similarity and intergroup relations. Then assume that A and B see themselves as, under some circumstances at least, acting alike and being treated alike in respect of their relations to a third set of groups, C. It is easy, given the previous observation, to see that a basis exists for A's assigning B, under these conditions, to its most immediate taxonomic category of social and cultural classification. That is, since, in any case, A and B, respectively, assign whatever they share in common culturally to their respective lowest, most intimate levels of intergroup similarities, they can for given purposes think of themselves as "the same people" even though the two groups remain substantially different in culture and recognize that difference. This, I think, goes a great way toward formalizing the facts adduced for Tai Lue by Moerman and the peculiar case of the Lisu-Kachin. The latter is dealt with further by La Raw Maran in his still unpublished paper on "The Algebra of Inter-acting Human Groups" (Maran n.d.).

Concluding this discussion, I want to make clear that I do not necessarily deny that ethnic categories generally contain culturally very similar groups, or that most ethnic categories have, at the very least, a distinctive language or dialect, or that most local groups, in fact, think of themselves as belonging to only one such lowest level category. Although these things may well describe the majority of cases in the world, that statistical fact is formally irrelevant, because it is not a necessary condition of ethnic identification but merely a sufficient one. I must also point out that I am really just expanding Stern's reference to principles. It seems clear that the use made by him of language as a criterion conforms perfectly with the paradigm I have just constructed.

Applications of the Theory to Karen Identity

How might the foregoing ideas help us understand how the category Karen is determined by its intergroup context and what relation Karen culture has to the cultures of neighboring peoples? At least the broad outlines of the theory can be used in an attempt at a proper definition of some of the subcategories of Karen, that is, Pwo and Sgaw, and Kayah. What we need here is help in untangling the bewildering problem of the apparent inconsistencies in the way different peoples apply ethnic nomenclature to a single population and/or to each other.

In his chapter, Stern points out that the Burmans called the Pwo "Talaing Karen" (*talaing* equals Mon, in Burmese), and that the Sgaw in contrast were called "Burmese Karen." I think, however, with Stern that it cannot be assumed that the two terms were used strictly in the same way: the Mon seem to have thought of the Pwo as their predecessors in control of the territory—and the spirits that ultimately "own" the land—and this seems to underlie the closeness of the relation between Mon and Pwo Karen intended by the notion of Mon Karen. I know of no evidence that the Burmans have any such idea with respect to the Sgaw. The Mon, who made the same terminological distinction as the Burmans did between Pwo as Mon Karen and Sgaw as Burmese Karen, may have thought that each civilized group was paired with its respective Karen group in the same way, but one cannot be sure of this.

The Burmese connection with the Sgaw appears to have considerable antiquity. Luce (1959A) cites very early Burmese inscriptions mentioning a people called, in the Old Burmese orthography, *cakraw*, being found or brought into the plains of central Burma. He tentatively identified these as Sgaw Karen, and we see that even today, in the Sgaw dialect, their word for themselves is /(pyakanyɔ) cə(k)gɔ/ (see also Iijima 1970). Yet, however long Sgaw may have lived in the plains, they seem never to have been ideologically associated with the foundation of a lowland kingdom as were the Pwo. The Taungthu, who are clearly linked with the Pwo, preserve the idea that they were directly involved with the founding of Thaton, the seat of the ancient Mon kingdom in Burma (see Hackett 1953).

Identification of Pwo as, in principle, lowlanders and Sgaw as hill people is also reflected in Kayah terminology, although in a curious and tortuous way. The Kayah call the Sgaw /pəky/,[10] which carries the connotation of hill Karen (Lehman 1967A). This term is applied to all Sgaw Karen,[11] especially to those around Toungoo, and to at least one subgroup of non-Sgaw-speaking hill Karen, the Geba.[12] The Pwo are not so designated; rather, insofar as I was able to elucidate the matter, their identity is almost wholly subsumed in that of the southernmost of the Kayah; thereby hangs a tale.

The southernmost, and maybe the oldest, Kayah State is that of Bawlakhè. The people there speak a language most closely related to either Kantarawady or Kyèbogyi Kayah; at any rate it is clearly one of the Central Karen (hill) dialects. The Burmese call these people Yintalè and the Shan render this as Yang Talai. The word *yin* or *yang* has been dealt with above in this chapter and I will not comment further on it. The second word corresponds to the Kayah word *taljà* or /talɛ/, in this instance denoting at once the south and the lowland country, the plains. It seems reasonably clear that the foundation of the Kayah State has a great deal to do with that of Bawlakhè. It is clearly through Bawlakhè and its people that the offshoots of the Mon messianism entered the area. In fact Kayah and Yangtalai tradition explicitly credit the founders with being charismatic figures coming up from the Mon country. In effect this makes the people of Bawlakhè at least symbolically "stand for" the southern civilization. What complicates the story is a bit of folk etymologizing, the implications of which are interesting.

Burmans have come to think of the Bawlakhè people, the Yang Talai or Yintalè, as being some sort of "Mon Karen," /(ka)yin təlaing/,[13] that is, Pwo. But why should the Burmese apply such a designation to a people they themselves knew so intimately?[14]

The following bears directly on this question. Stern observes, citing Peter Hinton, that in Northern Thai, the distinction between kinds of Karen is as between Pwo as "civilized" and Sgaw as "jungly" or "wild." This is not, according to my investigations of 1965, completely correct. Pwo are often called in Northern Thai *nyang piang* (Plains Karen) and Sgaw *nyang pa* (Wild Karen, Forest Karen). But Sgaw are themselves also called *nyang phüak* (White Karen, because of the color of an unmarried woman's dress), and a distinction is drawn, within this category, between *nyang dɔɔj* (Hill Karen), and *nyang baan* (Settled or Town Karen). The complication is that the last named word is often treated interchangeably with *nyang piang,* in which event remoter, ruder Sgaw *and* Pwo are lumped together as *nyang pa* (Wild Karen). The resulting ambiguity, even contradiction, in the way the Sgaw-Pwo distinction is made here, surely reflects just the facts adduced by Stern. For, on the one hand, it is generally understood, however dimly, that Pwo are to be associated with the civilization of the plains in some fundamental manner. On the other hand, it is mainly in the south, where Pwo-Mon associations are close, that this is reflected in actual Pwo life, whereas in the north of Thailand the Pwo seem to be relatively less integrated with (local) civilization. I suggest that in the north the Pwo are in an obvious sense out of their element, as Stern implies. The Sgaw, however, are more basically an isolate from civilization and therefore will more readily adapt and flourish in whatever civilizational context they may find themselves, as in northern Thailand.

This is reminiscent of a salient feature of Karen culture (see Marlowe's chapter in this volume). It is known that the traditional habit of the Sgaw Karen (and also of Pwo, although with a somewhat different function) of throwing up millennial movements and leaders seems to function to permit these people to reorient themselves radically to new contexts of social and cultural relations. It may also be the case that this makes possible the very great differences between the Sgaw of Chiang Mai Province and those of the Mae Sariang area in Mae Họng Sọn Province, in respect of things such as whether or not they recognize a Burma background in their past and whether or not they see themselves as basically people "belonging" to particular stream valleys, as they do in Chiang Mai (cf. Marlowe). Furthermore, Peter Kunstadter makes clear in numerous essays (e.g., in his chapter in this volume) that in the part of Mae Sariang district formerly subject to the Lawa under a vassalage to the old Northern Thai kingdom, the Sgaw Karen have managed to usurp the dominant position of the Lawa. The Lawa looked upon the hills as a resource to which they were traditionally and intimately attached as the basis of their claims to a recognized political standing vis-à-vis the Northern Thai state. The Karen seem to have evinced no such feeling, and they appear in this regard to have been willing, in a degree that the Lawa were not, to overexploit the hills in their swiddening. At the same time, they were provided with an opportunity to move in on the Lawa and in many cases to reverse local relations of dominance and subordination between the two, insofar as the old political paramountcy of the Lawa in the region ceased to be legally recognized after the absorption of northern Thailand into the kingdom of Siam. This all comes to the fact that the Sgaw tend to be oriented to local opportunism and to an interstitial position in the midst of other, more "autochthonous" peoples on the land. This, finally, is consistent with the distinction I tried to make earlier, according to which even the terminological connection between Sgaw and Burmans should not be taken as implying anything like the ideological symbiosis denoted by the terminological association of the Pwo with the Mon.

The Contemporary Dynamics of Karen Ethnicity: The Kayah Example

The previous section has tried to show that there is an overall pattern of adaptation to non-Karen peoples, set up for the most part in the context of Burma, that characterizes the general category of Karen. I further propose that as the intergroup context alters, so does the character of ethnic identity itself, as determined by that context. I shall document this proposal from the case of the Kayah of northwestern Thailand.

We have seen that the Sgaw, at least, have long been adapted to an interstitial place in the midst of several competing civilized societies: Burman, Shan, Northern Thai, and maybe even Mon. The non-Karen Lawa were more inflexibly situated, as vassal owners of a territory at the fringes of the Northern Thai kingdom of which it was mutually agreed that the Lawa were aboriginal owners and the Northern Thai ultimate successors *via* the Mon of Haripuñjaya. This ought in some measure to account for Karen expansion at Lawa expense. The devolution of the Lawa position gave the Sgaw Karen a distinct advantage in two ways: they felt themselves able to exploit the swidden lands massively, and they could, without substantially altering the basis of their ethnic identity, develop a novel mode of direct symbiosis with the Northern Thai. Neither of these options was open to the Lawa, because their ethnic self-image seems to have been more bound to a highly particular relation to both the land and the Northern Thai.

When the basis of these relations was eroded, the stage was set for a significant amount of passing of people from Lawa to other identities, and Kunstadter's chapter has given some indication that at least a part of the Karen population in the Mae Sariang area of northwestern Thailand has grown through accretion from ex-Lawa. Beyond that, it may of course be, as Kunstadter occasionally suggests, that the Lawa have come to have a lower birth and/or survival rate than the Karen, because the conditions of optimal function for their traditional institutional structure have to a great extent disappeared.

I know of at least one other case that may in part parallel these suggestions about Lawa. It is that of the Kayah of the northern part of Mae Hong Son province. I have elsewhere indicated (1967B) that Kayah identity is tied up with Kayah-Shan symbiosis. I have not the space here to elaborate on this claim, but I can say that in this region, where from the middle of the nineteenth century until quite recently almost the whole lowland population has been Shan, and much of the economy has involved connections westward with the traditional

Shan country of Burma (see especially Saimong Mangrai 1965: ch. 10; Keyes 1969; Phibun Borihan n.d.), the small Kayah population, however remote from the ken of even some of the local Shan villages, were wholly dependent on the Shan villages in whose hinterlands they were located. They looked to the Shan for recurrent assistance such as odd jobs and cast-off clothing, as a market for jungle produce and minor garden produce, and as a source of rice in addition to what they themselves could raise in their very poor hill fields.

For reasons that cannot concern us here, the last twenty years or so have seen the not-too-gradual incorporation of the region into the economy and network of communications of northern Thailand and a considerable turning away from a Burma orientation. An indirect consequence of these events has been a lessening concern on the part of the Shan villagers with their own immediate hinterland and with local ethnic interdependency. They are increasingly reluctant to develop patron-client relationships with the Kayah, if only because of the increasing dependence upon the cash-market economy of Thailand and the consequent reduction in nonmarket-oriented use of their capital and produce. Meanwhile, the Kayah population has also become seriously reduced, chiefly because of the decimating effects of the wartime (1943) smallpox epidemic, so it is difficult for them to make their swiddening economy work, given their current manpower resources, together with their own increasing involvement with Thai administration and the attractions of a cash economy.

The result is striking. In 1968 the people of one village cluster, the largest of the villages north of the provincial capital at Mae Hong Son, had more or less concluded that there was no great virtue in remaining Kayah any longer, although of course they were ambivalent about this conclusion. A delegation of them repeatedly urged me to find some persons or some institution to give them the financial assistance they required in moving off their hill slopes and setting themselves up in permanent, wet-rice cultivating villages; they had never known how to cultivate wet fields, had no ploughs, ploughlands, or plough animals, and they knew that the first few years would be terribly hard. While they set up as paddy farmers, they would also have to keep up their hill fields to be able to feed themselves during the transition. They put it to me again and again that, if anyone would help them in this way, they would be more than happy to take on the religion, customs, and even identity of their benefactors. They might, they said, still keep up some of their Kayah rituals for a while, but they left no doubt that their vision was of ceasing to be Kayah as they moved out of the ecological-symbiotic niche in which being Kayah made sense. As of July 1974, these Kayah were well established in a lowland village with permanent fields, thirty houses, and a school with two teachers. Of course, they still talk Kayah and answer to that identity, and I am told that they still practice the general run of Kayah rituals and ceremonies, even though they have also increasingly taken on Buddhist practices as well. The rapidity of their acquisition of Thai and Shan languages and the degree to which, in contrast to the situation as observed in 1968, they freely intermingled with Shan and Northern Thai are very striking. These Kayah have not been asked by anyone to change their identity now that they have moved into the lowlands and they themselves were probably unrealistic regarding their capacity to acquire a new identity simply by shifting ecological setting. But their announced expectations in 1968 were surely illustrative of their view of their situation all the same.

For the moment, however, the "constant ambivalence" that Marlowe's chapter notes as one measure of closeness and distance in the relationship between Sgaw Karen and Northern Thai is also characteristic of the relationship between the Kayah and the Shan in northern Mae Họng Sọn province. The Kayah living in the hinterland of the Shan village of Mọkˏ Tsam Pɛˏ, 15 kilometers north of Mae Họng Sọn town, provide us with a particularly striking example. I propose it as an instance not simply of ambivalence but also of the way members of such opposed but symbiotic ethnic categories play upon each other's partial understanding of the other's culture. They take advantage of what they rightly understand as the other party's dependence upon them, and of just the ambivalence that Marlowe is talking about (and the partial understandings that go with that ambivalence).

The Kayah here, probably for the reason that they both fear and respect the Shan, and partly because they obviously want to maintain a prominent symbol of an institutionalized place in the Shan social scheme, are nominal Buddhists. Their universal claim is to the effect that they are really Buddhists but are too poor and remote to be able to do anything about it. They are wholly ignorant of Buddhist doctrine and, to the best of my knowledge, no Kayah in this area has ever been either monk or novice; in fact not one of them is in the slightest literate. In many of their houses one can find a Buddhist shrine shelf with a vase of green leaves, and on this shelf, where there is almost never even an image, they will sometimes (mainly when a Shan or Thai is present) light candles in the evening and offer a bit of rice. No proper prayers are said, because they do not know any. Their explanation of the use of leaves (a kind of *Eugenia,* I think, a leaf that figures in Buddhist ritual) in place of images is instructive.

I have it from numerous informants that Shan have told them this is right for someone who is too poor to own an image or does not understand how to get one.[15] It is quite clear that the local Kayah view is that they do not know how to be proper Buddhists and have taken advice from "someone" who has somewhat condescendingly told them to do some second-best thing instead.[16]

There is a Kayah ideological paradigm for this attitude. First (cf. Lehman 1967A), it is consistent with the general Kayah view that wiser heads from outside ought to be listened to in case they come among the Kayah. Kayah may well be afraid of such people and they may not particularly like them, but if such a man comes and acts as Kayah suppose a real leader of men acts, they themselves say that they ought, for the time being at least, to follow. He has charisma and tends to be treated as the bearer of superior knowledge. In extreme cases, he is, in the case of the Western Kayah at least, the recurrent millennial figure, the *phré phrow*, although the Thailand Kayah say that this means a truly godlike figure who, at least these days, does not exist among men. This difference is, of course, quite consistent with the absence among them of the idea of a Kayah State.

Second, the Thailand Kayah have for *their* story of the origin of the cult of the *iylùw* (see Lehman 1967A) not a tale of a charismatic leader who appeared among them, but rather that of one who left them, who separated himself, his godliness, and his basically foreign, cosmopolitan wisdom from the Kayah once and for all. I cannot tell the whole rambling story here, but when he rose on his house platform into the sky, he called derisively down to his supplicating Kayah family and said, being disgusted with them, that since they were ignorant of how to treat him properly he was not going to stay in the world with them. He continued that since they did not know how to worship god properly (they had just asked him how they *ought* to act), they should just plant a big pole in the ground and worship that. Again, then, we have the second best, the substitute way, and clearly the Kayah believe they must be content with it, that anything better is, while they remain Kayah, beyond the capacities of their ignorance. Again, they tell us, with this tale, that the advice of an experienced outsider should be followed.

The Kayah "Buddhists" of northern Mae Hong Son never attend monastic services, save once in a while during a major ordination feast or something like a New Year festival, and then with the greatest hesitancy and obvious embarrassment. I have heard of one or two fairly Shan-ized Kayah (whom I knew slightly) keeping the Five Precepts when visiting the Shan village on an important holy day, but I have never seen it, and I expect that what was actually involved was the need both to impress the Shan they were trying to associate with and to be able to sit and talk with them at the one place they were on that day, the monastery. In any case, the Kayah here know exactly as much about Buddhist and related doctrine as they have picked up casually among the Shan and as the Shan have found it convenient to teach them—some of it deliberately fanciful.

Now during 1967-68 the village of Mǫkˬ Tsam Pɛˬ decided to put a new corrugated iron sheet roof on its monastery. The cost was many thousands of baht, and although there were one or two villagers, traders in cattle and other things, who could have afforded the entire cost, that is not the way things are done, if only because, for one thing, it is better to allow many people to make merit by contributing, and for another, there is more public aggrandizement in putting merit money into the more ceremonious festive occasions like ordinations. In any case, the village collected contributions over some months; not all households gave but many did, in varying amounts. It occurred to someone at one point that no Kayah had given anything. It is perfectly true that the Kayah villagers on the whole are extremely poor by their own and by Shan and Northern Thai standards, but there are among them a few men who, by working among Shan and Northern Thai for considerable periods, have become less poor than their fellows; these are the very men who are alleged on occasion to have kept precepts on a Buddhist holy day. But they are still Kayah; they are wholly illiterate, wholly ignorant of Buddhist ideas. They did not in fact want to give or to go back to their villages to try to collect anything there.

Then the Shan of our village said to them that if they did not give they would, by Buddhist doctrine, be reborn as *phỉ phāai*—untamed, wandering malevolent spirits, often thought to be the ghosts of those who have died a violent death or in childbed. It is important to understand that, as the Shan villagers who put this story forward told me later, the Shan knew perfectly well that there is no such doctrine; they were deliberately imposing on the credulity of the Kayah leaders, presumably the Kayah most eager to be thought of as at least nominal Buddhists. It worked. The Kayah were truly frightened. Bad spirits are something they understand and live with constantly, to their great sorrow and cost (in ever-present placation and curing rites), and *phỉ phāai* is on the lips of the Shan so often that the Kayah have a lively sense of its virulence. To be reborn as such a being is a terrible idea; they are solitary, homeless, rejected beings by ritual definition.

The Kayah leaders went back to their villages and collected from most households at least something, and gave it to Mǫkˬ Tsam Pɛˬ together with their own somewhat larger contributions. I never found out the amounts involved. I did, however, speak to the Kayah and Shan parties and one thing is clear about the transaction: the Shan were amused and took such slight trouble to hide it that the Kayah were at least suspicious of having been used, although too unsure and sheepish to look into the matter closely.

Now consider the other side of the matter. The Kayah regularly come down into the Shan villages peddling produce, begging handouts of cast-off clothing, making miniscule purchases at the village shops, mainly by barter, even taking or trying to find odd jobs among the Shan. The Shan, especially Shan women and children, tease them, sometimes are patronizingly kind to them, are amused by them or indifferent to them by turns and according to their different temperaments and moods. In any case, they do not trust the Kayah and it is thought unsafe to leave a house empty when Kayah are wandering about the village. This is especially troublesome at the time of monastery festivals, because the Kayah come down at such times to enjoy themselves at the fringes of the festivities and it is just on such days that whole blocks of houses together may be unoccupied for a couple of hours or more. What is uppermost in the Shan mind is that, as they see it, the Kayah are envious and jealous of Shan relative prosperity and constantly on the alert to avail themselves of some of it by any means.

In this respect, there is a pervasive Shan idea in these villages about the Kayah that makes at least those Shan villagers who have an unusual fear of spirits and sorcery fear and avoid the Kayah. Thus one woman I knew would simply hide in the inner room of her house when Kayah women came around to beg and her husband was away. Her husband and several other Shan with whom I checked assured me that she was correct in thinking the Kayah were to be feared because, if they were refused a handout or got something they believed was distinctly inferior in quality, they could send a certain spirit, the *ola,* against the offending Shan. This is the clearest sort of witchcraft fear, where one's hostility to others and one's consciousness of being in some sense oppressive to them leads one to impute, not unreasonably, a virulent jealousy to those others directed against oneself. That obviously the Kayah *are* envious of the Shan calls into question the thesis that the degree of fear implies a degree of projected guilt on the part of the Shan, but the issue is not crucial here.

What is important is the fact that the Kayah in their own cultural system control no such spirit that they can send against the Shan in this deliberate way. The Kayah, or some of them, were dimly aware that the Shan thought they could do this, and they found the idea faintly amusing and were not about to disabuse the Shan of their mistake. Once again the mistake was based upon imperfect and distorted information about one group on the part of the other, rather than upon outright ignorance.[17]

I should, in the light of this sort of situation, like to interpret Marlowe's notion of ambivalence in interethnic relations (see also D. Jones 1970) as follows. In interethnic systems where, by mutual agreement as well as objectively, the parties are of unequal status and have very unequal access to mutually desired economic resources and ecological "niches," ambivalence seems to be a function of the very fact of ethnic distinctiveness. That is, in many respects, the choice of a subordinate ethnic category is motivated by the perceived advantage of having alternate cultural standards as against competing with apparent promise of failure in the arena of someone else's cultural standards of achievement.[18] This involves people in at once envying and wanting what others have and at the same time denying themselves, categorially but not categorically, the chance to try to get what they envy. This is itself ambivalence of a high order. Moreover, people making this choice have, as Eric Wolf pointed out long ago (1955), to protect their integrity by keeping themselves relatively or selectively isolated from the counterpart society, therefore in structural ignorance of just the culture they are jealous of and on which they recognize a high degree of symbiotic dependence. This again is ambivalence of a high order and is the almost inevitable consequence of the structure of this sort of system of ethnic relationships.

Culture Change and Ethnic Identity: Some Conclusions

I have looked at the proposition that changing intergroup relations, for instance in the context of changing world political and economic conditions, determine changes in ethnicity. However, it is well known that cultural change is in large measure also a function of intergroup relations, if only because so much cultural change has to do with the diffusion of cultural traits from one people to another. Presumably, the course of cultural change among a people may be in part a function of the course of processes in intergroup relations, too. Then how should we see the relation of cultural change in general to ethnicity?

As a strikingly relevant example of cultural change, consider the impact of Christianity upon the Karen. Although not all Karen in Burma are Christian, Burma Karen have come to be identified by many with Christianity. As in the case of the Chin on the west of

Burma (cf. Lehman 1963), it is almost certain that the institution of the Church, in its international ramifications, has provided for the Karen a basis for dealing advantageously with Burmans as institutional equals rather than as a benighted tribe. They, too, now "have" a world religion.

Karen might just as well have become, and in fact many are, Buddhists, but it is clear that their interests do not lie that way. For that way their choice is to try to acculturate to the Burmans, which would mean, given their relatively backward and remote habitat, being, predictably, poor Burmans and thus relative failures at the very levels of aspiration they would be adopting. In fact, it can be argued that one of the very reasons for an historical and continued Karen identity is that peoples in relatively poor areas are often better off in their own eyes if they maintain cultural styles and aspirations distinct from those of their richer neighbors. The answer in recent times seems to have been both to maintain their separateness and to identify with a modern social and religious system, that is, to identify with Christianity, even while not necessarily adopting Christianity wholesale.

In closing, I have to make as clear as I can that, as this last observation about religion shows, cultural change itself, especially insofar as it is determined by intergroup relations, amounts precisely to a change in ethnicity, an alteration of identity. This is too frequently not understood. I will even go so far as to assert that the tendency for Karen, Sgaw, and Pwo in particular to develop millennial and messianic cults that seem to change their religion almost totally is exactly this, an alteration in ethnic identity in response to changing intergroup relations.

Acknowledgment

The field work upon which this report is based was conducted and the results were processed under Grant DADA 17-67-C-7058 from the United States Army Medical Research and Development Command.

Notes

1. The roman-letter transcription of Kayah words is almost identical with that I employed in Lehman 1967B, except that, now, a syllable without diacritics represents the low tone, and one followed by a hyphen represents mid tone; this has been done for convenience in typesetting. I use the letter y for a high, back, unrounded vowel and ə ("schwa") for the mid, back, unrounded vowel. For Shan ´ is the high-rising tone and ` the high-falling

(breathy) tone; ˉ, above a vowel, stands for the high-level tone. In a few Burmese place names and ethnonyms è is used as the standard nontechnical roman transcription for the lax, front vowel as in the English word bed. For the rest, I have tried to follow the usage established throughout the other chapters of the book for rendering the sounds and tones of Thai and Northern Thai, and the few additional phonetic symbols I have used in representing Karen and/or Kayah words are used in the internationally standard way: ɔ is the lax, back, rounded sound of the English vowel in the word law; γ stands for the voiced velar fricative; ŋ is what we write ordinarily as the digraph -ng. However, where I cite directly a foreign word from the literature, I cite it as the source in question writes it, which accounts for some inconsistencies of transcription in the text. There are only two letters that need interpretation in regard to my Burmese transcriptions: ṅ is the standard representation of Burmese and Pāli orthographical -ng, and N stands for spoken Burmese final nasalized vowel.

2. Brailey's whole enterprise is undertaken to try to explain who the Gwe were. The Gwe figure in eighteenth-century Burmese history as an insurgent hill people of some sort that came from the eastern hills but in part, for a time, had a settlement in the vicinity of the capital on the Irrawaddy plain. Michael Symes (1800: 13, 22, and 87) brings them from an eastern province of the north under the name of Quoi. Henry Yule (1968: 294–95), speaking of them as (ka)Kui, brings them from the region of Kengtung-Kenghung, and relates them to certain Kachin-speaking groups. Brailey wants to identify them with the Kayah or some closely related kind of Karen; he argues, then, that the Karen formerly lived where the Gwe were mentioned as living. But it is now clear that the terms Gwe, Kwe, and Kui—all variants of the same word—are the Kengtung Khu̱n name for the Yellow Lahu (Lahu Shi). See the observation by James Scott and J. P. Hardiman (1900: vol. I, part 1) and David Bradley (1974). Brailey in fact mentions Kengtung in his discussion of this word.

3. Burmese term for what the people themselves call /manə/ and the eastern Kayah call /panə/. This word means "western."

4. I speak here of a Kayah tradition that at least indicates the possibility of some ancient connection with vaguely Northern Thai territory, but I hold no particular opinion about this tradition. I think it possible that "Kayah," or at least ancestors of the present-day Kayah in Thailand, may have been here more or less under Northern Thai dominion. But the story of some sort of political partnership between these "Kayah" and the Northern Thai seems, from the way the Kayah invoke it and in the absence of any confirming evidence, self-justification and self-aggrandizement of the kind pervading the folk histories of tribal Southeast Asia.

5. His *kyay lateh* for the village of Kyèbogyi is, of course, *kéy ljà,* the "valley country" (Lehman 1967–68): from *ljà,* valley, downstream; or *taljà,* the south, the plain.

6. This is not quite as straightforward as I appear to make it. The dialect adverted to is the Kyèbogyi or Western Kayah. Now, in that dialect, the phonetic nucleus, /-ja-/, is easily shown to come from a front low plain vowel, /-ae-/, and one must furthermore reconstruct a rule for Kayah dialects generally according to which a low nonrounded vowel is fronted when it follows an initial consonant cluster of stop plus liquid. Thus, by rule, Western Kayah *phrja* would be reconstructed as *phra* (on high tone, as it happens),

and this is, of course, the Shan for Lord in the sense of Buddha or any deity. It is emphatically not the *fá* of the Shan for prince, *tsàu fá* (*sawbwa* in Burmese). However, there is a further still not fully explicable complication here. In Kyèbogyi Kayah, side by side with /sɔ́ phrja/, there is /sɔ́ phja/. The latter sometimes is interchanged with the former, but is probably just the formal word for prince, a ruler of a Kayah state, such as the great Kyèbogyi ruler whose name was /Sɔ́ phja Úw re/. It may be that *phja* is somehow from the Shan *fá*, but I am not certain. It is also possibly a derivative of *phrja* by cluster simplification. The likelihood is very slight that these Kayah words have their origin in either Thai or Northern Thai. The phonetically similar Thai word *phraya* is a formal title of rank (Wales 1965: 35), really not similar to either Kayah meaning given above; furthermore, there is no particular reason for postulating specifically Thai loanwords in Kayah. There are almost equally grave difficulties with respect to the Northern Thai word *phra*. In the first place, in Northern Thai this is used only for sacred personages, especially the Buddha and his images, never for secular statuses. The fact that in Kayah we have both sacred and secular usage does not help, because the latter usage in Kayah shows no evidence of implying that these princes were in themselves sacred persons. Moreover, in modern Northern Thai the -*r*- in *phra* is merely orthographic, and the word is pronounced *pha*. Furthermore, the wholly Shan series of parallels in the ceremonial apparatus surrounding the Kayah princes and the state cult of the *iylùw* argue against a source other than Shan for these terms.

7. Contrary, for example, to E. R. Leach (1954), the word, although given thus in Burmese form, has an ordinary Kachin source. It is true that the main Kachin group call themselves and their language Jinghpaw, but the word *ka-khyen* (Red Earth) also has currency, and "people of the Red Earth" refers to all Kachin in the light of their theory of the part of the country (the Red Earth country in the far northwest) they came from.

8. Critics may counter that for comparative purposes, for example, to find plausible solutions to Galton's problem of what counts as an independent case of "a culture" in cross-cultural studies of intracultural trait associations, we have to make use of so-called etic rather than emic descriptions of ethnic-cultural boundaries (Naroll 1964), but their position is equivocal.

They assume that the traditional ethnic categories that are used by both natives and ethnographers correspond in principle to just such discrete objective entities and that where they appear not to do so it is a question of a difference between native cognitive perception and observer's fact. But surely it is our task to find out what in the observers' world the traditional categories are related to, not to make gratuitous assumptions about it. Moreover, I find in Naroll's position a grossly pre-Chomskian notion of the emic-etic distinction, according to which the terms of a cognitive and of an objective description of phenomena, respectively, are possibly *arbitrarily* different, and according to which comparison cannot be effected at the emic level because it is perfectly culture-specific. This is not in fact what Goodenough means when he suggests that comparison is often best conducted in terms of etic distinctions.

Goodenough says (1970: 57) that we should think of etic levels of description as being essentially outputs of underlying cognitive-emic rules. This is like the Chomskian view that phon*etics* maps phon*emic* organization into its objective realization. But then unless we know what kind of a system of entities our rules are supposed to be about, we cannot speak about how and whether their output matches reality. Comparisons of the correlates of patterns of kin coresidence are instructive. We have every reason to believe that whatever the rules about such things in any given culture may be, their intended and actual effect upon behavior is to constrain the alignment of kinsmen on the ground in certain nonrandom ways. Since we can safely assume this, we are justified in comparing styles of residential alignment themselves, directly, even where different societies come to a given pattern of alignment on the basis of different rules or decision strategies. With cultures or societies the case is somewhat different, and it should be obvious that we cannot assume that native ideas about ethnic categories are intended either to align people in mutually exclusive, discrete culture-bearing collectivities or to describe such things.

9. Thus, for instance, while Burma proper (Upper Burma) was held to comprise the two countries (*detha, desa* in Pāli) of Tambadipa and Sunaparanta, the Shan country was Kamboza Taing, and so forth. The information on these points is scattered and confusing, but it can be found, for example, in Yule (1968: 298, 351–52). There, for Khemawara (Kengtung), read Khemarata (cf. Saimong Mangrai 1965), and see Symes (1800) for the fact that the old Mon kingdom of the delta could be either Ramaññadesa or Hanthawadi, the latter also the name of the capital province. For Maha Nagara, read Zodinagara. Luce (1959A, 1959B, and 1970) can also be consulted on these matters, as can Bernot (1967: vol. I) for Arakan as classical Dhañawadi. With these things in mind, consider Tin and Luce (1960) under the index-heading Macchagiri. In the first place, this was the old Thet (Sak) kingdom, but beyond that, in a wider sense, it seems to have meant that plus at least some of the Chin hills area (the southern part?), that is, the country of the western mountain frontier.

The fundamental idea seems to have been that, if your kingdom was a proper cosmographical module (Skt. *maṇḍala*), which as a "field of merit" it ought to be, it should, like the cosmos itself, contain as proper parts, entities that were themselves kingdoms. Thus, at the next lower level of hierarchical representation, a kingdom *not* taken as empire or seat of a major throne ought to contain, as proper parts, districts at the center of which again were to be found cosmographically interpreted capital towns (hence the classical names for provinces and their capitals too); and so on. (See Lehman 1978.)

10. Is the term /pəky/ in imitation of the Sgaw classifier for the pronoun "we"—/pa/ plus an affix—as both Sgaw and Kayah suppose?

11. LeBar, Hickey, and Musgrave (1964) notwithstanding, /pəky/ does not apply only to the Sgaw living in the hill country at the extreme south of the Kayah State, even though these are the Sgaw most intimately known to the Kayah.

12. The Geba, called /pəky dəne/ by the Kayah, live in the hills above Toungoo and appear, possibly, to be related to R. B. Jones's Palaychi (Jones 1961A).

13. In Kayah, as in Sgaw and Pwo, final nasals are absent and may conveniently be read in by those in whose languages such final nasals do exist for purposes of folk-etymological interpretation.

14. The word *talaing,* used to refer to Mon, is of problematical origin (see Yule and Burnell 1968). Although it is often considered to have something to do with the ancient Indian region of the Telengana, there are grave

objections to such an etymology, however popular it has become among historians. The Telengana etymology is founded on nothing better than the speculation found in Yule and Burnell; it has never really been established. Alternatively, *talaing* has been said to be a Mon word denoting the subjection of the Mon by the Burman king Alaungpaya in the eighteenth century. However, I do not know on what authority this etymology is based since the word is not found in Mon dictionaries. Moreover, it does not seem possible that the word was borrowed by the Burmans from Old Mon. Old Mon seems to have had no *ai* (Shorto 1965: 96) and its place was taken by *e* (or ε). Furthermore, OM *e* seems not to correspond with Burmese (closed syllable) *ai*, whereas, in words taken from or through Mon, *ai* corresponds to OM back unrounded vowels, frequently unstressed and often from understressed Indic or Dravidian *a*. If (Shorto 1965: 95) OM has had *ai* for which *e* was simply the graphic representation (just before velars), it makes no difference, since there seems to be no evidence of Burmese reflexes of this in loans as *ai*. Anyhow, whether we had, to begin with, Tel*i*ngana or, more likely, Tel*e*ngana, I find no way the vowel could have come into Burmese as *ai* via OM. Since in its original, Indian form, it seems not to have involved low ε, I cannot imagine how it could have come directly into Burmese from an Indian source with *ai* (see Lehman 1971): Modern Burmese open syllable ε and closed syllable *ai* both go back to Old Burmese *ai. Moreover, the traditional and inscriptional Burmese spelling of *talaing* is *tanlaing* (lit. *tanluiṅ*), the vowel and final of the first syllable casting yet greater doubt on the Telengana etymology.

15. Kayah have contact with Shan in several ways. Some Shan patron-traders will on occasion honor a Kayah settlement with a visit either during a Kayah festival or because of business. A few poor Shan spend some days working in Kayah upland fields. Kayah also seek out particular Shan in their villages to obtain their advice.

16. The belief that the leaves can be used on a Buddhist shrine in place of an image is, of course, widespread. For instance, Stern (personal communication) reminds me that even learned Buddhists of the Khwae Nọi use vases of leaves in this way. But it is worth remarking that the latter do not hold it to be an inferior practice and it does not mark them as being peripheral, although the Shan give the custom this interpretation and use it to marginalize the Kayah. Whether or not the custom has canonical sanction is beside the point.

17. There is a supernatural entity in Kayah culture from which the Shan get the notion of *ola*. It is called *rá* (Kyèbogyi dialect—Lehman 1967A: 71, 82). But as I pointed out in my published description of it, far from being something the Kayah believe they have any degree of control over, *rá* is an amorphous entity that the Kayah themselves are forever trying to placate (*sūw*), because of its habit of pervasive and diffuse interference with their health, welfare, and prosperity. In fact, among the Thailand Kayah I have more than once encountered a Shan or other outsider being asked to try to get rid of /(ɔ)-rá/, because, granted their greater knowledge and skill, they may be more successful than are the Kayah themselves. It is particularly important to understand that *rá* is, of all the spirits that Kayah belief recognizes, the least controllable or even conceptualized. It is not even clear that it represents a spirit at all; for it is absolutely denied that it falls under the class of *néy,* spirits and those who, consciously or not, are thought to cause evil *through* familiar spirits. All that is definitely alleged of *rá* is its contagiousness.

The Kayah do believe in jealousy witchcraft, mainly of the kind that is spontaneous and of which the agent is usually unaware. It is as often as not attributed to other Kayah, not projected onto, say, Shan. It is the most common source of misfortune, illness, and so on, but it is conceived of as containable rather than contagious and pervasive. It is /təphré/ (evils) and, characteristically, it is treated in a routine manner (see Lehman 1967A: 82) whenever need arises (almost daily somewhere in any sizable settlement) by putting out little open-work baskets with bits of food and a couple of tiny bamboo tubes of liquor at a trail or road junction. Outsiders need not be called in to do this and in fact as often as not /sūw təphré/ is done at odd times in the course of an otherwise ordinary working day, so, to the casual visitor, it is anything but a highly visible affair.

The Shan, then, may be expected to have heard in some sense of *rá* with more likelihood than to have encountered other Kayah ideas of spirits. Their contact with, and opportunities to know about, Kayah culture are highly selective. They overinterpret the *rá* on account of this selectiveness and in the light of their sense of Kayah envy of Shan relative well-being and prosperity. The Kayah are more than willing to capitalize upon this mistake on the part of the Shan, realizing, as they tell me, that that way they can extort more from the Shan villagers on occasion. It is the same game that the Shan have played upon the Kayah, and it is remarkable that neither party knows that the other is playing this game.

18. Compare the logic underlying Oscar Lewis's concept of a "culture of poverty" (Lewis 1970: ch. 4).

References

Aberle, David F. 1962. "A Note on Relative Deprivation Theory as Applied to Millenarian and Other Cult Movements." In *Millenial Dreams in Action,* ed. by Sylvia L. Thrupp. The Hague: Mouton, 1962. Pp. 209–14.

Andaya, Barbara. 1971. "Statecraft in the Reign of Lu Tai of Sukhodaya." *Cornell Journal of Social Relations,* 6 (1): 61–83.

Anderson, J. P. 1923. "Some Notes about the Karens in Siam." *Journal of the Siam Society,* 17 (2): 51–58.

Archaimbault, Charles. 1961. "L'histoire de Campasak." *Journal Asiatique,* 249: 519–95.

———. 1964. "Religious Structures in Laos." *Journal of the Siam Society,* 52: 77–96.

———. 1973. *Structures religieuses Lao.* Documents pour le Laos, 2. Vientiane: Vithagna.

Aung Thein, U. 1959. *Relationship with Burma.* Part 2. Selected articles from *Journal of the Siam Society,* vol. VI. Bangkok: Siam Society.

Backus, Mary, ed. 1884. *Siam and Laos as Seen by Our American Missionaries.* Philadelphia: Presbyterian Board of Education.

Bacon, George F. 1873. *Siam, the Land of the White Elephant.* New York: Scribner, Armstrong and Co.

Bagge, A. H. 1886. *Report on the Settlement of the Siam and Tenasserim Boundary.* Calcutta: Foreign Department Press (Selection No. 50 from the Records of Government of India, Foreign Department).

Barth, Fredrik. 1969A. Introduction. In *Ethnic Groups and Boundaries,* ed. by Fredrik Barth. Boston: Little, Brown and Co. Pp. 9–38.

———, ed. 1969B. *Ethnic Groups and Boundaries.* Boston: Little, Brown and Co.

Benedict, Paul. 1972. *Sino-Tibetan: A Conspectus.* London and New York: Cambridge University Press.

———. 1973. "Tibeto-Burman Tones, with a Note on Teleo Reconstruction." *Acta Orientalia,* 35: 127–38 (Copenhagen).
Berlin, Brent. 1971. "Speculations on the Growth of Ethnobotanical Nomenclature." Working Paper #39. Berkeley: Language-Behavior Research Laboratory, University of California at Berkeley.
Bernot, Lucien. 1967. *Les paysans arakanais du Pakistan oriental.* Paris and the Hague: Mouton.
Bharati, A. 1970. "The Hindu Renaissance and Its Apologetic Patterns." *Journal of Asian Studies,* 29 (2): 267–88.
Blackwell, Rev. George E. 1954. *The Anglo-Karen Dictionary (Based on the Dictionary Compiled by J. Wade and Mrs. J. P. Binney).* Rangoon: Baptist Board of Publications.
Blanchard, Wendell, et al. 1957. *Thailand: Its People, Its Society, Its Culture.* New Haven: Human Relations Area Files Press.
Blundell, E. A. 1836. "An Account of Some of the Petty States Lying North of the Tenasserim Provinces; Drawn from Journals and Reports of D. Richardson, Esq., Surgeon to the Commissioner of the Teanasserim Provinces." *Journal of the Royal Asiatic Society of Bombay,* 58: 600–25, 688–707.
Boonsanong Punyodyana. 1971. *Chinese-Thai Differential Assimilation in Bangkok: An Exploratory Study.* Southeast Asia Program (Data Paper No. 79). Ithaca, N.Y.: Cornell University.
Bọrihan Thepthani, Phra. 1965. *Phongsawadan chonchat thai [Chronicles of the Thai Peoples].* Bangkok: Pracak Witthaya Press.
Boserup, Ester. 1965. *The Conditions of Agricultural Growth.* Chicago: Aldine.
Bott, Elizabeth. 1968. *Family and Social Network.* New York: Barnes and Noble.
Bradley, David. 1974. "Lahu Shi Ban Lan." Paper presented at the 7th Annual Conference on Sino-Tibetan Languages and Linguistics, Atlanta.
Brailey, Nigel J. 1970. "A Re-Investigation of the Gwe of Eighteenth Century Burma." *Journal of Southeast Asian History,* 1 (2): 33–47.
Buchanan, Francis. 1792. "A Comparative Vocabulary of Some of the Languages Spoken in the Burma Empire." *Transactions of the Royal Asiatic Society of Bengal,* Old Series, vol. 18.
Bunchuai Sisawat. 1963. *Chaokhao nai Thai [Tribal People in Thailand].* Bangkok: Odeon Store.
Burling, Robbins. 1965. *Hill Farms and Padi Fields.* Englewood Cliffs, N.J.: Prentice-Hall.
Burma Reforms Committee. 1922. *Record of Evidence.* Vol. II. Rangoon: Superintendent of Government Printing.
Burney, Henry, et al. 1910–14. *The Burney Papers.* 5 vols. Bangkok: Printed by Order of the Vajiranana National Library.
Cady, John F. 1958. *A History of Modern Burma.* Ithaca, N.Y.: Cornell University Press.
Carpenter, C. H. 1873. "A Tour Among the Karens of Siam." *Baptist Missionary Magazine,* 53: 9–16.

Coedès, G. 1925. "Documents sur l'histoire politique et religieuse du Laos Occidental." *Bulletin de l'Ecole Française d'Extrême-Orient*, 25: 1–201.
Colquhoun, A. R. 1885. *Amongst the Shans*. London: Field and Tuer, Simpkin, Marshall.
Cooke, Joseph R.; J. Edwin Hudspith; and James A. Morris. 1976. "Phlong (Pwo Karen of Hot District, Chiang Mai)." In *Phonemes and Orthography: Language Planning in Ten Minority Languages of Thailand*, ed. by William A. Smalley. Pacific Linguistics Series C, No. 43. Canberra: The Australian National University, Department of Linguistics, Research School of Pacific Studies. Pp. 187–220.
Damrong Rajanubhab, Prince. 1957–58. "Our Wars with Burma." Tr. by U. Aung Thein (Phra Phraison Salarak). *Journal of the Burma Research Society*, 38 (2): 121–96; 40 (2): 135–240, 241–347.
———. 1962. *Thai rop Phama [Thai Wars with Burma]*. First published in 1920. Bangkok: Khlang Witthaya Press.
Dodd, William C. 1923. *The Tai Race*. Cedar Rapids, Ia.: Torch Press.
Douglas, Mary. 1970. *Natural Symbols*. London: Routledge and Kegan Paul.
Dumont, Louis. 1965A. "The Modern Conception of the Individual." *Contributions to Indian Sociology*, 8: 13–61.
———. 1965B. "The Functional Equivalents of the Individual in Caste Society." *Contributions to Indian Sociology*, 8: 85–99.
———. 1970A. "The Individual as an Impediment to Sociological Comparison and Indian History." In *Religion, Politics and History in India*, by Louis Dumont. Paris and the Hague: Mouton. Pp. 133–51.
———. 1970B. "The 'Village Community' from Munroe to Maine." In *Religion, Politics and History in India*, by Louis Dumont. Paris and the Hague: Mouton. Pp. 112–32.
———. 1970C. *Homo Hierarchicus*. Chicago: University of Chicago Press.
Emmons, Charles F., trans. and annotator. 1966. "The Ghehku, by Paolo Mann." M.A. Thesis, University of Illinois, Urbana.
Foster, Brian L. 1973. "Ethnic Identity of the Mons in Thailand." *Journal of the Siam Society*, 61 (1): 203–26.
Freeman, J. D. 1964. "The Iban of Western Borneo." In *Social Structure in Southeast Asia*, ed. by G. P. Murdock. Chicago: Quadrangle. Pp. 65–87.
Fürer-Haimendorf, C. von. 1960. "Caste in the Multi-Ethnic Society in Nepal." *Contributions to Indian Sociology*, 4: 12–32.
Furnivall, J. S. 1939. *Netherlands India*. Cambridge: Cambridge University Press.
———. 1956. *Colonial Policy and Practice*. First published in 1948. New York: New York University Press.
Fytche, Albert. 1878. *Burma Past and Present: With Personal Reminiscences of the Country*. 2 vols. London: Routledge and Kegan Paul.
Geddes, W. R. 1970. "Opium and the Miao: A Study in Ecological Adjustment." *Oceania*, 41 (1): 1–11.
———. 1976. *Migrants of the Mountains: The Cultural Ecology of the Blue Miao (Hmong Njua) of Thailand*. Oxford: Clarendon Press.
Geertz, Clifford. 1963. "The Integrative Revolution: Primordial Sentiments

and Civil Politics in the New States." In *Old Societies and New States,* ed. by Clifford Geertz. New York: Free Press. Pp. 105–57.

———. 1966A. *Agricultural Involution: The Processes of Ecological Change in Indonesia.* Berkeley and Los Angeles: University of California Press.

———. 1966B. "Religion as a Cultural System." In *Anthropological Approaches to the Study of Religion,* ed. by Michael Banton. Association of Social Anthropologists, Monograph No. 3. London: Tavistock. Pp. 1–46.

Gervaise, Nicholas. 1928. *The Natural and Political History of the Kingdom of Siam,* trans. by H. S. O'Neal. Bangkok.

Goodenough, Ward. 1970. *Description and Comparison in Cultural Anthropology.* Chicago: Aldine Press.

Gorman, Chester. 1969. "Hoabinhian: A Pebble-Tool Complex with Early Plant Associations in Southeast Asia." *Science,* 162: 671–73.

Gould, E. B. 1889. "Eastern Karennee and Siamese Claims." Letter to the Marquis of Salisbury, 27 March 1889. London: Foreign Office Archives, F.O. 69/132/4562.

Government of India, Foreign Department. 1890. "Proposals for Settlement of the Boundaries of the Trans-Salween State." Letter submitted to Her Majesty's Secretary of State for India. In "Political and Secret Letters from India." London: India Office Records, L/P and S/7/60. Pp. 1041–87.

Hackett, William D. 1953. "The Pa-o People of the Shan State, Union of Burma: A Sociological and Ethnographic Study of the Pa-o (Taungthu) People." Ph.D. dissertation, Cornell University.

Hall, D. G. E. 1950. *History of Burma.* London: Hutchinson.

———. 1968. *A History of South-East Asia.* 3rd ed. London: Macmillan.

Hallett, Holt S. 1890. *A Thousand Miles on an Elephant in the Shan States.* Edinburgh and London: William Blackwood and Sons.

Halliday, R. 1922. *A Mon-English Dictionary.* Bangkok: The Siam Society.

Hamilton, James W. 1963. "Effects of the Thai Market on Karen Life." *Practical Anthropology,* 10 (5): 209–15.

———. 1965. "Ban Hong: Social Structure and Economy of a Pwo Karen Village in Northern Thailand." Ph.D. dissertation, University of Michigan. (University Microfilms #66-6614.)

———. 1976. *Pwo Karen: At the Edge of Mountain and Plain.* The American Ethnological Society, Monograph 60. St. Paul: West Publishing Co.

Hanks, Lucien. 1972. "Upland and Lowland Village Relations in Northern Thailand." Paper presented at the annual meeting of the Association for Asian Studies, New York.

Harvey, G. E. 1967. *History of Burma.* First published in 1925. London: Frank Cass and Co.

Haudricourt, André. 1945. "Restitution du Karen commun." *Bulletin de la société linguistique de Paris,* 42: 103–11.

Hechter, Michael. 1971. "Towards a Theory of Ethnic Change." *Politics and Society,* 2 (1): 21–45.

———. 1974A. *Internal Colonialism: The Celtic Fringe in British National Development, 1536–1966.* London: Routledge and Kegan Paul; and Berkeley and Los Angeles: University of California Press.

———. 1974B. "The Political Economy of Ethnic Change." *American Journal of Sociology,* 79 (5): 1151–78.
Henderson, Eugenie J. A. 1965. "The Topography of Certain Phonetic and Morphological Characteristics of South East Asian Languages." *Lingua* (Indo-Pacific Linguistics Studies, Part II: Descriptive Linguistics), 15: 400–34.
Hinton, Peter. 1969. *The Pwo Karen of Northern Thailand—A Preliminary Report.* Chiang Mai: Tribal Research Centre.
———. 1978. "Declining Production among Sedentary Swidden Cultivators: The Case of Pwo Karen." In *Farmers in the Forest: Economic Development and Marginal Agriculture in Northern Thailand,* ed. by Peter Kunstadter, E. C. Chapman, and Sanga Sabhasri. Honolulu: University Press of Hawaii. Pp. 185–98.
Hymes, Dell. 1968. "Linguistic Problems in Defining the Concept of 'Tribe.'" In *Essays on the Problem of Tribe,* ed. by June Helm. Proceedings of the 1967 Annual Spring Meeting of the American Ethnological Society. Seattle: University of Washington Press. Pp. 23–48.
Iijima, Shigeru. 1965. "Cultural Change among the Hill Karens in Northern Thailand." *Asian Survey,* 5: 417–23.
———. 1967. "Karenzoku no Nominkakatei niokeru Kazokugirei" [Family-Cults in the Peasantization of the Karens]. *The Southeast Asian Studies* (Kyoto), 5 (2): 80–92.
———. 1970. "Socio-cultural Change among the Shifting Cultivators through the Introduction of Wet Rice Culture—A Case Study of the Karens in Northern Thailand." *Memoirs* of the College of Agriculture, Kyoto University (Agricultural Economics Series No. 3), 97: 1–41.
———. 1971. *Karen-zoku no shakai bunka hen'yô* [*Sociocultural Changes among the Karens of Thailand*]. Tokyo: Sobunsha.
Jones, Delmos J. 1970. "Village Autonomy, Cultural Status and Self-Perception." *Anthropological Quarterly,* 44 (1): 1–11.
Jones, R. B., Jr. 1961A. *Karen Linguistic Studies.* Berkeley and Los Angeles: University of California Press.
———. 1961B. "Laryngeals and the Development of Tones in Karen." *Burma Research Society, Fiftieth Anniversary Publications Number 1.* Pp. 101–6.
———. 1975. "The Question of Karen Linguistic Affiliation." Paper presented at the Eighth International Conference on Sino-Tibetan Languages and Linguistics, Berkeley, California.
Jordan, Marc. 1969. *Chin Dictionary and Grammar.* Paris: mimeo.
Judson, E. 1883. *Life of Judson.* New York: Anson D. F. Randolph and Co.
Keen, F. G. B. 1978. "Ecological Relationships in a Hmong (Meo) Economy." In *Farmers in the Forest: Economic Development and Marginal Agriculture in Northern Thailand,* ed. by Peter Kunstadter, E. C. Chapman, and Sanga Sabhasri. Honolulu: University Press of Hawaii. Pp. 210–21.
Kennedy, Victor. 1970. "An Indigenous Early Nineteenth Century Map of Central and Northeast Thailand." In *In Memoriam Phya Anuman Rajad-*

hon, ed. by Tej Bunnag and Michael Smithies. Bangkok: The Siam Society. Pp. 315–48.

Keyes, Charles F. 1966A. "Peasant and Nation: A Thai-Lao Village in a Thai-State." Ph.D. Dissertation, Cornell University.

———. 1966B. "Ethnic Identity and Loyalty of Villagers in Northeastern Thailand." *Asian Survey*, 6 (7): 362–69.

———. 1967. *Isan: Regionalism in Northeastern Thailand*. Southeast Asia Program (Data Paper No. 65). Ithaca, N.Y.: Cornell University.

———. 1969. "Tai-Tribal Relations in a Frontier District of Thailand: A Preliminary Report." Report to the National Research Council of Thailand, the National Science Foundation, and the University of Washington. Seattle: mimeo.

———. 1970. "New Evidence on Northern Thai Frontier History." In *In Memoriam Phya Anuman Rajadhon*, ed. by Tej Bunnag and Michael Smithies. Bangkok: The Siam Society. Pp. 221–49.

———. 1971. "Buddhism and National Integration in Thailand." *Journal of Asian Studies*, 30: 551–67.

———. 1973. "The Power of Merit." In *Visakha Puja B. E. 2516*. Bangkok: The Buddhist Association of Thailand. Pp. 95–102.

———. 1976. "Towards a New Formulation of the Concept of Ethnic Group." *Ethnicity*, 3: 202–13.

———. 1977. "Millennialism, Theravada Buddhism and Thai Society." *Journal of Asian Studies*, 36 (2): 283–302.

———. Forthcoming. "The Dialectics of Ethnic Change." In *Ethnic Change*, ed. by Charles F. Keyes.

Khanakamakan catphim ekkasan thang prawatsat [Committee for the Publication of Historical Documents]. 1971. *Tamnan phunmuang Chiang Mai* [*Local History of Chiang Mai*]. Bangkok: Office of the Prime Minister.

Khanakamakan prachasamphan lae ekkasan kancatngan chalong 25 phutthasatwat. 1957. *Cangwat Mae Hong Son* [*Mae Hong Son Province*]. Bangkok.

Kraisri Nimmanhaeminda. 1965A. " 'Put Vegetables into Baskets, People into Towns.' " In *Ethnographic Notes on Northern Thailand*, ed. by L. M. Hanks, J. R. Hanks, and L. Sharp. Southeast Asia Program (Data Paper No. 58). Ithaca, N.Y.: Cornell University. Pp. 6–9.

———. 1965B. "An Inscribed Silver-Plate Grant to the Lawa of Boh Luang." In *Felicitation Volumes of Southeast Asian Studies Presented to Prince Dhaninivat*, vol. 2. Bangkok: Siam Society. Pp. 233–38.

Kunstadter, Peter. 1965. *The Lua' (Lawa) of Northern Thailand: Aspects of Social Structure, Agriculture, and Religion*. Research Monograph No. 21. Princeton: Center of International Studies, Princeton University.

———. 1966. "Irrigation and Social Structure: Narrow Valleys and Individual Enterprise." Paper presented at the Pacific Science Congress, Tokyo.

———. 1967. "The Lua' and Sgaw Karen of Maehongson Province, Northwestern Thailand." In *Southeast Asian Tribes, Minorities and Nations*, ed. by Peter Kunstadter, vol. 2. Princeton: Princeton University Press. Pp. 639–74.

———. 1969A. "Hill and Valley Populations in Northwestern Thailand." In *Tribesmen and Peasants in North Thailand*, ed. by Peter Hinton. Chiang Mai: Tribal Research Centre. Pp. 69–85.

———. 1969B. "Socio-cultural Change among Upland Peoples of Thailand: Lua' and Karen—two Modes of Adaptation." In *Proceedings of the VIIth International Congress of Anthropological and Ethnological Sciences, 1968, Tokyo and Kyoto, Vol. II, Ethnology*. Tokyo: Science Council of Japan.

———. 1970A. "Integration and Assimilation of Minorities in Mae Hongson Province." Paper presented at the Annual Meeting of the Association for Asian Studies, San Francisco. Mimeo.

———. 1970B. *Natality, Morality and Migration of Upland and Lowland Populations in Northwestern Thailand*. Carolina Population Center Monograph 9. Chapel Hill: Carolina Population Center. Pp. 46–60.

———. 1971. "Ecological Change and Human Biology in Northern Thailand." Paper prepared for Symposium on Human Biology of Populations Undergoing Environmental Change, sponsored by the Human Adaptability Section of the International Biological Programme, University of Malawi, Bantyre, Malawi, April 4–10. Mimeo.

———. 1972. "Demography, Ecology, Social Structure and Settlement Patterns." In *Structure of Human Populations*, ed. by A. J. Boyce and G. A. Harrison. Oxford: Clarendon Press.

———. 1978. "Subsistence Agricultural Economies of Lua' and Karen Hill Farmers, Mae Sariang District, Northwestern Thailand." In *Farmers in the Forest: Economic Development and Marginal Agriculture in Northern Thailand*, ed. by Peter Kunstadter, E. C. Chapman, and Sanga Sabhasri. Honolulu: University Press of Hawaii.

———. 1979. "Ethnic and Ecological Differences in Migration, Marriage and Reproductive Success in Northwestern Thailand." Paper presented at Symposium on Population Structure and Human Variation: The Indo-Pacific Area. Post-Plenary Session of the 10th International Congress of Anthropological and Ethnological Sciences, Bombay, India, December 19–21, 1978. Revised February 1979, for publication in proceedings of the seminar.

———. In press. *The People of Pa Pae*. Accepted for publication as Monograph No. 2, Thomas Burke Memorial Washington State Museum, the University of Washington, Seattle.

Kuper, Leo, and M. G. Smith. 1969. *Pluralism in Africa*. Berkeley and Los Angeles: University of California Press.

Leach, E. R. 1954. *Political Systems of Highland Burma*. Cambridge: Harvard University Press.

———. 1960. "The Frontiers of Burma." *Comparative Studies in Sociology and History*, 3 (1): 49–68.

LeBar, Frank M. 1967. "Observations on the Movement of Khmu into North Thailand." *Journal of the Siam Society*, 55 (1): 61–79.

LeBar, F. M.; G. C. Hickey; and J. K. Musgrave. 1964. *Ethnic Groups of Mainland Southeast Asia*. New Haven: Human Relations Area File Press.

Lehman, F. K. 1963. *The Structure of Chin Society*. Illinois Studies in Anthropology No. 3. Urbana: University of Illinois.
———. 1967A. "Ethnic Categories in Burma and the Theory of Social Systems." In *Southeast Asian Tribes, Minorities, and Nations*, ed. by Peter Kunstadter. Princeton: Princeton University Press. Pp. 93–124.
———. 1967B. "Kayah Society as a Function of the Shan-Burman-Karen Context." In *Contemporary Change in Traditional Societies*, ed. by Julian H. Steward. Urbana: University of Illinois. Pp. 1–104.
———. 1967–68. Unpublished field notes.
———. 1971. "Some Diachronic Rules of Burmese Phonology: The Problem of the Final 'Palatals.' " In *Occasional Papers of the Wolfenden Society on Tibeto-Burman Linguistics*, Vol. II. Urbana: Department of Linguistics, University of Illinois.
———. 1975. "Formal Approaches to Ethnicity." In *Comparative International Studies*, ed. by R. L. Merrit and S. J. Brzezinski. Urbana: Center for Comparative International Studies, University of Illinois. Pp. 109–14.
———. 1978. "On the Vocabulary and Semantics of 'Field' in Theravāda Buddhism." Paper presented at the Conference on South Asian Languages and Linguistics, University of Illinois, Urbana, July.
———. 1979. "Etymological Speculations on Some Chin Words." *Linguistics in the Tibeto-Burman Area*, 4 (2). In press.
Lévi-Strauss, Claude. 1949. *Les Structures élémentaires de la parenté*. Paris: Presses Universitaires de France.
Lewis, J. L. 1924. "The Burmanization of the Karen People: A Study in Racial Adaptability." M.A. thesis, University of Chicago.
Lewis, Oscar. 1970. *Anthropological Essays*. New York: Random House.
Li, Charles N., and Sandra A. Thompson. 1975. "The Semantic Function of Word Order: A Case Study." In *Word Order and Word Order Change*, ed. by C. N. Li. Austin: University of Texas Press. Pp. 163–96.
Loo Shwe, Thra. 1962. "The Karen People of Thailand and Christianity." Typescript, n.p.
Luce, Gordon H. 1953. "Mons of the Pagan Dynasty." *Journal of the Burma Research Society*, 36 (1): 1–19.
———. 1959A. "Geography of Burma under the Pagan Dynasty." *Journal of the Burma Research Society*, 42 (1): 32–51.
———. 1959B. "Introduction to the Comparative Study of Karen Languages." *Journal of the Burma Research Society*, 42 (1): 1–18.
———. 1959C. "Chin Hills Linguistic Tour." *Journal of the Burma Research Society*, 42: 19–31.
———. 1965. "Danaw, a Dying Austroasiatic Language." *Lingua*, 14: 98–129.
———. 1970. *Old Burma, Early Pagan*. 3 vols. Locust Valley, N.Y.: J. J. Augustin, for Artibus Asiae, Ascona, Switzerland.
McGilvray, D. 1912. *A Half Century Among the Siamese and the Lao*. New York: Fleming H. Revell.
McLeod, W. C. 1869. "Journal of 1836–37." In *Copy of Papers Relating to*

the Route of Capt. W. C. McLeod from Moulmein to the Frontier of China and to the Route of Dr. Richardson on his Fourth Mission to the Shan Provinces of China, comp. by Great Britain, India Office. London: House of Commons.

MacMahon, A. R. 1876. *The Karens of the Golden Chersonese*. London: Harrison.

Maran, La Raw. 1970. "Some Thoughts on Sino-Tibetan as a Genealogical Classification." Paper presented at the Third Annual Meeting on Sino-Tibetan Reconstruction, Cornell University.

———. 1971. "Tone in Burmese and Jinghpo." Ph.D. dissertation, University of Illinois.

———. n.d. "The Algebra of Inter-acting Human Groups." Ms.

Marlowe, David H. 1969. "Upland-Lowland Relationships: The Case of the S'kaw Karen of Central Upland Western Chiang Mai." In *Tribesmen and Peasants in North Thailand*, ed. by Peter Hinton. Chiang Mai: Tribal Research Centre. Pp. 53–68.

———. 1970. "The S'kaw Karen of Chiang Mai." Paper presented at the Annual Meeting of the Association for Asian Studies, San Francisco, April.

———. 1973. "Notes on a Mountain Flower: Thoughts on the Epidemiology of the Cultivation and Use of *Papaver Somniferum* in Certain Hill Areas of North Thailand." Washington, D.C.: Division of Neuropsychiatry, Walter Reed Army Institute of Research. Mimeo.

Marlowe, G. W. 1965–68. Unpublished field notes.

———. 1972. "Under Chiang Mai Wall: Networks and Boundaries in a Circum-Urban Area." Paper presented at the Annual Meeting of the Association for Asian Studies, New York.

Marshall, Harry I. 1922. *The Karen People of Burma: A Study in Anthropology and Ethnology*. Columbus: Ohio State University.

———. 1945. *The Karens of Burma*. Burma Pamphlets, No. 8. London: Longmans, Green.

Mason, Francis. 1852. *Tenasserim*. Maulmain: American Mission Press.

———. 1860. *Burmah: Its People and Natural Productions*. Rangoon.

———. 1882–83. *Burmah, Its People and Productions*. 2 vols. Revised and enlarged edition by W. Theobold. Rangoon.

———. 1884. *The Karen Apostle, or Memoir of Ko Thah Byu, the First Karen Convert, with Notices Concerning His Nation*. Bassein, Burma: Sgau Karen Press. (Originally published in Boston by Gould, Kendall, and Lincoln, 1843.)

Matisoff, James A. 1972. "The Tones of Jinghpo and Lolo-Burmese." Paper presented at the Fifth International Conference on Sino-Tibetan Languages and Linguistics, Ann Arbor.

Mendelson, E. Michael. 1961A. "A Messianic Buddhist Association in Upper Burma." *Bulletin of the School of Oriental and African Studies*, 24: 560–80.

———. 1961B. "The King of the Weaving Mountain." *Journal of the Royal Central Asiatic Society*, 48: 229–37.

———. 1963. "Observations on a Tour in the Region of Mount Popa, Central Burma." *France-Asie*, 179: 780–807.
Moerman, Michael. 1965. "Ethnic Identity in a Complex Civilization: Who Are the Lue?" *American Anthropologist*, 67: 1215–30.
———. 1968. "Being Lue: Uses and Abuses of Ethnic Identification." In *Essays on the Problem of Tribe*, ed. by June Helm. Proceedings of the 1967 Annual Spring Meeting of the American Ethnological Society. Seattle: University of Washington Press. Pp. 153–69.
Moore, A. W. 1879. "Burma: The Question of Karennee." In "Political and Secret Memoranda of the India Office." London: India Office Records, l/P & s/18/B20.
Mouhot, Henri. 1868. *Voyage dans les royaumes de Siam, de Cambodge, de Laos et autres parties centrales de l'Indochine*. Paris: Hachette.
Murdock, George P. 1949. *Social Structure*. New York: Macmillan.
Naroll, Raoul. 1964. "On Ethnic Unit Classification." *Current Anthropology*, 5: 283–9, 306–12.
———. 1968. "Who the Lue Are." In *Essays on the Problem of Tribe*, ed. by June Helm. Proceedings of the 1967 Annual Spring Meeting of the American Ethnological Society. Seattle: University of Washington Press. Pp. 72–79.
Notton, Camille, trans. 1926. *Annales du Siam. Première partie: Chroniques du Suvanna Khamdeng, Mahathera Fa Böt, Suvanna K'om Kham, Sinhanavati*. Paris: Impr. Charles-Lavauzelle.
———, trans. 1932. *Annales du Siam, IIIe Volume: Chronique du Xieng Mai*. Paris.: Libr. Orientaliste Paul Geuthner.
O'Riley, F. G. S. 1857. "Notices on Karen Nee, the Country of the Kaya or Red Karens." In "India Political and Foreign Consultations." London: India Office Records, IPF/26/202, No. 102. (Also published in *Journal of the Indian Archipelago*, n.s., 4 (1889): 1–25.)
Penth, Hans. 1977. "Historical Notes on the Region West of Chiang Mai." *Journal of the Siam Society*, 65 (2): 179–88.
Phibun Borihan, Phra. n.d. c. 1935. *Prawat muang Mae Hong Son* [*History of Mae Hong Son*]. n.p. (Typescript copy obtained in Mae Hong Son in 1968.)
Pho Saemlamciak, comp. 1970. *Prawat amphoe ngao, chiwaprawat cao pho pratu pha (Phraya Mulek), tamnan Muang Nakhon Lampang, chiwaprawat Cao Phraya Sulawalu Chaiyasongkhram (Nan Thip Chang)* [*History of Ngao District, Biography of the Lord of the Cliff Pass (Phraya Iron-hand), Accounts of Muang Nakhon Lampang, Biography of Cao Phraya Sulawalu Chaiyasongkhram (Nan Thip Chang)*]. Lampang: Khana Chao Amphoe Ngao.
Phra ratchaphongsawadan krung Ayutthaya [*The Royal Chronicles of Ayutthaya*]. 1962. (Version of Somdet Phra Phanarat.) Bangkok: Khlang Witthaya Press.
Poriyat Thammathada, Phraya (Phae Talalak) and Phra Yanwicit (Sitthi Locananon), trans. and ed. 1967. *Camthewiwong phongsawadan muang*

Haripunchai [*Camadevi Dynasty, Chronicle of Haripunjaya*], by Bodhiramsi. Thai translation, first published in 1920. Bangkok: Published on the Occasion of the 72nd birthday of Mrs. Kimho Nimanhemin.

Prachakitcakoracak, Phraya (Saem Bunnak), comp. 1964. *Phongsawadan Yonok* [*Yonok Chronicle*]. First published in 1907. Bangkok: Khlangwitthaya (National Library Edition).

Prani Sirithon na Phatthalung, comp. 1963. *Phet lanna: sankhadi chiwaprawat bukkhon yuk thong khong Lannathai* [*Lanna Jewels: Biographical Essays of Men in the Golden Age of Lannathai*]. 2 vols. Chiang Mai: Suriwong Kanphim.

Purtle, Dale I. 1970. "Reconsidering the Position of Tibeto-Burman within Sino-Tibetan." Paper presented at the Third Annual Meeting on Sino-Tibetan Reconstruction, Cornell University.

Richardson, Dr. 1839–40. "Journal of a Mission from the Supreme Government of India to the Court of Siam." *Journal of the Asiatic Society of Bengal*, 8 (96): 1016–36; 9 (97): 1–30.

———. 1869. "Journal of 1836–1837." In *Copy of Papers Relating to the Route of Capt. W. C. McLeod from Moulmein to the Frontier of China and to the Route of Dr. Richardson on His Fourth Mission to the Shan Provinces of China,* comp. by Great Britain, India Office. London: House of Commons.

Ryley, Horten. 1899. *Ralph Fitch*. London: J. Fisher Unwin.

Saimong Mangrai, Sao. 1965. *The Shan States and the British Annexation*. Southeast Asia Program (Data Paper No. 57). Ithaca, N.Y.: Cornell University.

Sangermano, Vincentius. 1885. *A Description of the Burmese Empire*, trans. by W. Tandy. First published in 1833. Rangoon: Government Press.

Sanguan Chotisukkharat, ed. 1972A. *Nangsu phunmuang Chaing Mai* [*Local Chronicle of Chaing Mai*]. Anthropological and Cultural Series, No. 1. Chiang Mai: Lanna Thai Research Center.

———, comp. 1972B. "Banthuk kantham sanya maitri Chiang Mai kap muang yang daeng" ["Records of Treaty Making between Chiang Mai and the Red Karen Country"]. In *Prachum tamnan Lannathai* [*Collected Accounts of Lannathai*]. Bangkok: Odeon Store. Pp. 545–50.

Sarkisyanz, E. 1961. *Buddhist Background of the Burmese Revolution*. The Hague: Martinus Nijhoff.

Scott, James George, and J. P. Hardiman. 1900–1901. *Gazeteer of Upper Burma and the Shan States*. 5 vols. Rangoon: Superintendent of Government Printing.

Seidenfaden, Erik. 1967. *The Thai Peoples*. Bangkok: The Siam Society.

Shorto, H. L. 1962. *A Dictionary of Modern Spoken Mon*. London: Oxford University Press.

———. 1963. "The 32 *Myos* in the Medieval Mon Kingdom." *Bulletin of the School of Oriental and African Studies*, 36: 572–91.

———. 1965. "The Interpretation of Archaic Writing Systems." *Lingua*, 14: 88–97.

Shway Yoe (Sir James George Scott). 1963. *The Burman: His Life and Notions*. First published c. 1909. New York: Norton.
Siamese Legation in London. 1880. In "Boundary Between Siam and Upper Burmah: Memoranda and Supplementary Memorandum." London: Foreign Office Records, F.O. 69/135/4585, November.
Skinner, G. William. 1957. *Chinese Society in Thailand: An Analytical History*. Ithaca, N.Y.: Cornell University Press.
———. 1958. *Leadership and Power in the Chinese Community of Thailand*. Ithaca, N.Y.: Cornell University Press.
———. 1964. "The Thailand Chinese: Assimilation in a Changing Society." *Asia*, 2: 80–92.
Smeaton, D. M. 1887. *The Loyal Karens of Burma*. London: Kegan, Paul and Trench.
Smith, M. G. 1960. "Social and Cultural Pluralism." *Annals of the New York Academy of Sciences*, 83: art. 5.
———. 1965. *The Plural Society in the British West Indies*. Berkeley and Los Angeles: University of California Press.
Sophon Ratanakorn. 1978. "Legal Aspects of Land Occupation and Development in Thailand." In *Farmers in the Forest: Economic Development and Marginal Agriculture in Northern Thailand*, ed. by Peter Kunstadter, E. C. Chapman, and Sanga Sabhasri. Honolulu: University Press of Hawaii. Pp. 45–53.
Spiro, Melford E. 1967. *Burmese Supernaturalism*. Englewood Cliffs, N.J.: Prentice-Hall. (Expanded edition, Philadelphia: Institute for the Study of Human Issues, 1978.)
———. 1971. *Buddhism and Society*. New York: Harper and Row.
Steinberg, Joel, et al. 1971. *In Search of Southeast Asia*. New York: Praeger.
Stern, Theodore. 1965. "Research upon Karen in Village and Town, Upper Khwae Noi, Western Thailand. Selected Findings." Report to the National Research Council of Thailand. Bangkok: mimeo.
———. 1968A. "*Ariya* and the Golden Book: A Millenarian Buddhist Sect among the Karen." *Journal of Asian Studies*, 27 (2): 297–328.
———. 1968B. "The Cult of the Local 'Lord' among the Karen." Paper presented at the 67th Annual Meeting of the American Anthropological Association. Mimeo.
———. 1968C. "Three Pwo Karen Scripts: A Study of Alphabet Formation." *Anthropological Linguistics*, 10 (1): 1–39.
———. 1971. "Karen on the Khwae Noi in the Nineteenth Century." Eugene, Ore.: University of Oregon. Mimeo, June.
Stern, Theodore, and Theodore A. Stern. 1971. " 'I Pluck My Harp': Musical Acculturation among the Karen of Western Thailand." *Ethnomusicology*, 15 (2): 186–219.
Stewart, John. 1909. *Burma Through the Centuries*. London: Kegan, Paul, Trench, Truebner and Co.
Suwan Ruenyote. 1969. "The Hill Tribe Programme of the Thai Government." In *Tribesman and Peasants in Northern Thailand*, ed. by Peter Hinton. Chiang Mai: Tribal Research Centre. Pp. 12–14.

Symes, Michael. 1800. *An Account of an Embassy to the Kingdom of Ava, Sent by the Governor-General of India, in the Year 1795*. London: W. Bulmer. (Reprinted, England: Gregg International, 1969.)
Tadaw, Saw Hanson. 1961. "The Karens of Burma: A Study in Human Geography." In *Studies in Human Ecology*, ed. by George A. Theodorson. Evanston, Ill.: Row, Peterson and Co. Pp. 496–506.
Tambiah, S. J. 1970. *Buddhism and the Spirit Cults in North-east Thailand*. Cambridge Studies in Social Anthropology, 2. Cambridge: Cambridge University Press.
Tej Bunnag. 1968. "The Provincial Administration of Siam from 1892 to 1915." Ph.D. dissertation, Oxford.
Thiphakọrawong, Cao Phraya (Kham Bunnak). 1962. *Phraratchaphongsawadan krung ratanakosin ratchakan thi 3 lae phraratchaphongsawadan krung ratanakosin ratchakan thi 4* [*Royal Chronicles of the Third and Fourth Reigns of the Bangkok Era*]. Bangkok: Khlang Witthaya (National Library Edition).
Tin, Pe Maung, and Gordon H. Luce, trans. 1960. *The Glass Palace Chronicles of the Kings of Burma*. Rangoon: Rangoon University Press.
Tinker, Hugh. 1957. *The Union of Burma*. London: Oxford University Press.
Truxton, Addison Strong. 1958. "The Integration of the Karen Peoples of Burma and Thailand into Their Respective National Cultures: A Study in the Dynamics of Culture Contact." M.A. thesis, Cornell University.
Wales, H. G. Quaritch. 1965. *Siamese Government and Administration*. First published c. 1934. New York: Paragon Book Reprint Corporation.
Walker, Anthony. 1969. "Red Lahu Village Society: An Introductory Survey." In *Tribesmen and Peasants in North Thailand*, ed. by Peter Hinton. Chiang Mai: Tribal Research Centre. Pp. 41–52.
Wayland, Francis. 1853. *Memoir of Rev. Judson*. Vol. I. Boston: Phillips Sampson and Co.
Witz, Klaus R. n.d. *Abstract Algebra Course*. University of Illinois. Ms.
Wolf, Eric R. "Types of Latin American Peasantry." *American Anthropologist*, 57 (3): 452–72.
Worsley, Peter. 1968. *The Trumpet Shall Sound*. 2nd ed. New York: Schocken Books.
Yule, Henry. 1968. *Narrative of the Mission to the Court of Ava in 1855*. London: Oxford University Press.
Yule, Henry, and A. C. Burnell. 1968. 2nd ed. *Hobson-Jobson: A Glossary of Anglo-Indian Colloquial Words and Phrases*. First published c. 1903. London: Routledge and Kegan Paul.

Notes on the Contributors

Peter Hinton is Lecturer in the Department of Anthropology, University of Sydney, Sydney, Australia.

Shigeru Iijima is Professor of Social Anthropology, the Institute for the Study of Languages and Cultures of Asia and Africa, University of Foreign Studies, Tokyo, Japan.

Charles F. Keyes is Professor of Anthropology and Asian Studies, University of Washington, Seattle, Washington.

Peter Kunstadter is Research Associate in the East-West Population Institute, East-West Center, Honolulu, Hawaii.

F. K. Lehman is Professor of Anthropology and Linguistics, University of Illinois, Urbana, Illinois.

David H. Marlowe is with the Division of Neuropsychiatry, Walter Reed Army Institute of Research, Washington, D.C.

Theodore Stern is Professor of Anthropology, University of Oregon, Eugene, Oregon.

Index

Aberle, David F., 91
Acculturation, 66
Administration: administrative reforms in Thailand, 22, 53, 103, 122, 128, 146, 160–161, 207; local administration in Thailand, 93, 183–184
Adoption: by Karen, 86; of Karen by others, 136, 156. *See also* Children, Karen attitudes toward
Agricultural rituals, 106
Agriculture: among Karen, 14, 15, 46, 51, 65, 66, 68–69, 70, 75, 103–105, 106; among Kayah, 87. *See also* Land; Swidden cultivation; Wet-rice cultivation
Akha, 147, 195, 211
Alaungpaya, King of Burma (1752–1760), 34, 42, 56, 65, 85, 202, 252
Alcohol: *See* Liquor
American Baptist Mission, 50, 90, 112, 132. *See also* Christianity
Ancestral spirit cult: among Pwo, 68, 70; among Sgaw, 50, 107–113, 115, 116, 118, 131–134, 138, 162, 173, 178, 179
Ancestral spirits: *See* Spirits, ancestral
Andaya, Barbara, 238
Anderson, J. P., 100–101
Anglo-Siamese Border Commission of 1890, 40, 41, 51, 52, 59, 60, 61
Animism: *See* Ancestral spirit cult; Locality spirit cult; Spirit beliefs among Karen; Spirits, ancestral; Spirits, locality
Archaimbault, Charles, 27, 30, 55

Archer, W. A., 41, 60
Assimilation, 6–7, 207, 211; in Thai society, 122; of Karen to Thai society and culture, 15, 19, 21, 22, 116, 145, 158, 162; of Kayah in Thai society, 19. *See also* Karen ethnic adaptation and change
Aung Thein, U, 44, 55, 60
Auxre, 179. *See also* Ancestral spirit cult
Ava, 33, 34, 39, 40, 42, 64, 79, 93
Awkre, 131–134, 138, 162. *See also* Ancestral spirit cult
Ayutthaya (Ayuthia), 27, 33, 34, 36, 55, 56

Backus, Mary, 206
Bacon, George F., 201
Bagge, A. H., 52, 53
Baht, 80
Ban Hong, 68, 69, 70, 71, 72, 76, 79
Ban Huai Phung, 128, 129
Barth, Fredrik, 3, 4, 7, 23, 29, 78, 120, 121, 160, 191, 202, 232
Bawlakhè, 223, 227, 239
Benedict, Paul, 219, 220, 229
Berlin, Brent, 236–237
Bernot, Lucien, 250
Bgha, 106–111, 113, 115, 118. *See also* Spirits, ancestral
Bharati, A., 234
Biculturalism and multiculturalism, 177; among Karen, 78
Bi Khi Pwo: *See* Waplonkhu

269

Blackwell, George E., 229
Blanchard, Wendell, 55
Blaw (blǫ), 100, 162, 163
Blundell, E. A., 43, 128, 199, 200
Bǫkeo, 181, 192
Boonsanong Punyodyana, 122
Border between Thailand and Burma: Anglo-Siamese demarcation of and debates over, 40–42, 51–53, 207; closing of, 148. *See also* Anglo-Siamese Border Commission of 1890
Border Patrol Police in Thailand, 73, 147
Bǫrihan Thepthani, Phra, 55
Boserup, Ester, 104
Bradley, David, 249
Brailey, Nigel J., 33, 34, 39, 56, 57, 59, 79, 223, 225–227, 249
Brè, 224
Buchanan, Francis, 198, 202
Buddhism: as practiced by Karen, 12, 21–22, 50–53, 61, 79–80, 84, 248; as practiced by Kayah, 226, 243–245, 256; as practiced by Pwo, 51, 52, 66, 69, 70, 72, 76, 77, 82, 84–86; as practiced by Sgaw, 110–112, 116, 117, 132–134, 153–154, 162, 175, 184, 186–189, 192, 193, 210; Buddhist missionary work among tribal peoples, 19, 61, 154
Bunchuai Sisawat, 26, 44, 52
Burling, Robbins, 166
Burma Reforms Committee, 168, 203
Burmans, 6, 213, 234–235
Burmese, 6, 203
Burnell, A. C., 251–252
Burney, Henry, 49, 60, 61

Cady, John F., 56
Capitalist activity among Karen, 15, 69
Carpenter, C. H., 44, 45, 51, 52
Cekosi, 12, 21, 132–133. *See also* Tattooing cult
Central Thai: *See* Thai, Central
Cetiya, 112, 154
Chakasi, 110, 112–113, 132. *See also* Tattooing cult
Chang Phụak, Phraya, ruler of Chiang Mai (1813–1821), 42, 43, 59
Chao khao: *See* Hill tribes
Charismatic leaders, among Kayah, 224, 239, 244. *See also* Khruba Khao; Millennialism
Chiang Mai (city and province, formerly capital of autonomous principality), 38, 54, 56–60, 127, 189, 211, 214; Karen in Chiang Mai province, 10, 16, 20, 21, 28, 32, 36, 40, 42–43, 46, 48, 49, 54, 56, 61, 65, 72, 118, 134, 143, 150, 151, 161, 162, 168, 176, 187, 198–200, 205, 212, 240; treaty with Kantarawady, 40–42, 47, 60–61; wars with Burma and Siam, 36–37, 39–40
Children, Karen attitudes toward, 135, 182–183. *See also* Adoption
Chin (Tibeto-Burman speaking people in Burma), 23, 168, 169, 219–221, 232, 247, 250, 251; relations with Burmans, 30
Chinese: as minority in Thailand, 5, 7, 122, 127, 136, 155, 175; Haw, 174, 206; Nationalist Chinese in Thailand, 94
Christianity: adoption by Karen, 12, 16, 20, 21, 50, 61, 82, 90–92, 109, 110, 112, 131–134, 149, 157, 247–248; and education among Karen, 17–18; and Karen identity, 22, 149, 157, 247; Christian missionary work among Karen, 17, 20–21, 50, 51, 90, 112–113, 156, 157
Chulalongkorn, King of Siam (1868–1910), 53
Church of Christ in Thailand, 21, 157
Citizenship: and ethnicity, 5; for Karen in Thailand, 15, 17, 22, 23, 50, 54, 76, 147–149; of tribal peoples in Thailand, 13, 17
Class: and ethnicity, 6, 7, 12; and Kayah, 246; and Pwo, 69; and Sgaw, 136, 196–197. *See also* Income; Wealth and poverty
Coedès, G., 20
Collins, Dr., 200
Colquhoun, A. R., 214
Cǫm Thǫng (town and district), 177, 181, 185, 187, 189, 192, 198, 209, 212, 214
Communal meeting room or house in Sgaw villages, 100, 162, 163
Conflict: in interethnic situations, 6, 22, 247; involving Karen, 124–125, 142, 155, 184. *See also* Rebellion by Karen in Burma
Cooke, Joseph R., 8, 79
Cooperative labor, 106, 140
Cotton production, 66
Courting customs, 140, 171
Craft production, 69
Credit available to Karen, 142, 143, 151, 185, 186
Curing rituals, 68, 138, 144–145, 193, 194. *See also* Illness

Da muxha, 173. *See also* Spirits, locality
Damrong Rajanubhab, Prince, 31, 32, 55
Danaw, 230, 231
Death, Karen ideas of, 172
Diet, 125

Divination, 144, 206–207
Dodd, William C., 55
Dong Luang, 68, 70, 71, 72, 79
Dopuweh, 107–113, 115. See also Kin groups
Dosuda, 114. See also Ritual head
Douglas, Mary, 91
Dress, 126
Dumont, Louis, 203, 213–214

Ecological adaptation of Karen, 14, 15, 121, 136, 211
Economy: among Karen, 14, 15–16; among Pwo, 68–69, 75–77, 82; among Sgaw, 134–136, 142, 150–153; economic change, 242. See also Agriculture; Cooperative labor; Credit available to Karen; Land; Lumber industry; Mining; Productive resources; Swidden Cultivation; Teak trade; Trade; Wage labor; Wealth and poverty; Wet-rice cultivation
Education: among Karen, 15, 16, 21, 76, 78, 135, 148, 157, 159, 163; hill tribes schools, 19, 148, 161; schools in Karen communities, 82. See also Literacy
Elections, Karen participation in, 16, 149–150
Elephants owned by Karen, 83, 142, 151, 152, 201
Elias, Ney, 59, 60
Emic-etic distinction, 250
Emmons, Charles F., 224
Employment: See Wage labor; White-collar occupations
Endogamy: See Marriage patterns
Entrepreneurship: See Capitalist activity among Karen
Ethnic adaptation and change, 6–7. See also Acculturation; Assimilation; Karen ethnic adaptation and change
Ethnic boundaries, 5, 120, 194; between Karen and others, 21, 54, 77, 78, 122, 208
Ethnic category, 168, 176, 190, 215–216, 232, 233, 235–236, 250; definition of, 119–120, 123; formal model of structure of ethnic categories, 236–237; hill tribe as ethnic category, 8, 13; Karen ethnic category, 54, 126, 147–148, 187, 199, 229, 232, 238–240. See also Ethnic labels
Ethnic consciousness among Karen, 157
Ethnic group, definition of, 3, 4, 5, 119, 120, 121
Ethnic group relations, 8, 29; dichotomization as hill (upland) and valley (lowland), 166, 167, 193, 195, 196, 212, 213; dichotomization as "sown" and "wild," 170, 172, 180, 192–196, 200, 201, 205, 207, 208, 212; encapsulation in, 212; hierarchical structure of, 166, 176, 189–202, 205, 207; structural opposition in, 3, 5, 7, 8, 29, 190, 191; symbiotic structure of, 30, 33, 45, 55, 64, 90, 231, 232, 241. See also Karen ethnic group relations; Kayah ethnic group relations; Plural society; Pluralism and pluralistic society
Ethnic labels, 231; for Karen, 25–26, 29, 31, 45, 54, 55, 60, 73, 79, 80, 126, 229–232, 238–239; for Pwo, 23, 64, 198; for Sgaw, 23, 73, 80, 198, 230, 239; used by Karen for Thai and northern Thai, 194; used by Karen for tribal peoples, 196. See also Ethnic category; *Yang*
Ethnic stereotypes and images: of Karen by Lua', 143–144; of Karen by Thai, 147–148, 197; of non-Karen by Karen, 154–155, 177. See also Hill tribes; Karen ethnic group relations
Ethnicity and ethnic identity, 4, 6; and access to resources and power, 5, 14, 29, 136; and class, 6, 7, 12; ascribed by others, 120; behavioral basis of, 168–169; 176, 233; cognitive basis of, 234–236; cultural basis of, 1, 4, 5, 8, 29, 191, 216, 232–235, 237; definition of, 119, 120, 216; ecological basis of, 201; linguistic basis of, 7; multiple and hyphenated identities, 4, 5, 19, 204; primordial basis of, 1; saliency of, in northern Thailand, 180; self-identity, 120; situationally determined, 160; symbolic expression of, 6. See also Karen ethnicity and ethnic identity

Finch, Ralph, 214
Food taboos, 125–126
"Foreigner": See Westerner
Freeman, J. D., 102
Fukui, Hayao, 117
Fürer-Haimendorf, C. von, 116
Furnivall, J. S., 5, 56, 165, 167, 203
Fytche, Albert, 64

Geba, 239, 251
Geddes, W. R., 155
Geertz, Clifford, 3, 6, 30, 104
Gervaise, Nicholas, 213
Goodenough, Ward, 250
Gorman, Chester, 221
Gould, E. B., 60, 61
Gwe, 56, 249

Hackett, William D., 8, 238
Hae mai kham, 187–188, 191, 192, 193, 208. *See also* Thai rituals
Hall, D. G. E., 33, 231
Hallett, Holt, 47, 102
Halliday, R., 60
Hamilton, James W., 8, 68, 69, 71, 72, 79, 80
Haṁsavati: *See* Pegu
Hanks, Lucien, 180, 186
Hardiman, J. P., 27, 56, 57, 249
Haripuñjaya, 26, 235, 241
Haudricourt, André, 219
Harvey, G. E., 57, 79, 197, 202, 203, 228
Haw, 174, 206. *See also* Chinese
Headmen, village: in Pwo villages, 82–85; in Sgaw villages, 102, 103, 140, 149, 181, 184, 185, 189. *See also* Ritual head; Village social organization
Health services, 82, 157, 173. *See also* Curing rituals; Illness
Hechter, Michael, 5, 23
Henderson, Eugenie J. A., 64
Hickey, G. C., 23, 214, 251
Hill tribes (*chao khao*) in Thailand, 14, 19, 53, 122, 146, 161; category applied to Karen, 8, 13, 53, 121, 147–148, 158, 211; category used by Thai officials, 8, 13, 147, 211; stereotype based on Meo, 148, 156
Hinton, Peter, 10, 11, 19, 20, 50, 57, 61, 64, 67, 71, 80, 82, 100, 162, 214, 239
Hmong: *See* Meo
Hti k'cha ko k'cha, 106, 114, 116. *See also* Spirits, locality
Hudspith, J. Edwin, 8, 79
Hymes, Dell, 7

Iijima, Shigeru, 10, 12, 15, 61, 68, 71, 80, 157, 162, 229, 238
Illness, 242; Karen ideas of, 173. *See also* Curing rituals; Health services
Income: of Pwo, 75; of Sgaw, 153. *See also* Economy; Wealth and poverty
Indians, overseas: in Burma, 6, 168; in Thailand, 106, 122, 127, 136
Inheritance of property: among Pwo, 68, 70, 71, 72; among Sgaw, 105, 138, 182. *See also* Land
Inthanon, Cao, 59
Inthara Khiri (Eindagiri), 31, 55
Iwata, Keiji, 103, 117
Iylùw, 226, 244, 250

Jinghpaw (language and people), 220, 233, 250. *See also* Kachin
Jones, Delmos J., 247

Jones, R. B., 8, 10–11, 13, 23, 29, 55, 219–221, 251
Jordan, Marc E., 219
Judson, Adoniram, 50
Judson, E., 202

Ka ja pado, 181. *See also* Spirits, locality
Kachin, 3, 5, 93, 120, 167, 182, 203, 232, 233, 237, 250; relations with Shan, 30, 107, 203
Kalang (karang), 73, 80, 230
Kanchanaburi (town and province), 44; Karen in province, 8–9, 16, 20, 21, 45, 51, 52, 53, 66, 67, 69, 176, 230
Kantarawady (Eastern Karenni), 36, 40, 42, 45–48, 59, 61, 221, 224–226, 239. *See also* Karenni
Karen: as autochthonous population in Thailand, 26–31; origins of, 26–31, 55, 217, 219–221, 223, 228–229, 231
Karen Baptist Church, 16, 18, 21, 22
Karen ethnic adaptation and change, 8, 18–22, 46, 65, 67, 78, 99, 107, 111, 113, 115–117, 122, 123, 130, 131, 159, 160, 174, 207, 247–248; assimilation to hill tribe category, 8, 13, 53, 121, 147–148, 158, 211; assimilation to Thai society and culture, 15, 19, 21, 22, 116, 145, 158, 162; change through marriage, 141, 142; individual change in identity, 135–136; Kayah ethnic adaptation and change, 19, 242–243; Pwo ethnic adaptation and change, 73, 77, 78. *See also* Karen ethnicity and ethnic identity
Karen ethnic group relations: with Burmans and Burmese, 11, 30, 33, 85, 123, 157, 159, 166, 168, 203, 238; with "foreigners" (Westerners), 156–157; with Haw Chinese, 206; with Khamu, 179; with Lao, 74; with lowlanders, 11, 12, 13, 30, 64, 81, 82, 86, 87, 89–91, 241; with Lua', 48, 50, 100, 104, 106, 121, 123–125, 128, 130, 131, 141–146, 151, 162, 196, 240, 241; with Meo, 123, 138, 155–156; with Mon, 30–33, 45, 51, 64, 66, 76, 79, 123, 239, 240; with non-Karen, 14, 123, 159, 169, 170–171, 187; with northern Thai (Khon Muang, Yuan), 12, 13, 26, 31, 36–39, 43, 45–46, 48–50, 64–66, 90, 104, 106, 115, 125, 128, 145–146, 150, 153–155, 176, 179, 185–189, 191–194, 199–200, 206–208, 210–211, 229, 241, 243; with other Karen, 137–138; with Shan, 30–33, 106, 113, 225; with Siamese (Central Thai), 12, 13, 26, 43–46, 51–53, 65–67;

with Tai, 29, 35, 228; with Thai, 12, 13, 53, 54, 74, 77, 78, 82, 85, 116, 122, 123, 135, 143, 145–155, 158, 161, 174, 194, 208–210; with tribal peoples, 196. *See also* Ethnic category; Ethnic labels; Ethnic stereotypes and images; Kayah ethnic group relations

Karen ethnicity and ethnic identity, 1, 8, 10, 18, 78, 123, 125, 157–158, 159–160, 173–174, 212, 291; and class, 69, 196–197; ascribed by others, 10, 12, 13, 64, 121; behavioral basis of, 174, 175, 176, 187; cultural basis of, 10, 11, 12, 136; descent and Karen ethnicity, 107, 116, 117, 138, 169, 170, 172; diet as basis of, 125; dress as emblematic of, 126; ecological basis of, 126; language basis of, 10, 11, 63, 77–78, 109–110, 125, 126, 137, 143, 155, 163; locality and ethnicity, 126, 138, 176–177, 190–192, 193; multiple and hyphenated identities, 16, 19, 20, 77, 198; politico-economic conditions for, 15–16, 73–74, 135; religious basis of, 12, 107, 109, 110, 115, 123, 157; self-identification, 10, 13, 14; symbolic expression of, 73, 140. *See also* Ethnic boundaries; Ethnic category; Ethnic labels; Karen ethnic adaptation and change; Karen ethnic group relations; Kayah ethnic group relations

Karen National Defense Organisation, 92

Karenni (pre-modern Kayah state in Burma), 36, 40, 48, 199, 228; border with Chiang Mai, 40–42, 59. *See also* Bawlakhè; Kantarawady; Kayah; Kayah State; Kyèbogyi

Karennic language family: *See* Language, Karen

Kariang (Thai label for Karen), 25, 26, 31, 45, 54, 55, 60, 73, 80, 229, 230, 231

Kawila, ruler of Chiang Mai (1782–1813), 37–40, 57–59

Kayah (Red Karen), 8, 36, 47, 88–89, 128, 137, 216, 223, 224, 249–250; in Thailand, 48, 60, 61, 87, 102, 221, 225, 241–247, 249; origins of, 28, 228, 249. *See also* Karenni

Kayah ethnic group relations: with lowlanders, 89, 94; with northern Thai (Khon Mµang, Yuan), 36, 39–42, 45, 47, 48, 60–61, 199–200, 250; with Shan, 28, 87–90, 224–226, 241–247, 250, 252, 253; with Thai, 223

Kayah State in Burma, 34, 36, 48, 223, 226. *See also* Karenni

Keen, F. G. B., 156

Kennedy, Victor, 45

Keyes, Charles, F., 4, 10, 19, 20, 43, 56, 58, 61, 65, 79, 80, 84, 87, 102, 103, 117, 221, 225, 227, 229, 230, 231, 235, 242

Kha, 30

Khae Chae Uae: *See* Khruba Khao

Khamu, 15, 122, 179, 214

Kho lae, 86, 93. *See also* Westerner

Khon Mµang: *See* Thai, northern

Khruba Khao (White-robed monk), 20, 84, 85, 87, 92, 93, 154, 159, 186–187

Khruba Siwichai, 84

Kin groups: among Pwo, 68, 70–72, 75, 83, 86; among Sgaw, 102, 107–113, 115, 137, 177–178. *See also* Communal meeting room or house in Sgaw villages; Long houses; Marriage patterns; Residence, post-marital

Kings of Siam and Thailand: patronage of Karen, 17, 23, 53, 79

Kinship nomenclature: among Pwo, 72; among Sgaw, 177–178

Koloa, 156. *See also* Westerner

Kǫn Kaeo, Upparat (Viceroy) of Chiang Mai, 37, 49, 57

Kraisri Nimmanhaeminda, 30, 128

Kunstadter, Peter, 10–16, 30, 48, 55, 61, 65, 83, 90, 100, 103, 107, 122, 128, 131, 196, 240, 241

Kuper, Leo, 167, 204

Kyèbogyi, 223, 226, 227, 239, 249, 250, 253. *See also* Karenni

Labor exchange: *See* Cooperative labor

Lahu, 14, 147, 184, 191, 249

Lamphun (town and province, called Labong in older literature), 43, 48; Karen in province, 20, 28, 118, 199

Land: alienation by Karen, 183, 186; disputes about, involving Karen, 138, 140, 155; land rights and tenure among Karen, 82, 83, 105, 128, 130, 138, 142, 145–147, 181–182, 183; Thai government policy towards, 14, 145–147, 163. *See also* Inheritance of property

Language: and ethnic differentiation, 7, 23; Northern Thai language as *lingua franca,* 143, 177

Language, Karen, 10–11, 28–29, 217, 219–221, 223–224, 228; as ethnic marker, 10, 11, 63, 77–78, 109–110, 125–127, 155, 163; Kayah language, 223–225, 228, 248–249

Lannathai, 25, 30, 54, 55, 65, 235. *See also* Chiang Mai

Lao, 4; in Kanchanaburi province, 73, 74, 75, 77. *See also* Thai, northeastern

274   Index

Law: *See* Citizenship; Legal rights
Lawa, in Kanchanaburi province, 73, 74. *See also* Lua'
Laykawkey, 161
Leach, E. R., 3, 5, 30, 63, 93, 107, 120, 130, 165–168, 181, 182, 195, 203, 213, 226, 250
LeBar, Frank M., 23, 122, 214, 251
Legal rights: ethnic basis for access to, 5; Karen adaptation to Thai law, 113, 131, 147–149; relating to land use in Thailand, 14. *See also* Citizenship
Lehman, F. K., 3, 8, 10, 11, 19, 23, 29, 30, 40, 55–57, 59–61, 79, 87, 88, 93, 118, 120, 136, 168, 169, 191, 195, 198, 203, 214, 217, 219, 221, 223–227, 229, 232, 238, 244, 248–250, 252, 253
Leke sect, 51
Lévi-Strauss, Claude, 5, 165
Lewis, J. L., 103
Lewis, Oscar, 253
Li, Charles N., 220
Liquor, as used by Karen, 113, 149, 163
Lisu, 14, 167, 195, 196, 211, 232, 233, 237
Literacy: among Karen, 170–172, 192, 193; among Kayah, 243–245; in Thai, 18; scripts used by Karen, 17–18, 73. *See also* Education
Literature, Karen, 17. *See also* Myths and folklore
Locality: as basis of Karen social organization, 106, 190–194. *See also* Village social organization
Locality spirit cults: among Pwo, 68, 70, 76, 93; among Sgaw, 106, 113–116
Long houses, among Karen, 68, 80, 100–103
Loo Shwe, Thra, 53
Lua' (Lawa), 14, 48, 55, 73, 74, 100, 122, 124, 127, 128, 130, 141–147, 151, 159, 196, 199, 221, 223, 240, 241; agriculture practiced by, 6, 131; as autochthonous population in northern Thailand, 26; change in ethnic identity, 6, 15, 128, 141–147; ethnic identity of, 6; intermarriage with Karen, 121; relationship with northern Thai, 6–7, 11, 30, 31, 37, 48, 214; religion among, 6, 84, 144, 154; village social organization among, 131
Luce, Gordon H., 10, 28, 64, 80, 219–221, 225, 229, 236, 238, 250
Lue, 6, 7, 12, 79, 185, 214, 237
Lumber industry: Karen involvement in, 15, 54, 66, 70, 78, 85, 140, 143, 151–152; Kayah involvement in, 89; *See also* Teak trade

McGilvray, D., 200
McLeod, 197, 199, 200, 202, 211, 214
MacMahon, A. R., 170
Mae Ha Ki, 99, 100, 102–104, 106, 110, 112, 113
Mae Họng Sọn (town and province), 57–59, 211, 221, 223; founding of, 42, 60; Karen in Mae Họng Sọn province, 10, 15, 21, 50, 54, 60, 65, 82, 99, 103, 117, 199, 240; Kayah in Mae Họng Sọn province, 19, 41, 42, 60, 61, 87, 225, 226, 241–244
Mae Klọng, Phra, 52, 67
Mae Sariang (Mụang Yuam, Mein Lun Ghee), district and town, 47, 57–59, 85, 93, 103, 113, 127, 130, 141, 143, 152, 153, 199; elections in, 16, 149–150, 152; Karen in district, 11, 15, 19, 21, 22, 43, 48–49, 54, 61, 68, 84, 99, 100, 102, 104, 106, 107, 116, 117, 121, 123, 126–128, 130, 137, 140, 146, 150–153, 162, 163, 185, 199, 240, 241; Meo in district, 155; Pwo in district, 50, 82, 102
Mae Tia Glo, 192
Manumanaw, 223–224
Maran, La Raw, 219, 220, 237
Marlowe, David A., 10, 11, 13–15, 49, 61, 65, 72, 83, 90, 117, 132, 143, 150, 161, 162, 174, 183, 186, 187, 195, 196, 211, 229, 240, 243, 247
Marlowe, G. W., 179, 180, 214
Marriage patterns: among Pwo, 68, 71, 74; among Sgaw, 130, 137–139, 174–175, 178–179; intermarriage of Kayah with non-Karen, 225; intermarriage of Sgaw and Pwo with non-Karen, 14, 71, 77, 106, 116, 121, 128, 136, 141, 143, 145, 156, 174–175, 177, 179, 180, 185, 214. *See also* Courting customs; Residence, postmarital
Marshall, Harry I., 55, 61, 101–103, 109
Mason, Francis, 28, 51, 61, 64, 65, 202, 227
Matisoff, James A., 220
Mendelson, E. Michael, 56
Meo (Hmong), 14, 15, 49, 61, 93, 130, 138, 146, 147, 155–156, 158, 161, 174, 186, 195, 196, 211; and opium production, 155; as stereotypical hill tribe, 13, 156
Migration: and ethnic change, 7; Karen migration legends, 27–28, 64; migration of Karen from uplands to lowlands, 115, 138; of Karen, 121; of Karen in Burma, 56; of Karen in Thailand, 29, 43–46, 48, 65, 79, 85, 100, 102, 121, 139, 162, 178, 231; of Karen to eastern Thailand, 44, 45; of Karen to Thai towns, 73, 74, 76,

78; of Kayah, 224; of Kayah east of the Salween River, 42, 48; of non-Karen tribal peoples to northern Thailand, 211
Millennialism, 33, 34, 56, 224; among Karen, 12, 20–22, 35, 40, 45, 50, 51, 53, 57, 61, 64, 67, 70, 72, 73, 81, 90–93, 240, 248; among Kayah, 40, 224, 226, 232, 244. *See also* Charismatic leaders; Khruba Khao; Rebellion by Karen in Burma
Mining, 15, 143, 147, 186
Missionary work among Karen: *See* Buddhism; Christianity
Moerman, Michael, 3–7, 12, 23, 29, 63, 79, 214, 233, 237
Mọkˏ Tsam Pẹˏ, 243, 245
Mon, 195, 251–252; in Kanchanaburi province, western Thailand, 74
Moore, A. W., 39, 47
Morris, James A., 8, 79
Mouhot, Henri, 44
Moulmein, 43, 46, 65, 67
Muang Mọk Mai (Mawkmè), 42
Muang Nai (Moné), 34, 42
Muang Pai (Mobyè), 32, 34, 38, 56, 57
Muang Yọng, 55
Muang Yuam. *See* Mae Sariang
Murdock, George P., 72, 177
Musgrave, J. K., 23, 214, 251
Myths and folklore, Karen, 11, 13, 17, 27–28, 86–87, 90, 94, 137, 140, 144, 153, 156, 159, 163, 169, 170–172, 244; Kayah myth of charismatic leader, 244; myth of "Golden Book," 153, 156, 163; myth of lost book, 11, 17, 170–172; myth of orphan, 86; origin and migration myths, 27–28, 63, 86, 90, 169, 170

Naga, 232
Narini, Father, 202
Naroll, Raoul, 3, 250
Nationalism, Karen, 22, 92. *See also* Karen National Defense Organisation; Millennialism; Rebellion by Karen in Burma
New Year, Thai, as celebrated by Karen, 74, 112, 116, 162, 187–189
Notton, Camille, 26, 55, 57, 227
Nyang. *See* Yang

Okpo, 79
Opium, 13–15, 93, 94, 155, 174; and Karen, 13, 14, 125, 152, 156, 174, 186
Oral tradition: *See* Myths and folklore
O'Riley, F. G. S., 224, 226, 227
Orphans in Karen society, 86. *See also* Adoption

Oxe, 107–113, 115, 116, 118. *See also* Ancestral spirit cult

Pagan, 235
Palaychi, 251
Pa-o: *See* Taungthu
Papawgyi (Papaw), 42, 59
Papun (town and district), 37–39, 57, 58, 132
Patron-client relations, 180, 182, 242
Pegu (Haṁsavati), town and former Mon kingdom, 33, 35, 45, 56
Penth, Hans, 221
Phamalọ, 99, 105, 106, 110, 112, 113, 118
Phibun Borihan, 60, 242
Phibun Songkhram, 73
Pho Saemlamciak, 56
Phré phrow, 244
Phumiphon Adunladet, King of Thailand (1946–), 23
Plural society, 167, 168, 203, 204, 207
Pluralism and pluralistic society, 203, 204–205, 207, 208, 211
Po, San C., 168
Political organization: of Kayah society, 36, 40–42, 47, 48, 60–61, 87, 88, 90, 92, 224–228, 239; of Pwo and Sgaw society, 16, 45, 68, 82–84, 91, 92, 102, 103, 140, 184. *See also* Conflict; Political status of Karen; Village social organization
Political status of Karen: in British Burma, 168, 203; in dominant lowland societies, 89, 91, 93; in modern Burma, 6, 8, 16, 20–22, 92–94; in modern Thailand, 13–17, 19, 22, 23, 53–54, 77, 82, 85, 87, 93, 145–150, 152, 160–161, 182–185, 194, 195, 206–212, 225, 249; in pre-modern Burma, 32, 33, 35, 38, 85; in pre-modern northern Thailand (Chiang Mai, Lannathai), 31, 32, 36–39, 43, 49, 50, 53, 55–56, 102, 122, 145–146, 182, 198–200, 226; in pre-modern Siam, 16, 22, 23, 51–53, 66–67, 79, 128, 130, 200–201; *See also* Legal rights
Population, Karen, 1, 23; expansion of, 35, 103, 104, 123, 128, 129, 131, 142; in Burma, 23; in Thailand, 23, 127, 162. *See also* Migration
Pọriyat Thammathada, 26
Poverty: *See* Wealth and poverty
Power: ethnic basis for access to, 5, 30; powerlessness of Karen, 206–211
Prachakitcakọracak, Phraya (Saem Bunnak), 32, 37, 41, 43, 47, 55–58
Prani Sirithọn na Phatthalung, 49, 50, 58
Productive resources: ethnic basis for access to, 5, 29, 30; Karen control of,

82, 131, 134–135. *See also* Economy; Land
Purtle, Dale I., 220
Pwo Karen, 10, 67, 232; called "Talaing" or "Mon" Karen, 198; compared with Sgaw, 63–66, 68, 79, 109, 118, 198, 238–240; origins of, 28

Rá (ola), 252–253
Rai, defined, 79
Ramtri, 31
Rebellion by Karen in Burma: pre-modern, 32, 33, 38, 85; since Burmese independence, 6, 8, 16, 20–22, 92–93. *See also* Millennialism
Red Karen: *See* Karenni; Kayah
"Red-turbaned" Karen, 37, 39, 227
Refugees: Karen in Thailand, 16, 17, 148. *See also* Citizenship
Relative deprivation hypothesis, 91
Religion: among Karen, 12, 35, 50–54, 90–93; among Kayah, 88, 92, 225, 244–247; among Pwo, 68, 70–71, 76, 82–85; among Sgaw, 106–115, 130–134, 153–155, 162, 175; religious change, 20–22, 46, 112–115; Sgaw and Lua' religion compared, 144–145. *See also* Ancestral spirit cult; Buddhism; Christianity; Curing rituals; Divination; *Iylùw*; Millennialism; Spirit beliefs; Thai rituals; Witchcraft and sorcery
Residence, post-marital: among Pwo, 68, 71–72, 76, 80; among Sgaw, 130, 137–138, 177
Rice cultivation: *See* Agriculture; Land; Swidden cultivation; Wet-rice cultivation
Richardson, D., 43, 66, 80, 127–128, 198–200, 202, 213, 232
Ritual head: among Pwo, 68, 83; among Sgaw, 100, 102, 110, 113, 114, 130, 173, 181, 188. *See also* Headman, village
Rituals: *See* Agricultural rituals; Ancestral spirit cult; Divination; *Iylùw*; Locality spirit cults; Tattooing cult; Thai rituals
Ryley, Horten, 214

Saen Phumilokaphet, 31
Sahai, 143, 150, 185, 186
Saimong Mangrai, Sao, 61, 93, 94, 235, 242, 250
Samoeng, 185, 192
Sangermano, Vincentius, 1, 12, 79, 198, 202
Sangkhlaburi (town and sub-district), 73; Karen in, 53, 69, 73–78, 179, 213. *See also* Suwan, Phra

Sanguan Chotisukkharat, 32, 37, 39, 40, 57–60
Sapga, 100, 102, 113, 114. *See also* Ritual head
Sapwaa zii kho, 181. *See also* Ritual head
Sarkisyanz, E., 56
Sawbwa (saohpa, caofa), 57–58, 88, 250
Sawlapaw, 61, 225
Sawlasa, 42, 60
Schools: *See* Education
Scott, James George (Shway Yoe), 27, 41, 47, 56, 57, 59, 60, 169–170, 249
Seidenfaden, Eric, 53, 60, 79
Sgaw Karen: compared with Pwo Karen, 63–66, 68, 79, 109, 118, 198, 235–240
Shan, 87–89, 213; in Mae Hoṇg Sǫn province, 127, 216, 221; relation to Kachin, 3, 5
Shan states in Burma, 235, 251. *See also* Muaṇg Mǫk Mai; Muaṇg Nai; Muaṇg Pai; Muaṇg Yǫng
Shorto, H. L., 56, 64, 80, 252
Shway, Yoe: *See* Scott, James George
Si-so, 185. *See also* Trading partners
Siamese: *See* Thai, Central
Siamese Legation in London, 61
Sii kho muu xha, 173, 178, 179. *See also* Spirits, ancestral
Sisawat, Phra, 52, 66–67
Skinner, G. William, 7, 122
Slave trade, 36, 43, 65, 200, 231
Smeaton, D. M. 43, 44, 65, 202
Smin Htaw Buddhaketi, 33–34, 56
Smith, M. G., 167, 204
Social structure and organization of Karen society, 136. *See also* Class; Headmen, village; Kin groups; Locality; Marriage patterns; Political organization; Political status of Karen; Residence, post-marital; Ritual head; Village social organization
Songs, Karen, 171–172
Sophon Ratanakorn, 163
Sorcery: *See* Witchcraft and sorcery
Spirit beliefs, 83; among Kayah, 245, 246, 252–253; among Sgaw, 134, 135, 138, 144–145, 153, 154, 163, 175, 176, 201, 209. *See also* Spirits, ancestral; Spirits, locality
Spirit mediums: absence of, among Karen, 206; Northern Thai mediums consulted by Karen, 206
Spirits, ancestral, 50; among Pwo, 68, 70; among Sgaw, 106–113, 115–118, 131–134, 138, 162, 173, 178, 179
Spirits, locality: among Pwo, 68, 70, 76,

93; among Sgaw, 106, 113–116, 173, 181, 182
Spiro, Melford E., 56, 234
Steinberg, Joel, 33
Stern, Theodore, 10, 12, 16, 20–22, 27, 28, 44, 45, 50–53, 55, 56, 60, 61, 65, 66, 70–73, 76, 79, 81, 93–95, 113, 176, 179, 198, 213, 224, 229–231, 237–240, 252
Stern, Theodore A., 73
Stewart, John, 202
Sukhothai, 235
Surr do ta, Sgaw curing ritual, 193. *See also* Curing rituals
Suwan, Phra (Phraya Si Suwannakhiri), 12, 53, 66, 67
Suwan Ruenyote, 13, 14, 19
Swidden cultivation, 13, 14, 131; by Karen, 46; by Kayah, 242; by Pwo, 65, 68–69, 70, 82, 84; by Sgaw, 100, 102, 103, 105, 106, 115, 140, 142; Karen and Lua' practices compared, 144; Thai government policy toward, 14, 53, 85, 93, 146, 147, 163
Symes, Michael, 79, 198, 249, 250

Ta mu xha pado, 181. *See also* Spirits, locality
Tadaw, Saw Hanson, 86
Tai, 30, 54
Tak (town and province), 55; Karen in province, 15, 20, 45, 51, 54, 61, 67
Taksin, King of Siam (1767–1782), 34, 36, 37, 57
Talaing, 251–252. *See also* Mon
Talutaphadu, 106, 113–116. *See also* Locality spirit cults
Tambiah, S. J., 71
Tattooing cult, as practiced by Sgaw, 12, 21, 110, 112–113, 131–134
Taungthu (Tǫngsu, Pa-o), 8, 11–13, 28, 54, 63, 64, 73, 74, 77, 137, 140, 229, 238; relationship to Shan, 11
Tayuu (tayzuu), 209
Taxes and tribute: collected from Karen by Lua', 48, 50, 128, 146; from Karen in Burma, 56, 88; from Karen in modern Thailand, 82, 85, 130, 146, 162; from Karen in pre-modern northern Thailand, 49, 53, 60, 117, 145, 162, 182, 198; from Karen in pre-modern Siam, 52
Teak trade: and Karen, 15, 16, 21, 36, 46, 47, 50, 51, 54, 61, 142; and Kayah, 89, 224. *See also* Lumber industry
Tej Bunnag, 16
Telakhon sect, 20, 51, 67, 90–93

Tenasserim (peninsula and state), Karen in, 32, 64–66
Thai, as a national identity, 4, 5, 7, 194, 207; for Karen, 15, 19, 21; religious basis for, 19
Thai, Central (Siamese), 4, 54, 127
Thai, Northeastern (Isan, Thai-Lao), 4, 5, 7
Thai, Northern (Khon Mųang, Yuan), 25, 54; migration of, from frontier areas, 58, 65
Thai rituals, Karen participation in, 74, 112, 116, 162, 187–189, 191–193, 208
Thipakǫrawong, Cao Phraya (Kham Bunnak), 52
Thipokawkesa, 130. *See also* Ritual head
Three Pagodas Pass, 66
Tin, Pe Maung, 250
Tinker, Hugh, 94
Tǫngsu: *See* Taungthu
Toungoo, 34, 228
Trade, 148, 151, 199, 207; by Kayah, 89; by Pwo, 69, 82; by Sgaw, 140, 143. *See also* Slave trade; Teak trade; Trading partners
Trading partners, Karen with non-Karen, 143, 150, 185, 186
Tribute: *See* Taxes and tribute
Truxton, Addison Strong, 8, 50

Umluk, 31, 55
Utah, 171–172

Village social organization: among Pwo 68–70, 82–84, 93; among Sgaw, 102–104, 137, 140, 180–181, 183, 184. *See also* Locality; Long houses

Wage labor: by Karen, 15; by Pwo, 69, 70, 75–76; by Sgaw, 140, 143, 151–153, 156
Wales, H. G. Quaritch, 250
Walker, Anthony, 184
Waplonkhu, 69–73
Watson, James B., 23
Wayland, Francis, 202
Wealth and poverty: among Pwo, 82–83; among Sgaw, 134, 135; ethnic differentiation of, 5, 30. *See also* Economy; Productive resources
Westerner ("foreigner"), 86, 93, 156–157
Wet-rice cultivation, 15, 131; by Pwo, 68–70; by Sgaw, 142; introduction of wet-rice cultivation among Sgaw, 103–106, 115
White-collar occupations filled by Karen, 16

White-robed monk: *See* Khruba Khao
Witchcraft and sorcery: among Karen, 125; among Kayah, 246–247, 252–253; ascribed to Karen by others, 205–206, 246–247, 252–253
Witz, Klaus R., 236
Wolf, Eric, R., 247
Worsley, Peter, 22

Xeho, 110

Yang (nyang), 25, 26, 29–31, 37, 54, 176, 187, 194, 198, 199, 209–210, 229–231, 239
Yang Suai Krabang, 43, 58
Yangtalai, 227, 239
Yanwicit, Phra (Sitthi Locananon), 26
Yao, 49, 147, 195, 211
Yuan: *See* Thai, Northern
Yule, Henry, 239, 250–252
Ywa, 11, 90–92